Reproducing Period Furniture
and
Accessories in Miniature

Other Books by Virginia Merrill

The Complete Book of Making Miniatures
with *Thelma R. Newman*

Needlework in Miniature
with *Jean Jessop*

Reproducing Period Furniture and Accessories in Miniature

by Virginia Merrill
and Susan Merrill Richardson

CROWN PUBLISHERS, INC.
NEW YORK

To: Robin, Derek, Gordon, and Ted

Inquiries should be addressed to Crown Publishers, Inc., One Park Avenue,
New York, New York 10016

Printed in the United States of America

Published simultaneously in Canada by General Publishing Company Limited

Library of Congress Cataloging in Publication Data

Merrill, Virginia.
   Reproducing period furniture and accessories in
  miniature.

   Bibliography: p.
   Includes index.
   1. Miniature craft. 2. Miniature furniture. 3. Needlework—
Patterns. I. Richardson, Susan Merrill, joint author. II. Title. III. Title:
Period furniture and accessories in miniature.
TT178.M48   1980   749'.1'0228   80-14777
ISBN: 0-517-538164 (cloth)

10 9 8 7 6 5 4 3 2 1

First Edition

Design by Patricia Smythe

All photographs by Virginia Merrill unless otherwise noted.

Contents

ACKNOWLEDGMENTS

We wish to express our sincere gratitude to the many people who have contributed their time and knowledge toward making this book possible, and for the opportunity of working with Brandt Aymar, a superb editor at Crown Publishers, Inc.

To the museums and libraries whose help we sought in researching our material—special thanks to Katherine Kavaraceus, a curator of the Museum of Fine Arts, Boston, who granted us special permission to adapt in miniature, for inclusion in this book, designs from their collections, and to Margaret Davis of Woodlawn Plantation for allowing us to reproduce the "Puppy Chasing a Butterfly" stool.

To Rose Barell and Linda Wexler for their expertise in furniture making and decoration; to Lois Sterling, Stephanie Matthews, Kay Weiger, Jean Holty, and Claudine Wilson for their talents with the needle; to Harry Tower and Jim Barry, our illustrious illustrators; to Herb Haber, Nancy Van Roosen, Gloria Hurme, Pam Johansen, Karen Bishop, Raquel Gavel, Don Buckley, Edward G. Norton, Donald Buttfield, and Ron Terrill, a round of hearty thanks.

And last but never least, to Eugene Kupjack who has set us upon our most challenging course—that of keeping up to his standards of workmanship and expert detail as to authenticity and correct period arrangements—always our very grateful thanks for his help and inspiration.

Preface

Women in America have been doing needlework for almost four centuries. During different periods the requirements and uses for this needlework changed. At first, needlework was considered totally utilitarian. It was used for creating and marking household linens and for clothing construction. Practical stitchery could often be treated in a decorative way. For example, quilts, bed rugs, and bed hangings were necessary for warmth during the night, but they were created with exquisite foliage or landscapes. Even during hard times, handwork was treated as a leisure pastime because women sat together and chatted as they accomplished their sewing. Daughters were always present to learn sewing techniques at these needlework sessions. Rich and poor alike considered mastering the needle arts the main emphasis of a young woman's education, a talent which she would either use as a wife or teach her servants.

The nineteenth century saw handwork much more as a diversion. Intellectual and social challenges took women out of the home. Household management was left to servants. Needlework did continue, however, with a purely decorative emphasis.

Today, although industrialization relegates the needle arts to ornamentation, mothers still teach their skills to daughters, as mine has done. Being a lady with a proven artistic talent, Virginia Merrill instilled in me her standards of quality and perfection. As her interests leaned toward miniatures, our needlework took on the challenge of being reduced to miniature scale for rugs, upholstery, and accessories.

Mother's ability to create flawless miniatures also has been shared with many students and readers. Now mother and daughter have, in this book, joined together to share their craft of miniature reproduction. Having visited museums, restored houses, and palaces in the United States and in Europe, we find our perspective broadened. Our book carries the precision of miniature making one step further, as it takes on the challenge of historical accuracy. Historical accuracy includes the careful copying of not only a single piece of furniture and its upholstery, but also the environment into which the furniture is to be placed. We selected for reproduction appealing pieces of period furniture, needlework, and accessories. The plans are original. The instructions for making these pieces will follow a discussion of their coordination into appropriate surroundings. We invite you to join us as we attempt to recover the past for present-day miniaturists.

SMR

Introduction

As the miniaturist sets about to design a period room, he or she wants not only to emphasize accuracy in the design of each piece of furniture or accessory but to suit the combination of individual items to their surroundings. Every feature of the room should be in keeping with the style of the time. But as a visit to a restored home will demonstrate, people who lived during the periods with which we will be concerned could rarely afford to refurnish their homes completely in the current style. They added pieces of furniture and accessories, even a contemporary room, to what they already possessed. In order that a replica be realistic, the designer ought to include features of contiguous periods, especially elements of the preceding style. Thus, in a Queen Anne room, one could have articles of furniture and accessories, or even architectural details, from the William and Mary period and perhaps a Chippendale chair imported from England.

That is not to say that a miniature room cannot be designed in one style exclusively. However, the proper mixture of styles is completely acceptable, if not preferable. The combination of elements of two contiguous styles occurred in furniture also. Furniture is called transitional when the elements of a preceding or newly emerging period are incorporated with those of the dominant contemporary style. A Queen Anne hoop back might have been retained on a Chippendale chair. This mixture occurred because stylistic features were continually borrowed from abroad, especially from England and France, and reinterpreted by the American cabinetmaker. Fabrics, furniture, silver, porcelain, glassware, and other furnishings were imported from Europe and the Orient, with the result that elements of style were often being influenced and changed.

There were regional differences and preferences within the United States. First of all, there were differences of national culture between the early settlements—English, Dutch, and French. Second, the larger coastal cities were more fashionable and affluent than the rural towns. The flow of trade and commerce brought exposure to European fashions and the availability of desired items. Third, there was a difference between the North and the South in the degree of independence from England. Uniquely American forms and styles were created by Northern craftsmen who exported them to the Middle Colonies. However, the South maintained a stronger dependence on England for its household items. Because of the success of tobacco exportation, Southern colonists could well afford to import English goods. Tobacco ships were larger than the Northern trade ships and could return with many imports. Finally, the ebb and flow of peace and war exerted its influence on the progress of different areas of the country.

In spite of regional differences, there are certain basic elements of style which characterize each successive period of design described by the following text: Jacobean, William and Mary, Queen Anne, Chippendale, Federal, Empire, and Victorian. Descriptions of each period will include interior architecture, furniture, and accessories. The architectural account will include wall, window, and door treatment, fireplace style, drapery technique, flooring, and floor covering. Furniture will be discussed in terms of style, upholstery, and unique forms of the period. The examination of accessories will cover metalware, glassware, ceramics, and objects common during the period.

Following the historical discussion, there will be a chapter with kinds of tools, basic methods, and working plans, which will include actual-size patterns for specific reproductions. As a sequel to furniture construction, charted needlework will be offered. A selection of miniatures by talented artisans will be presented at the conclusion of the book.

After the text, there will be a series of charts for quick reference in period research and a glossary complete with terms with which the reader may not be familiar.

A transitional chair shown with a Chippendale dressing table created by Stanley Jameson.
Collection of Claire Dinsmore

1 Periods and Their Characteristics

The Jacobean Period   1600–1700
The William and Mary Period   1700–1725
The Queen Anne Period   1725–1760
The Chippendale Period   1760–1790
The Federal Period   1790–1825
The Empire Period   1810–1840
The Victorian Period   1830–1870

The Jacobean Period   1600–1700

Jacobean Interior Architecture

Housing progressed from tents, huts, or caves carved in hills to frame dwellings consisting of one multipurpose room. Other rooms were added later either on the second-floor level or on the first. Additions included a room on the opposite side of the entry from the multipurpose room and/or a lean-to at the back of the house. Wooden chimneys became brick; thatched roofs became shingled. Both improvements lessened the incidence of fire. Window openings went from solid wood shutters to framed glass panes.

The entrance of a typical home of this period faced stairs that led to a second-floor bedroom. The stairway was built against the wall. The open side was flanked by a wooden banister, supported by turned balusters. Each section of the stairway ended in a simple, square newel post, topped with a fat, round knob. Opposite the staircase was a massive, dark room with a low ceiling generally not more than six feet high. The "hall" or "great room," as it was called, was decorated and used

in the manner of the medieval hall in England. The strong oak frame structure of the building was evident in the exposed beams. A heavy central "summer beam" ran the length of the ceiling of the room, usually perpendicular to the fireplace wall. This beam supported all the ceiling joists, which were spaced about three feet apart, usually parallel to the fireplace wall. Corner and intermediate posts along the wall supported the horizontal beams on which the ceiling joists rested.

The wall surface between the exposed beams was plastered, and occasionally whitewashed. There was no interior painting of either wood or plaster in the seventeenth century. The ceiling voids were filled by oak planking which created the flooring for the second-floor bedroom overhead. The same wide oak boards covered the floor surface of the "hall." Medieval windows were made of diamond-shaped panes set with molten lead into iron frames. These small panes of glass were the largest size made until the beginning of the

A Thorne room depicting a living room and kitchen in an early Massachusetts house 1675–1700. *Courtesy: Thorne American Rooms in Miniature, The Art Institute of Chicago*

eighteenth century. The windows were either stationary or double casement, opening from the middle outward to the side.

A massive fireplace dominated the room. It was about three-quarters of the height of the hall and as much as eight feet wide. A simple rectangular opening was constructed of either brick or fieldstone. The matching hearth was level with the wooden floor. High above the flames, in front of the built-in wall oven, there hung a green stick (or iron pole) from which pots and kettles were suspended on chains or adjustable trammels. A plain wide oak board (set in flat against the wall) served as a lintel across the top of the fireplace opening, which typically had no vertical supports.

This one room was used for every indoor family activity—working, cooking, eating, and even sleeping. Furniture and decorative accessories were sparse at first. As the house enlarged, there were more rooms for sleeping: the children and servants could sleep on the second floor or in the lean-to rear room; the master bedroom would be located on the other side of the entry from the hall.

Jacobean Furniture

American craftsmen did not start to make furniture until the last quarter of the seventeenth century, at which time their styles lagged behind those of England by twenty-five to thirty years. Furniture construction

Early fireplace with accessories.
Courtesy Harry Smith,
Barnstable Originals

was performed by turners and joiners, rather than cabinetmakers. The furniture in early colonial houses followed the trends set in England in the first half of the seventeenth century. A few pieces, called Jacobean after the reigning James I, came over on the ship with the early settlers; others·were sent over or imported on trade ships.

Oak was the principal wood used; maple and pine were in evidence. The use of turned members was the distinctive characteristic of furniture of this period. Ornamentation consisted of painted floral and heraldic designs, intricate carving, and applied moldings. Carved motifs included fluted arches, horizontal foliated S-scrolls, palmate panels, and low-relief tulip and rosette forms. The moldings were round or oval knobs and spindles cut in half and frequently painted black for application to the surface. Strong massive turned legs, called balusters, supported many pieces of furniture. Columnar legs were sometimes cut on a lathe to form ball shapes on the shaft, known as ball turnings.

There was little variety in the furniture forms available. They consisted of seats, beds, tables, and storage pieces. Seating was not designed for comfort in these early times. Except for the father and, perhaps, the mother, who were given a chair, the family sat on chests, benches, stools, and settles. (It is the honorary chair set at a long table, often called a "board," that gives us the expression "chairman of the board.") Benches and stools were very primitive, consisting of a horizontal board supported by either two vertical boards or columnar legs, perhaps turned with stretchers. These basic pieces were probably constructed by the master of the house. The stool was the first individual seat at the dining table for a family member. A joint stool occasionally had a rush seat and raked legs connected by four rectangular stretchers. This miniature form of the stretcher table stood twenty to twenty-two inches tall. A settle was often found by the fire. It was a bench with a plain high paneled back and paneled sides and arms. The tall back and sides enclosed the heat from the fire and blocked the cold drafts which came rushing through the room. The seat was often hinged, forming a lid for a storage chest underneath.

The actual chairs in the family were limited. Armchairs, "great chairs," were made in several forms. No upholstering was used, but loose cushions provided some comfort. The Brewster chair, named after Elder William Brewster of the Plymouth colony, was an open armchair, made with tiers of vertical turned spindles in the back, under the arms, and below the seat. The Carver chair, named for Plymouth's first governor, John Carver, was similar, but it did not have vertical spindles below the seat or arms. The wainscot chair was made with a solid paneled back of ornately carved oak. The arms were open. The wainscot style was also made in England in a bench form. The slat-back or ladder-back chair was made with turned upright supports joined by three or four horizontal slats for the back. Sometimes

A Brewster chair created by Elena Lamb. *Courtesy: Elena Lamb Designs*

Carver chair made by Warren Dick.

A typical wainscot chair of the Jacobean period.

A pair of slat-back (ladder-back) chairs. *The Hoffman Collection*

A Cromwellian chair.

the slats were curved for more comfort. The front leg supports ended in a round knob or, occasionally, a large flat mushroom-shaped terminal. The terminal occasionally had a recess in the top surface to hold a candle for reading. The Cromwellian chair was angular with turned leg supports and a turned front stretcher. The plain side and back stretchers were close to the floor. American forms had no arms. The seat and raised back panel were slightly upholstered.

American-made beds began often as straw-filled mattresses on a pallet, or board, the frame of which was probably built into a corner of the room. This form became a separate piece when simply turned posts and a plain headboard and footboard were added to the rectangular frame. Rope was tied to the frame for mattress support. Stump, or low, bedstead was the name

A country bed with a rope-tied mattress support made by Ron Terrill. *Courtesy: Ron Terrill*

under which this bed was listed in seventeenth-century inventories. Elongation of the legs led to the canopied form called a tester bed. The beds were high off the floor so that a trundle could slide underneath should additional bed space be needed. The trundle consisted of a rope-tied frame on wheels. Given a choice, sleeping in the higher bed was preferred because sleeping on the floor was colder. As the century progressed, American beds were made of maple. English bedsteads were evident in many seventeenth-century homes. They were always tester beds with four tall turned posts supporting the canopy. The headboards were more ornate than American versions. Both were heavily draped with curtains.

Table use in the hall was always temporary. Surface space needed at a meal would crowd the room when other family activities were taking place. Thus, the table needed to be designed with a removable top or collapsible sides. The trestle table provided a detachable top on footed supports which were joined by a horizontal stretcher. After the meal, the top would be placed against the wall, and the trestle, which occasionally folded, was moved aside. The family could then continue with the day's activities or gather in front of the fire for the evening. A chair table was a chair with a hinged back projecting above the arm supports. When the back was moved forward, it became a table surface supported by the arms. (The settle was also designed to serve this dual function.) The stretcher table was usually a smaller table with raked turned legs and rectangular "box stretchers," which joined all four legs to form the shape of a box.

Drop-leaf tables were space-savers also. The butterfly table had a rectangular surface when closed, but when two side leaves were opened the rectangle either was enlarged or became oval. The two side leaves were each supported by a wing bracket that looked like a butterfly wing. The legs were often turned and splayed, angling out as they neared the floor. The gateleg table had the same surface design as the butterfly table. The difference between the two was the leaf support device. This support swings out from the table base like a gate. The gate leg was eventually replaced by a single swing leg in the early eighteenth century.

There were very few closets and built-in cupboards in seventeenth-century houses. The storage space for clothing, linens, and other belongings for the sea voyage and later life in the settlement was provided by chests, court cupboards, and press cupboards. Early chests were low lidded boxes, supported by baluster legs or the extension of the corner posts of the box. They were plain, painted, carved, or decorated with

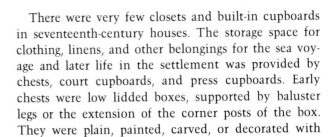

An early trestle table.

A chair with a hinged back that forms a table surface.

A butterfly table with turned raked legs. *Roger L. Gutheil, Inc.*

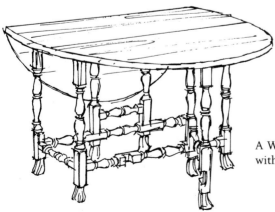

A William and Mary drop-leaf gateleg table with turned members and Spanish feet.

applied moldings. The more elaborate decoration was used on court and press cupboards. The court cupboard had an enclosed section for the storage of utensils and an open shelf above and below this section for the display of household accessories. The press cupboard, on the other hand, had no shelves. The enclosed cupboard for clothing and linen storage was located above drawers. Only the top surface provided space for display. The blanket chest was a conventional lidded box with drawers below. As time passed, the more efficient storage of the drawers increased in importance until the chest became merely the frame to support many drawers.

A smaller storage form is the Bible box. It held valuables, books, and the family Bible and could be locked for security. This storage piece was always given a place of honor in the hall, often set on the court or press cupboard or on a table or chest. Sometimes the Bible box had a slanting lid and could serve as a writing surface or a reading stand. As this box grew in size, it was placed on a frame and became a desk. A miniature chest was used as a cabinet for the storage of luxurious spices. This also was placed on a piece of furniture for display.

In England, new furniture forms were created which were soon to appear on the American scene—the daybed, tall-back chairs, high chests, drop-front desks, tall case clocks, and upholstered wing chairs. Walnut had become the predominant wood. New decorative techniques were employed, such as oriental lacquer, the painting in gold of Chinese scenes, and marquetry, the creation of veneered designs with thin pieces of wood.

Jacobean Upholstery

The only upholstered piece of furniture existing during this period in America was the Cromwellian chair. The seat and back were covered either in leather with

A Jacobean cupboard for the storage of clothing, linens, and household accessories made by Elena Lamb. *Courtesy: Elena Lamb Designs*

A Bible box in which were stored the family Bible and valuables.

A Jacobean storage chest with hinged top and bottom drawer made by Elena Lamb. *Courtesy: Elena Lamb Designs*

A tall-back English chair with velvet
upholstery made by Denis Hillman
and available from Paige Thornton.

A drop-front desk with applied moldings and turned
members made by Elena Lamb.
Courtesy: Elena Lamb Designs

brass mushroom-shaped tacks or in turkey work with
occasional metallic trim on the lower edge of the back
and around the seat. Turkey work was a form of needlework or weaving designed to imitate carpets that
were imported from the countries of the Near East, one
of which was Turkey. Wool may have been stitched
through a canvas and knotted to form a pile. The designs were mostly floral. In England later in the century
there was needlepoint upholstery on a few open armchairs with solid high backs. But only the Cromwellian
type was listed in American inventories.

Furniture was softened through the use of knife-
edged cushions placed on the seats. These were sometimes made of velvet and satin but more often of linen,
which was decorated with handwork. Tent stitches
formed patterns of family crests, flowers, people in
landscapes, and even damasklike geometric patterns.
The stitching was fine, detailed, and much like the tap-
estries of the time. Large flame patterns, not as time-
consuming as other stitches, were created by vertical
Irish, or brick, stitches.

Jacobean Drapery Treatment

Fabrics and needlework pieces were used in drapery
treatments for windows and bed hangings. There was
much reliance upon imported fabrics, especially from
Italy, though these were expensive and came through
trade with England. There were brocatelles (satin patterns on a twill background), brocades (silver and gold

patterns on a silk background), and damasks (lustrous
designs on a shaded silk or satin background). Less expensive were the Jacobean-style crewel embroideries,
stitched on an even-weave linen. Simple panels of fabric were hung on a rod at the top of the window frame
and pulled to the side. No needlework fabrics decorated windows at this time. The fabrics that were hung
at the windows often matched covers for the bed located in that room.

The only form of elaborate drapery was on the tester
bedstead. Early colonial beds were located in the main
room of the house. Guests were entertained in this
room so it was important to have a fine set of hangings

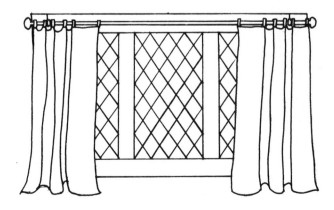

A casement window with simple fabric panels.

to indicate social status and wealth. A set of hangings included: a headcloth, which was slightly gathered as it hung from the tester to the floor; six side curtains, which fell straight to the floor and completely enclosed the bed when drawn; a bedspread or coverlet; three valances; and three bases, which were suspended from under the mattress to the floor. The valances and bases hung smoothly with no gathering. Their hems had straight edges.

Jacobean Floor Coverings

The only floor coverings in the early colonial days were animal skins. Otherwise the floor was left bare. Occasionally sand was spread over the floorboards, sometimes in a design. This helped to control the amount of dirt brought into the house. What carpets there were in the colonies were placed on a table according to English custom. Even though seventeenth-century carpets were used on the floor on occasion, their permanent place, with possibly a few exceptions, was on the table. Carpets were imported by England from countries in the Near East, such as Persia (Iran) and Turkey. England had developed its own rug industry by this time. Copies of Near Eastern carpets were produced along with English carpet designs consisting of masses of gaily colored garden flowers, which were hand-knotted or embroidered.

Jacobean Needlework

Because of the high cost of imported materials, crewel-embroidered linen was the typical fabric for bed hangings. Crewel designs were based on tree of life panels brought to England by the East Indian Company in the seventeenth century. The design consisted of a large central tree from which many different types of flowers and leaves grew. The tree rose up out of a very hilly terrain. People, flowers, animals, and birds were perched on top of the many little hills. No attention was paid to scale or proper proportion. There were a variety of patterns on the hangings of this period. One, for example, is an allover design of small trees. Another equally popular pattern was a single large tree placed on a small series of hills on the headcloth or spread. Borders of large vinelike arrangements of flowers trailed along bases, valances, and curtains. A third treatment showed long, narrow bucolic landscapes which served as borders for hangings. Finally, there was an instance of a set of flame-stitched valances with plain green hangings.

A record of the different needlework stitches and designs was kept on a strip sampler. This long, narrow embroidered fabric was rolled up and stored when not

A strip sampler used by women in the Jacobean period as a reference for their handwork. Stitched by Susan Richardson.

in use. The sampler consisted of rows of letters and numerals separated by lines or narrow borders of stitches. These patterns were referred to when the lady of the house was marking the household linens. Wider border patterns and various design motifs were reserved for use on upholstery, bed hangings, and other projects. Silk or linen thread formed the cross-stitched patterns which were often unfinished in appearance and in fact. New ideas were added as they were invented or learned from a friend. These needlework pieces were never framed because they served a more practical use than the display of the stitcher's ability.

Sewing excellence was seen in the quilts used to cover beds. Early American forms were made from a single colored material. Several widths of loomed fabric were assembled to make the top layer. Designs were stitched through the top fabric, the filler, and the lining. A simple running stitch was used to create the lovely floral and geometric patterns. Quilts were not only decorative but also practical because they provided warmth.

Woolen stockings and mittens, made by younger family members who had learned to knit by the age of six, also provided warmth. Boys as well as girls spent many an evening knitting by the family fire. Initials and numbers for easy sorting were either knit into the item or embroidered later.

Jacobean Silver

Although the interiors of early colonial homes were not crowded with silver pieces, occasional objects were brought by families from England. American silver began to appear around 1650. By the end of the seventeenth century, pieces of silver were often found in the homes of successful and well-to-do families. The silversmith became a banker of sorts because he melted down a gentleman's silver coins and created an object of unique design. In the case of loss or theft, the silver piece could be easily identified by the gentleman's design, as well as the silversmith's mark. The style of seventeenth-century silver was architectural, based on Italian Renaissance models. The shapes were essentially rectilinear. Simplified decoration took the form of raised panels, chased floral patterns, and engraved heraldic designs.

There was a great variety of silver forms serving many different functions. The greatest diversity was seen in the drinking vessels. Their ornamentation often consisted of flat chasing in allover designs or single engraved crests. Cups came in many styles. The caudle cup was a two-handled cup often made with a lid. It had either a straight-sided or gourd-shaped body and stood about six inches high. A narrow ring served as a base, and the two handles were curved ear shapes. The surface was either smooth or decorated with flat chasing. This cup was used to serve spiced wine drinks, such as syllabub, posset, or caudle, a warm beverage made of oatmeal, water, lemon juice, and wine, with sugar, nutmeg, and mace as spices. The cup was used at festive occasions, such as christenings or during visits to a new mother.

The dram cup was much shallower than the caudle cup. Its diameter was two to three inches and held a dram of liquid. The bottom was flat, and the sides curved slightly. A simple chased pattern of a stylized flower was set in a series of panels placed around the outer surface. A single row of chased punchwork encircled the rim of the cup. Two ear-shaped handles were formed from twisted silver wire and soldered to the top and bottom edges of the cup. Distilled liquors were served in this form.

The punch bowl was a larger version of the caudle cup. There was no lid. A circular bowl had rather straight sides decorated with flat chasing. There were two handles and a low shaped base. Punch was mixed and served in the bowl, and then it was passed around the table so that each person could drink.

Standing cups had almost straight sides with a slight flare to the rim. Puritan simplicity was seen in the design of the plain cup shaped from a single piece of metal. The cup was supported by a stem that imitated the baluster shape seen in the furniture of the period.

A shallow dram cup with twisted wire handles and decorative chased designs.

Goblets were used more in churches than in homes until after the Revolutionary War.

Beakers had no stems and, typically, no handles, though there were a few single-handled forms. They were large cylindrical drink containers. The sides tapered only slightly outward as they approached the mouth. The base was flat. Early forms were decorated only by a wide middle band of punchwork. Later forms were decorated with either allover flat chased patterns or simple crests. Tumblers were shorter vessels with weighted rounded bottoms. They had straight sides with neither handles nor lids.

Small cups were made during all periods of silver production. They often followed the style of the beaker with a single handle or the caudle cup with two. Handles were ear-shaped and were made of flat thin lengths of silver called "flat strapped" handles. A spout cup was used during the seventeenth century for feeding liquids to children and invalids. A thin curving spout was located at right angles to the handles. These cups often had a flat lid with a finial. The cup had a globular body with a wide neck decorated with reeding. Reeding was a very narrow semicylindrical molding applied to surfaces in a varied number of bands. The use of the spout cup ceased at the beginning of the eighteenth century.

Tall cups with one handle and a lid were called tankards. The cylindrical bodies tapered slightly in the opposite direction from the beaker; the narrower portion was at the rim. The scroll-type handle was made in the shape of an S with the lower half smaller than the top. The handle had a shield placed at the end. Another handle style was the flat strapped handle which was decorated on the top surface with reeding or graduated beading. Lids were flat and protruded out beyond the rim of the container. Beginning at the origin of the handle and tapering about halfway down the tankard side was an applied decoration piece in the shape of a rat's tail. This silver ridge was used either as decoration or as a reinforcement for the joining of two pieces of silver. Occasionally there was a coin or medal set into the lid. A protruding thumbpiece was located at the spot where the handle joined the top edge of the container. The thumbpiece, often in the shape of a lion, was used to raise the lid. The surfaces varied from being very plain to having raised designs on the handle surface and a molded strip of vertical leaves around the base. Occasionally on the inside surface of the tankard, a vertical row of about five pegs was placed in line with the handle. The pegs were spaced at intervals to indicate the quantity that each could drink as the cup was passed around the table. Mugs had no lids, but followed the style of the tankard.

A common silver object was the porringer, a shallow bowl with a single flat handle soldered horizontally to the top edge. It came in many different sizes, the most popular of which were the half-pint and the pint. The seventeenth-century forms had flat bottoms and almost straight sides. These became rounded toward the end of the century. The solid U-shaped handle became pierced and more ornately shaped around the edge. The bowl was used for holding berries, cereals, and other foods.

Seventeenth-century flatware consisted mainly of only one form: a medium-sized spoon, which served many different functions. Silver-handled knives were not made in America until the nineteenth century. Bone-handled steel knives were used. Silver forks were only rarely made before the nineteenth century also. Forks simply were not used for eating. There were only two tines on the few forks created in the seventeenth century. More common in this century was the English-made sucket fork. This piece had a two-tine fork at one end and a spoon at the other. This device was used for the eating of sweetmeats: the fork end was used to pierce the preserved fruit and the spoon for drinking the thick syrup in which the fruit was served. This form vanished early in the eighteenth century.

The earliest spoon style in the seventeenth century was the "slip end" spoon. The bowl was fig-shaped with a V-shaped drop on the underside at the point where the handle joined the bowl. The polygonal handle was slim with the end cut at an angle (chamfered) so that it looked like the stalk of a cut plant, or "slip." The cut surface faced the top side of the handle. Another style of this period was the "Puritan" spoon. The handle was flattened and squared at the end. The bowl was larger and more oval than the earlier style. At the end of the century, the trifid spoon appeared. The flattened end of the Puritan spoon was divided into three lobes. The back of the bowl had a slight relief decoration along the edge of a long pointed drop called a "rattail." This drop originated at the joint of the bowl and the handle and tapered toward the end of the bowl. The concern for the decoration on the underside of a spoon was caused by the fact that spoons were set on the table for meals with this side facing up. This fashion disappeared at the end of the eighteenth century when spoons were placed with the bowl cavity turned up.

Table salt was a luxury item. It was set in a fancy container on the table nearest the place of honor. The standing salt container had a round base, a spool or trumpet-shaped body, and a shallow cavity, with four scrolled projections to support a covering napkin or dish. By the end of the century, salt became less dear. The salt containers on the table were reduced in size and increased in number. They were placed next to each person's plate, or trencher. The name dates back to the Middle Ages when food in England was cut into pieces and served on a thick slice of bread called a trencher. Later the trencher became a flat piece of wood or metal, usually round in shape. In spite of the

A standing salt with spool-shaped body.

more modern development of earthenware, pewter, or silver objects, plates continued to be called trenchers. Thus, the name for the salt container set next to each guest's plate is "trencher salt."

Sugar, as well as spices and sweetmeats, was contained in an elliptical box with a lid, about eight inches in length. It closely resembled the version on page 22. The sugar boxes were brought on when wine was being served because additional sugar smoothed out the unpredictable quality of the wines. By the end of the century these boxes were ornately embossed. They had a single handle on the top in the form of a snake, coiled at each end and elevated in the middle.

A salver with a trumpet-shaped foot from Eugene Kupjack.

Salvers were used to present filled drinking containers to guests. They were flat circular trays set on a trumpet-shaped foot. The rims were decorated with simple reeding. By the end of the century they had acquired broad rims with an engraved vine with flowers.

Chafing dishes were used at the end of the century to keep foods or liquids warm at the table. Hot coals were placed in a pierced pan with three brackets around the edge to support the solid pan. The brackets ended in a bird's claw foot holding a wooden ball. The silver pan had a heavy wooden handle. Chafing dishes were often made in pairs.

In the seventeenth century, candles were very expensive, even though many were dipped at home. Candles became less messy and smoky. As a result, candlesticks were made of silver instead of only the baser metals. The style from 1660 to 1670 had a shaft formed by a cluster of thin columns with a large square, or, on occasion, circular, base. Protruding horizontal "trays" were placed midway up the shaft to catch the dripping wax. These mirrored the base and shaft in shape. Later can-

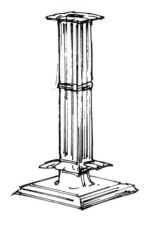

A silver candlestick with a shaft of clustered thin columns.

dlesticks had columns of the more simple Doric style with a mid drip pan. These were made during the last quarter of the seventeenth century and had gadrooned borders. Gadrooning was a wider form of reeding which resembled a twisted rope. During the last twenty years of the century, baluster stems became a form for the candlestick shaft. This style continued into the eighteenth century.

Jacobean Pewter

During the early settlement days, there was very little pewter. Woodenware was used to hold and serve food. Woodenware was brought over on the ship with the settlers in very simple forms, such as platters, dishes, trenchers, and spoons. As the living conditions improved, pewter became more plentiful in homes. It was certainly more abundant than silver. Pewter pieces were considered the basic household items for the well-to-do family. The family collection was often displayed on the shelves and top surfaces of furniture.

Little pewter was made in America until the eighteenth century. The English discouraged pewter production through a high duty on raw tin, which had to be imported from England, and a low duty on finished English pewter pieces. Pewter forms were created in America only by recasting broken pieces, a part-time, not full-time, occupation.

Pewter styles and forms followed those of silver pieces, but the decoration, if present at all, was cruder and simpler. Spoons were the most common form of pewter. Porringers were considered one of the most important pewter household items. But of all the containers in the house the standing saltcellar was held in the highest esteem. Such honor was inherited from the feudal age, when salt was considered an item of extreme luxury. The standing salt was probably the first piece of pewter purchased for the home. Only one was needed, and it lasted forever. Tankards and mugs of pewter were often seen on cupboard shelves. They followed the basic silver models, except for an occasional ornamental form called "wriggle work," patterns cut by rolling a gouge from side to side. The designs were bold

and free. The flat lid style of the pewter tankard was sometimes crenelated around the edge so that it was characterized by a wavy line. Toward the end of the century the crenelated edges disappeared, and the lids became domed and double domed.

In England, candlesticks, whether of silver, brass, or pewter, were designed in popular styles of the day. America followed English trends. Few pewter candlesticks were used before 1830, as compared with the many iron and brass varieties imported from England. Early pewter candlesticks had a heavy bell-shaped base with a prominent mid drip pan. In the middle of the century there appeared a square pillar stem with the same obvious drip pan. It became less prominent on the new round pillar forms that appeared in the last quarter of the century.

There were a few forms that were more typical in pewter than in other metals. Flagons were tall and cylindrical in the manner of the tankard. They had a short domed lid and a spout that was formed by the extension of the rim. These vessels were used in homes to carry cider or beer to the table and in churches to hold the wine for communion. Examples existed with a finial on the lid and a slightly spreading foot at the base. Liquid measures, a set of graduated mugs or pitchers for measuring, were frequently made of pewter. The capacity of the containers in a set ranged from one-quarter of a gill to a gallon. Though they may have been found in a few well-to-do kitchens, they were used more often in American taverns than the home. Measures were used extensively in English homes, but in the colonies mugs of various sizes sufficed.

The largest quantity of imported pewter during the seventeenth century was sadware, one-piece objects cast in two-piece molds. These consisted of large numbers of stackable items and were usually sold by the pound. "Saucers" were plates less than six and one-half inches in diameter; "plates" were six and one-half to ten inches; deeper "soup plates" were seven and one-half inches; "dishes" were ten to thirteen inches; much deeper "basins" with narrower brims were six to twenty inches in diameter; and round or oval platters of thirteen to twenty-eight inches were "chargers." Early English sadware had a wide, smooth rim with a narrow reed just under the edge. At the middle of the century, the rim became very narrow. Finally, by 1675, the narrow rim became triple reeded.

Jacobean Ceramics

The earliest objects for kitchen, table, or dairy use in America were made of wood or pottery. Eventually, "treen" (wooden) items were created in pewter; but red earthenware, or redware, pottery continued to be used even during the nineteenth century.

Redware was made from common brick clay and was red or reddish brown. A clear lead glaze was applied to the inside or over the entire piece creating a shiny, streaked, and mottled surface of orange, green, brown, and red. Some pottery was brown or black if manganese was added to the glaze. Mugs, jugs, pitchers, and teapots were treated in this manner.

Besides the glaze technique, potters decorated with trailed slip, an application of clay thinned with water. Patterns were also created by incised or tooled lines.

Redware forms were simple and practical, including such items as bowls, mugs, jugs, cooking and baking dishes, and mold pans. In Staffordshire, England, slipware (redware with slip decoration) was made with lively trailed designs. Dots were applied to emphasize the pattern of light slip on dark ground and vice versa.

Stoneware was made both in America and in England. The clay for these objects was finer; they were fired at a higher temperature; and the only glaze was salt, applied while objects were in the kiln. The pieces were more durable. Tablewares were the main product of this process. In England some busts and figures were made.

Americans depended on England for the importation of finer ceramics. The most popular form was English delftware, a fine white earthenware pottery with blue designs. Globular wine bottles were inscribed with the name of the wine. On chargers, blue dashlike strokes surrounded a central polychrome painting, ranging in subject from biblical scenes to royal portraits. "Merryman" plates were made in a series of six, each of which was decorated with a line from a rhyming verse. Other drink containers were barrel-shaped mugs; cylindrical tygs with from one to twelve handles; and fuddling cups, three, five, six or more of which were connected on the inside. Barber's bowls and tablewares were also made. The decorative motifs and shapes were greatly influenced by the oriental porcelains imported into England. Some delftware was decorated more primitively with freehand peasant designs applied in bright colors with a brush and a sponge. This style was especially popular during the William and Mary period.

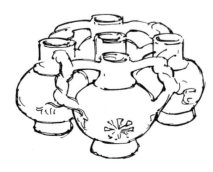

A fuddling cup.

Jacobean Glassware

The struggle for existence so occupied the early settlers that there was no time to create glass. The ability to produce glass objects was not mastered in England until the 1680s, so very little glass existed in the colonies during the seventeenth century. Occasional glasshouses made glass windowpanes, or perhaps bottles and everyday glasses. But they did not produce for any length of time. In England, when the skill of making lead glass was finally mastered, wineglasses were created with nicely proportioned baluster stems and either round or V-shaped bowls. Knops, small rounded shapes, were added to the stems in the shape of an acorn, an egg, or a mushroom. A few knops contained a coin. Verre églomisé became a late-seventeenth-century English decoration for looking glass frames. This decoration was achieved by painting the underside of a piece of glass and backing the design with a piece of metal foil, gold or silver leaf. Because it was such a new industry in England, the achievements in glassware and verre églomisé probably were not shared to any degree by the colonists until the eighteenth century.

Jacobean Metalwares

Brass objects appeared in seventeenth-century America in many forms, such as skimmers (ladles with holes in the bowl), thimbles, pins, pots, and kettles. Late in the century there appeared trivets; plate warmers (only for the well-to-do); warming pans, into which fireplace coals were placed to warm the bedclothes before retiring; mortars and pestles for grinding food; and candlesticks.

A unique brass item of the times was the lantern clock, so called because of its close resemblance to a lantern. This clock was created in England in the early seventeenth century. A round brass dial was supported by a brass structure made up of four columns. Heavy brass straps rose up from each of the columns and intersected above the clock. Sometimes the intersection was topped by a finial. The brass face was engraved and oftened crowned by a pierced plate of metal called a crest.

The pendulum clock housed an elegantly engraved brass backplate which could be viewed through a glass door.

Furniture utilized brass decor in the form of handles and key escutcheons. These were conservative in the use of simple drop handles hanging from small, round, and delicately engraved plates. The plates around the keyhole were larger and more ornate in shape and engraving.

Brass chandeliers of the seventeenth century had a globular base with a series of progressively smaller

A bed warming pan.

A seventeenth-century lantern clock with engraved face and pierced crest made by and available from Virginia Merrill.

signed with a baluster shaft which supported an urn or flame-shaped finial.

The fireplace provided the best source for warmth and the only means for the preparation of food. Herbs were hung across the ceiling beam in front of the heat for better drying. Copper pots and kettles were interspersed among many iron utensils: cranes to support hanging pots inside the fireplace; a mechanical spit with weights to keep it turning; thongs; mortars; skillets; pots; caldrons; and andirons. Metal objects hung within the fireplace, from the lintel, or sat on the hearth. Evening light was provided by the fire, candles, or open wrought-iron lamps. But wicks for the lamps were difficult to keep evenly trimmed and in place. They smoked and smelled so badly, whether burning tallow, fat, or grease, that they were not popular. Wrought-iron hardware in the form of door hinges and

globes mounting the shaft. These were topped by a finial or hanging hook. Encircling the shaft were one or more tiers of S-curved arms at the end of which were placed candles. Later in the century, the Dutch baluster shaft was used in place of the earlier globes.

Candlesticks of brass followed the same styles as those of pewter. They had a domed base, an obvious drip pan, and a plain shaft. As the century progressed, the base became lower, the stem baluster in shape, and the drip pan less prominent.

Although British andirons were made of brass, steel, or the more utilitarian iron, they always had an iron base on which the logs rested. The andirons were de-

A Thorne room depicting a great hall in the miller's house in Millbach, Pennsylvania. *Courtesy: Thorne American Rooms in Miniature, The Art Institute of Chicago*

A parlor in the Sam Wentworth House in Portsmouth, New Hampshire. *Courtesy: Thorne American Rooms in Miniature, The Art Institute of Chicago*

latches were in use in seventeenth-century homes. Wooden products were also seen on shelves and around the fireplace. One unique form was the wooden bread peel used to remove baked bread from the wall oven (see page 26).

Jacobean Furniture Arrangement

The typical Jacobean hall contained a central table covered with a rug, surrounded by benches, stools, and at most two or three arm or Cromwellian chairs, none of which matched. On the table was placed the Bible box. The rest of the furniture was placed around the

edge of the room. A settle or table chair, a child's chair, and a spinning wheel flanked the fireplace. Against the walls were the court and press cupboards, a chest, miscellaneous chairs, and in the corner or with its headboard against the wall, a bedstead. On the cupboard and chest surfaces were found pewter, ceramics, and silver of the times. Next to, or at the foot of, the bedstead was a cradle; under the bed, a trundle on which the children slept. An engraved map in a simple wooden frame, a small portrait, a wooden box to hold clay pipes (see page 25), and simple tin candle holders hung on the plastered walls. On the fireplace lintel rested a firearm of the time.

The William and Mary Period 1700-1725

William and Mary Interior Architecture

When William and Mary took the throne in England, they brought with them continental tastes in architecture and in the decorative arts. The baroque style characteristic of Italy after the Renaissance was the basis for the style popular during their reign. In reaction to the classical purity and disciplined perfection of the Renaissance, the artistic style adopted large massive forms, the use of contrast through an emphasis on the three-dimensional, and a feeling of constant vitality and motion.

The look of the interior of colonial homes became more refined during the William and Mary period. Emphasis turned from basic structural elements to ornamentation. The height and size of rooms increased. Ceilings became about eight feet in height. The rough-

hewn ceiling beams of the Jacobean period were boxed with finer wood which was painted or covered with plaster. Finally, no beams could be seen at all as the ceiling became a smooth plastered surface.

Wooden wainscoting with raised panels covered the lower part of plastered walls. The rectangular panels were in high relief to create the desired play of light and shadow so characteristic of this period. The same paneling covered the entire fireplace wall. The pattern of the wood surfaces provided a large rectangle over the fireplace on which was often painted a landscape. The fireplace in the main room was greatly reduced in size now that cooking for the household took place in a separate, more primitive, room called a kitchen. The opening of the fireplace was framed no longer with simple sheathing, but with bolection molding, protruding from the panel in the sweep of a continuous double curve, convex toward the outside and concave toward the inside. The inside edge of this framing was lined with a single or double row of delft tiles or with the brick of the fireplace itself. In rare cases, the paneling treatment of the fireplace wall was continued on the other three walls of the room, as it was done in England. Most paneling in colonial homes of this period was painted. Some of the colors used were blue, light brown, and green. Often the molding paint was applied in a way to imitate the marble in Italian and French palaces. The plastered walls occasionally had a wall covering of flocked canvas made to look like velvet.

Double-sash windows with panes six by eight inches in size replaced leaded casement windows. This arrangement allowed much more light into the room. Typically, there were four panes in a row and five or six tiers (always with three tiers in the bottom sash). The windows were framed with wider sheathing than the Jacobean casements, but the wood remained flat. Often, paneled shutters, painted to match the window trim, were hung on the inside to provide protection from Indians, soldiers, and other dangers. The flooring remained the same as that in Jacobean homes with pine or oak floorboards for the surface. But now some of the floors were painted or spattered with paint. Rooms were more specialized; there were separate rooms for cooking, sleeping, and "living" (eating, reading, or working). Bedrooms followed the architectural style and had all of the decorative elements of the main room. The kitchen received a more primitive treatment: it lacked the finishing touches of paneling, wall coverings, and draperies. The kitchen fireplace continued to be large because of the need for cooking space. Cupboards and built-in shelves were added for storage. The wood was either left natural or painted.

William and Mary Furniture

The style of furniture in the William and Mary period emphasized beauty and comfort as well as practicality. Walnut and maple rather than oak were used for furniture construction. Pieces became lighter in appearance as slim turnings replaced heavy balusters. Furniture was still basically rectilinear, except for certain stylistic features such as the curved borders of aprons on tables; the arched curves on the tops of chairs; the sinuous cross-form stretchers; shaped, or spoon, backs on some chairs; the occasional cabriole leg later in the period; and the sometimes bulbous turning of almost all supports and stretchers. Vase, trumpet, ring, ball, and block shapes appeared on these turned pieces. Arches and scrolls replaced the geometric rigid elements of the earlier period. Flemish scrolls were formed by reverse C-curves coming together at an angle The turned legs ended in a ball, a bun (a flattened ball), or a Spanish foot. The Spanish foot was a carved scroll with

A William and Mary high chest made by Donald Dube and hand-painted by Linda Wexler.

vertical grooves; the scroll curved backward to turn at the bottom. Late in the seventeenth century, a slightly curved cabriole leg appeared. The foot was in the shape of a hoof or a small pointed slipper. The ball-and-claw foot was used with the cabriole leg in England around 1700. Arms came from the chair back with a slight downward curve and rose up again to wind into ram's-horn terminals.

Flat surfaces were no longer carved; they were decorated only with veneers, marquetry, and chinoiserie. Veneering was the superimposing on or the setting into a wood surface of a thin layer of wood that had been carefully selected for its superior grain. English veneers took the form of cross and herringbone bands bordering drawer fronts and other flat surfaces. Cross banding was formed by laying strips of veneer so that the grain would run crosswise to the main surface grain. Herringbone banding created a feathered effect by placing two strips of veneer side by side with opposing grain diagonals. Marquetry, as well as veneer, was more popular with the English cabinetmaker who had completely mastered the skill. This mastery was seen clearly in the seaweed marquetry on oblong cabinets, chests of drawers, tall case clocks, and small decorative tables. The seaweed design was created by a pattern of minuscule scrolls cut from boxwood or holly and placed in a walnut ground. Chinoiserie was the painting on a black background of Chinese figures and scenes as they were interpreted by English artists from the many imported products from that country. The motifs were oriental buildings, towers, steeples, figures, and rocks.

Stools (see page 182) were still in evidence in the colonies during this period, though the focus for seating had definitely turned to chairs. Rectangular seats were upholstered, vertical legs turned, and stretchers curved and crossed.

Chairs were more widely used in the colonies during this period. The desire for more comfort was evident: chair backs were high. An allover upholstered chair finally made an appearance in the form of a wing chair (easy chair). The chair had a side panel that ran perpendicular to the solid back panel from its top edge to the top of the solid chair arm. It was this wing panel that gave the chair its name. The early wing chair had an arched crest at the top of the back panel and was narrow in appearance. Later, the crest became a gradual curve. The arms were rolled horizontally on the early chairs. This style was retained by Philadelphia, but not by New York or Massachusetts, which adopted the vertically rolled arm. Turned median and side stretchers joined the front legs, which had a vase turning, a block, and then a Spanish foot. The square rear legs were plain. There was an upholstered apron which was straight along the edge of an earlier chair and curved on a later version.

A chair form unique to the colonies was the banister-back chair. This simple form was generally painted black. The high back consisted of a series of turned banisters which were flat, or split, with a rounded surface on only one side. If arms were present, they were open and curved with ram's-horn terminals, and supported by a turned spindle which grew from the front leg. The chair back was topped by a pierced crown-shaped crest. The banisters rested on a straight or curved slat above the level of the seat. Richly turned stretchers were placed across the front and lower at the sides, perhaps with a median stretcher joining the two side stretchers. At the rear was a plainer stretcher on the same high level as that at the front. The rush seat might have had a cushion for added comfort. The front legs were turned, but the rear were plain.

The Boston chair was made in New England and exported to the Middle Colonies. It had for the back a tall spoon-shaped upholstered panel above an upholstered seat. A flat horizontal crest curved into the back supports. Typical William and Mary arms curved into ram's-horn terminals. The vase-and-block turned front legs ended in a Spanish foot. This chair was generally upholstered in leather with brass tacks.

Chairs with caned seat and back surfaces were made in England at the end of the seventeenth century. The prototype for this chair design was that of the Jacobean chair popular during the reign of Charles II. The upholstered velvet surface was replaced by cane panels. This decorative idea came from the many oriental imports inundating England at that time. Many of these chairs were exported to the colonies. They were made of beech with some maple and ash included. The back was tall with a cane panel. The panel was topped by a

A banister-back armchair made by Martha Dinkel, with a petit point cushion by Susan Richardson.

An English tall-back side chair with a scrolled crest supported between upright supports. *Collection of Rose Barell*

A corner chair with a rush seat. *The Hoffman Collection*

pierced crest either held between or placed on top of the upright supports of the chair. These chairs were used typically around the tea table as the drinking of tea became fashionable.

Corner (roundabout) chairs came into existence during the William and Mary period. This form was used at a game table and, most frequently, at a desk. A low crest rail extended to become arms. This single curve was supported by turned chair supports located at three of the four seat corners. A double row of stretchers formed a box frame. The square seat had a covering of wrapped or woven rush. The open front was designed to accommodate the cumbersome skirts worn by ladies and the long coats and swords worn by men.

The daybed (see page 124) was a new form introduced during the William and Mary period. This form was a chair whose seat was extended to the length of a small bed. Usually there were four pairs of turned legs. Three pairs of ornate lengthwise stretchers were seen along the side, and four plain lower stretchers joined each pair of legs. The back was either adjustable or canted (slanted backward). The back panel was topped by a solid crest and was held between turned supports. Caned panels were typical on the back and lounging surfaces. A set of cushions was usually found on the daybed: a squab (a long box cushion) with a round tubular pillow or a flat knife-edged pillow tied to the back.

A typical bed form of the William and Mary period was the folding trestle bed. This bed had a shortened tester at the head. There were six legs so the bed could be folded against the wall under the tester. The bed was then concealed behind the tester curtains. The short foot and tall headposts were turned; the headboard was plain.

Tables of the William and Mary period came in diverse sizes and served various functions. The gateleg table was seen in many dimensions, from twenty-four to seventy-one inches in length when opened. The form was the same as that of the Jacobean period, but the legs had vase-and-ring or ball-and-ring turnings and ended in ball, vase, or Spanish feet.

The butterfly table was a most popular form. The legs were splayed, that is, all four pointed out in four different directions. Much turning was evident on the legs and the stretchers. The top was oval or rectangular when opened. The bracket stood from the undersurface of the leaf down to the stretcher as it formed the shape of a butterfly's wing. The outside edge was curved beautifully, leaving the bracket wider at the top than at the bottom. The inside perpendicular edge was straight.

Medium-sized tables were created for reading, writing, breakfast, cards, or tea. These different furniture requirements indicated the more comfortable standard of living of the period. The hutch table was a rural descendant of Jacobean chair tables. The top was supported on paneled trestle ends which became the arms of the chair when the top was lifted. The chair seat was either a box with a lifting lid or a support for two drawers with small round wooden handles. The tavern table was a light table set easily next to a customer at an inn. These tables were used also in homes. There may have been a drawer with a small round wooden handle set in the apron beneath the plain table surface. Four turned legs had either turned box stretchers or a median joining two side stretchers. The tavern table was soon replaced by the butterfly table. The splay-legged table had raked legs going out in four different directions. The turned legs were joined by plain box stretchers and ended in Spanish feet. The apron was slightly curved with the plain top surface projecting well beyond it. The porringer table was so named because of the round protruding corners of the top surface. The extended porringer-shaped surfaces supported candlesticks, keeping them out of the way of any activity on the oblong table surface. The skirt was curved, and turned side stretchers were joined by a median stretcher. The mixing table was probably the most unique table form. It had a slate or marble top framed by a wide inlay border of marquetry or strapwork panels. The slate or marble surface was resistant to hot or strong liquids. This sophisticated form was made of walnut or fruitwood. The dramatic curve of the apron, which supported one or more drawers, arched in the middle. A turned vase-shaped (dropped) knob was suspended from the apron on either side of the central arch. The legs were typically turned in the trumpet shape. Serpentine cross stretchers supported a ball finial at the intersection, as seen previously on the William and Mary stool.

Case pieces seemed to have undergone the greatest

change during the William and Mary period. Court and press cupboards were replaced as the most important storage furniture by the high chest. This form began as a chest of drawers with a pair of drawers on the top level and a support piece of furniture with a single long drawer. Eventually the support piece acquired an apron and more drawers. Flat surfaces were often covered with walnut and ash burl veneers. The top of the high chest was flat. The number of turned legs varied from four to six, with the extra legs standing across the front. Flat curved stretchers formed either a rectangle or an **X** when joining the legs. A ball finial was sometimes placed at the intersection.

The support piece could have been used as a separate piece of furniture. Eventually one was made to match the high chest in a bedroom. The separate piece was called a dressing table. The skirt had a central arched opening which allowed a person to sit comfortably while using toilet articles contained in the drawers. There was a pair of deeper drawers on either side of a shallow middle drawer.

There was an increase in letter writing during the seventeenth century. Desks became popular first as a desk box, a large Bible box placed on a simple turned box frame. The box might have also rested on a frame of legs joined by one median and two side stretchers. The slanting top surface of the box was stationary for the standing writer or hinged so that it would fall toward the seated writer, supported on slides housed in

Curved cross stretchers strengthen cup-turned legs on this William and Mary dressing table made by Ernie Levy.

the front surface of the box. A single drawer may have been located under the hinged lid. The slant-top (slopefront) desk involved the placement of the desk box on a chest of drawers. These more sophisticated versions were often decorated with burl veneer and had ball or bun feet. The desk and bookcase (secretary) added a cupboard to the top of the slant-top desk. This form was rare in the colonies until the Queen Anne period, but a few examples were made. The cupboard had a flat top. Each door had a panel with a top curved in the manner of the aprons of tables and case pieces.

Looking glasses became more important as decorative pieces during the William and Mary period. They became longer in size, forecasting the very long, slender pier glass placed on the wall space (pier) between two windows. These became longer in England, not because the skill of making longer pieces of glass had been perfected, but because two pieces of glass, one above the other, could be framed. The elongated mirror hung over a "pier" table in a more formal room. In colonial rooms the looking glass was framed in a simple rectangular frame and also in a more ornate frame with pierced crests.

Brasses appeared on furniture at the end of the Jacobean period. Teardrop handles were suspended from diamond-shaped plates. The key escutcheons were larger and more ornate because of engraved decoration. At the end of the William and Mary period the Queen Anne "batwing" form was used. A wide **U**-shaped handle hung from a plate that resembled a bat with its wings spread open.

During the first quarter of the eighteenth century in England, furniture styles had progressed through the Queen Anne and into the Early Georgian styles. In the Georgian tradition, the chair backs were lowered, splats

Brass hardware in appropriate scale on a walnut high chest by Douglas Kirtland.

became pierced, the Queen Anne cabriole leg had a
claw-and-ball foot, and the mahogany wood recently in
use was carved.

William and Mary Upholstery

Upholstery was more widely used during the William and Mary period. The Boston chair and the wing
chair had padded surfaces. Cushions were used on the
daybed and on chair seats (see pages 124 and 16). During this period the loose seat cushions on chairs were
tied with tasseled cords to the back chair supports and
to the front legs. Metallic fringe might have been
placed around the edge. Bright-colored silk velvet; Italian brocades, brocatelles, and damasks; China silks;
embroideries; chintzes; painted calico; and blue-and-
white "furniture checks" were used as upholstery.
Leather covers with brass tacks were also common.

Needlework coverings were tapestrylike allegorical
scenes framed by flowers executed in the tent stitch, or
they were large flame patterns in the Irish stitch. The
flame design was seen frequently on the daybed squab
with a round end pillow or a matching pillow tied to
the back.

Printed linens often covered wing chairs. For example, blue resist designs were created by applying wax to
linen, which was then dipped into indigo dye. The
areas covered with wax remained linen-colored, while
the uncovered floral design was dyed blue. Copperplate-printed linens were crowded with floral designs.
Colors were limited to red, purple, chocolate, and black
printed on a beige ground.

Wool coverings were used, especially in the colonies
after the Wool Act of 1699, by which England refused
to import any colonial wool. These fabrics were red,
green, gold, or blue in color.

William and Mary Drapery
Treatment

Draperies were seldom used in more than two or
three rooms, except in the homes of the extremely
wealthy. Only the parlor and the bedroom had curtains
at the windows. Draperies were now hung in a more
decorative fashion. Instead of window-length panels
drawn to the side on a rod, side panels, if present,
reached the floor. Across the top edge of the window
hung a flat valance with a straight top edge and a curvilinear bottom edge. The regular arched design of the
bottom edge echoed the lines of the aprons of chests
and tables of the period. In more formal rooms, Venetian curtains were used. In this curtain style a fabric
panel was hung from the top edge of the window and
drawn up in the manner of venetian blinds. With the

Floor-length draperies hung under a scalloped valance.

Fabric panel drawn to the top of the window in a Venetian
drapery treatment.

tightening of the cords, puffs of material formed a valance or hung under a valance. All of the fabrics, except
leather, which were used for upholstery were also hung
as draperies.

Bed hangings seen on the tester bed were the same
style as those of the Jacobean period. The expensive
fabrics from Italy such as brocatelles, brocades, and
damasks became more widely used in bed draperies.
Crewel-embroidered linens with the Jacobean tree of
life motifs were seen on both tester and trestle-foot
beds. The trestle-foot bed had a three-sided valance
around the shortened tester with a vinelike floral
motif. The head curtain, the skirt, and the spread were
placed as they were on the tester bed. The curtains,
however, hung from the side of the tester and could be
pulled around the bed when it was closed against the
headcloth.

William and Mary Floor Coverings

Carpets were not completely limited to the tops of
tables during the William and Mary period. As the
quality of life improved, they began to be placed on
floor surfaces more often. Table and floor carpets of the
William and Mary period consisted of Near Eastern
imports and products of English looms. English carpets
were either copies of Turkish rugs or original designs of
country garden flowers. The Near Eastern carpets were
more common on the tables and floors of colonial
homes.

William and Mary Needlework

As was mentioned earlier, canvas work was used for
upholstery and cushions. The tent-stitch tapestry de-

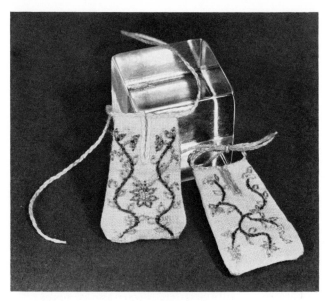

Crewel-embroidered linen fashioned ladies' pockets worn at
the waist. Made by Virginia Merrill.

signs were seen mainly on English furniture, while the
colonial ladies emphasized the less time-consuming
flame patterns. These women also created hatchments
to hang over the fireplace or on a wall (see page 192).
The coat of arms design was placed on a dark lozenge-
shaped ground. The work was done in the tent stitch
on canvas or in silk and metallic embroidery on a dark
silk ground. In England the coat of arms was painted on
wood and hung outside the home or in the church of a
person who died. The embroidered version was created
for home decoration. Hatchments gradually disappeared by 1800.

A William and Mary setting
composed of a banister-back
armchair by Marty Dinkel, a strip
sampler on a corner chair by
Warren Dick, a table carpet by
Susan Richardson, set with a
porcelain bowl by Priscilla Lance
and Deborah McKnight, and
candlesticks by Eugene Kupjack.

Strip samplers were still on hand for consultation as clothing and linens were marked and crewel embroideries were stitched. Bed hangings were not the only projects using crewel stitching. Clothing, especially petticoat borders and pockets, were decorated in this way. Fashion called for a top skirt that parted in the front from the waist to the hem. This opening revealed linen petticoats with gathered embroidered borders around the bottom edge. Long (12 by 18 inches) flat, U-shaped pockets, each with a vertical slit at the top for entry, were tied at the waist by a tape. One pocket was placed at each hip under the open top skirt. It was in these pockets that a lady kept her personal items, such as sewing or keys. The pockets were made of patched fabric, needlepoint, and, most often, linen on which a vinelike floral design had been embroidered with crewel yarn.

One-piece quilts were still the only style seen on the bed. This same quilting method was used for petticoats worn during the cold weather. There was a bit more time for women and girls to spend making items that were not only useful but pretty to see. The knitting of stockings and mittens continued to be necessary as the only means of creating fabric with the proper stretch and warmth. Knit items were still initialed and numbered.

William and Mary Silver

Silver during the William and Mary period followed baroque trends rather than the earlier Renaissance style. The emphasis here was on the bold contrasts of heavy three-dimensional details and on the motion of curves and reverse curves. Pieces were larger and more ornately decorated. Gadrooning, a common decoration at this time, was a decorative border of parallel concave and/or convex lobes. These lobes moved vertically, at an angle, or radiated from the edge. This technique especially suited the desired play of light and shadow. It was often contrasted with a plain surface. Repoussé designs were executed by the hammering of the inner surface to create a three-dimensional motif on the outside of the piece. These designs and plain surfaces were often juxtaposed. Cast elements were applied to silver surfaces, often in the form of ornate handles of leaves with graduated beading. The richness of the style was achieved by the frequent combination of a number of decorative methods on one piece of silver.

Most Jacobean cups continued to be produced during the William and Mary period. The exception was the spout cup. This form was replaced in the eighteenth century by the shallow papboat, elongated in shape with a wide rim at one end. It had no cover, no foot, and no surface decoration. The caudle cup changed its ornamentation from chased designs to re-

A selection of silver pieces characteristic of the William and Mary period by Eugene Kupjack.

poussé and from panels to gadrooned borders around the base. Coats of arms were sometimes engraved on plain surfaces. Handles became cast caryatid forms. They were still ear-shaped, but now were molded in the shape of an arched lady with graduated beading. One form of caudle cup made in New York had three finials on the lid. The finials became the base for the inverted cup so that it could be used as a dish to hold sugar lumps often served with brandy. The caudle cup was no longer used by the second quarter of the eighteenth century.

Another cup that became obsolete during the Queen Anne period was the dram cup. Before its disappearance, it became larger (four or five inches in diameter). The twisted wire handles were replaced by flat ear-shaped strap handles. Some dram cups were created with curved sides and no paneling.

Cast caryatid handles
on an early-eighteenth-century caudle cup.

Eighteenth-century beakers developed more curved lines, and by the Queen Anne period adopted the shape of an inverted bell. On the various smaller cups, the flat strapped handle was replaced by a cast handle in the shape of the letter *C* with an occasional single row of graduated beads along the side surfaces.

Tankards during this period became more ornate. Cut-card decoration, a design cut from a thin sheet of silver, was applied to the tankard lid and in bands at the base. The lid, though still flat, had a slightly higher stepping. The rims of the lid continued to protrude and were crenelated with larger scallops. Gadrooning was placed around the step of the lid. Reeding, graduated beading, or applied designs lined the length of the handle on the top surface. A cast cherub's head replaced the earlier shield at the handle terminal, and the rattail spine became shorter or disappeared altogether. The shape of the thumbpiece was a scroll, a ram's horn, a dolphin-and-mask, or a cocoon. The plain bodies of the tankards were occasionally engraved with a coat of arms on the front.

Mugs followed the style of the tankards. However, about 1720, the cann made its appearance. The cann differed from the mug only in that it had a tulip-shaped body on a rounded, domed, circular foot. It was heavy-looking at first. There was a large drop under the handle intersection and, at the spot where the handle originated, a flat, curved piece of silver had been applied to the top surface.

Porringers of this period developed rounded sides and a narrow lip which turned out (see page 21). The bases were flat around the outside edge and slightly raised at the center. Handles were pierced in several patterns according to where the bowl was made.

A new bowl form called a monteith had deep notches along the rim from which wineglasses hung by the foot. This arrangement allowed the glasses to cool in liquid contained in the bowl. The container was named after a Scotsman, who wore a cloak scalloped at the bottom with the same notches that lined the top of the bowl. The bowl ranged from nine to ten inches in diameter. The outside surface of the bowl was lavishly decorated with baroque motifs: scrolled arches and

cherubs' heads formed an ornate band around the notches in the rim; flat fluting, a two-dimensional gadrooning, covered the lower surface of the bowl; gadrooning probably encircled the foot.

The medium-sized spoon of the Jacobean period continued to be the only flatware form used in the colonies at the beginning of the eighteenth century. At this time, the end of the trifid handle on the spoon curved. The engraving disappeared from the underside of the bowl, and only the rattail remained.

Trencher salts, placed at each guest's plate, were made in New York and Boston. Gadrooned borders edged bell-shaped bodies at both the top and bottom. Standing salts, though outmoded, continued to be made during this period. Bases and bodies became octagonal in shape. A molded midband decorated the body, which stood about five inches high.

Shakers for condiments, such as mustard, pepper, and sugar, were used to "cast" spices on food during this period. These "casters" were made in sets of two or three, with a larger container reserved for sugar. The body was a two-part straight-sided cylinder held together by a banded joint. The rounded lid was topped by a finial and was pierced in a decorative pattern. Other decoration consisted of a band around the joint, some gadrooning on the top and bottom edges of the body, cut-card decoration, and an occasional engraved coat of arms. At the end of the period, it became pear-shaped (see page 21). Another caster style had a flatter lid with less decorative piercing and a scrolled handle.

A caster for mustard, pepper, or sugar by Eugene Kupjack.

A monteith with notches at the rim to support wineglasses made by Eugene Kupjack.

An elliptical sugar box with ornate decoration.

All of the baroque decorative elements were brought together on the elliptical sugar boxes with the hinged lid. These boxes, copied directly from English boxes of this type, were decorated with large bosses, gadrooned bands, and repoussé acanthus leaves. The surfaces of the circular bosses were engraved with a heraldic shield or a repoussé knight in battle. The earlier snake-coil handle became a scrolled handle with leaves. Sugar bowls or dishes replaced the sugar box during the Queen Anne period.

Salvers maintained the style of a round tray on a trumpet foot. The only addition was a gadrooned border around the edge of the tray and around the bottom edge of the foot.

Tea, coffee, and chocolate came to be enjoyed socially in the colonies around 1700. Tea was used initially for medicinal purposes and was extremely expensive. One pound of tea was equivalent to many barrels of rum and even to a piece of furniture. As these beverages began to be incorporated into the colonial social life, silver forms were designed in which to serve them. The teapot of this period was globular with a straight spout, a domed lid, and a ball finial. It was decorated with bands of gadrooning. The C-shaped handle was made of dark wood. Contemporary English teapots were made in the Queen Anne style. It would not have been unusual to use imported Queen Anne style silver pieces for serving tea, coffee, or chocolate. These imports might have been copied by American silversmiths. The Queen Anne teapot seen at this time in the colonies had a squat pear-shaped body, a spout curving up close to the body, a C-shaped wooden handle, and a high domed lid topped by a ball finial. Coffeepots and chocolate pots were usually tall and cylindrical (see page 21). The body was vase- or pear-shaped. Early coffeepots were probably used for serving chocolate. The chocolate pot was unique because of a small hole in the lid, covered by a removable finial that was chained to the pot to ensure against loss. It was through this hole that a stirring rod was placed to stir the chocolate which often settled to the bottom of the

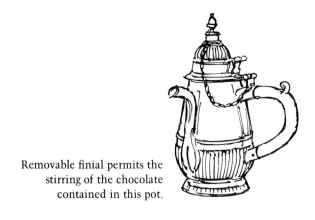

Removable finial permits the stirring of the chocolate contained in this pot.

pot. The spout was placed at right angles to the handle.

At the beginning of the period, round stop-fluted columns replaced the square cluster columns of silver candlesticks. The columns had bands at each end that "stopped" the vertical fluting. Because the column rested on an elevated square base, drip pans at the socket and two-thirds the way down the shaft were square. Baroque ornamentation was evident in the bands of gadrooning and the engraved oriental motifs. The corners of the bases and drip pans might have been chamfered. At the end of the period, octagonal candlesticks were created without the baroque ornamentation. Candlesticks gradually lost their drip pans, which were replaced occasionally by removable bobeches set on the candle socket to catch dripping wax.

The inkstand (standish) was made at the end of the seventeenth century as an accessory for the new desk form (see page 21). Three cylindrical containers stood on a tray, supported by lion's feet. The tray had at the center a vertical post topped by a ring so that it might be carried easily from place to place. One of the cylinders contained pounce, a fine powder which was sprinkled on wet ink to keep it from spreading. The second box held wafers, dried paste disks used to seal letters. The third container was an inkwell.

Small boxes made of silver were created to store tobacco, snuff, and small decorative patches worn early in the eighteenth century by women to enhance their beauty. The boxes varied in size from less than two inches to several inches in length. They were round or oval in shape with engraved tops.

Baby rattles called coral-and-bells or whistles-and-bells were made in silver or gold during the eighteenth century. A whistle was located at one end and a coral stone for teething at the other. Rows of bells were attached around the middle of the shaft. The rattles were hung around a child's neck or waist on a chain or ribbon. Most of these rattles were imported from England, and by the nineteenth century, few, if any, were created by American silversmiths.

A globular teapot with a straight spout.

William and Mary Pewter

Pewter became more abundant in colonial homes during the William and Mary period. The same objects continued to be imported from England. Along with ceramics, pewter forms served as eating utensils and food containers. Porringers were used frequently to hold cereals, berries, and many other foods (see page 26). The sides were now rounded and the handle pierced and curved in outline. Stackable sadware plates, dishes, and chargers were still purchased by the pound. The rim was edged with triple reeding. Drink containers, such as flagons, tankards, and mugs, were cast in graduated sizes with a midband (see page 26). Lids were domed and crenelated. The standing salt, once the most important pewter piece in the home, was replaced at the end of this period by a trencher salt for each place at the table. When damaged, spoons were easily recast by a local craftsman. The end of the handle was trifid in design.

Many forms which were plentiful in other metals were made in small numbers in pewter. Pewter shapes followed those of silver, but ornamentation was much simpler. Candlesticks were made more frequently with brass or silver, but a few pewter versions had mid drip pans. Though chandeliers were uncommon during this period, there might have been a few pewter examples as well as brass.

William and Mary Ceramics

America persisted in importing ceramics from England, except for kitchen, dairy, and other useful wares. American redware remained primarily unchanged during this period. England's preoccupation with the imported objects from the Far East led to a continuation of the imitation of oriental porcelains. The blue-and-white delftware of the Jacobean period became multicolored, with reds, greens, purples, and yellows added to earlier blue monochrome designs. The Dutch influenced the decorative style on this earthenware with the use of trek, a dark blue green outline filled with lighter colors. The trek method was used for the first ten to twenty years of the eighteenth century. Plates and dishes had many shapes, such as round, octagonal, scalloped, or, most commonly, wavy. Following the William and Mary interest in surface variation, delft tiles with oriental motifs or scenes framed some fireplaces.

Delftware forms provided drinking and dining accessories for the early-eighteenth-century home. Pots were made for tea, coffee, and chocolate, as well as cups and straight-sided mugs with which to drink them. Sugar bowls, creamers, tea caddies, sauceboats, tureens, monteiths, and labels for the necks of wine

bottles were more delft items. Hollow "bricks" held cut flowers in the holes in the top. Two-handled posset pots became punch bowls with ladles. Puzzle jugs had several holes in the neck. A playful challenge was issued to drink without spilling by covering all of the neck holes with your fingers.

Although oriental items were in great abundance in England at this time, authentic Chinese porcelain was brought into the colonies in very small amounts. Far Eastern scenes and figures surrounded by floral borders were seen on tea caddies, globular teapots, platters, and bowls of various sizes. Armorial designs covered the center of the plate and were framed with a floral border inside geometric bands.

Europeans continued the quest for the reproduction of porcelain. White salt-glazed stoneware was cautiously potted so that objects were thin enough to serve as a substitute for porcelain on colonial tables. The color was really buff and pieces were sprigged, decorated with applied stamped clay shapes.

The more primitive lead-glazed earthenwares continued in demand as more practical forms. Applied designs were still used for ornamentation. Slip patterns incorporated tulips and formal flowers as motifs, as well as imprinted geometric designs. Liquid clay was applied with a stick to create feathered and combed designs on the surfaces of posset pots, jugs, cups or mugs, and dishes.

William and Mary Glassware

During the William and Mary period in the colonies, glassware was still not much in evidence. There may have been a few glasshouses making window glasses

Delft ceramics consisting of mantel garniture, a monteith, a flower brick, and several tiles.

Holes in the neck of the puzzle jug present a challenge to the drinker.

Kitchen accessories consisting of an iron candle mold, a tin wall sconce, a brass kettle, and clay pipes in their box.

and bottles, but fine glass objects were imported from England. Monteiths, punch bowls, cordial and dram glasses, and decanters were created in glass as well as in ceramics and silver. Wineglasses were the most common glass form. The English wineglass was simple in design. The bowl came in three shapes: cone, round, and waisted, with the cone bowl tapering inward halfway down. The stem strongly resembled the turned legs of furniture with the shape of a baluster (a balanced carrot shape) and knops (wads of glass in many shapes). An air bubble, or tear, was often placed in the baluster stem. The rounded foot was flat or domed-shape with edges either plain or folded under. Simple flowers, fruit, or scrolled designs were either engraved or painted with enamels of blue, red, yellow, and green. While English glassware had simple decoration, German and Bohemian versions were more intricate and sophisticated.

William and Mary Metalwares

Brass, copper, and iron housewares were extremely durable and passed from one generation to another. Thus, the same style and many of the same forms were seen in early and later colonial rooms. Metalware became more plentiful and was seen not only in the kitchen: in spite of the fact that the cooking area had been moved from the main room, brass, copper, and iron items continued to be seen in the main room and in the bedchamber. Fireplace furnishings such as tools, andirons, fenders, and firebacks were used. The tools were created from iron, brass, or a combination of the two, with brass handles on iron tools. Brass or steel andirons had a baluster shaft with a ball finial. Again the horizontal bar that supported the burning logs was iron. A pair of creeper (shorter) andirons may have been set between the taller andirons to support kindling under the logs. During the William and Mary period, brass fenders were placed in front of the fireplace to protect the flooring from sparks. These short metal walls were straight across the front and curved

back toward the fireplace at the end. The fender surface was either pierced or engraved. Iron firebacks were cast with molded decoration, usually a coat of arms, and set against the back of the fireplace to protect the rear stone or brick wall. In less formal rooms, iron grates held the logs, and iron and tin wall candle sconces provided light.

A tea kettle was in the main room where water could be heated in the fire for a cup of tea. The tea kettle was made in many sizes, but in one standard shape during the entire eighteenth century. The body was globular, moving out from the circular base to a gradually rounded shoulder. The cover was set down into the body. A flat strapped handle curved up over the kettle. Bed warmers (see page 13) were kept in the main room or in the bedchamber so that at bedtime hot coals from the fire could be carried in the pan to the bed and placed under the covers to warm them. The long wooden handle was attached to a shallow pan made of silver, copper, or, in most cases, brass. The hinged lid was round and flat with engraved, chased, or repoussé flowers, animals, or geometric patterns.

An eighteenth-century copper tea kettle.

Kitchen equipment including a wooden bread peel, a pewter porringer, an iron skillet and kettle, a pewter tankard with a midband, and a foot warmer.

Candles were supported on various metal stands which varied in height from forms set on tables to those tall enough to stand on the floor. Candlesticks, as andirons, retained the baluster shaft. The bases were round, square, or octagonal. The drip pans located midway down the shaft gradually disappeared. A chandelier might have been hanging in the main room but was used infrequently because of the cost of candles. It was typically made of brass, though there were some pewter and silver forms. The style continued to be the Dutch baluster shaft with one or more rows of S-curved arms. Finally, tall wrought-iron candlestands were supported on a tripod or a four-footed base. The stand had either a single or an American double arm. The candle sockets, knops, and finials were sometimes brass.

The kitchen fireplace was equipped with even more objects, as metal kitchen tools were either made in the colonies or imported from England with greater frequency. Various metals formed large spoons and ladles, pots, saucepans, and toasters. Goffering irons were cylindrical rods for pressing ruffles; hollow irons had a back door for hot coals from the fire. Hanging on the top edge of the fireplace was a clock jack which turned the spit. This device was propelled by the same system of weights as the clocks of the period. Large brass and copper kettles were used for dyeing, brewing ale, cooking fish, and making apple butter. Foot warmers were tin metal boxes framed with wood. They had a wire handle for carrying. The sides were pierced. Coals from the fire were placed in the box to provide warmth for the feet at church or in a wagon or carriage. Wooden kitchen objects seen around the fireplace included a bread peel and bowls in various sizes and shapes.

William and Mary Room Arrangement

The main room became a more formal room now that cooking and sleeping had been relegated to separate chambers. There were a greater number of furniture pieces and accessories. A central table covered with a table carpet might have had on its surface a delft bowl framed by a pair of candlesticks. On the other hand, the table could have been set for a meal with beakers, tankards, a standing salt, delft plates or pewter porringers, pewter or silver spoons, a caster, and a colored globular wine bottle. At the table was placed a banister-back chair, with a flat cushion on the seat, belonging to the master of the house, as well as a joint stool and a Boston chair with a curved back. On one side of the fireplace was a wing chair with a splay-legged table next to it. On the table was a less formal candlestick and a book. On the other side of the fireplace stood a caned armchair with an iron candlestand next to it providing light. On the cushion of the chair rested some needlework. A partially rolled strip sampler lay on the floor at the foot of the chair. Against one of the walls of the room was positioned an open slant-top desk with a corner chair drawn up to it. On the desk were displayed a pair of candlesticks, an inkstand and quill pen, and an open book. A high chest also stood against a wall with a pair of banister-back side chairs on either side. A daybed projected from a corner of the room. Jacobean storage pieces, tables, and chairs could have been present. On the walls hung sizable portraits, engravings with simple wooden frames, a pipe box, a spoon rack, and a lantern clock resting on a narrow wooden shelf. Furniture surfaces were embellished with delft earthenware from England or Holland, pewter and silver pieces, and, perhaps, a glass or two. At the fireplace a brass tea kettle was suspended from a stand.

The kitchen displayed most of its cooking equipment at the fireplace opening and on the walls, though there might have been a built-in cupboard or two. A rustic table was set in front of the fireplace to provide a surface for food preparation. The table surface was covered with more utensils and tools. An open-arm chair was situated next to the fireplace so that the lady of the house could sit to do some of her work. A cradle, a child's chair, or a primitive walker might have been present because children would have been with their mother as she worked in the kitchen. A spinning wheel, a winder, and a butter churn were some of the pieces of larger equipment needed for household chores.

The family might be fortunate enough to have a separate room for sleeping. The bed was placed with its head against the wall, or maybe in a corner. A storage

This spinning wheel by Ron Terrill could be found in an eighteenth-century kitchen. *Courtesy: Ron Terrill*

A winder by Ron Terrill. *Courtesy: Ron Terrill*

chest was placed along its foot. Next to the bed was a side chair or perhaps a table with a candlestick resting on it. The fireplace was less formal in its accessories. A bed warmer leaned on one side of the opening. Miscellaneous chairs and storage pieces lined the walls. A table surface with a side chair drawn up to it was provided for reading or writing. A more formal bedroom would have had a high chest and a matching dressing table for storage pieces.

The Queen Anne Period 1725–1760

Queen Anne Interior Architecture

The colonists now had time to look to England for architectural styles. Printed guidebooks described styles and set standards followed by English carpenters. Many Georgian features presented in these books were incorporated in the more elegant homes of this period. The Queen Anne interior showed a definite classical influence. The walls were fully paneled above and below the chair rail. The fielded panels were large and recessed as opposed to the raised panels of the William and Mary period. Paneling was painted all one color, for example, soft blue, pale blue green, grayish white, or medium green. In less formal rooms, the wall surface above the chair rail was left unpaneled. Some of these surfaces were covered by flocked or hand-painted canvas. Flocked paper had a monochromatic stylized floral design in relief on a contrasting ground. The hand-painted designs might have been floral with S-curved stem designs moving vertically up the wall. Stop-fluted pilasters were present in the room's corners, at intervals across the wall surface, and flanking the fireplace. The heavily molded cornice had become wider and filled the entire space between the top of the window and the ceiling. It jutted out from the wall over windows, doors, fireplaces, and pilasters. Paneled doorways were framed in bolection molding with a narrow panel on the wall across the top.

The fireplace in some homes had been relocated to the corner of the room. The corner fireplace indicated

27

a new trend for chimneys to be placed at each end of the house rather than in the center. The pair of chimneys allowed all four rooms on each level in the newer floor plans to be heated, each with a corner fireplace. The opening of the fireplace was framed by tiles and the bolection molding of the William and Mary period. Contemporary tiles might now have been plum and white, or, to the earlier blue-and-white patterns, purple might have been added. Occasionally, the tiles were carried into the inside of the fireplace opening. On either side of the fireplace, or in a corner, were built-in cupboards, arched at the top and framed with bolection molding and stop-fluted pilasters. An interior shell formed a concave arched ceiling. Occasionally, an arched door with glass panes covered four shelves located above an enclosed cupboard.

Some floors were painted with black and white squares to imitate the marble floors of Europe; others were finished in natural wood. Some parquet work was seen at this time.

The hallway in these elegant homes was characterized by the use of classical arches. The arches were either paneled or had carved keystones and brackets supported by fluted pilasters. On the staircase, risers and gracefully shaped balusters were painted white. Two of the balusters on each step had a tight spiral design, while a third was more loosely turned. The steps and railing were stained in a wood tone. The newel post was slender and curved in shape. The wall surface under the rising stairs was paneled with shapes that conformed to the angle of the stairs. A scalloped strip of wood, which fit into the shape of the steps,

Round brass and glass hall lantern.

topped this paneling. The staircase rose against the wall and might have curved out at the bottom. Lighting for the hall was provided by a round or square lantern hanging from the ceiling. The lantern was composed of glass sides and a brass frame.

The kitchen of the Queen Anne period was located either at the back of the house or, as in the South, in a separate building because of the danger of fire. As in the past, this room was much less formal than any other room in the house. Corner and ceiling supports were exposed. An imaginary wainscot might have been painted, but the upper wall and plastered ceiling were simply whitewashed. The fireplace was still large and primitive. Although some built-in cupboards were present, kitchen equipment and other tools used by the housewife crowded the room. Again, a worktable and chairs stood in front of the fireplace opening. If the kitchen was removed from the main house, the floor was often dirt or unfinished wood. The brick fireplace might have had an arched opening. The ovens were still placed in the interior fireplace wall.

Queen Anne Furniture

The general style of Queen Anne furniture was lighter and more curvaceous than the large-scale architectural forms of the William and Mary period. Practicality was combined with comfort and grace. The S-curve, or cyma curve, was the central theme in the design of this furniture. It was seen in the vase-shaped back splat on chairs, the scalloped edges of tabletops, and in the design of the cabriole leg. The top of a cabriole leg curved outward, forming a knee. It then bent inward until just above the floor, where it moved out again to form a foot. This balance of curves created an extremely strong support. The cabriole leg ended in a pad foot, a pointed slipper foot, a trifid three-toed foot, or, at the end of the period, a claw-and-ball foot. Ornamentation changed in emphasis from William and Mary veneering techniques to a display of the wood grain of the furniture itself. Japanned painting decorated many wood surfaces, and carving was limited to the popular shell motif. Transitional furniture pieces were plentiful during this period as William and Mary stylistic elements, and later Chippendale, were combined with the Queen Anne (see Introduction). Not as many new forms were added to the cabinet-maker's repertoire as during the William and Mary period, but many of the stylistic modifications made on Queen Anne furniture continued through the succeeding period.

The Queen Anne open-back side chair epitomized the stylistic changes of this period. A recurving line was seen throughout the entire piece. The back was curved like a spoon to better accommodate the human

A Queen Anne side chair with japanned ornamentation.

Gold chinoiserie decorates a black secretary.

Japanning on a round tea table by Eugene Kupjack.

A tall case clock and a Queen Anne armchair
with oriental motifs made by Eugene Kupjack.

Four Queen Anne side chairs around a dining table by Deborah Churchill and Lenore Kovolisky of R-Stuff.

body. The rear chair supports remained in one piece as they formed the continuous curve of the hoop back. If present at all, the crest was merely a carved shell, a rosette, or acanthus leaves. The rear legs bent away from the chair as they approached the floor. Framed by the hoop back, a vase-shaped splat rested securely on the back edge of the seat on a support called a shoe. The combination of the curves of the splat and the hoop sometimes created the silhouette of two birds facing each other. The horseshoe form of the seat moved from the back in a sinuous line to be supported by the front cabriole legs. The legs ended most commonly in the pad foot, the location of the cabinetmaker determining the foot style.

Arms were sometimes included in the open-back chair design. They curved out from the rear supports to rest on curved vertical front supports. The flat curve of the arm might have ended in a vertically or horizontally rolled spiral. The arm supports might have curved toward the back of the chair or out to the side to accommodate the ladies' hooped skirts. A looped arm might have been used where the arm surface proceeded from the back support and curved back again before it joined the vertical arm support.

Though many characteristics were standard in the design of the Queen Anne chair, regional differences in furniture design first became obvious during this period. Massachusetts pieces were narrow and tall in appearance. Chairs were rather straight. The curves of the vase-shaped splats and cabriole legs were more gentle. Tall, delicate legs were supported by stretchers long after other areas discontinued their use.

Newport, Rhode Island, favored mahogany for its furniture construction. Cabinetmakers adopted the claw-and-ball foot earlier than other areas. The claw-and-ball became oval in shape, and the talons curved

out from the ball in a pierced effect. The shell carved on the crest rail was silhouetted because it had no background wood behind it. The narrow splat on Massachusetts chairs was more scrolled in its design.

Furniture in New York appeared more sturdy and vigorous. Their chair back was more square than rectangular. The cabriole leg was heavier, while the rounded rear legs tapered as they ended in small squared feet. The claw-and-ball foot was square in shape.

Philadelphia furniture was the most ornate, with its rhythmic curves and rich carving. On the hooped crest rail stood a panel with an S-shaped spiral silhouette. The shell on this crest rested on a wooden background rather than standing free. The splat was characterized by curving scrolls and volutes. The horseshoe seat was recessed at the center to display a carved shell. The same shell could be seen on the knee of the cabriole leg. A trifid foot was used almost exclusively in Philadelphia, as was the paneling treatment of the trifid, slipper, and pad foot. A paneling treatment caused the foot to end abruptly with its edges perpendicular to the floor. The rear stump leg was plain, rounded, and occasionally chamfered.

A new upholstered chair form replaced the open hooped back with an upholstered one. The tall upholstered back rested on an upholstered seat. This form was created with or without open arms. The back was rounded or squared at the top, or it might have had an upholstered crest in the shape of the reverse cyma curve seen on the wooden hooped back. A slipper chair was designed in this manner. The seat on this form, however, stood twelve to fourteen inches from the floor. This low side chair was designed for women.

The corner chair now had a vase-shaped splat on each side of the central back support. The flowing curve of the back supports were echoed by the rounded

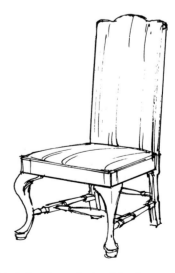

A lady's slipper chair with a low seat.

Wing-back easy chair by Paul Runyon; japanned high chest by Harry Smith; basin stand by Virginia Merrill.

front corner, the curved back rail, and the four cabriole legs. The back rail ended in a spiraled knuckle. Occasionally, a combed back was mounted on this rail. The combed back was in the form of the top half of a hooped back with a vase-shaped splat. This added back support increased the comfort of the corner chair.

The basic design of the easy chair remained the same throughout the eighteenth century. The leg treatment changed with the period. A short cabriole leg ended in a pad foot. New England continued to use stretchers with this form. The regional differences of the William and Mary period persisted in the style of the arms. New York and New England used the vertically rolled style, while Philadelphia favored the horizontal roll.

The settee made its appearance during this period. This elongated chair form provided seating for two persons. It was slow to gain popularity in the colonies although the easy chair was used extensively. Chair-back settees had a double wooden hooped back. This form was used more in England until the Chippendale period. The upholstered settee followed the style of the tall-back upholstered chair, with upholstered armrests and padded backs which rested on padded seats. The top edge of the backs of some settees were scalloped (see page 32), but most had a straight horizontal line.

The sofa was seen rarely, and only at the end of the Queen Anne period. It could accommodate four to six people and was long enough for reclining. On this form not only the seat and the back were padded, but also the arms. The upholstered arched back was lower than that of the settee. Horizontally rolled arms rose up from the seat and curved out at the level of the back. Four cabriole legs crossed the front of the sofa and were

connected to the rear legs by flat, arrow-shaped stretchers. Simple flat stretchers joined the four rear legs.

Stools were rare in the colonies during this time. Chairs were now plentiful enough to make stools unnecessary, except in wealthier households where a stool might have accompanied a chair as a set. The connotation of the earlier Jacobean use for stools caused them to be looked down upon. They stood twelve to eighteen inches in height and had a rectangular slip-seat frame with a cabriole leg curving out from each corner (see page 32).

A pair of Queen Anne easy chairs by Deborah Churchill and Lenore Kovolisky of R-Stuff.

A Queen Anne settee with a scalloped back is placed in a period room by Eugene Kupjack.

The daybed continued to be popular during the Queen Anne period. It followed the style of the open-back side chair, except that the hooped crest rail was supported by two scrolled splats, and the squared seat extended to form a bed. Six to eight legs served as supports. These, too, followed the chair style. By the middle of the eighteenth century, the daybed was no longer needed because houses were larger and could accommodate a greater number of standard beds in extra rooms.

Queen Anne beds used cabriole legs at the foot and sometimes at the head for support. Headboards had straight or scalloped edges. Field beds, which had arched testers, could also be found during this period.

Originally, the field bed was used during war or travel because it could be readily dismantled and transported. More permanent models were used in homes because the curved testers could accommodate low ceilings or sloping attic roofs. Low-post beds were also made at this time with the Queen Anne headboard and leg characteristics. Corner posts, each consisting of an oblong block with a ball finial, rested on cabriole legs.

A field bed of the Queen Anne period made by Deborah Churchill and Lenore Kovolisky of R-Stuff.

Queen Anne stools with tent- and Irish-stitch upholstery by Donald Buttfield.

A dish-top tea table with sliding candlestick supports.

Ron Terrill made this tilt-top tea table. *Courtesy: Ron Terrill*

Tables continued the same specialization that began in the William and Mary period. By 1730, tea drinking had become an everyday practice. Tea tables became popular at this time. They were made with either a rectangular dish top or a round tray top. The elevated edge of the dish top prevented teawares from sliding off the table surface. The edge was created by cutting a flat depression in the table surface, leaving only a narrow elevated band around the outside edge. The rectangular tea table was created with a plain edge around the dish top. The narrow frieze supporting the top was either scalloped or rested on a convex scalloped skirt. Long, slender cabriole legs stood at the corners. Set in the frieze at each end of the table might have been flat,

rectangular extensions which supported candlesticks when drawn out. The round tea table had a tray top with a plain elevated edge. The top was supported by a tripod base with either a baluster shaft or a simple tapering shaft set on a flattened ball. The shaft might have been topped by a square bracket, which served as a transition from the shaft to the horizontal rail of the tabletop. This device enabled the top to tilt to an upright position.

The William and Mary gate leg was replaced at this time by a cabriole leg attached to a swinging gate. Drop-leaf tables were seen in various sizes. The larger versions could be used for dining, while the smaller provided a collapsible surface for breakfast, tea, writ-

The hinged device allows the round top to move to a vertical position. *Courtesy: Ron Terrill*

A front view of the round dished top of the tea table in a vertical position. *Courtesy: Ron Terrill*

A Queen Anne swing leg supports a rounded leaf on this dining table. The table surface is oval when completely opened.

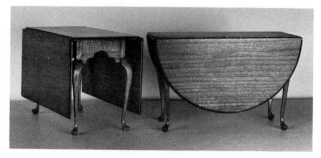

A pair of Queen Anne dining tables. The surface of one is oval when opened, the other rectangular. They were made by Edward G. Norton. *Courtesy: Edward G. Norton*

Edward G. Norton created this drop-leaf handkerchief table and candlestand in the style of the Queen Anne period. *Courtesy: Edward G. Norton*

ing, cards, or candlesticks. The opened table surface was typically oval, although some rectangular forms exist. One drop-leaf form was the handkerchief table. The base was triangular with three stationary legs. A fourth leg pivoted to support a triangular folding leaf. The top surface was square when the leaf was in use.

A new form created during the Queen Anne period was the folding card table. The square top folded in half when the table was not in use. The opened surface was square with rounded turret corners that projected outward to accommodate the round candlesticks of the period. An oval depression at each side of the table surface held counters, fish, or other game equipment. The opened top was supported by a rectangular base and a pivoting leg or by an accordion-action extension. An insert of leather or needlework protected the wood of the table surface (see pages 183 and 230).

Marble-topped tables followed the design of the rectangular tea table, with the exception of the treatment of the top surface and the candlestick extensions. A marble slab served as a top surface; no extensions for candles were provided. This longer table was finished on all four sides for use in the center of a room. It was also used against the wall under a mirror as a pier table.

Other tables served specialized functions. A small round table, modeled after the larger tea table, was a candlestand. A table resembling the rectangular tea table had tiles on the entire top surface and was used as a mixing table.

Freestanding cupboards replaced the earlier court and built-in cupboards. A popular form was the corner cupboard with a cyma-scrolled broken pediment and a shell radiating over the interior ceiling. It was here that

fine ceramics and glassware were displayed. The kas, another storage piece, was a wardrobe of Dutch origin made predominantly in New York and New Jersey as early as the seventeenth century. This enormous cupboard had two long doors and ball feet. This form was paneled and often painted with brightly colored designs.

The high chest of drawers of the Queen Anne period was unique to the colonies, the concept not based on an English model. This form was used until the end of the Chippendale period. A nicely molded crown in the form of a broken scrolled pediment replaced the flat top of the William and Mary period. The pediment received this name because the peak was cut away. A finial sat on each of the top front corners. In the central opening, a matching finial often took the shape of a flame, an urn, or a corkscrew. It stood on a tall base. Finials were wooden, brass, or painted to resemble brass. The occasional use of a stepped pediment provided surfaces to display chinaware. On a flat William and Mary top rested an often separate piece in the form of two steps that tapered inward. The second step took the form of a small, broken scrolled pediment with a single central finial. Ceramic objects were placed on the top edge of the high chest and on the first step of the

A freestanding corner cupboard with the Queen Anne shell over the top shelf made by Donald Buttfield.
Courtesy: Donald Buttfield

A green kas with paneled doors that lock by Virginia Merrill.

Mary S. Kebbon made this eighteenth-century kas.
Courtesy: Mary S. Kebbon

pediment. Turned wooden pendants replaced the William and Mary legs that had been used for additional support. The design of the cabriole leg provided enough strength to support the weight of the high chest with only four legs. The leg bracket on either side of the top of the cabriole leg was scrolled. A carved shell, sometimes gilded, decorated the central top and bottom drawers. Occasionally, when the shell motif became more geometric, it was called a fan. When it was completely round, it became a sunburst. A small, rounded convex molding framed either the edge of the drawers or the case opening into which the drawers were set. There was some use of inlay on drawer fronts or in the form of a variegated star on the side of the piece. The apron beneath the drawers was often arched.

The dressing tables imitated the stylistic elements of the high chest because they were often made as a set. Now the case held two tiers of drawers, which made the piece more boxlike than the William and Mary form. But the curves of the scalloped apron and the cabriole legs gave the piece the grace necessary for this period and the next.

Many high chests and their matching dressing tables

Corkscrew finials ornament the broken scrolled pediment of this Queen Anne high chest by Harry Smith.

Dr. Frank Renna made a Queen Anne high chest and a Chippendale side chair from a kit produced by X-ACTO®, HOUSE OF MINIATURES®.

The Queen Anne dressing table has turned drops in place of the two extra front legs on the William and Mary form. It was made by Edward G. Norton.
Courtesy: Edward G. Norton

Queen Anne desk on frame by Paul Runyon.

Inside view of Paul Runyon's desk
shows the complex arrangement of
drawers and cubbyholes.

were decorated with chinoiserie painting and finished
to a hard, shiny surface by the japanned technique (see
page 31). A tortoiseshell ground was created for the
gold designs by the streaking of red and black.

The desk on frame of the Queen Anne period placed
the desk box on a dressing table. The box had many
cubbyholes and drawers inside. This form succumbed
to the more convenient slant-top desk, which provided
three or four drawers for storage space beneath the
desk box. Shortened cabriole legs supported the piece.
When a bookcase was set on the slant-top piece, the
shortened cabriole legs were occasionally replaced by a
flat bracket foot having a straight corner edge and a
scrolled inner edge. Finials and the pediment of broken
scrolls seen on the high chest crowned the bookcase.
Decoration was often in the form of inlaid stars or veneered banding. The desk and bookcase (or secretary)
form was used through the Federal period.

Furniture brasses of the Queen Anne period were
used for drawer pulls and key escutcheons. The backplate was in the shape of a bat with its wings spread
open. The U-shaped handle hung from the wing tips.
The key plate matched the drawer pulls exactly.
Toward the end of the period, the plates increased in
size and were occasionally pierced.

The William and Mary tall case clocks had a domed
hood, but the top of the dome and the cornice over the
arched dial were flat. During the Queen Anne period,
the cornice over the dial was arched, as was the dome.
The clocks were often painted with chinoiserie and
finished in the japanned technique.

The looking glass was now elongated and required,
usually, two pieces of silvered glass to fill the frame.
This glass had to be imported from Europe throughout

William and Mary tall case clock
characterized by a flat domed hood
over an arched dial and a flat base.

Queen Anne tall case clock with an
arched hood over the arched dial
and bracket feet at the base.

the eighteenth century. The frame was convex with a scrolled crest at the top. A scrolled apron might have been present at the bottom. The frame was often painted black and decorated with gold chinoiserie designs (see page 170). Or, the frame could have been veneered and decorated with applied rococo gilded ornaments characteristic of the contemporary Georgian period in England. The looking glass often served as a pier glass hung over a side table against the wall between two windows. This arrangement was often seen in pairs with a central window.

Contemporary English cabinetmakers were creating furniture in the Georgian style. Mahogany replaced walnut by 1730. Forms took on the new emphasis of the chest of drawers, the desk, and the console table, which was designed to fit against, or to be fixed to, a wall. The stylistic elements included the claw-and-ball foot, the ogee bracket foot, and bold carving with masks and shells.

Queen Anne Upholstery

During the Queen Anne period, many more pieces of furniture required upholstery. The coverings of this period consisted of canvas work, crewel embroideries, printed linens (especially the blue-and-white resist linen), leather, velvets, silks, brocades, and brocatelles.

The horseshoe-shaped slip seats of the open-backed chairs were covered with a variety of fabrics. A unique treatment was the tent-stitch design of a pastoral scene, framed by a border of flowers (see page 258). Irish-stitched canvas designs became smaller during this period. The patterns became more geometric in shape as opposed to the simple wave of earlier flame patterns. Miniature examples of the Queen Anne Irish stitch designs are seen on pages 206 and 207. Crewel embroidered floral and scenic designs on linen were also used. A few of these pieces were worked so that none of the background was revealed.

On the wing chair and on the rare settee and sofa, the upholstery was carried over the frame. Occasionally, this treatment was trimmed with brass tacks. Wing chairs were covered in Irish- or tent-stitch scenic canvas designs, as well as crewel-embroidered fabrics.

Gaming tabletops were protected by an insert of leather or needlework. The tent-stitch design might have been a crowded pastoral scene created in brightly colored wool, as that seen on page 183.

Queen Anne Drapery Treatment

Windows of the Queen Anne period were covered, in many instances, by wooden interior shutters. After 1750, venetian blinds were used. Window coverings of

A pair of festoon drapery panels, each drawn up to a corner at the top of the window.

drapery fabrics existed only in the more formal rooms of the house. Drapery materials were the same as those used for upholstery, with the exception of leather. Drapery treatments seen during the William and Mary period persisted during the Queen Anne years. Floor-length side curtains were topped by a scalloped valance, or fabric was puffed at the top of the window in the Venetian style. At the end of the Queen Anne period, the festoon style of drapes emerged. Festoon curtains were made with two straight pieces of cloth. Diagonal rings and cords ran from the bottom inner corner to the top outer corner. When the cords were drawn, the curtain gathered at the upper outside corner of the window, creating a double swag with tails, or points, hanging down the sides.

Until the middle of the eighteenth century, entertaining was done in the room housing the master bedstead, so the bed hangings still served as an indication of prosperity. Tester, half-tester, and field beds were draped with upholstery fabrics. Side curtains were no longer drawn around the three exposed sides of the bed, but were hung at the head for purely ornamental reasons. Many sets of crewel-embroidered bed hangings were passed down from a previous generation. Different pieces were divided among the offspring. It was not unusual to use valances and pieces of side curtains to drape windows during the Queen Anne period. Beds were decorated with embroidered pieces combined with solid colored fabrics to complete the set. Newly embroidered Queen Anne hangings were created during this time as crewel embroidery was very popular.

Queen Anne Floor Coverings

Turkey carpets were still used as table covers during the Queen Anne period, but this fashion was disappearing. The use of carpets on the floor was much more common. Carpets were imported from the Near East. A rare floor covering was an English needlework carpet. These carpets were made by individuals in the more durable cross or tent stitches with English worsted wool on a sturdy linen canvas. The stitcher often included dates and family crests. The designs showed borders created by an abundance of large, realistic flowers with complicated foliage, in the contemporary English style. A central floral motif was often framed by a cartouche or a medallion. A tree of life would have been a suitable central motif for an English needlework carpet or for a Near Eastern import. On page 234, the central motif included whimsical animals seen in the needlework pictures of the times. The central design was framed by a border of S-curves which were so characteristic of this period. While it was not a copy of an actual piece, this rug might have been designed and stitched in the colonies.

Floorcloths of thickly painted linen or canvas also covered floors. These cloths were often painted heavily with oil paint to resemble black-and-white marble tiles.

A Queen Anne floor carpet.
Designed by Susan Richardson.

Rag woven carpets were created by weaving torn strips of cloth with a durable cotton, linen, or worsted warp. This technique resulted in colorful striped patterns. Rag or list carpets such as these were used more as protective covers for the more valued oriental or needlework carpets and for parquet floors.

Queen Anne Needlework

Because of the increase in leisure time, colonial ladies were able to create more decorative needlework. A large part of a young lady's education was taken up with the acquisition of stitching skills. During her schooling, she produced a sampler. Rather than serving as a reference for future needlework projects, this piece became a demonstration of accomplishment, which was framed and hung on the wall. Samplers were no longer created by adults, but by girls five to twelve years of age as part of their education. More decorative motifs were added to the alphabet and numeral forms. By the middle of the eighteenth century, a pictorial emphasis was adopted. The shape more closely resembled a square and borders were introduced to frame the work. As time progressed, the borders became wider and more obvious. Samplers became plentiful as the custom was established for a young lady to attend a residential finishing school.

Canvas-work pictures were created by these same young ladies as graduation projects. These sizable works were often as long as three or four feet. They, too, were beautifully framed, sometimes with a "dog-eared" wooden frame decorated with gilt. A brass candle holder might have been placed at each lower corner (see page 193). These needlework pictures were hung in a place of honor over the mantel. The subject of mid-eighteenth-century tent-stitch pictures was a pastoral setting of human figures in a landscape. For example, a lady might have been seated by a stream, fishing. Fishing had been established as a proper courting activity. A number of pictures with this particular theme apparently originated in the Boston area. They were called "Fishing Lady" pictures. The landscape was presumed to be the Boston Common. Mrs. Susannah Condy, who owned a needlework shop and a boarding school in Boston, was reported to be the designer of a large series of these pictures. Another typical figure in the scene was a lady with a drop spindle. The weighted sticklike whorl twirled as she dangled it so that yarn fibers became wound. This portable device allowed ladies to do their spinning out of doors while visiting with friends. Also in these pictures were sheep, dogs, birds, deer, houses, and other ladies and gentlemen. Proper proportions were not considered. Other pastoral motifs were borrowed from printed sources.

There were sources other than schools for needlework designs. Professional designers in England and America created drawn patterns on linen or canvas, and supplied enough silk or wool with which to stitch the design. Lessons in drawing needlework designs were available. Various motifs were also shared or sketched by amateur friends.

The Irish stitch was popular in the colonies because the stitching of a piece could be accomplished much more quickly. Flamelike patterns were devised, such as a diamond within a diamond, a zigzag, a carnation, or whimsical geometric designs. Many items were created with these patterns: chair seats, easy-chair upholstery, bookcovers, folding pocketbooks, wall pockets, standing or hand fire screens, tablecloths, and candlescreens. A needlework cover was applied to a Bible for its protection and as a decorative touch when it was on display (see page 206). Pocketbooks (see page 207) were like envelopes in which valuables were kept. Currency, IOUs, deeds, important documents, and wills that were not hidden in secret compartments in furniture could be carried around with the owner. Ladies carried jewelry, sewing tools, and small articles. Their pocketbooks were smaller than the men's. Wall pockets (see page 209) were open envelopes hung on the wall, perhaps next to a bed or chair, in which papers or a book might be kept. Hand fire screens (see page 208) were less convenient than adjustable pole screens on a tripod base. Nonetheless, they were used to protect the face from the fireplace heat when a standing screen was unavailable. Irish-stitch tablecloths, often designed as a sampler of different Irish-stitch patterns, were used as the table carpet had been. The rectangular surface of the candlescreen served as a shade for the light from the flame (see page 208).

Crewel or silk embroidery were used as they were during the William and Mary period, but had become more prolific. Hatchments, bed hangings, window draperies, upholstery fabrics, pockets, petticoat borders, clothing decoration, and pictures were all created with wool or silk embroidery on a linen or silk ground. The tree of life motif was still in evidence and was joined by large peonies, stylized acanthus leaves, carnations, the Tudor rose, parrots, pineapples, and cypress trees. Small pictures were plentiful. Crewel embroidery continued to be used to create bold looped designs on bed rugs during this period.

Colorful woolen stockings and mittens were still knit by small children. Men's stockings were in view and were decorated with clocks, elaborate bell-like objects. Women's stockings were colorful also, although they could not be seen. The owner's initials were still knit in the design of the stockings. Many continued to be numbered as well.

One-piece quilt techniques persisted until around 1750, when pieced quilts were created. Quilts not only covered mattresses but were made into petticoats, bodices, jackets, and coats for added warmth during the cold months. Pieced quilt designs were made into bedcovers and pockets.

Queen Anne Silver

Silver pieces were more abundant in homes of the Queen Anne period. Increased prosperity allowed the colonists to display their wealth in the form of silver. Because a separate dining room rarely existed, silver pieces were displayed on furniture in the parlor, such as the shelves of freestanding shell cupboards.

Silver produced during the Queen Anne period discarded the heavy, molded ornamentation of the William and Mary style. Queen Anne silversmiths relied on the curvilinear silhouette of the piece for a decorative effect. The Englishman William Hogarth described the perfection of the S-curve in his book, *Analysis of Beauty*. He considered the S-shape the most beautiful, graceful line because it had just the right amount of roundness, being not too curved and not too straight. This curve was seen in S-shaped spouts on pots, S- and C-scrolled handles, the pear shape of containers, and in engraved motifs. The design of all silver objects of this time was created by the joining of several continuously flowing, curving lines. Decoration was limited to the engraving of delicate floral or shell borders and central, foliated cyphers (initials) or heraldic insignias.

Round shapes were predominant in Queen Anne sil-

Several Queen Anne silver objects: a coffeepot on a stand, a salt cellar (1768), a tea caddy (1706), a teapot, a creamer, a candlestick, and a presentation cup.

ver, but the octagonal was also much in evidence. Candlestick bases supported baluster-shaped shafts with no drip pans or bobeches. At the base of the shaft was an octagonally shaped base with either straight sides or lobes (see page 40). The octagon was also used in the design of an eight-sided, pear-shaped teapot (see page 40).

Hogarth also noted the importance of closely tying in practicality with beauty. Practicality was clearly seen in the design of the Queen Anne teapot. The pear shape of the body distributed the greatest amount of water to the bottom of the pot where the tea leaves had settled. The high cost of tea encouraged the creation of small teapots. The handles were large enough to accommodate the hand and were curved rather than angular for an easier grip. They were wooden to prevent the conduction of heat from the pot.

Bowls of the Queen Anne period followed the round shape of Chinese porcelain. The simple flared bowl now rested on a circular domed foot instead of on a silver band. The bowl was used for the preparation and serving of punch. By the middle of the eighteenth century, the same bowl shape was used in a smaller circular or octagonal form during the presentation of tea. Cold tea was poured into the "slop bowl," as it was called, before fresher hot tea was poured into the cup.

Innovation during the Queen Anne period emphasized new shapes rather than new forms. Drinking vessels continued to be made but followed the decorative trends of the Queen Anne period. Round-bottomed tumblers were no longer made after this period. The loving cup, used earlier as a communal drinking vessel, with a lid, became a presentation piece. The rounded body became urn-shaped (see page 40). The two handles were retained. The silver goblet was still reserved for church use. Mugs and tankards were taller and more tapered. The base moldings were wider. A midband was introduced, and the rattail disappeared. The lid on the tankard was slightly domed with no finial. The pear-shaped cann was popular.

Porringers retained the same shape, while the pierced handle design became keyhole. In England, the American porringer form was called a "bleeding bowl." The English "porringer" was a caudle cup. In England, porringers ceased to be used early in the eighteenth century. Therefore, the keyhole-handled porringer became a form unique to America.

Silver flatware remained limited to the spoon form, although a few three-tined forks might have been produced. The underside of the spoon still faced up when set on the table. The rattail had been replaced by a shell or a spatula shape. Spoons became more specialized. Large spoons were made for serving, small spoons for eating custard or stirring tea or chocolate. Strainer spoons had pierced bowls and skimmed the leaves out

A footed sauceboat with a curved handle
made by Eugene Kupjack.

A globular Queen Anne teapot with a wooden handle.

of tea or solid ingredients from punch. Tea tongs appeared at this time. They were in the form of scissors with a round, flat hinge and shells at the ends for pincers.

Spice container forms remained the same. Salt trenchers were widely used at each place as salt became less scarce. The solid octagonal trenchers became rounded, and the bodies were lifted to rest on three or four curved legs. Casters with handles were octagonal and had a molded base or rested on three or four feet. By the middle of the century, these casters fell into disuse. Pear-shaped casters continued to be made in sets of three (see page 84). The curve of the pear shape became more exaggerated while the top section became more slender. The caster acquired a midband.

Salvers continued in use. Instead of the trumpet foot, three or four little feet supported the tray surface. The rims of these footed trays were composed of a series of curves, creating a variety of edge shapes. The tray surface was decorated by engraving. An engraved border might have followed the inside of the curved rim, and a central motif of an insignia or initials ornamented the center of the plain tray surface.

Silver dining equipment was growing in sophistication and specialization. The chafing dish with its pierced pan was used at this time to keep dishes and teapots hot. Sauceboats made an appearance during this period. One end terminated in a single long lip and the other end supported a scrolled handle. The bowl sat on three curved legs.

The Queen Anne tea service included more pieces, which were now coordinated in terms of design. The teapot might have had the round or the pear shape. The pear shape was either circular or octagonal in section. The domed foot followed the shape of the section. The round pot extended the S-shaped spout outward more and had a lid with a finial that sat flush with the shoulders of the pot. A domed lid with a finial topped the pear-shaped teapot. Chocolate drinking was falling out of favor at this time, though it continued to some degree. Coffee and chocolate pots were tall with tapered cylindrical bodies and domed lids. The coffeepot might have mirrored the teapot in shape, though, as today, it was taller. Milk was now served with tea. By the middle of the century, the milk pot had a spout created by the curved elongation of the mouth of the pot. The pear-shaped body sat on three small curved legs (see page 40).

Sugar bowls followed the Chinese design. They were circular or octagonal. A circular ring on the top of the lid allowed it to be inverted and used as a small salver. Before the middle of the century, the bowl shape became an inverted pear. The lid became domed with a finial.

A Queen Anne sugar bowl whose lid becomes a dish when inverted.

Tea caddies stored dried tea leaves. The kati was an early unit of weight by which tea was sold. The vertical, rectangular boxes with all four corners curving inward had round necks with fitted lids. The caddies were made in pairs with perhaps a third for the storage of sugar. The name of a particular tea was engraved on each piece. Finally, a large tea kettle on a stand with three or four legs contained water to be heated by a lamp built into the stand (see page 40). A large rotating handle curved over the top of the vessel. The handle could rotate because it was attached to the pot with hinges. Though it was larger, the tea kettle followed the shape of the teapot.

Candlesticks of the Queen Anne period were characterized by a baluster shaft and by the absence of a drip pan. The bases of candlesticks might have been octagonal or rounded with lobes or curves at the edges (see page 40). Silver candlesticks were not plentiful in colonial homes during this period because they were now cast and very expensive. A candlesnuffer on a small tray was produced at this time. The scissor form snuffed the flame, cut the burned wick and, with a pointed end, pried loose the remaining candle stub.

Candlesnuffer and stand by Eugene Kupjack.

Silversmiths appeared in the smaller towns in the colonies, rather than being found only in the larger cities. With increased prosperity, silver became more plentiful and was used for more objects. Miscellaneous personal items appeared in silver such as knee and shoe buckles, rings, buttons, thimbles, lockets, snuff and tobacco boxes, sword hilts, and inkstands.

Queen Anne Pewter

Pewter making in the colonies was discouraged by an English tax on imported tin. The tax on the purchase of English pewterwares was low. Pewter was soft and easily damaged. Thus, after a century of colonization, a need arose for the melting down and recasting of damaged pewter pieces. Necessary items, such as basins, plates, spoons, and mugs, were cast. While the pewter metal cost nothing, the brass molds used in the casting process were costly. Molds were passed from one generation to the next. As a result, the style of pewter changed very little.

In England, pewter was produced in greater variety. The consistency of the metal and the casting process required simplification in the style of the pewter form. Fashionable shapes were incorporated in pewter designs, but much of the ornamentation was left to the silversmiths. Tablewares, such as plates and serving dishes, spoons, mugs, tankards, beakers, and porringers, were made. Plates and dishes had a single-reeded rim; spoons, trifid ends; mugs and tankards, a midband. Tankard tops were domed. Beakers were made in several standard sizes. Their sides flared and they had midbands. Porringer handles were pierced. Teawares were produced in pewter—teapots, sugar bowls, creamers, tea stands, and teaspoons. The teapot followed the silver style in its pear shape and domed lid. The sugar bowl was an inverted pear with a lower domed lid. Pewter was used to make other items, such as clockfaces, lighting fixtures, chamber pots, nursing bottles, buckles, and buttons.

Queen Anne Ceramics

During the Queen Anne period, colonists continued to rely on local artisans for their kitchen and dairy pottery pieces, while good china was imported from England. Stoneware and redware pottery, such as tall pots, jugs, and plates, were created in simple, pleasant shapes. Ornamentation consisted of incised bands of straight and wavy lines or stylized trailed slip decoration. The sgraffito technique was used to decorate pottery made by the Pennsylvania Germans (see page 63). In this method, the brownish red clay surface was covered entirely with a thin coating of diluted clay, or slip. A design was then scratched through the slip surface, which was usually gold in color. The cut design appeared in the color of the red clay underneath. Sgraffito motifs were a rider on horseback, a courting couple, stylized tulips, and decorative birds. Pottery forms with sgraffito ornamentation were plates, bowls, mugs, lidded jars, jugs, barber bowls (whose rims were concave at one point to accommodate customers' necks), and bird whistles.

From Staffordshire, England, informal earthenwares with variegated surfaces were seen at this time. Agateware and tortoiseshell wares were created either by the blending of clays under a clear glaze or the streaking of a variety of glazes on a single clay. Tableware were made with this technique. Small sculptures called "image toys" were also produced in this manner. The figures were created in the form of musicians and soldiers as they were seen in the country in England.

Delftwares and salt-glazed stonewares were formed into more formal ceramic pieces. A greater variety of table and tea pieces were seen now that tea had become such an important part of social ritual. Ornamentation was multicolored on a white ground. As in earlier periods, Chinese shapes and motifs continued to be used. Plates had wide rims that were round, octagonal, or scalloped around the edges. A central pattern might have been surrounded by a decorated rim of a contrasting color, or a Chinese landscape might have covered the entire plate surface, including the rim. Pots, creamers, and bowls followed those seen in contemporary silver.

An assortment of Queen Anne delftware.

Staffordshire salt-glazed stoneware was used not only for tablewares but also to form small statues called "pew groups." A group of seated figures might have shown a single English peasant woman framed by two men playing fiddles. The pew groups and the image toys were early examples of purely decorative ceramics.

Dutch delft and English delft tiles were imported into the colonies to cover table surfaces or to frame fireplace openings. The designs were blue, purple, or polychrome on a white ground. Animals, stylized flowers, or scenes were framed by a square, diamond, or circle.

German salt-glazed stoneware was used in the colonies for informal dining. Blue ornamentation was placed on a light gray ground.

China trade porcelain continued to be rare in the colonies. Pieces were obtainable only through England. Examples of beautiful European ceramics also had difficulty making their way across the Atlantic. France and Germany, in particular, were getting closer to duplicating the fine quality of Chinese hard-paste porcelain.

Queen Anne Glassware

During the Queen Anne period, the colonies depended on England for most of its glassware. Up to this point, no colonial glasshouse survived, so the only locally produced glass products were windowpanes and bottles. In the 1730s, the first successful glass foundry was established in Southern Jersey. Besides bottles and windowpanes, useful items such as bowls, pitchers, and jars were created in greens and ambers.

From England came drinking glasses and decanters. The wineglasses had bowls engraved with flowers. The bowl was shaped like a tulip or a funnel. The funnel shape flowed directly out of a straight stem, or, as did the tulip, rested on a baluster stem with one or two knops. The straight stem might have had a white spiral air twist twirling through its length. English decanters were onion-shaped with low, thick bodies that tapered to thin necks.

Other glasses were designed for elegant entertaining. The ratafia glass, used to serve a fruit-and-nut liqueur, had a narrow cylindrical bowl that tapered to a very tall stem. Syllabub, a punch made with milk and wine, was

Glasses with a funnel-shaped bowl and with a knopped and a plain stem.

properly drunk from a small jelly or syllabub glass. Its waisted conical bowl rested on a knop sitting directly on a slightly domed foot. These glasses might have had two handles and might have been called posset glasses. Sweetmeat glasses, or champagne glasses, were footed cut-glass bowls in which to present desserts. A popular way to serve dessert at this time was to assemble on a footed glass plate a sweetmeat glass with syllabub glasses surrounding it. Another dessert dish arrangement was a pyramid of graduated footed plates on which small dishes filled with sweetmeats had been arranged. Sweetmeats were candied or crystallized fruits.

Chandeliers, sconces, and candelabra were made of glass in the style of contemporary brass models. Because of the expense of candles, these objects were not plentiful in the colonies, in spite of their exquisite beauty in the soft glow of candlelight.

A glass tax levied in 1745 in England forced glassmakers to make their wares thinner. They placed their emphasis on ornamentation instead of on the simpler, weighty shapes.

Queen Anne Metalwares

During the Queen Anne period, articles for the home were made from copper, brass, iron, steel, and tin. Tin was the only metal that was not durable. Undecorated tin articles were considered expendable and could easily be replaced. Decorated tinware was held in greater esteem. Candlesticks, teapots and tea caddies, trays, and different sized boxes were often decorated with painted ornamentation. Gold chinoiserie was applied to a red, black, or tortoiseshell background and lacquered. These japanned tinwares were imported from England.

Brass, copper, and iron household equipment could be melted down and recast in the same way that pewter was repaired. As with pewter, the styles remained the same over a long period of time. Saucepans, dippers, bed-warming pans, kettles, and a great variety of other kitchen tools were made in the colonies from local raw materials. Saucepans were tin-lined with flat bottoms and gently curved sides. The tea kettle retained the same round body with gently curved sides. Arching over the inset lid was a flat handle. The angular spout was shaped like a goose's neck. European tea kettles did not follow the same style, that is, the bodies were made in different shapes. The spout might have been covered and the handle might have been cast.

Fireplace equipment remained unchanged from the William and Mary period except that the low fenders that protected the room from sparks had become bow or serpentine in shape. They were still decorated with pierced openwork or engraving. Cast-iron firebacks

were still in evidence. Andirons typically retained the baluster shaft and the cabriole legs with claw-and-ball, snake, or penny feet. In the 1740s, Benjamin Franklin gave his name to a cast-iron stove that had a hearth. The efficient distribution of heat made this a popular item in the colonial home.

Lighting was provided by candles set in candlesticks, candlestands, chandeliers, wall sconces, and lanterns. Candlesticks were produced in many metals, such as silver, pewter, tin, iron, and, most commonly, brass. Queen Anne candlesticks were created with a baluster shaft rising from a lobed foot. The mid drip pan of the William and Mary period had completely disappeared. Candlestands were wrought iron with one or two arms extending to support a candle. Bases had three or four legs. Brass was used occasionally to form finials, candle sockets, and round knops for ornamentation. Chandeliers and wall sconces were made of pewter or silver. But the most popular metal for these was brass. The stem of the chandelier was globular while the arms stretched out in S-curves. The wall sconce followed the chandelier style with only two arms. Lanterns hung in the central hallway of the colonial home. Four or six glass panes were framed with brass and set into a square or a hexagon. They might have been round also (see page 28). Portable candlesticks, rather than chandeliers, wall sconces, and lanterns, were more frequently used in the colonial homes because of the expense of candles.

Arched clock dials were made with brass. The surface was engraved. Since clockworks were also cast in brass, clocks were costly.

Queen Anne Room Arrangement

The use of the rooms of a Queen Anne home varied with the economic level of the owner. In grand houses of the Queen Anne period, a separate dining room removed the centrally placed dining table from the parlor to a separate room across the central hall at the front of the house. The master bedroom was moved to the second floor. The parlor was used for tea and other social events. More typical, however, was the parlor where most family activities took place, except sleeping. Built-in or corner shell cupboards flanked the fireplace, upon which pewter, ceramics, silver, and a few pieces of glassware were displayed. Hanging over the fireplace was a tent-stitch fishing lady picture with a brass candle holder at each bottom corner. An armed open-back chair and a wing-back easy chair framed the fireplace opening. Next to the open-back chair was a wrought-iron candlestand. Light was provided for the easy chair by a candle in a lobed brass candlestick set on a round candlestand. A mahogany drop-leaf dining table stood closed against the wall under a window. An open-back

Queen Anne side chair was situated at each end of the table. Over each chair hung a framed quillwork picture with a silver candle arm extending from the lower edge. Between the two windows on another wall was placed a pier mirror painted black and decorated with gold chinoiserie. Under the mirror against the wall was a pier table. In the corner, a game table had been opened, with two side chairs providing seating for players. Lobed brass candlesticks were set in the turret corners. Ivory fish rested in the recesses of each place. Cards were positioned for a game. A rectangular tea table had been moved from against the wall. The table, set for serving tea, was placed in front of the two fireplace chairs. A silver teapot, sugar bowl, creamer, teaspoons, and sugar tongs were displayed with colorful delft cups and saucers. A medium-sized needlework carpet was positioned on the center of the parlor floor.

The master bedroom served as a study and a room in which to entertain friends for tea—if these activities could not take place in other rooms of the house. A high chest stood majestically against one bedroom wall. A pair of side chairs flanked this piece. The tester bed

was placed with its head against another wall. A mixing table to the left of the bed had on its surface a round brass candlestick and a book covered with Irish-stitched canvas. A dressing table to the right of the bed displayed another candlestick and a lady's Irish-stitched pocketbook. A slant-front desk was located between two windows. A pair of silver lobed candlesticks and a silver inkstand accompanied a variety of papers on the opened desk. A Chinese porcelain bowl decorated the top surface of the desk. Seating was provided by a corner chair. A round basin stand was situated in front of one of the windows. A porcelain bowl rested in the ring and a clear glass bottle was seen on a lower shelf. A handkerchief table was folded in a corner with unfinished handwork on its surface. A crewel-upholstered slipper chair stood next to the fireplace. A bed warmer and a copper tea kettle embellished the hearth. An engraving of a map hung over the desk. In the same manner, samplers and tent-stitch pictures were placed on other wall surfaces. A long oriental carpet spread the length of the room, from the fireplace to under the tester bed at the opposite wall.

The entrance hall at Carters Grove, James City County, Virginia, 1751. *Courtesy: Thorne American Rooms in Miniature, The Art Institute of Chicago*

A replica of the drawing room in Wilton, Henrico County, Virginia, shows the addition of Chippendale decorative features and furniture pieces to a Queen Anne room. *Courtesy: Thorne American Rooms in Miniature, The Art Institute of Chicago*

The Chippendale Period 1760–1790

Chippendale Interior Architecture

As the colonists continued to look to England for architectural guidelines, they were exposed to the Palladian and rococo features as described in Thomas Chippendale's *The Gentleman and Cabinet Maker's Director*. The colonial architect of the Chippendale period created a stage for the display of elegant furnishings. Many of the same decorative techniques used in interior design were seen on furniture, especially the case pieces. The formal life-style of the colonists was reflected in the balanced use of purely classical elements. Rococo motifs were limited to carved ornamentation of moldings. The floor plan remained the same as the Queen Anne period, with a square of four rooms bisected by a large central hallway.

The white plastered ceiling might have had a stucco curvilinear relief design. The cornice was molded with modillion blocks or dentil molding. The walls were fully paneled in the more formal rooms and probably in the master bedroom. Other rooms were paneled only to the chair rail. Wallpaper usually covered the unpaneled upper portion of the wall surface. Fluted pilasters

were used more frequently to square the corners of the room, to frame windows, doorways, fireplaces, and cupboards, or to divide the paneled wall into sections. The capitals were Corinthian with curved leaves, Ionic with scrolls, or Doric with a plain surface. Paneled doors were, at times, topped by triangular pediments. Pediments also might have been placed over cupboards or windows. Windows were still recessed but often framed by an elliptical arch. The arched Palladian window used during this period consisted of three windows, the center one rounded at the top. A fireplace was flanked by two cupboards. The rounded cupboards resembled those of the Queen Anne period. The fireplace best utilized the Roman portico theme, especially when the entire chimney breast projected out into the room. The overmantel was framed occasionally by a simple molding, by rococo carved ornamentation, or by a triangular pitch or a broken scroll pediment supported by fluted pilasters. A mantel now protruded beyond the fireplace opening. The frieze under the mantel might have been carved with naturalistic motifs. The fireplace opening was framed with marble or transfer-printed tiles and a bolection molding. The hearth was marble. Floors continued to make use of the narrower planking and were usually finished in a natural wood tone.

The Chippendale staircase was more curvilinear than the Queen Anne. The stairway in the central hall still rose against the wall surface. More attention was given to decorative details. The newel post was either a fluted square or a twisted column. The spiraled balusters formed a rhythmic pattern as they progressed up the steps because the front one of the three on each step was twisted more loosely. Sometimes all three of the balusters on each step varied, forming a different repeated pattern. The handrail curved up to the newel post as it reached the landing. At the foot of the staircase, the handrail and balusters turned out to accommodate a wider first step.

Woodwork was often painted during this period. Imported colors were listed as deep olive, Spanish brown, Prussian blue, Venetian red, and white. Ocher, cream, and gray were also used. Stairs were painted with buff and gray to simulate marble. Plastered walls were often covered with wallpaper. Chinese designs might have depicted scenes of daily life in a village; exotic birds set in trees of peonies, chrysanthemums, and cherry blos-

soms; or floral designs. The colors were muted green, rose, white, and gray blue. English artists copied oriental motifs on wallpapers. Rococo wallpaper styles used curvilinear leaflike motifs to frame romantic scenes, Roman ruins, or seascapes with sailing vessels.

Chippendale kitchens were often located in a separate building or at the rear of the house, as in the Queen Anne period. Again, these had very primitive furniture and interior architecture. If the kitchen was attached to the rear of the house, the interior architecture, though informal, was more finished. Sometimes the attached kitchen was used only during the cold winter months because the heat generated by the fireplace could help warm the entire house. The rustic cooking fireplace was smaller, with wall ovens located next to, rather than in, the fireplace opening. Kitchen equipment was plentiful, but some of the dishes and pewter were artfully displayed in the cupboards and on the mantel. Older furniture continued to be used in this room, but because of their practicality, contemporary Windsor chairs might have been present also. Wainscoting and wood trim framing windows, paneled doors, and overmantels gave a finished appearance to the room.

A stucco relief design is seen on the ceiling of the drawing room of Mount Pleasant, Philadelphia, Pennsylvania, 1761. *Courtesy: Thorne American Rooms in Miniature, The Art Institute of Chicago*

In the drawing room of the Jeremiah Lee Mansion, Marblehead, Massachusetts, the fireplace is decorated with rococo carving on the overmantel and on the frieze. *Courtesy: Thorne American Rooms in Miniature, The Art Institute of Chicago*

Windsor chairs are seen in the kitchen of the Governor's Palace in Williamsburg, Virginia, eighteenth century. *Courtesy: Thorne American Rooms in Miniature, The Art Institute of Chicago*

Chippendale Furniture

The furniture style guiding colonial cabinetmakers between the years 1760 and 1790 was called Chippendale, after the English cabinetmaker Thomas Chippendale. His *Director*, first distributed in 1754 in England, described the current English fashion in furniture and interior design. While he did not create unique pieces of his own, he coordinated the trends in furniture design being used in England at the time, including Gothic, Chinese, French rococo, and Georgian features. An interest in the past brought about the use of Gothic elements, such as cusps, pointed arches, tracery, trefoils, and crockets (bunched leaves) on pediments. The

Chinese influence was seen in the use of the straight leg on chairs and tables and in the decoration technique of lattice and fretwork. French rococo inspired the ornate, asymmetrical carved decoration seen on Chippendale pieces. Rococo meant rock and shell as seen in gardens in France. Lively naturalistic plant and animal forms were placed amid curving and recurving lines. The cabriole leg was used in French furniture of this period. The **S**-shape became freer and less disciplined than in the Queen Anne period. An unbalanced framework of curves, called a cartouche, was used frequently.

The Georgian period popular in England many years earlier had filtered into America by the 1760s, as seen in the use of the baroque broken scrolled pediment and the pierced vase-shaped splat. Many elements of this style, not included in Chippendale's work, were adopted by American cabinetmakers, such as the claw-and-ball foot, no longer in vogue in England. American Chippendale furniture was more Georgian in style, but included even Queen Anne features, such as the arched panel doors and the pad foot in rural furniture. In many cases, Queen Anne forms were merely decorated in the Chippendale style.

Colonists, especially in the Northern and Middle Atlantic areas, depended on American craftsmen for their furniture pieces. Because of the high price of English furniture, colonial pieces continued to be custom-designed. A patron worked with the cabinetmaker in planning each piece, selecting features to be included from a "menu" of stylistic elements, each individually priced. A cabinetmaker usually established his workshop in the same city in which he had done his apprenticeship because he would already have established a reputation. This practice perpetuated and even emphasized the regional differences of the Queen Anne period.

In Newport, Rhode Island, Townsend and Goddard brought furniture design to perfection. The blockfront treatment of a chest of drawers was their creation. Drawers and frames were cut so that a recessed central vertical surface was framed on either side by a projecting surface. This theme was carried beautifully through the three-part division of the upper portion of tall pieces. The concave or convex carving of the shells was determined by the raised or depressed surface on which they were located. This factor was reflected in any shells on the upper portion of the piece. A small spiral scroll was located on the bracket foot, which had taken on a slight curve at the outside edge. On the secretary and the double chest, the broken scrolled pediment was backed by a solid panel, and paneling was used on the pediment surface. The Newport claw-and-ball foot was oval in shape. On Goddard pieces, the slender talons were undercut at the point where the leg should have touched the ball and under the arch of the claw.

A Newport blockfront chest of drawers by Paul Runyon.

The broken scrolled pediment on Paul Runyon's Newport secretary is backed with a solid panel. The three-part division of surfaces is carried throughout the entire piece.

A Massachusetts chest of drawers with the characteristic bombé shape made by Douglas Kirtland.

Philadelphia characteristics are evident in this second-size high chest made by Stanley Jameson. *Collection of Claire Dinsmore*

Massachusetts continued to feature slender forms. The cabriole leg was still slim, and block-and-spindle stretchers were retained on chairs. The claw-and-ball foot was precisely carved with the side talons pointing backward to create, with the center claw, a triangular surface seen easily from the side. Rectangular table forms were supported by a characteristic tall, thin cabriole leg. The frieze under the top surface was plain. A form unique to Massachusetts was the turreted tea table. The top surface was rectangular but had semicircular projections along all four sides to accommodate individual cups and saucers. The secretary and the chest-on-chest used engaged pilasters to frame the upper section. Corkscrew finials were typical. The shape given to the lower chest was bombé (kettle), in which the sides gradually curved outward as they moved toward the floor. The same silhouette was given to chests of drawers. The Newport blockfront on Massachusetts furniture was somewhat flat in treatment.

New York produced squarer and heavier furniture. On the chair splats were seen a tassel and ruffled curves. Heavy gadrooning, which looked like a twisted rope, lined the edges of chair and table skirts. The claw-and-ball foot was boxlike and squared. The rear legs of chairs and sofas tapered rapidly to a squared foot. The secretary was usually flat-topped, but examples could be seen with a broken pitch pediment, having straight slanted sides in contrast to the scrolls used in other areas. The sides of the card table tops were curved, with squared projecting corners to accommodate candlesticks.

The carved ornamentation, as described by Chippen-

dale, was developed to its fullest in Philadelphia. The Gothic arch and trefoil were seen on chair backs. Gothic frets were incorporated on case pieces, as were inset corner columns. Rococo pierced shells decorated surfaces, and pierced cartouches served as the central finial on high chests. A flattened ball was placed at the base of a baluster that supported the piecrust-edged top of a round tripod tea table (see page 52). The foot at the base of the cabriole leg might have been precise claw-and-ball or a hairy animal's paw. The cabriole leg was decorated at the knee with an acanthus leaf in low relief or a kidney shape called a cabochon. The Marlborough leg was straight and ended in a block (plinth). If no plinth was present, the leg was called a Chippendale leg. The surface of these straight legs was plain, fluted, or carved. The straight leg was used on chairs and tables.

Connecticut cabinetmakers often studied with Philadelphia and Rhode Island craftsmen. On case pieces, the surface of the pediments was composed of lattice (see page 296). The skirts were scalloped. The blockfront furniture had a flatter surface and shells with lower relief. Carved sunbursts were a decorative motif, often in the end of a scroll. The corners of case pieces were chamfered (cut off at an angle), and the cut surface was fluted. The Queen Anne pad foot was retained, or the claw-and-ball foot was crudely carved.

Furniture was produced in Charleston, South Carolina, and, in the tradition of the South, was closely related to English style. The chest-on-chest was emphasized rather than the American high chest form. A flat top was placed over a fret-carved frieze. Mahogany was used rather than walnut.

Chippendale side chairs were characterized by a pierced splat set into an elevated shoe on the back seatrail. A bow-shaped crest rail curved up at the end to form ears. The crest rail sat on top of rear chair supports, which curved slightly backward as they approached the floor. The front legs were either cabriole, ending in a claw-and-ball foot, or straight, perhaps sitting on a plinth. A pierced curvilinear bracket might have been located where the straight leg met the seat frame. Set into the frame was an angular seat which differed from the Queen Anne horseshoe shape. A ladder-back chair was not shown in Chippendale's *Director*. The American design repeated a horizontal pierced crest rail three more times down the back of the chair. The straight leg and plain stretchers were used with this back design. The look of this piece was one of strength and simplicity.

A Chippendale side chair showing the beautiful carving technique of Harry Cooke. *Collection of Virginia Merrill*

Two more Chippendale side chairs, this time with the straight Chippendale leg.

On some chairs, the back and seat might have been upholstered over the frame. The backs of the upholstered form varied in height and were curved with round shoulders, or straight and squared at the top. Arms on these chairs were curved outward, resting on an incurved arm support, or, with a straight leg, were straight with a convex arm support (see page 135). The straight arm might have had some upholstery.

The settee was a double chair constructed along the same lines as the open-back chair (see page 229) or the upholstered-back chair. The sofa, long enough to seat three people, had become a popular seating form in spite of its great cost. The back was serpentine, as was seen on the rare Queen Anne form. Sofa crest variations included a reverse curve or a triple arch. The arms typically had a horizontal roll, though a form with a side wing and a vertically rolled arm was made.

Corner chairs and wing chairs changed little; Chippendale elements were added to the Queen Anne form. The cabriole leg now ended in a claw-and-ball foot and was carved with a shell or an acanthus leaf at the knee. The corner chair had pierced splats (see page 56). This roundabout or desk chair disappeared at the end of this period. Wing chairs could be seen with straight, Marlborough, or cabriole legs.

As in the Queen Anne period, stools were rare in America. There was no need for them because there was no royalty or hierarchical seating in this country. Should a stool have been constructed, the seat would have been rectangular with over-the-frame upholstery, and the legs cabriole with a claw-and-ball foot.

The four posts of the Chippendale tester beds were supported by either Marlborough legs or cabriole legs

The Chippendale piecrust tea table by Paul Runyon has the claw-and-ball foot and a carved acanthus leaf at the knee.

A view of Paul Runyon's birdcage device that allows the table surface to revolve and to tilt to a vertical position.

with claw-and-ball feet. The end of the bed was treated in a more decorative manner now that curtains were hung only at the head of the bed. The tall posts were fluted with unbroken concave lines. A straight or scalloped edge outlined the headboard. An upholstered or carved and gilded cornice was set on top of the tester. Mahogany low-post beds stood on Chippendale cabriole legs with foot posts topped, perhaps, by terminals of carved heads.

Because of the increased desire for specialized furniture forms, the table became available in many sizes and designs to fulfill many different needs. The most popular Chippendale table was the round tea table. The plain rim of the Queen Anne period was now molded and curved and was called a piecrust edge. The baluster shaft was supported on a flattened ball that rested on a tripod base consisting of three cabriole legs ending in claw-and-ball feet. The birdcage device enabled the top to turn and tilt vertically, making the table easy to move aside when not in use. A smaller round table of this design, which may not have included the birdcage device, served as a candlestand.

The rectangular tea table of the Queen Anne period now incorporated Chippendale stylistic forms, such as a claw-and-ball foot. The dished top of the Massachusetts table included a turreted edge, or in Newport, a cyma-curved edge. The rectangular tea table was also called a china table. Around the edge of the top might have been a scalloped or pierced gallery designed to keep the displayed china from slipping off the surface. The gallery form often had the straight leg and pierced or arched cross stretchers (see page 297).

The larger center or pier table now had the Chippendale cabriole leg and foot with a scalloped apron under the top frame. It was this piece which preceded the sideboard in formal dining rooms. It was placed near the drop-leaf dining table. The marble top provided an excellent surface upon which hot foods could be set before serving.

Card tables became ornately carved on the cabriole legs, and heavy gadrooning often edged the apron. Projecting round or square corners for candlesticks might have been present. Some top edges were serpentine. Card tables with squared folding tops were seen with a straight leg and a pierced leg bracket. These forms reflected the Chinese influence and were sparingly decorated.

The drop-leaf dining table continued the Queen Anne form with the use of Chippendale stylistic features. The opened top became rectangular in shape in many instances, although the oval shape was used also. The handkerchief table now had a scalloped apron and its cabriole leg had a claw-and-ball foot. A new drop-leaf form was the small Pembroke table, used for breakfast. Unlike earlier drop-leaf tables, the leaves were narrower than the top. The legs were straight, often with casters for easy relocation. The cross stretchers and brackets were arched or pierced. A

Fine craftsmanship on a miniature scale is seen in this drop-leaf Pembroke table by Paul Runyon. The curved arched stretchers are topped by a finial.

The underview of Paul Runyon's Pembroke table shows the leaf supports.

drawer was set in the frieze at one end. The spider gateleg table was a small drop-leaf form. This table had a rectangular top surface and slender legs, as compared with the earlier William and Mary piece. The English developed this design from the heavier gateleg style. Few were made in the colonies, and those only in New York.

Kettle stands with a square or triangular top surface occasionally had a pierced gallery and brackets. Legs were straight or Marlborough with no stretchers, but had an occasional lower shelf. It was on this table that the silver tea kettle or urn was displayed. Another form with a squared top surface was the wash or basin stand. The top surface was supported by a curvilinear apron. Four columns rested on a drawer, which in turn was supported by four Marlborough legs. The more popular form for the basin stand had a round molded rim that held a porcelain wash basin (see page 31). The rim rested on three supports which were placed on a tripod base. Within the rim support system a drawer and shelves were constructed to accommodate articles used for washing.

Pole fire screens (see page 212) continued to be used to protect those sitting by the fire from popping coals or intense heat. A rectangular screen slid along a long thin pole so the level of the screen could be adjusted by sliding it up and down the pole, which rose from a Chippendale baluster shaft and a tripod base.

Chippendale case pieces were more ornate than Queen Anne forms. The high chest retained the tall broken scrolled pediment and the shell carved on top and bottom center drawers. According to the regional

styles, this piece was decorated in varying degrees with carved rococo motifs. The earlier arched apron with drop pendants of the Queen Anne pieces was replaced by a curvilinear scalloped design on the apron. The dressing table echoed the treatment of the high chest and was often made to match for bedroom use.

A triangular kettle stand with a fretwork gallery by Eugene Kupjack.

The elegance of the high chest of the Chippendale period is seen in this piece created by Paul Runyon.

This view of Paul Runyon's high chest shows the detail of the egg and dart carved decoration trimming the top of the support piece. Convex shells embellish the knees and apron; a concave shell is carved on the middle drawer. The claw-and-ball foot is finely carved.

Flame finials decorate the broken scrolled pediment on this Chippendale high chest by Paul Runyon.

A form that received new emphasis during the Chippendale period was the chest of drawers. The front of this piece might have been flat, but more typical were the serpentine, the reverse serpentine, or the blockfront. The serpentine surface moved from concave to convex to concave; the reverse serpentine from convex to concave to convex. The blockfront showed a recessed vertical surface framed by projecting surfaces. Corners might have been canted (cut at an angle) and fluted, or left plain. The case was supported by claw-and-ball feet on shortened carbriole legs or by ogee (curved) bracket feet. All sides were perpendicular except on the Massachusetts kettle-base bombé form, where the sides bowed out and then in as they approached the floor (see page 50). The chest-on-chest, popular for some time in England, now made an appearance, combining Chippendale chest-of-drawer elements in the lower portion with high-chest elements in the upper.

A new form of desk or dressing table was the knee-hole chest of drawers, in which the central portion below the top drawer was recessed to accommodate the knees of a person seated in front. A small door was set in the back wall of the recessed area for entry into a shallow cupboard. The slant-top desk was a continuing Queen Anne form. The Queen Anne bookcase was placed on top of the slant-top desk to form the secre-

Drawing room, Queen Anne period by Eugene Kupjack.

Fine pair of Queen Anne side chairs with petit point seats by Susan Richardson.

Louis XVI gilded canapé. Embroidered silk covering by Stephanie Matthews.

Louis XV bergère, upholstered with silk embroidered fabric, by Virginia Merrill.

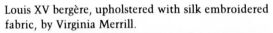

Susan Richardson's petit point adaptation of "Noah's Ark," covering a Queen Anne stool.

Martha Dinkel's banister-back chair, covered with a petit point cushion by Susan Richardson, who also designed the petit point English carpet. Dower chest from Hillhouse Miniatures, tiny shoes by The Doll's Cobbler.

Important cherrywood Chippendale secretary desk, by Ernie Levy.

Hepplewhite side chair, adapted from a chair in the collection of the Museum of Fine Arts, Boston.

Fine six-panel screen with delicate hand-painted design by Nancy Weaver. Available from Dearring Tracy Ltd.

Antique dollhouse.

Horse tricycle by Alex Fried, available from Dearring Tracy Ltd., with an antique bisque doll.

Gaming table with designed inset petit point
by Susan Richardson.

Victorian desk, hand decorated by Linda Wexler.

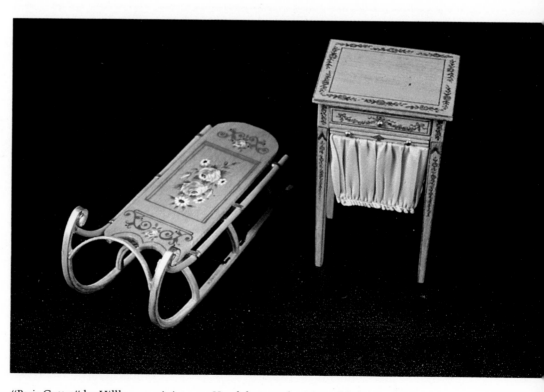

"Paris Cutter" by Hillhouse miniatures. Hand-decorated sewing table by Emily Good.

Oil painting by Karin Hardy. 2″ × 2½″.
Private collection.

Ernie Levy's adaptation of a William and Mary lowboy stands 2½″ high.

Greenhouse with live plants, assembled by Jane Hotchkiss and Kathleen Pitney.

Lacquer cabinet delicately painted with chinoiserie design, by Virginia Merrill.

Stephanie Matthews's lovely hand-embroidered
silk fabric covers a bergère with curved back.

"Bird of Paradise" quilt embroidered by
Deanna Mayer Vondrak of Cantitoe Corners.

Standing clocks are dwarfed by a gentleman's pocket watch. Lantern and elephant clocks by Virginia Merrill.

"The Princess and the Pea," a framed vignette to hang on the wall, by Susan Sirkis.

William and Mary daybed. Pad and pillow are covered with a petit point flame stitch design.

A well-designed stove by Jim Marcus.

The Chippendale chest of drawers by Edward G. Norton is given a front shaped in a reverse serpentine curve. Claw-and-ball feet serve as supports. *Courtesy: Edward G. Norton*

Edward G. Norton also made the blockfront version of the Chippendale chest of drawers. *Courtesy: Edward G. Norton*

A Chippendale side chair and kneehole dressing table or desk beautifully executed by Paul Runyon.

A loop-back Windsor chair stands in front of a Chippendale desk, which is opened to reveal the intricate drawer arrangement inside. These pieces were made by Edward G. Norton. *Courtesy: Edward G. Norton*

tary. Again, a Queen Anne piece received Chippendale decorative features and was fashionable. A bookcase consisting of an upper cabinet with paneled glass doors over a lower enclosed section, often with a projecting center, was called a breakfront. They first appeared in America during the Chippendale period, though they were scarce because of their cost.

Handles and key escutcheons on case furniture continued to be made of brass. Large batwing-shaped brasses were imported from England. These were pierced or latticed on Philadelphia pieces. Another brass style showed each end of the U-shaped handle hanging from a small round disk. When this second type of handle was used, the keyhole was merely edged with a thin brass fitting. During this furniture period, brass handles might have been located also on the sides of a case piece for easier carrying, should it have had to be moved.

The arched dial of the tall case clock was usually topped by a broken scrolled pediment and three finials. The bracket feet were now ogee. The clocks were ornamented with Chippendale features. The bracket clock made its first appearance in the colonies during this period. This small clock sat on a wall bracket, a table,

Ernie Levy's skill is demonstrated by this tall case clock with its delicate inlay.

Virginia Merrill's tall case clock shows the ogee curved bracket feet of the Chippendale period and the eagle motif of the Federal style. *Collection of Susan Richardson*

or a mantel. The clock was set in a veneered wooden case with a sarcophagus-shaped top above which stood a brass loop handle. The surface was occasionally painted.

The larger, more impressive mirrors of this period come in three forms: fret, architectural, and rococo (see page 169). The fretwork looking glass was a continuation of the Queen Anne form. The crests at the top and bottom of the frame were curved even more, and gilt or ormolu might have been applied for decoration. The architectural style used the broken scrolled pediment as its crest. The rococo mirror was composed of sculptured Chinese and rococo gilt ornamentation in intricate and lively arrangements.

The pierced splat of the Chippendale period is seen in Virginia Merrill's corner chair, which has been drawn up to Ernie Levy's elegant secretary. Fine details have been beautifully executed on the secretary, which displays corkscrew finials, rosettes on the scrolls, and an intricate arrangement of shelves, cubbyholes, and drawers.

A bracket clock by Lois Sterling.

Flatware is stored in a wooden knife box
made by Richard Simms.

Painted Pennsylvania dower chest by Virginia Merrill. The
miniature detail is clearly executed.

The case housed sets of knives, forks, and spoons.

An independent style of furniture design, the Pennsylvania German, coincided with Chippendale creations. The furniture consisted of memory pieces of the Germans and the Swiss who came to the colonies in the seventeenth and early eighteenth centuries to take advantage of the religious liberty espoused by William Penn. Typical pieces were wooden scrolled-back chairs (resembling the chair on page 151), often with pierced heart shapes in the back; dower chests of painted tulipwood; dressers and cupboards of yellow pine, walnut, and oak; and wardrobes with painted decoration. There were several preferred motifs. The tulip was derived from sixteenth-century Germany. The heart was painted on chests, pierced in chairbacks, shaped in iron trivets, and embroidered on samplers. A pomegranate, paired birds, a vase of flowers, unicorns, horsemen, and geometric stars were used in Pennsylvania German ornamentation also.

Another form that does not fit into the Chippendale style is the Windsor chair. The chair was so named because it was originally produced in the early eighteenth century in the area around Windsor Castle in England. The chair created in the colonies was uniquely American. This graceful, flexible construction was executed by a joiner rather than a cabinetmaker. Unseasoned wood was used for all parts except the pins. Steamed hoops and spindles were assembled. The pieces contracted as the wood dried. The result was a very strong piece of furniture. The seat was saddle-shaped. Because different woods were used in the construction, the chair was almost always painted, usually green, but also red, yellow, and black. The legs were turned. Windsor chairs were used predominantly in public buildings and inns. The six types of Windsor

Mahogany knife cases were made in New York during the Chippendale period. Silver side handles, if present, allowed for the easy carrying of the case, and a top ring facilitated the lifting of the lid. The wooden case had a serpentine front surface and a sloping hinged lid.

Authentic stenciled designs decorate this black eighteenth-century chest of drawers. *Collection of Mary Lee Dearring Tracy*

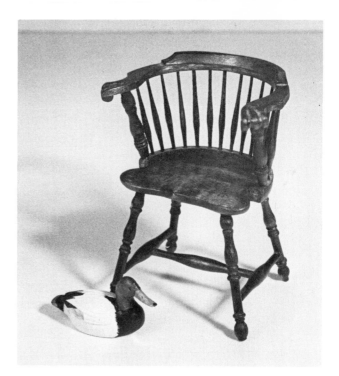

A low-back Windsor chair shows a curved crest rail that becomes a support for the arms.

Two comb-back Windsor chairs made by two top artisans, Paul Runyon on the left and Donald Buttfield on the right.

Edward G. Norton executed these Windsor chairs. On the left is a fan-back version, on the right a bow-back. *Courtesy: Edward G. Norton*

chairs were determined by the style of the back. The low-back had a horizontal horseshoe-shaped back that curved around to provide arm support. The comb-back added a section of vertical spindles and a horizontal crest rail to a low-back Windsor chair. The bow-back showed a horizontal circular armrest that cut through vertical spindles. The spindles were held in place by an arched hoop which sat on the armrest. In the fan-back,

vertical spindles rose smoothly out from the seat to a horizontal curved crest rail. The loop-back had an arched hoop that curved in before the ends reached the seat. The arm of the New England Windsor chair flowed continuously into the hoop back. After 1800, this chair style came under the influence of Thomas Sheraton in its design.

By the last quarter of the eighteenth century, neo-

This bow-back Windsor chair has a desk surface on one of its arms. It was made by Edward G. Norton. *Courtesy: Edward G. Norton*

Three fan-back chairs were executed by Edward G. Norton. The central child's chair is flanked by two adult chairs, one of which is turned to reveal the back structure. *Courtesy: Edward G. Norton*

Another combination of a child and an adult chair utilizes the loop back. The problem of duplicating these delicate chairs from the full size reflects Edward G. Norton's talent. *Courtesy: Edward G. Norton*

classicism was dominating English furniture design. Inlay, controlled carving, and painting replaced the Chippendale motifs. Disciplined classicism supplanted the unrestrained rococo style. Because of the Revolutionary War, communication with England was interrupted. Thus, the neoclassical style was not used in America until after the 1783 peace treaty which entitled America to be a nation in its own right.

The continuous arm of the New England–style Windsor chair curves above a deep saddle seat, rakishly splayed legs, and bold turnings. This chair was made by Don Buckley. *Courtesy: Don Buckley*

Chippendale Upholstery

All Chippendale seating forms required upholstery. The smallest amount was applied to the squared set-in seat of the open-back chairs and settees. Occasionally, the seats of these pieces were upholstered over the seat frame and attached by round brass tacks. The seat and back of other chairs and settees were upholstered over the frames. Some of the arms were padded, leaving only the handrests, arm supports, and legs unupholstered. The wing chair and the sofa were completely covered, with the exception of the legs. These pieces were occasionally trimmed with brass tacks along the bottom edge of the apron. This trim might have framed the front apron and the front surfaces of the horizontally rolled arms of the sofa.

Upholstery fabrics used at this time were many. Blue, red, or green silk damasks continued as covering, as did velvets and leather. Blue resist-dyed linens were still used. New printed cottons were seen in abundance. Copperplates were printed with blue chinoiserie motifs on a beige ground or other monochromatic documented prints. Needlework covers were not as necessary at this time because colonists could well afford imported fabrics. Crewel embroideries were either cut from old sets of bed hangings or created for a specific piece. Jacobean floral arrangements prevailed. Canvas work appeared mainly on slip seats. The most popular tent-stitch design was a variety of flowers arranged in a vase (see page 228). Robert Furber's *Twelve Months of Flowers*, published in 1732, inspired this motif. The background was typically dark blue. Allover floral patterns were also executed on a dark (black, blue, or green) ground to upholster the back and seat of chairs. Canvas-work inserts in gaming tabletops persisted during this period (see page 230). Floral motifs in the Chippendale style were popular, as were game-equipment designs such as cards, coins, dice, or fish. Fire screen panels were covered with a piece of fabric or a piece of needlework depicting a flower-filled vase or a pastoral scene (see page 213)

Chippendale Drapery Treatment

Damasks, velvets, and printed textiles were also used for drapery arrangements. At the windows in formal rooms hung the Venetian drapery and the scalloped valance with floor-length side panels seen during the Queen Anne period. The festoon drapery style, which had recently appeared, was extremely fashionable. Many windows were trimmed with double swags created by a pair of panels drawn up in opposite directions by the festoon technique. Some windows were draped with only a single panel.

Tester bed hangings showed a more curvilinear valance and a flat skirt using the same scalloped-edge design. Draperies and a headcloth hung only at the head of the bed, more for ornamentation than for warmth. Printed textiles were the most popular fabric for bed hangings during this period. The edges were trimmed with decorative tape. A fabric-covered scalloped cornice might have been superimposed on the tester frame.

Chippendale Floor Coverings

Carpets were no longer seen on tables. The most popular floor carpet was that imported from the Near East. These were listed in house inventories as "Turkish carpets," but came from many different countries in the region, such as Ushak, Kuba, and Ispahan. A few English needlework carpets graced colonial homes of this period, as did those produced by English textile manufacturers. Bright colored floral motifs on a dark ground characterized the manufactured pieces. The florid patterns were composed of borders of cartouche-framed flowers surrounding a busy arrangement of flowers and fruit. A small central area might have been decorated by two or three birds. Striped rag-woven carpets served as protection for finer floors and floor coverings at this time. A double-woven Scotch carpet was seen in two tones of diamonds, squares, or other geometric shapes. Designs were painted on woven cloth, which was varnished or waxed for more durability. These patterns, too, were geometric and, in some cases, imitated tile or marble designs. During the warmer summer months, a grass mat might have replaced the heavier carpet.

Chippendale Needlework

During the Chippendale period, leisure time continued in abundance, so handwork was prolific. Samplers were executed by daughters in school and framed with pride. There was more awareness of the overall composition of the piece, and elements were often joined by a scene and a wide decorative border. Sampler compositions reflected the style of the school in which they were designed.

Canvas needlework was used to create pocketbooks, seat and chair upholstery, pincushions, hand and standing fire screens, wall pockets, and tablecloths. Aside from the tent-stitch upholstery motifs already discussed, the style of canvas work remained the same as that of the Queen Anne period.

Crewel and silk embroidery on linen or silk provided the material for pockets, petticoat borders, padded potholders, hatchments, and clothing. Queen Anne patterns continued until sometime after the Revolutionary War.

In 1773, a knitting machine was invented. As a result, the knitting of mundane items, such as mittens and stockings, was left to a mechanical device. More decorative knitted items, such as purses, drew the attention of colonial ladies' knitting needles. Knit purses were designed with rows of patterned borders and included the date and the owner's name. Knitting needles were inserted through a silver device and worn at the waist. They had decorative ends of fish or heart motifs.

Quilting techniques during this period included one-piece, pieced, and appliqué. All three methods of quilt construction were often combined in one project. A central appliqué might be framed by a pieced strip, and the whole quilt stitched with an overall geometric pattern. One-piece quilts were still made into articles of clothing for cold-weather warmth.

Three examples of Chippendale silver by Eugene Kupjack: a salver, an inkstand, and a ladel.

Chippendale Silver

By 1750, the rococo style was adopted by colonial silversmiths. Attention was now focused on decorative detail rather than on shape and line. Curves became playful and undisciplined. Naturalistic forms, such as flowers, leaves, and animals, were combined with ruffles and a now asymmetrical scallop shell. Surfaces were covered with an overabundance of three-dimensional ornamentation created by repoussé, cast pieces, and gadrooning. Engraved heraldic or cypher motifs were surrounded by an asymmetrical cartouche. Piercing was another decorative effect used at this time. As on furniture, Chinese and Gothic influences were seen in the openwork of silver bread or cake baskets. Pierced hinged handles arched over these gracefully curved containers.

The shapes emphasized during this period were pear and inverted pear. The upside-down pear shape was called "double bellied" because the wider rounded section surmounted a narrower rounded section. This body rested on a domed foot. Globular teapots became apple-shaped. Handles became double scrolled, that is, the Queen Anne C- or S-scroll rested on another curve. Tops were rounded into a single dome or a double dome, in which one rounded shape seemed superimposed on a wider rounded shape. The Queen Anne spout was decorated with scrolls and curls. Finials were cast to resemble naturalistic forms rather than the earlier rounded shapes. Many silver pieces rested on short, curved legs. The legs resembled those seen on furniture, even to the point of having claw-and-ball feet. Shells might also have served as feet.

As in furniture design, Queen Anne forms and shapes were retained in the design of silver. Rococo ornamentation was merely applied. At the beginning of the eighteenth century, beakers had lost their straight sides and had taken on the shape of short, inverted bells: they were footed and had outward curved lips. During the rococo period, these vessels were elaborately engraved with humorous scenes. At the end of the American Revolution, silver goblets appeared in homes. Earlier straight sides became curved and the baluster stems more regularly shaped. The bowl was engraved. Silver canns were pear-shaped. Tankards now had rounded bodies as well as cylindrical. The domes on the lids rose gradually, so that now some were even double-domed with a naturalistic cast finial.

Porringers continued to be popular during this period of silver design. Occasionally, this bowl form was created with a lid. While the shape of the bowl did not change, the lid reflected the style of the times. Punch bowls closely resembled the Queen Anne form in shape. Rococo ornamentation characteristic of the period was applied. The monteith continued to be used for the drinking of wine. After 1771, this form disappeared until the second quarter of the nineteenth century.

A silver cann by Eugene Kupjack.

A Chippendale tankard with a midband and a domed lid by Eugene Kupjack.

In flatware, knives and forks continued to be rare. If present at all, forks had only three tines. Pistol-handled knives were imported from England. These two forms were not produced in America until the nineteenth century. Spoons continued to be created in the variety of sizes seen in the Queen Anne period. Ornamentation on these spoons was diverse. In place of the rattail, a double drop, which combined the spatulate drop with the shell, was used. The earlier spatulate handle was replaced in the 1760s by a handle that arched down from the concave bowl in a volute (curve). The top surface of the handle might have been edged with gadrooning. On this new handle style, initials were placed on the top surface rather than on the underside. Thus, when these spoons were placed on the table, this top surface faced up. The strainer, or mote, spoon had a pierced bowl for the skimming of refuse in tea. This spoon also had a thin, pointed handle used for removing clogged tea leaves that had gathered in the strainer at the base of the teapot spout. Punch ladles now had scalloped shell-like bowls (see page 61). Tea tongs were seen in two forms. The scissor style continued with arms made of curled curves. A hinged round disk concealed the intersection of the two arms. Shells were located at the end of each arm to grip sugar cubes. In the 1760s, arched spring, or bow, tongs with pierced straight arms were used.

Dining accessories became more plentiful. A punch strainer appeared with a shallow pierced bowl and two flat handles. The curvaceously shaped and pierced handles followed the style of the porringer handles. They were long enough to allow the strainer to straddle the punch bowl. Salts continued as round trenchers with three or four legs that bent inward. The legs ended in shell or claw-and-ball feet. The body was repoussé, and the bowl edges were gadrooned. Casters had a taller domed lid with a flame finial. The body adopted the inverted-pear shape. The circular foot was domed. During this period, the three casters were often combined with two cruets, glass bottles for vinegar and oil. These vessels were placed on a small footed tray with a tall central handle. Receptacles for the bottles were created by a thick gadrooned wire.

Silver chafing dishes continued to warm foods at the table. Silver saucepans and skillets contained the foods and drink to be served hot at the table. Saucepans were rounded with an abrupt inward curve at the top. A straight wooden handle was placed perpendicular to the side of the bowl. The handle extended at right angles to the small spout formed from the top edge of the pot. Saucepans were created in a great variety of sizes to accommodate everything from stews to warmed brandy or wine.

Rococo sauceboats retained the Queen Anne boat shape, though they were more slender. The handle was composed of connecting curves that were attached to the boat at only one low point; the upper portion stood free. Cast shells and acanthus leaves ornamented the curved legs, feet, and handles. Dish rings supported hot dishes to protect the table surface. They were pierced and curved in at the middle. Salvers continued to be supported by curved legs. Now they ended in the claw-and-ball or shell foot (see page 61). The tray surface resembled the top of the piecrust table with its cast curves. Cast decoration of shells and gadrooning were included in the edge design.

The rococo tea service included a teapot with an inverted-pear shape. The lid was slightly domed. Coffeepots mirrored the teapot, but they were taller. Their lids had higher domes. Coffeepot handles included another curve at the bottom to accommodate the height of the piece. Tea kettles, milk pots, sugar bowls, and slop bowls all retained the Queen Anne form and incorporated rococo ornamentation techniques. Handles were more scrolled; lids had higher domes; surfaces were more ornate. Tea caddies became cylindrical in imitation of those seen in Chinese porcelain.

Candlesticks showed an abundance of lively decoration. Square, leaf-decorated, portable bobeches were placed in the socket to collect the wax from dripping candles. Gadrooning and leaves decorated the baluster shaft. The squared base had corner leaves that framed a molded inward curve along the side edges. Candlesnuffers set on trays continued to be used.

Silver inkstands (see page 61) were included in the list of the multitude of silver items produced during the rococo period of silver design. Containers for ink, seals, and pounce were supported on a tray with a tall handle. A container might also have been provided for pens and, occasionally, for a candle (or taper) to apply seals.

Chippendale Pewter

During the Chippendale period, pewter was prolific in colonial homes. Pewter forms remained very simple. Because of the preference for rococo and oriental ornamentation, silver and fine ceramics were procured whenever possible. Pewter teapots, sugar bowls, and creamers followed rococo shapes. The teapot adopted a round neoclassical silhouette. The lidded sugar bowl was circular and formed to resemble an inverted pear. The pear-shaped creamer stood on a foot. Plates had smooth rims. Tankards and flagons had midbands and domed or double-domed lids. The taller flagons often had spouts, so they could serve as pitchers. Mugs and flared beakers also had bands around the middle. Spoons had oval bowls and rounded handles. Porringers reached the peak in fashion in the colonies as they were disappearing in England. The bowls remained unchanged, while the handles were either solid tabs or pierced, curved metal pieces.

Chippendale silver coffee and tea pieces showing the pear shape in the coffeepot and creamer and the inverted-pear shape in the teapot and sugar bowl. Rococo ornamentation covers the surface.

A sgraffito plate with several Toby jugs.

Chippendale Ceramics

Pottery produced in America during the Chippendale period was still predominantly practical. Painted and trailed slip decorated redware. Sgraffito continued to be used by the Pennsylvania Germans. Forms consisted of plates, tea bowls, mugs, platters, cooking utensils, and pitchers.

English earthenwares increased in variety. In Liverpool, the process of transfer printing was perfected. A design was engraved on a copperplate and inked with an enamel color. The enamel was transferred to the surface of a ceramic piece through a thin piece of paper. This method allowed for finer detail in the designs on ceramics and was immediately put to use on ceramic tiles. Other decorative forms in Liverpool were "Fazackerly" and "bianco sopra bianco." Fazackerly delftware was decorated with large polychrome floral decoration. Bianco sopra bianco patterns showed opaque white stylized motifs placed on a ground of pale blue or gray. This last style of ornamentation was usually seen as a rim border pattern. Jackfield wares were covered red earthenware forms with a shiny black glaze. These pieces were decorated with gilding on occasion.

Staffordshire saw the creation of pottery in the form of cauliflowers or pineapples with bright green and yellow glazes. Toby jugs and figures were treated with the same lively enamel colors. The small jugs were shaped to resemble a man seated while holding a pipe and a mug. The hat on his head might have been re-

movable so as to serve as a cup. Josiah Wedgwood perfected the ivory-colored "creamware" process so well at this time that he attracted Queen Charlotte as a customer. After her patronage, Wedgwood's creamware was called "queensware." The forms for this earthenware varied from tile, kitchen, and dairy wares to everyday dishes for the table. Transfer-printed designs were used for decoration. Wavy edges of plates might be trimmed with a narrow blue fringed border. Pierced decoration characteristic of contemporary silver pieces was also utilized around the rim.

The art of creating hard-paste porcelain was perfected at a few establishments on the European continent. Though these wares did not reach America until the nineteenth century, they served as a basis for English soft-paste porcelain forms. Porcelain production continued to be influenced by oriental creations. Japan, as well as China, provided prototypes. The Japanese Kakiemon style emphasized the shape of background areas as much as those that were decorated so as to achieve an underlying imbalance. Imari techniques created red, blue, and gilt designs that resembled brocades. The fine quality of hard-paste porcelain allowed for fine detail and frivolously decorative forms, even for useful items. Meissen soup tureens were seen in the shape of fruits, vegetables, animals, or birds. Painted decorative motifs such as fruits, insects, and butterflies were painted on white grounds. Decorative figures were created in the round for use on a table. From 1760 on, they were designed with front views only because they were displayed on a mantel or in a cabinet. Bowers of leaves provided a background for sculpted human figures. Vibrant enamel colors were given gilt highlights. Sèvres porcelain was characterized by the use of colored backgrounds of blue, turquoise, pink, green, and bright yellow. These colors surrounded smaller white areas decorated with landscapes or unusual birds. Strong enamel colors and gilding helped to create these decorative motifs. The most common form for Sèvres porcelain was the tall vase form.

The Sèvres color technique and the Meissen design

An assortment of Japanese Imari porcelain exquisitely painted by Priscilla Lance and thrown by Deborah McKnight.

motifs were seen in English soft-paste porcelain produced in Chelsea and Worcester. In Chelsea, tureens took the form of animals. Fruits and insects decorated white porcelain forms. Rococo pieces used the colored background of Sèvres. Figurines had leaved bowers in the background. Small containers and boxes were also created in Chelsea porcelain. Worcester emphasized practical everyday ceramic forms. Oriental shapes dominated, but some dishes were shaped into leaves.

Chippendale Glassware

It was during the Chippendale period that colonial glasshouses produced glasswares sophisticated enough to equal European pieces. Clear and colored glass in shades of green, purple, amethyst, and blue were free-blown or pattern-molded and then blown. Typical patterns were diamonds, ribs, and flutes. Decoration took the form of engraving and enameling in paints of yellow, white, red, blue, and black. Motifs were naturalistic birds, flowers, and leaves. Wavy lines provided

borders. Forms made in the colonies were large tumblers, mugs, wineglasses, decanters, salt containers, sugar bowls, and creamers. Other colonial glass products were jars for pickles and preserves, and various bottles.

In spite of the glass output from local glasshouses, colonists continued to import drinking glasses, such as wine and water goblets, and decanters. Because of the English Glass Excise Tax mentioned earlier and the stylistic requirements of the Chippendale period, glassware was lighter in weight and appearance. Ornamentation was emphasized. Chinese motifs provided the trend for engraved and enameled decoration. Baluster stems were replaced by straight stems on wine and water glasses. An air twist or faceting decorated this vertical support. The plain funnel bowl was the most typical, although a bowl in the shape of a bucket with a flat bottom and straight or S-curved sides was also seen. Decanters flowed gracefully from the round stopper down the tall neck over the sloping shoulders.

English glass was also made in a deep blue and an opaque white, characteristic of Bristol glass. Forms such as bottles for toilet water, patch boxes, finger bowls, and wine coolers were made of the deep blue glass, sometimes decorated with gold. The opaque white glass was made into vases, bottles, tea caddies, candlesticks, mugs, basins, cruets, and plates to resemble Chinese porcelain. As a result, they were printed with oriental motifs in enameled colors.

The Chinese influence was also seen in the chandelier with its canopy set high above the rest of the piece. Chippendale chandeliers and candelabra were also characterized by hanging drops, spires, and V-shaped indentations on the arms. Candlesticks had straight stems like the wine and water glasses.

A Chippendale decanter and two wineglasses with straight stems decorated with air twists.

Fine detail is achieved by Mary O'Brien in her painting of japanned tinware (toleware).

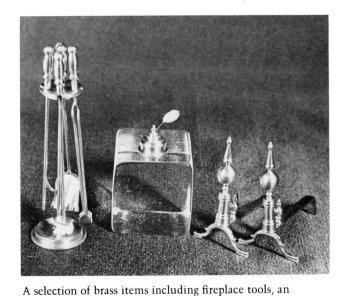

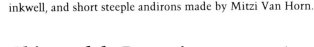

A selection of brass items including fireplace tools, an inkwell, and short steeple andirons made by Mitzi Van Horn.

Chippendale Metalwares

As with the style of furniture, Chippendale ornamentation was added to Queen Anne metalwares. Japanned tinwares incorporated colors into the gold chinoiserie decoration. Trays were oval, square, rectangular, and scalloped. Candlesticks, tea caddies, and boxes were still in evidence.

Household equipment made of brass, copper, and iron continued to be abundant. Kitchen tools and the more mundane (copper, iron, and undecorated tin) articles were relegated to the kitchen. Highly polished brass objects were in evidence in the more formal rooms of the house because they better complemented the Chippendale interiors, as did silver, porcelain, and glass. Clock dials and works were still made of brass. Candlesticks showed curvilinear baluster shafts and rococo decoration on the shaft, the round base, and the socket. Candlesticks and candlestands were used more often than chandeliers, sconces, and lanterns because they consumed only one, or at the most, two, candles and could be brought close to a person's activity. Lighting fixtures were used to light an entire room only at large social gatherings. The arms of the chandeliers and sconces became curved and recurved. Brass frames on hall lanterns were ornamented with rococo naturalistic motifs.

Fireplace equipment also emphasized the use of brass in more formal rooms. Fenders remained bowed and serpentine. The top edge became curved. Pierced and engraved designs provided the ornamentation. In the 1760s, andirons adopted the style of a columnar shaft with an urn finial. Short andirons, which resembled a church steeple, appeared during the Chippendale period and remained in use into the nineteenth century.

Chippendale Room Arrangement

During the Chippendale period, a separate dining room became more common, but was by no means a requirement, in the arrangement of rooms within the home. The parlor became more ornate and formal. A crystal chandelier was suspended from the middle of the ceiling. Matching glass sconces were hung over the mantel shelf. A garniture of five blue-and-white delft ceramic pieces lined the mantel. A serpentine-back sofa was placed at right angles to the fireplace. Separating the sofa from the fireplace wall was a pole screen with a tent-stitch panel. A china table with a curved gallery stood in front of the sofa. Behind these pieces was a game table with four open-back side chairs in the Chippendale style. Cards and other game equipment were scattered over the needlework insert on the tabletop. Wineglasses rested at each place while a silver candlestick shed light from each of the four corners of the table. On the other side of the fireplace stood a wing-back easy chair. Situated on the fireplace side of the chair was a silver kettle on a stand with a pierced gallery and a tripod base. A piecrust tea table displayed a silver candlestick and a tray with a teapot, a creamer, and a sugar bowl. A silver "slop bowl" rested near four scenic ceramic cups and saucers. A blockfront chest of drawers stood between two windows. Two Chinese export vases and a bowl adorned the top surface of the chest. Flanking the window on another wall were a pair of pier glasses and tables. A ceramic figurine was placed on each table. Oil paintings of individuals or landscapes and needlework pictures decorated the walls. A large oriental carpet covered the floor.

The master bedroom again had a high chest against the wall flanked by two open-back side chairs. These pieces now displayed Chippendale stylistic elements. Located between two windows was a kneehole dressing table on which were placed a mirror and a wig stand holding a white wig with its hair tied back in a black ribbon. A corner chair was positioned in front of the dressing table. Close by was a washstand with a blue-and-white delft bowl set in the ring and a matching bottle on a lower shelf. The tester bed was placed with its head against the wall. A dressing table that matched the high chest supported a brass candlestick and an Irish-stitched pocketbook. Hanging on the wall at the side of the bed was an Irish-stitched wall pocket, in which were deposited a book and a letter. Under the wall pocket stood a round candlestand with a brass candlestick. An open-arm chair with an upholstered back was located in front of the fireplace. A needlework hoop on a stand was next to the chair. On a nearby Pembroke table was a small, wooden handloom used to make tape and trim. Several floral tent-stitch carpets were scattered over the floor.

Located at the back of the house was a study where a man might have conducted his business. A tall secretary stood with its doors and slant front open. Books lined the shelves. Letters filled the cubbyholes. A silver inkstand and a pewter cann rested on the desk surface with an open book and some papers. A bow-back Windsor chair provided seating at the desk. A wing-back easy chair upholstered with needlework was positioned next to an iron candlestand. A painted floor-cloth resembling black-and-white marble tiles was placed on the floor.

The dining room was small. The rectangular drop-leaf dining table had been opened. Six Chippendale open-back side chairs were placed around it. The table had no cloth. A silver monteith supported wineglasses and a silver candlestick stood on either side. Each place was set with a folded napkin, a pewter plate, a wine-glass with an air-twist stem, a bone-handled knife, and a silver spoon placed in the fork position so that the concave bowl faced downward. A marble-topped serving table stood against the wall under a wooden wall shelf with pierced sides. A decanter and four wine-glasses, two candlesticks, and a salver were set on the side table; fine ceramic plates of various sizes embellished the wall shelves. An oriental carpet covered the floor.

The Federal Period 1790-1825

Federal Interior Architecture

House interiors during the Federal period were adapted from the antique designs of Robert Adam. In England, Adam created his designs after carefully studying ruins, such as those at Pompeii and Herculaneum. In America, English styles were adapted to local needs because Americans lacked the necessary materials and were limited in the amount of money they could spend. The general floor plan of the house remained the same as that of the Chippendale period, with a square of four rooms on the first and second floors. Instead of the half story on the third level seen in houses of the Chippendale period, a full third story was incorporated in the house design.

Little relief ornamentation was seen on ceilings or walls. Plain moldings framed ceilings, windows, and doors. Ceiling surfaces were flat, except for a few instances when scalloped borders were applied and the framing surface was painted a color contrasting with the white central area. The only relief decoration on the wall surfaces was a paneled wainscoting and the framework of windows, shelved recesses, and entranceways. Plaster walls were painted in soft shades such as white, off-white, shell pink, pale green, dove gray, and soft beige. Hand-painted French papers became the fashionable wallcovering. Delicate floral motifs were seen on wallpaper, as were Etruscan motifs. One of the popular themes was a large-scale scenic design in which actual buildings in France or Italy served as a background for figures in a pastoral setting. Since few Americans could afford these scenic papers, itinerant painters would paint wall scenes for a fee.

Windows continued to be recessed into the wall. They were framed by an arch with a central keystone resting on pilasters, which were reeded, a convex treatment as opposed to the concave fluting. Windows might have also been framed by a molded rectangle, often topped by a frieze. The Palladian window seen during the Chippendale period was given special emphasis now, especially in academic architecture. The rectangular side windows were framed by a flat-topped pediment on pilasters in high relief, and the central window arched between them. The arch of the shelved wall recess had a central keystone and rested on pilasters. Entranceways into formal public rooms might have been arched in this manner with no door. If present, doorways were rectangular and might have had a frieze above the molded frame.

Plaster ornament and decorative moldings were largely limited to the treatment of the fireplace. An overmantel was not necessarily included in the fireplace design. If present, it remained a simple framework for whatever might have hung over the mantel, such as a mirror or a painting. The fireplace opening was framed either by marble or tile. The hearth was marble. The mantel was supported by reeded pilasters or by columns in semirelief. The plaster decoration ranged from a very simple classical framework to the finely carved and molded ornament of Samuel McIntire, a professional carver. Ornamentation was delicately rendered in contrast with the heavy voluminous decoration of Chippendale rococo. Classical motifs were used, such as wheat sheaves, drapery swags, leafed garlands, reeded panels, or baskets of flowers. The center of the mantel frieze might have had an oval frame surrounding a historic scene or a basket of flowers. Swagged garlands of leaves might have hung on either side.

The staircase in the large central hall became very graceful, with the handrail curving gently, without stopping, from the second floor into a spiral above a simple columnar newel post. The steps flowed in the same rounded path. Some examples stood independently from the wall, both sides of the handrail curving out to be supported by a pair of newel posts resting on the flared bottom step. Balusters became straight supports that were round or square in section.

Floors were wooden or, in hallways, marble. The floor planks were narrow and stained in a natural wood tone.

Federal Furniture

In reaction to the rococo, Chinese, and Gothic trends of the Chippendale period, Robert Adam introduced a fresh selection of classical motifs to England in the 1760s. In his presentation, Adam stressed the coordination of the designs of architecture and furniture. He advocated perfection in his strict adherence to the earlier classical style. Straight or gradually curved lines took the place of serpentine. Rectangles, squares, ovals, and circles served as the basic designs for furniture. Forms under Adam's influence became lighter in scale and linear in quality. All ornamentation became balanced and delicate. Decorative techniques included controlled carving, inlay, decorative painting, reeding, and veneering. Satinwood was used as inlay to provide a contrast to the dark-toned mahogany wood surfaces. Some of the popular classical motifs were urns, swags, and husks. Straight furniture legs became tapered. They were either round with fluted or reeded surfaces,

or square, ending in a spade foot. The spade foot was a tapering block, wider at the top than the leg. Its sides were spade-shaped. Chairbacks were now suspended above the seat-rail, gently supported by stiles. Pilasters and delicate moldings edged furniture pieces. Case furniture became rectangular, while commodes and side tables were semicircular in design.

America was not exposed to the neoclassical style until the renewal of communication with England in 1783 after the Revolutionary War. At this time, the less formal neoclassical designs of Adam's followers, George Hepplewhite and Thomas Sheraton, greeted Americans. It was their publications that influenced American cabinetmakers. Hepplewhite's designs showed a square tapering leg, often ending in a spade foot. He stressed delicate inlay as a decorative technique, rather than carving, although a silhouette of the feathers motif of the insignia of the Prince of Wales was seen set in the back of a chair. Curved lines were present in his work. The shape of the chairback was that of an oval, a heart, or a shield. The upholstered seat might have had a curved front. The rear legs leaned inward slightly as they approached the floor. The tall and slender bracket feet of his case pieces flared out at the bottom. On the other hand, Sheraton's patterns emphasized square backs on chairs and sofas, and round legs which were often reeded. The ends of case pieces were convex with decorative colonettes projecting at the sides.

American cabinetmakers of the Federal period selected details from the publications of Sheraton and

The back of Denis Hillman's side chair has a shield back.

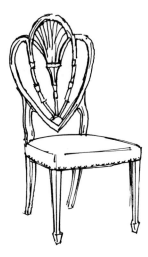

A Hepplewhite side chair
with a heart-shaped back.

Hepplewhite and combined them in their own ways to create pieces characterized by grace and beauty. The open back of side chairs during this period was shield, heart, oval, or square in outline. The splat was carved in the form of classical motifs such as urns, feathers, and drapery. The square backs had a carved central splat, a series of pointed arches resting on columns, or several crossed arches within the exterior framework. Painted oval-back chairs with Prince of Wales feathers were considered the most luxurious chair form (see page 145). The upholstered seat might have been straight or bowed across the front. The legs were selected from the two English styles. Arms on this form moved from the back, often in an unbroken line, to the side of the chair seat or to the top of the front leg.

Simple back stools, upholstered over the frame, were reminiscent of the Jacobean Cromwellian chair. The chairs were stools with tall serpentine crested backs. Upholstered open-arm chairs with tall backs were called Martha Washington, or lolling, chairs. (The meaning of the word "loll" is to recline in a relaxed manner.) This chair became popular in New England as a comfortable chair. It continued in use even after it fell out of favor in England. Wing chairs, or easy chairs, continued to be fashionable. The serpentine wings were more exaggerated and open. They slanted diagonally inward and perhaps stopped at the arms, in contrast to the continuous flow of the Chippendale easy chair. The squared legs were slightly tapered. A barrel-shaped easy chair was a new form emerging during this period. The height of the back varied, but an unbroken line, perhaps emphasized by wood trim, moved from the leg support up over the arm, around the back, to the other arm, and down to the other leg. An upholstered armchair with a low back was seen occasionally in America at this time. This chair mirrored the style of the Federal sofa and often matched it in a set.

The Windsor chair now had bamboo-type turnings on the legs. This design was created with vase turnings bisected by a groove. Sheraton designed a new Windsor back, replacing the curved bow with horizontal cross rails on a raked back.

Sheraton "fancy chairs" were open-back arm or side chairs with painted decoration. Pictorial scenes or other motifs adorned a flat, wide back rail. The seats were woven with rush or cane. The chairs themselves were painted and gilded. These fancy chairs inspired the design of the American stenciled Hitchcock chair. In 1825, Lambert Hitchcock was one of the first to manufacture furniture with an assembly-line method. He also manufactured the painted and stenciled Boston rocker. This rocker had a comfortable shaped seat that rolled up in the back and down in the front. The high back was bowed and made of spindles.

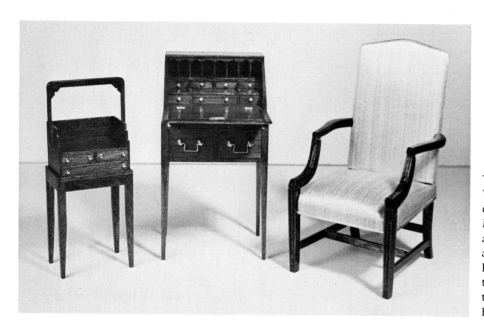

The graceful lines of the Martha Washington, or lolling, chair are carefully followed by Virginia Merrill. Pictured with the chair are a ladies' desk by Bill Robertson and a portable bookstand by Terry Rogel. These two pieces have met the challenge of the gracefully tapered legs so characteristic of the Federal period.

A pair of black Hitchcock chairs decorated with the standard gold designs. William Severback reproduces caning very nicely on the chair to the left; Harry Smith's gold stenciled design is very authentic on the chair to the right.

An angular view of Betty Valentine's Federal sofa shows the arm resting on a freestanding support that rises from the front leg. This design is characteristic of the style of Thomas Sheraton.

The sofa was still an expensive and rare item. The low back was straight or slightly arched. It had a wooden top rail that was carved or inlaid. The rail either echoed the top edge of the back or formed a graceful crest. It flowed along the high upholstered arms that sloped at right angles from the back. The arms occasionally rolled over in a graceful curve. The wooden framework of the arm might have flowed directly into the front leg. Occasionally, the end of the upholstered arm was supported by a freestanding baluster. The baluster was an extension of the front leg, which was turned and reeded. This arm treatment was characteris-

tic of Sheraton pieces. A cabriole sofa style, made in Baltimore, showed the back curving around to form arms. The front edge of the seat was serpentine. These gently curved lines created a fluid quality.

Samuel McIntire introduced a mahogany bench for use in front of the window in his Federal interiors. A back was absent but upholstered armrests curved up from the ends of the seat. The fan shape of the seat caused the arms to open outward. The wooden line of the leg continued up the front and the back of the arms, and spiraled into a rosette.

The tester and field beds were still the popular bed

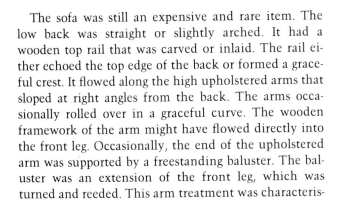

Red moiré covers this exquisite mahogany Sheraton sofa made by Paul Runyon.

The sewing table is so named because it was designed to house a lady's handwork and accessories. English brown oak is used for the lovely burled top. Sewing implements were stored in the drawer and sewing in the silk bag suspended from a drawer frame. Made by Jose F. Rodriguez and available from the Washington Doll's House and Toy Museum.

Paul Runyon's Pembroke table has Sheraton leg supports and gracefully curved leaves.

forms. Often, a decorative cornice crowned the top of the tester bed. The reeded posts were supported by a vase-shaped section that rested on a tapered square leg ending in a blocked foot. The reeding might have been interrupted at the base by delicately carved wheat ears. A round brass disk was mounted on the outside surface of the squared leg. The headboard was plain with a slight arch or a straight line across the top.

Tables continued to be specialized, but now they also became intricate in their construction. The worktable was a new form designed to meet the needs of the needleworker. Often, a pouch was attached to a sliding frame under an upper drawer. The pouch might have been made of wood and covered in pleated silk, silk lined with a more durable fabric, or wood lined with a decorative paper. Occasionally, the table surface lifted to reveal a compartmentalized area for the storage of needlework tools. Later worktables replaced the pouch

Paul Runyon overcomes the difficulty of inserting drawers in a round frieze. The circular drum table is set on a tripod base consisting of curved legs that end in brass casters.

The rent table has a more complicated support that also ends in brass casters. The drawers are well executed on this piece. Available from Paige Thornton. *Collection of Theodore Merrill*

Denis Hillman's fine craftsmanship is exemplified by this sofa table with perfectly executed burled veneer and satinwood inlay.

The drum table, a round library table, might have had drawers set in the apron, with Sheraton's vase pedestal form for a base. The incurved legs were reeded and ended in a square brass foot on a caster for easy movability. The drum table was similar to a rent table whose drawers were numbered so as to provide a file for a landowner's tenant paperwork. A sofa table, set in front of the sofa, aided ladies engaged in needlework, reading, or writing. These tables were used more frequently in England, but a few were found in America. This form showed the same incurved leg seen on the vase pedestal.

Side tables and card tables adopted either the Hepplewhite semicircular surface or the Sheraton shape with round D-shaped ends and projecting sides. A variation of the Sheraton surface was the cloverleaf top whose sides and corners were lobed. The top surface of the side table might have continued to be marble, but a wooden surface decorated with wood inlay was also used. The wooden card table surface was expanded by opening the top and turning it so that the opened surface was supported by the apron framework. The semicircular table had tapered square legs, each with a spade foot or an inlaid cuff or band. The Sheraton vase pedestal was seen on card tables. The legs of the base were spaced to allow the table to stand against the wall when closed.

device with an additional drawer and required heavier legs to support the added weight. The Federal period was the first in which furniture was made solely for women.

The Pembroke table, introduced during the Chippendale period, was used for serving tea during the Federal period. Now with rounded leaves, it opened to form an oval surface. Oval was a popular shape during this period.

Larger dining furniture was designed during the Federal period because a sizable room on the first floor of the house was designated solely for eating. Before this time, eating had taken place in a parlor or a sitting

The emergence during the Federal period of a large dining room is typified by the Thorne reproduction of a dining room in the Hammond-Harwood House in Annapolis, Maryland, 1770–1774. *Courtesy: Thorne American Rooms in Miniature, The Art Institute of Chicago*

Larger dining tables were placed in these sizable rooms, as exemplified by Paul Runyon's extension table. The shield-back arm and side chairs surrounding the table are made by Denis Hillman.

room. Dining tables become larger and sectioned. The oval table surface was created by the addition of a leaf to a pedestaled extension table, by the arrangement of two semicircular portions, each with a rectangular drop leaf, or by a rectangular drop-leaf table to which two semicircular side tables were drawn.

The basin stand, now designed to stand in the corner, had slightly curved legs. A small shelf for the ewer served as a stretcher. The circular opening in the upper shelf held the Chinese porcelain bowl used for washing.

Candlestands and fire screens were created in the Hepplewhite and Sheraton styles. Candlestands were small and had tilt tops. Fire screens might have been

equipped with a collapsible candlestand. Hepplewhite showed an oval screen or table surface with an urn-shaped baluster shaft. The base was comprised of three curved legs ending in a snake foot. Sheraton, on the other hand, proposed an octagonal surface and a tripod base with a convex foot. A few rectangular fire screens were also seen during this period. Unlike the broad shield on the moderately tall pole of the Chippendale period, these pole screens were very tall with small shields. Music stands followed the same style as the pole screen. They often had one or two brass candle holders so that candles could provide the proper light for reading sheets of music.

The simplified curves of the Federal period are incorporated in this basin stand by Paul Runyon.

A ring of satinwood inlay echoes the shape of the top of a Federal candlestand supported by three convex feet.

On a Baltimore mixing table circa 1800, a Sheraton roll top shaped by a waterfall enclosure opens to reveal a marble surface resistant to stains from the alcoholic drinks mixed on its surface. This piece was made by Rose Barell.

The same convex foot is seen on the mahogany music stand created in the style of Sheraton by Paul Runyon. *Collection of Virginia Merrill*

Intricate storage forms appeared during the Federal period. The cellarette was a small piece of furniture for the storage of liquors. It had a drawer for cutlery with a storage space above that was sectioned for bottles. The hinged lid was equipped with a lock. There might have been additional space for sugar and spices. This piece was seen more often in Southern homes. The mixing table provided the same storage and had a marble surface for the mixing of drinks. Other specialized tables were the drawing table and the dressing table. The drawing table had a drawer whose top lifted to reveal an easel that could be elevated. The dressing table had small drawers for cosmetics and accessories and a folding box lid that lifted to reveal a compartmentalized box and an easel mirror.

The Federal period brought a new emphasis in the form of case pieces. The concepts of the high chest and the dressing table had been discarded. The chest-on-chest form was utilized with a low broken triangular pediment and carved freestanding classical figures and urns. Carving decorated the frieze with classical motifs. The chest of drawers was the most popular replacement for the high chest during this period. American

The inlay on this Hepplewhite sideboard is superbly done by Paul Runyon. It moves down the leg to form stockings around the leg. The inlaid circles on the doors follow the shape of the handle; tambour doors enclose a central storage area under the shallow central drawer.

designs generally followed those of Hepplewhite and Sheraton. The Hepplewhite pieces had a flat, bow, or serpentine front, a shaped apron, and a curved French foot. Sheraton included, at the sides of a straight or bow-front chest, small projecting columns that continued below the bottom drawer to form a short leg. A dressing chest with an attached mirror was created in New England. These lighter chests of drawers foreshadowed the Victorian bureau. The rectangular or oval mirror might have been supported on a recessed tier of drawers by an S-shaped frame or by obelisks. Semicircular commodes (chests of drawers) came into use. Four columns in the Sheraton style divided the semielliptical front surface into three parts. Each side section provided cupboard space and the center section accommodated drawers. Decoration of the top surface might have consisted of rays of inlay emanating from a semicircular motif.

Side tables were no longer used with dining tables for the serving of food. A larger furniture piece called a sideboard was introduced for this purpose. The sideboard was a wide chest of drawers on tall legs used for storing and displaying dining equipment. It looked well with the larger sectioned dining tables.

Desks appeared in more numerous forms during the Federal period. The slope-front desk was still made with a lower chest, following the contemporary style. However, the tambour desk was more popular. A tambour was a vertical or horizontal sliding door made of thin wood strips glued to a heavy fabric. It followed the

A Sheraton ladies' desk, 1810–1820, was made by Donald Buttfield from Cuban mahogany. The complicated drawer arrangement is beautifully executed. The desk surface closes to an upright position. *Courtesy: Donald Buttfield*

A *bonheur du jour* by Denis Hillman is a French ladies' desk. The storage section on the desk surface inspired the tambour design seen during the Federal period. The marquetry on this piece is extraordinary.

shape of the groove into which it was set so it was either flat or curved when closed. The desk might have been rectangular with tall legs. A case of two drawers might have supported a recessed upper cabinet with flat vertical tambour doors. The prototype for the tambour desk was the French *bonheur de jour*, a desk developed for ladies during the letter-and-diary era of the period of Louis XVI and later. A smaller desk, made in America specifically for ladies, had a narrower single drawer supported by tall legs. The separate desk box might have used a slope front or a rounded tambour opening (see page 161). The upper section of the ladies' desk also might have been recessed with a desk surface that closed vertically. The use of portable sections for a ladies' desk was more popular in the South.

The desk and bookcase (secretary) was still produced during the Federal period. The doors no longer had wooden panels, but had glass panes framed in an intricate geometric pattern. Panels of verre églomisé might have been set in the doors. Gathered fabric covered the interior surface of the glass panels. The piece was crowned with a broken pediment that was triangular rather than scrolled. The top might also have been flat or had brass finials of classical or patriotic symbols perched on a gently curved pediment. Legs were either French with a curved apron or longer and turned with

The Federal piano case was simple and rectangular. Stringlike inlay emphasized the purity of the lines. Square sectioned legs were tapered gracefully to brass casters. A satinwood panel painted with delicate flowers might have been set on the surface above the keys. A shelf with a recessed front edge might have been placed under the case for the storage of sheet music.

During the Federal period, tall case clocks were also expensive and rare. They were characterized by an elegant use of inlay on the case surface. The Chippendale molded base with the ogee bracket foot disappeared. The base of the Federal clock was less obvious. It had a gracefully scalloped apron with the smaller curved French foot. The hood had an arched head topped by a broken scrolled pediment, perhaps having a pierced crest. The corners on the hood were columned. Simon Willard designed a case-on-case clock as a precursor to the banjo clock. The long rectangular case hung on the wall and was divided into two parts: the lower half housed the pendulum; the top had a door with a

The pedimented secretary desk by Jerry Hodgson is another fine example of inlay work as the satinwood lines frame drawer fronts, including those in the interior whose fronts are not only flat but curved.

reeding. The desk had a slant front, a wooden cylinder, or a tambour opening. The larger breakfront was predominantly a bookcase with a hidden center desk surface. It was called a breakfront because it originally had a lower front surface that was broken by a central protruding section. This massive piece was expensive and rare, although it was made more frequently at this time than in the Chippendale period. The most popular form for this piece during the Federal period was the Salem secretary made in Salem, Massachusetts. This New England creation was divided into three parts, with a desk hidden behind the top drawer of the middle section.

Brasses seen on Federal case pieces were typically round or oval in shape. They came in two types. Oval or round backplates supported swinging handles attached at each side, or flat circular handles protruded to allow a drawer to be pulled open. Placed on this hardware were decorative motifs such as rosettes, baskets of flowers, or eagles.

A Simon Willard tall case clock by Ron Terrill is not only a fine reproduction, but it also keeps time. The dial decoration is photo etched in brass; the key fits and locks the door. *Courtesy: Ron Terrill*

kidney-shaped glass pane. The bell, located over the movement, could be seen. A pierced crest was framed on each side by a small brass finial. The banjo clock showed a round clock face topped by a brass eagle. A long neck connected the mechanism to the rectangular section which enclosed the end of the pendulum. Decorative glass panels covered the two lower sections. The girandole clock resembled the banjo clock, except that the bottom area had a round painted scenic panel in a frame decorated with gilt balls. The resemblance to the fashionable girandole mirror influenced its name. Pillar and scroll clocks by Eli Terry were made to sit on a shelf. The decorative case was characterized by its bro-

Another Eli Terry shelf clock was made by Ron Terrill. His also keeps time. The finials are brass turned.
Courtesy: Ron Terrill

A banjo clock.

Two pillar and scroll clocks based on the designs of Eli Terry. The clock to the left is by Paul Runyon; the example to the right is a working clock by Dave Usher.

ken scrolled pediment and side columns. A painted glass panel filled the lower portion of the door. Terry produced many clocks until 1840.

Looking glasses became more varied during the Federal period. Some followed the Hepplewhite style in that they were pedimented with a broken scroll. The earlier Chippendale form became more graceful and was adorned with more gilding. It was topped with a brass finial and wire ornament. In some cases, the upper and lower crests were constructed entirely of gilded "French putty" and wires. Sheraton's design of a tabernacle mirror had a flat cornice and a molding comprised of gilded balls. Under the cornice was a painted glass panel with a landscape design. Columns, or later a twisted rope molding, framed the sides of the mirror. Occasionally, three urns with wire and gesso forming bouquets of flowers and wheat topped the cornice. Chains with dangling gilded balls were occasionally hung within the decorative framework above the cornice. A larger Sheraton mirror was styled to hang over the mantel. This gilt chimney glass was divided into three sections by reeded columns. A frieze of carved and painted classical motifs separated the cornice from

A scrolled mirror decorated with ormolu mounts and a gilt vase. Virginia Merrill captures the grace of the original wired flowers seen on mirrors of the Federal period.

This Hepplewhite mirror is completely gilded. Wire and putty ornamentation becomes even more prominent.

A brass girandole mirror.

A wine cooler for the storage of wine before serving made by Paul Runyon.

A canterbury with beautifully turned members made by Paul Runyon.

the glassed portions. The girandole mirror made an appearance during the Federal period, although it was used frequently in Empire interior decoration. The term girandole originally applied to any wall light with sections of mirrored glass. The form became a round convex mirror with an ornate carved gilded frame. The circular frame had molding decorated with round balls. It was typically crowned by an eagle.

During the Federal period, small wooden forms served specialized functions. The wine cooler was an oval or hexagonal container on tapered legs. Wine bottles were kept in the metal-lined tub to cool before wine was served. The canterbury was named for a cleric who first ordered a piece of this type. It was a portable stand with sections for storing sheet music or a dinner tray, plates, and cutlery. Knife cases, often made of satinwood, became vase-shaped.

After the Revolution, less time elapsed between the creation of European fashions and their incorporation into American design. European techniques were introduced to America by emigrating craftsmen, who found a great demand for their skills in American cities such as New York, Philadelphia, and Baltimore. General stylistic trends were followed throughout Europe, although they were interpreted differently in the various countries. Although most of the influence on American designs came from England, America had established a mutually supportive relationship with France. The French championed the American cause during the American Revolution. Later, the Americans were sympathetic as the French experienced their own revolution. American ministers were sent to France and returned with pieces of furniture and an awareness of the current fashions in that country. Philadelphia, the temporary national capital at the time, incorporated some French designs in its furniture. Furniture pieces created with Louis XVI lines and gilded decoration resembled the sofa (canapé) on page 154 and the tub chair (bergère) on page 140. The English influence in Philadelphia inspired square-backed chairs with a central urn motif and looping drapery. Sideboards in Philadelphia typically had rounded ends.

Regional differences were less obvious during the Federal period because of the ease of communication between cities. However, other areas of the country differed from Philadelphia in their preference for certain details. New York chairbacks were characterized by drapery and Prince of Wales feathers. Sideboards were often decorated with a quarter fan inlay. The front inner legs were set on a diagonal to conform with the curving front surface.

New England furniture forms were still extremely slim and delicate. As a result, chairs retained the stretchers characteristic in this region during earlier periods. New England Hepplewhite-styled chairs had heart-shaped backs. Chests of drawers had bow fronts. Designs relied on the contrast of inlaid woods against mahogany for ornamentation. In Salem, Massachusetts, chairs had a shield back with a carved urn and drapery swags that reached to the outer edge of the shield. This city promoted the dressing chest with an attached mirror and the breakfront secretary that bore its name. Samuel McIntire designed interiors and furniture in Salem. His carved and cast motifs were cornucopias, baskets of flowers, rosettes, and water leaves. He used punchwork as a background technique on furniture and house interiors.

Baltimore suddenly became a prosperous city at this time. An influx of English cabinetmakers caused the design of furniture to follow closely that of London. A unique regional furniture style was created here. Baltimore furniture was characterized by a sophisticated use of inlay. Large ovals were placed on mitered panels. Bellflowers with elongated central petals hung down chair and table legs. Tassels and medallions with classical and patriotic motifs decorated flat and rounded surfaces. The inlay technique also used painted églomisé glass panels decorated with allegorical figures. The kidney shape was favored for table surfaces. Over-the-frame seat upholstery covered only half the seat-rail. The painting of London's "fancy furniture" was perfectly executed in Baltimore.

Most of the Southern furniture characteristic of Charleston, South Carolina, was destroyed or scattered during the Civil War. Sideboards made in this area are six-legged with D-shaped ends and inlaid ovals on the doors. Reeding on bedposts framed delicately carved clusters of ears of wheat. These were executed so finely that they resembled rice. Thus, the Southern technique adopted the name "rice carving."

Federal Upholstery

Thomas Sheraton defined the drawing room of an elegant house as the room to which guests withdrew after dining and in which callers were entertained in a formal manner. It was these bright and delicate interiors that were enhanced by the glow of silk fabrics hanging at the windows and covering pieces of furniture. The silks were plain, as seen on Virginia Merrill's Martha Washington chair on page 68, or decorated with brocade or silk-embroidered designs. The colors were muted. Classical motifs were used, such as urns, swags, and baskets of flowers. Stripes were common. They were solid or patterned, in which vertical geometric borders alternated with a column of classical ornamentation.

Silks and damasks were used exclusively in the wealthier homes, and then only in one or two of the more formal rooms. Dining rooms and libraries were decorated in more somber colors. Leather was used often to upholster chair seats in the dining room because of its resistance to spills and on easy chairs in the study because of its durability.

Less expensive fabrics, such as horsehair, chintzes, and copperplate-printed toiles, were used for upholstery also. Horsehair was made with a cotton, linen, or woolen warp, and a weft of long hairs from the mane and tail of a horse. This extremely durable fabric was dyed and woven to resemble many of the silk fabrics. Floral-patterned chintzes were used in the bedroom and in the public rooms of the house. Red copperplate patterns of historical scenes were produced by the English and the French for the American market. Monochromatic scenes were scattered on a cream-colored toile ground. Unless horsehair was used to upholster a furniture piece in the bedroom, the same fabric was used for draperies, bed hangings, and upholstery.

Chair seats were generally upholstered over the frame. In Baltimore, however, the material was pulled only halfway down. A single row of brass tacks, placed so closely together that they touched, secured upholstery fabric. Another row of tacks might have proceeded around the top edge of the chair rail also. Occasionally, additional tacks were applied to the front seat-rail in a scallop or swag design. Later in the period, narrow borders of floral tape or contrasting cord replaced tacks.

Federal Drapery Treatment

While we think of shimmering silks as the most appropriate fabric for Federal interiors, printed cottons and chintzes were more commonly used for drapes and bed hangings. The fashionable drapery treatment of this period was the French style. A pair of fabric panels were drawn together on rods with rings, pulleys, and cords. This mechanism operated in much the same way as traverse rods do today. The floor-length panels hung open and straight or were closed and drawn back at the middle with tasseled cords. The valance treatment varied. A gilded or wooden cornice might have crowned a fabric valance. The valance was a flat scalloped piece of material. Festoons were hung over the French curtains, or material supported by a pole was draped in swags. Fringe trimmed valance fabrics and the inner and bottom edges of drapery panels.

A white gauze, or mull, fabric appeared at windows during the Federal period. This fine, sheer material was embroidered with spots of design or left plain. It was hung at the window in single or double panels tied back with tasseled cording attached to a small round brass wall fixture. Occasionally, only one of a pair of panels was tied back; the other hung straight to the floor.

Field and tester beds supported many styles of drapery. During the winter months, floor-length panels and liners enclosed the bed. On field beds, hangings were

A bed with a bow-shaped cornice and arrow-filled quivers is seen in the bedroom at Oak Hill in Peabody, Massachusetts, 1800. *Courtesy: Thorne American Rooms in Miniature, The Art Institute of Chicago*

designed to enclose the bed at night, while during the day, panels were looped in graceful swags and were tied with cords. Bed hangings of colored mull fabric served during warm weather because it allowed air to circulate and acted as a mosquito netting. Other fabrics were hung so as to leave the bed open day and night during the summer months.

The old straight or scalloped canopy styles continued through many fashion periods, especially in less expensive cotton printed fabrics and furniture checks. Fringes and tapes could be added and removed as the current fashion dictated. Scallops were seen on the edges of valances. A straight-edged canopy might have been decorated with tasseled swags of cording. Fringed silk or satin embroidered spreads covered the bed. The gathered or flat skirt had a straight edge. An ornate bed treatment showed a scalloped cornice on the tester bed. Festoons of drapery hung from it. The same festoons were used in the design of the bed skirt. At the foot might have been a horizontal bow with crossed arrow-filled quivers at the center (see page 79).

Federal Floor Coverings

During the Federal period, there was an abundance of floor carpets. Direct trade with the Far East made orientals available to the many who could afford them. Baku, Ferghana, Bukhara, and Khorasan were some examples. As a friendly relationship with France developed after the American Revolution, French tapestry and tufted-weave carpets became very popular in America. Savonnerie tufted carpets were made for the French court. The flatter tapestry-weave Aubusson carpets were sold to the general public and, as a result, were the more plentiful of the two in America. The delicate floral and classical designs were very well suited to the American Federal style. Fragile designs

consisted of shells and ribbons (see page 235), scrolls, moldings, flowers, acanthus leaves, bouquets, urns, and rosettes. Soft, pale colors enhanced the delicacy of the pattern. It was not uncommon to see Aubusson carpets in sets of three. The color scheme and motifs from a larger central carpet were repeated differently in each of the carpets on either side.

Families who could not afford the expensive oriental or French carpets purchased less expensive English-manufactured rugs, which copied the techniques and styles of the more costly floor coverings. In England, manufacturers of carpets were thriving. The most popular in America, Thomas Whitty's Axminster rugs, imitated oriental carpets and created designs with Greek and Roman motifs. Many of his carpets consisted of classical arrangements of garlands, bouquets with ribbons, and medallions.

Needlepoint carpets continued to be produced at this time. The designs became fine, controlled, and balanced. Classical motifs were used often in the striped arrangements seen on some furniture upholstery. A linear or geometric stripe alternated with a vertical sinuous floral or grape pattern (see page 247).

Less formal carpets such as the striped rag-weave and the geometric Scotch carpets were still used, but in less formal rooms. Hooked rugs were American in origin. They were made during this period in New England but reached their peak of popularity during the middle of the nineteenth century. At this time, brilliant designs, crudely imitating French Aubusson carpets, were hooked in wool or cotton.

Federal Needlework

To complement the delicate and shimmering furniture in the classical interiors, needlework of the Federal period incorporated new techniques and adopted a

A set of three similar Aubusson carpets arranged as they might be in a large room in a Federal home. Carpets designed by Susan Richardson and stitched by Lois Sterling.

new emphasis in materials. Finer embroidery eclipsed tent-stitch canvas work. Worsted embroidery yarns became glowing silk threads. Oval or rectangular pole screen panels and pictures were designed with classical motifs. Pictures embroidered with silk were set with black, white, and gold églomisé mats into gilt or black and gilt frames. At the end of the eighteenth century, scenic views and still lifes were popular. Scenes of local buildings in specific cities revealed the patriotic pride evident during this period. By 1800, embroidered pictures were enhanced by watercolor painting. This technique was seen in the painting of the faces of embroidered figures. Earlier, people had not been allowed to dwell on life's sadnesses. Now, mourning was permitted to such a degree that it became a theme in needlework. Tombs were set among weeping willows, angels, and sad, bereaved women were dressed in neoclassical Empire-styled gowns (see page 218). There developed great interest in memorializing individuals, whether they were alive or dead. In needlework, as well as through other media, patriotic figures were eulogized and mourned on a national scale.

During the late eighteenth and early nineteenth centuries, samplers were made almost exclusively in ladies' finishing schools. These boarding schools had become prolific. Samplers were used for learning and as reference tools. The finished product was usually framed and put on display. The samplers of the Federal period were usually wider and shorter and, by the end of the eighteenth century, might have even been square. There was a stitched border all the way around the piece, which was signed with the stitcher's name, birthday, and the date of the completion of the work. Samplers depicted family trees, globe-shaped maps, darning techniques for invisible mending, and lacework designs. Lacework samplers served as a reference for trim used on baby caps, aprons, and handkerchiefs.

As soon as machines created the more practical knitted articles, such as stockings and gloves, ladies were able to use their knitting ability to create more decorative items such as imitation lace edgings for tablecloths, pillowcases, and collars.

Tambour work became fashionable the last quarter of the eighteenth century. For about fifty years, chain-stitched patterns were worked from the top of fine Indian muslin with special hooks. Hoops were used to hold the fabric tight. Silk, metallic, linen, cotton, and woolen yarns were used. This technique was most popular around 1800 for embroidering sheer fabrics for drapes, bed hangings, scarves, and women's dresses. By 1830, the style of dress had changed to stiff wide skirts, which did not suit this type of ornamentation. By the mid-1840s, machines created tambour patterns.

Bedspreads were decorated with fashionable handwork. Candlewicking used thick, soft, white yarns that resembled the wicks of candles to create large embroidery stitches on heavy white cotton fabric. By 1840, this too was done by machine. Marseilles quilting was the technique of stitching together two pieces of fabric and stuffing selected areas of the design with cotton batting or candlewick yarn. This work was done in a factory after 1830.

Quilts were now created by using all three of the quilting techniques, which were often combined on one project. One-piece quilting showed a design stitched through two layers of fabric with cotton batting between them. Pieced quilts had a top layer formed by assembling different pieces of fabric. Appliquéd quilts were decorated with cutout designs stitched to a background fabric. Two quilting motifs during this period were birds and vases of flowers.

During the Federal period, as much emphasis was placed on needlework tools as on the handwork itself. Ivory, mother-of-pearl, and whalebone were used to create implements such as a sewing clamp, a bodkin, a needle, a thimble, and cases to hold these items. Chatelaines were chained jewelry pieces worn at the waist on which sewing accessories were hung for easy accessibility. A silver heart was worn at the waist in which to sheathe knitting needles. Intricate boxes were created from fine, often inlaid, woods in which to house the many sewing tools belonging to Federal ladies.

Federal Silver

Silver designed during the Federal period followed the classical trend initiated by Robert Adam in London. The florid, opulent, rococo style was replaced by one of simplicity, symmetry, precision, and proper scale. Unbroken curves were more controlled. Gently scrolled French feet replaced the earlier claw-and-ball or shell feet. Machinery now supplemented the silversmith's tools, so silver pieces were designed on the basis of a machine's ability rather than on a creative design.

Classical shapes were applied to the designs of an expanding number of forms. The Roman urn appeared in its own right and as a shape for other vessels and containers. Ovals were seen in the silhouette of trays, teapots, and tea caddies. The shape of the inverted helmet of a warrior was used for small pitchers.

Ornamentation was limited to beading, reeded molding, fluted sides, cast finials, and engraving. Beading often trimmed the openings of silver pieces. Convex reeded moldings were used to edge or band surfaces. Concave fluting added a decorative shape to the otherwise plain surfaces of straight-sided pieces. A small bead topped a cone finial, which rested on a slightly domed lid. Pineapple and urn finials were also typical.

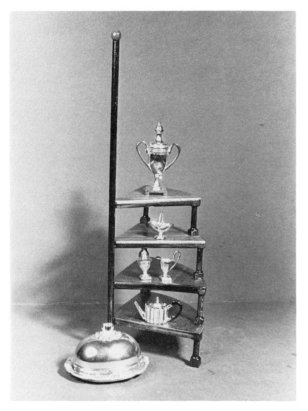

An arrangement of silver seen during the Federal period: a coffee urn, a cake basket, a sugar bowl and creamer (1791–1793), a teapot, and a covered platter.

Engraving was emphasized as the decorative technique. The asymmetrical cartouche framework for initials was replaced by a balanced shield, wreath, or swag. Rosettes supported classical motifs such as restrained floral festoons.

The number of objects produced in silver increased considerably during the Federal period. There was now an emphasis on sets of items such as oval goblets with trumpet-shaped feet. The cup was simple and smooth with beading and engraved borders. Beakers again had straight sides and flat bottoms. These, too, were made in sets and simply decorated. Mugs became barrel-shaped with squared and scrolled hollow handles. Tankards also adopted hooped bodies with either flat or slightly domed lids. Canns remained unchanged, except that the rococo decorative engraving designs became classical. By the nineteenth century, ceramic and glass drinking containers replaced silver mug, tankard, and cann forms.

Flatware production now included knives and four-tine forks. By 1783, the increased variety of spoons had completely incorporated the down-turned handle. The underside of the bowl was decorated with a fine engraving of a bird holding a branch in its mouth. The top surface of the spoon handle was engraved with delicate initials and flowers. Occasionally, the initials were written sideways from the end of the handle. At the close of the eighteenth century, the handles were pointed, and the bowls were more egg-shaped. Around 1800, the end of the handle was canted to create a coffin shape. Knives, forks, and spoons were made in sets so that all spoons were one pattern, forks another, and knives a third.

The types of specialized spoons increased. Caddy spoons, for removing tea from tea caddies, had very short handles and scallop-shaped bowls. Marrow spoons were very narrow with channels shaped at each end to collect marrow from bones. Bone marrow was held in high regard at eighteenth-century dinners. Small spoons were made for salt. Long, thin-handled, small spoons were used to serve mustard. The bowls of ladles became oval in shape and were more widely fluted.

Condiment containers incorporated classical features. Salt cellars became oval, pierced frameworks for blue glass liners. They also were made in a boat shape supported by an oval or a rectangular foot. Two handles might have been located at the ends. Casters became urn-shaped with an urn finial. The body portion was taller, the neck shorter, and the dome of the lid lower. A circular or oval domed foot or a square block called a plinth served as a base. This form was quickly replaced by glass casters with silver pierced lids. Mustard was now stored in a straight-sided pot. A hole in the lid accommodated the long-handled mustard spoon. The pot was pierced to display the color of the glass liner inserted to protect the silver from tarnish.

Serving pieces abounded at this time. They were often made in sets for display on the dining room sideboard. Chafing dishes continued to keep foods warm at the table. A saucepan now had straight sides with beading around the rim and a shaped band around the base. The sauceboat became sleeker. It rested on an oval foot or on a molded band. A papboat was made in the same form. It was introduced during the seventeenth century to hold pap for feeding infants, and now closely resembled a Roman lamp. Small tureens, also made for sauces, came in sets of two or four and were oval with a shaped lid. The lid might have had a hole at the opening for a ladle. Each end had a handle for easier passing. Soup tureens were larger models of the sauce tureen. They were rectangular in shape with rounded corners. A cast handle was placed at each end and vertically on the lid. Eagle claw-and-ball feet supported the rectangular base. The punch bowl retained the Chinese bowl shape and was set on a collet foot that was created with a band of metal. The sides curved smoothly. A punch strainer, resembling the tea sieve, was still used with the punch bowl, as it was during the Chippendale period. Beaded decoration surrounded the top edge. The handles at each side of the pierced round bowl were thinner and only slightly curved in outline. Bread and cake baskets, now made in great quantity, had either a hinged bail handle or a stationary handle at each end

Silver tea sieve circa 1792
by Eugene Kupjack.

Silver basket to serve cake
circa 1813 by Eugene
Kupjack.

Barrel-shaped silver pitcher
circa 1820 by Eugene Kupjack.

of the solid oblong form of the body. The base was a rectangular or oval domed foot. Toast racks, used to keep toast crisp at the table, were created with shaped silver wire. A shallow, circular serving dish was made from one sheet of silver so that it could withstand the heat of a baking oven. Large pitchers were barrel-shaped with a triangular spout. Later the pitcher took on a ewer form.

During the Federal period, porringers continued in use. In 1825, they were no longer produced because they were not in vogue.

Large sets of tea and coffee serving pieces became fashionable. The Federal teapot was elliptical with a straight spout (see page 82). The sides were straight and were either smooth or fluted. The wooden handle was D-shaped. This vessel had a flat base with no base molding or foot. It was set on a small fitted tray elevated from the table surface by four French feet. The heavy coffeepot was urn-shaped, resting on a plinth base. The sides were fluted or smooth to match the teapot. The creamer was made in the shape of an upside-down warrior helmet (see page 82). It was accompanied by a lidded sugar bowl whose body was urn- or boat-shaped. The urn shape had no handles (see page 82). The slop, or waste, bowl became a larger basin on a pedestal base. Tea tongs were made in a bow shape from one strip of

silver. The tapering arms were decorated with engraving. The grips were oval or acorn-shaped. The earlier tea kettle form became an urn with two handles at the sides (see page 82). There was a short spout with a valve on the front surface. A warming lamp might have been concealed in the base, which was elevated from the table surface by four ball feet. A pierced area in the upper portion of the foot provided further ventilation.

Trays were produced in a wide variety of sizes. Oval was the preferred shape, but circular trays and rectangular trays with canted corners were also created. French feet supported some tray surfaces, while others were flat. A large, oval, flat tray with handles at the ends was used to present the tea service. Rims might have been beaded or pierced or trimmed with machine-stamped edging or gadrooning.

Candlesticks were more common during the Federal period. Fluted or reeded columns stood on square bases. Circular or oval bases were also seen. The columnar shaft was slightly shaped and tapered as it approached the base. The socket and bobeche were combined to form a graceful urn shape.

Many miscellaneous objects were made in silver at this time. Inkstands continued to be produced, but with urn-shaped containers and French feet. Silver sewing items were thimbles, hooks, needle cases, bodkins with an eyelet at the end to pull tape through a hem, and heart-shaped chatelaine hooks from which scissors and other equipment hung. Silver was formed into brooches, crosses, earrings, armbands, and medals. Presentation pieces such as tureens, punch bowls, and tea sets were made to honor war heroes, especially after the War of 1812.

Federal Pewter and Britannia

After the Revolutionary War, there was a rapid decline in the demand for English pewter. Silver, Sheffield plate, ceramics, and glass were preferred by the more affluent urban families of the Federal period. American pewterers located in more remote areas carried on a prolific business with less affluent and more rural families. The mug replaced the tankard after 1800. The rim of the plate again became decorated with a single reed. Neoclassical shapes were made until the middle of the century. Pressed glassware eliminated the demand for pewter at that time.

In the 1790s, a harder metal than pewter was developed. It was called "britannia." This bright metal eventually replaced pewter completely in England and America during the nineteenth century. Britannia was a fine quality pewter that contained no lead. Because of its durability, it could be rolled into thin layers and either shaped on a lathe or cut into parts to be as-

A display of Federal ceramics consisting of two
China Trade bowls, a transfer-printed teapot, and
several Wedgwood pieces.

sembled. Traditional pewter forms, such as plates, mugs,
and porringers, were produced along with the great variety of metal objects demanded at this time. The
forms remained simple and were rarely decorated with
engraving. But the public enjoyed the diversification of
forms, the durability, and the finish, so britannia ware
remained popular until well into the Victorian period.

Federal Ceramics

As in the other decorative arts of the Federal period,
ceramics adopted the neoclassical style. Fine colored
stoneware was produced in England by Josiah Wedgwood in the form of busts, seals, plaques, and classical
vases. Black basalt was polished with a wheel used by a
lapidary. But more typical was his unpolished jasper
stoneware that was seen in light blue and sea green
with white molded decoration. The white ornamentation of classical figures and motifs was designed by a
professional sculptor. Later, more colors were added to
the spectrum of background shades, such as sage and

olive green, lilac, dark blue, black, and, rarely, yellow.
Useful and ornamental forms, including jewelry and
opera glasses, were made in jasper.

Ivory-colored English creamware replaced delft for
everyday use. Transfer prints in blue or black served as
the ornamentation. To regain the American market
after the Revolution, English transfer designs represented American victory scenes, even though the van-
quished were British. American heroes such as George
Washington, Thomas Jefferson, and Benjamin Franklin, American ships, and patriotic emblems such as the
eagle decorated these wares. Also serving as motifs were
armorials, romantic scenes, and pictorial excerpts from
a literary series, such as *The Adventures of Dr. Syntax*.
The mass production of transfer printing made it possible to create large sets of matching dinnerware. Dish
shapes followed those of silver.

Leeds creamware occasionally received enamel or
transfer-printed decoration. But, more often than not,
its only form of decoration was a bright, perfect glaze,
pierced designs in wide bands around rims or openings,
and handles that were molded into twisted stems with
leaves or flowers at the end.

Lusterware made an appearance at the beginning of
the nineteenth century. The technique of creating luster was very old, with beginnings in the Near East. The
Arabs took it to Spain in the seventh century. From
there, it filtered into the other countries of Europe. Its
use died out in England after the eighth century until
the end of the eighteenth century. There was a great
variety of luster shades. Film colors included gold, copper, silver, purple, orange, and rose. An early use of
luster was to create "poor man's silver" by coating ceramics completely with a film of silver luster. Later, the
various lusters were combined on earthenware or porcelain with transfer printing and enamel ornamentation. Pieces were considered a novelty. Mugs, bowls,
pitchers, and plates were some of the forms made.

Direct trade with China brought a variety of porcelains to American homes. Wares ordered by Amer-

Copper lusterware made by Priscilla Lance
and Deborah McKnight.

icans were simpler and less diversified than those going to Europe. Selections were made from three basic underglaze designs. Fitzhugh china produced a wide border composed of latticework, pomegranates, and butterflies. At the center were four medallions of emblems and flowers. Chinese patterns from the cities of Nanking and Canton were similar. A central scene of an island or a landscape was surrounded by a wide border of latticework. Nanking porcelain was often gilded. The predominant pattern color was blue, but the Fitzhugh design might have used green, orange, rose, and brown as overglaze colors. Stock patterns could be obtained. Monograms, ships, flowers, armorials, and emblems such as the eagle (see page 84) were ordered as central motifs with narrow decorative borders framing the rim. The porcelain was smooth and white. Large dinner and tea services were ordered, as well as punch bowls, mugs, pitchers, and flagons. Five-piece garnitures or pairs of covered urns for the mantel were imported, but rarely.

Large ornamental urns were procured from France. French wares became fashionable, so polychrome and gilded urns from Sèvres were popular. Flowers, scenes, and portraits of prominent people decorated the central medallion. Sèvres colors of rose, blue, turquoise, green, and yellow provided the overall color for vases.

American artisans continued to produce only practical pottery. Redware and stoneware objects were decorated in the traditional techniques of trailed slip, incised patterns, or sgraffito.

Federal Glassware

During the Federal period, the number of American glasshouses grew. While these factories all provided windowpanes and bottles for the American market, they also created free-blown and pattern-molded pieces for nearby residents. Bowls, pitchers, and dishes were created in traditional, practical shapes for everyday use. The colors were predominantly green and amber, the natural glass colors. Some blue and amethyst were created by artificial means. Small compotes, sauce dishes, and lidded sugar bowls followed the shapes of contemporary silver.

Free-blown and pattern-mold techniques were used. Glass could be blown directly or after being placed in a small mold to create surface designs. Patterns on the surface took the form of vertical or swirled ribbing or a broken swirl created by placing a vertical design on top of the swirl. Diamond shapes could also be created on pieces through the pattern molds. Free-blown glass of the Southern Jersey type applied glass ornamentation to the surface in the form of threads, patterned trails, and ornamental pieces of glass. Lids on Southern Jersey objects were topped by a bird finial.

Because of the immigration of European craftsmen,

the American industry was able to produce, in a few factories, close approximations of fine European wares. John Frederick Amelung established a business at the end of the eighteenth century that produced glassware of good quality. His pieces were characterized by engraved neoclassical designs, decorative handles, and beautifully shaped bird finials. Clear glass was used as well as green, amber, blue, and amethyst. Objects were free-blown and pattern-molded. Presentation pieces were created in the form of an engraved round-bowled goblet with a lid. Drinking vessels consisted of wine and dessert glasses, mugs, and tumblers in various sizes. Tumblers and goblets had lids. Stoppers were made for bottles and decanters. Flasks and decanters were produced along with the standard bottles and windowpanes.

In spite of the remarkable achievements in American glass production, wealthy Americans continued to import glass from Europe. European glasswares of this period received ornate decoration by such methods as églomisé, stippled diamond-point engraving, and engraved foil medallions placed between two layers of glass.

It was during this period that Ireland began its production of cut glass. A great number of English craftsmen emigrated to Ireland after the second glass tax in 1777. Because the Irish levied no tax on glass, pieces could be as heavy as the designer wished. It was this heavy glass that lent itself to the cutting technique. English stylistic trends were continued in Ireland. Elongated classical shapes were cut in varied diamond and sunburst patterns. Many forms were made in the cut-glass method: decanters, glasses, jugs, salt cellars, dishes, bowls, punch glasses, and cruets. Wine vessels had faceted short stems decorated with thin bands of diamonds. Tumblers were cylindrical. A new type of glass was a rummer. It had a tall, wide bowl that tapered to a very short stem. The decanter had gently sloping shoulders and a long neck encircled by neck rings and topped with a mushroom-shaped stopper. Candlesticks were tall, classical columns that were urn-shaped with square bases. The globe on the shaft was replaced by an urn.

Cut-glass objects were created in America by Benjamin Bakewell. He established a glass factory in Pittsburgh, Pennsylvania, in 1808 that produced the standard glasshouse products but also cut-glass pieces of high quality. Decanters, drinking glasses, large punch bowls, and centerpieces to hold fruit were some of his exceptional forms.

Federal Metalwares

In Federal homes there was greater use of silver, glass, and ceramics for household equipment than of the

Landscape motif hand-painted with trees, a building, and two figures on a red tray shows incredibly fine detail of japanned tin (or tole) ware circa 1820. Made by Marietta Payne Slayton.

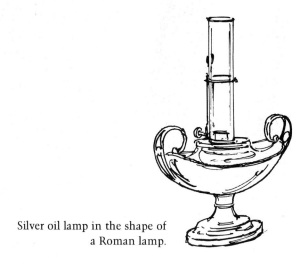

Silver oil lamp in the shape of a Roman lamp.

more mundane metals like iron, copper, brass, and undecorated tin—except in the kitchen, of course. Japanned tinware began to be produced in America at the end of the eighteenth century. Landscapes, flowers, and designs based on architecture served as motifs on trays, boxes, tea caddies, and candlesticks.

Fireplaces continued to be equipped with brass pieces. Andirons still had classical columns for shafts. Finials were urn-shaped. Short steeple andirons were popular, their finials taking the shape of an urn, a lemon, a ball, or an acorn. Bowed or serpentine fenders were much more carefully decorated with fine, intricate openwork and engraving. Engraving was occasionally worked on andirons. Artisans concentrated on detail.

Clocks became more reasonably priced and, thus, more prolific. The arched face was still an engraved brass surface, but the works were now made of wood.

Lighting fixtures emphasized glass, although brass chandeliers were made at this time. The globular shaft was replaced by one that was urn-shaped. Hall lanterns were glass urn shapes set in a brass ring and suspended from a brass chain. Brass wall sconces supported a tall, tapering glass globe. Candlesticks and candelabra were controlled and careful as they followed uncomplicated classical lines. A new form of brass candle holder, the bouillotte, appeared during the Federal period. A shaft, which rested on a flat base shaped like a saucer, supported two or three candle arms extending from its middle. A painted metal shade, of green for example, was suspended near the top of the shaft.

Lamps were plentiful at this time. Metal, glass, and ceramics were combined to create containers for whale oil, or some other fuel, and a saturated wick. A brass oil lamp might have had a band of Wedgwood's jasperware around the base. An urn-shaped glass container for fuel rested on the brass shaft. A single arm extended to form a short column that supported the wick sheltered inside a tall glass globe. Oil passed through the shaft and the arm to moisten the wick. The most successful wick design was invented about 1782 in Geneva, Switzerland, by Amié Argand, a Swiss physicist. His cylindrical wick burned more brightly because of a draft of air blowing up from a central location. Lamps employing this wick arrangement were made in many styles with many metals, such as Sheffield plate, brass, and cast iron. Glass shades were plain or decorated with etching or cut surfaces. Argand and oil lamps were often made in pairs for use on the mantel.

Federal Room Arrangement

An increase in the size of the houses of the Federal period allowed for even more specialization in the use of rooms. The parlor was used solely for entertaining. A Federal sofa was placed at right angles to the fireplace.

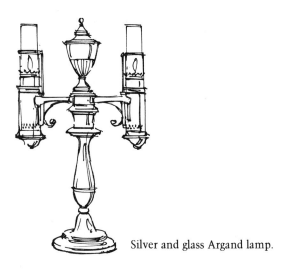

Silver and glass Argand lamp.

A pole screen with an oval silk-embroidered shield separated the sofa from the fireplace wall. At the other end of the sofa was a small, square tilt-top stand with a tripod base and snake feet. A silver candlestick was placed on the top surface of the stand. A pair of back stools faced the sofa. A round table with graceful convex feet forming a tripod base stood between them. A Chinese porcelain bowl filled with flowers was placed on this table. A statue of George Washington embellished the gilded bronze French clock at the center of the mantel. At either end stood brass and glass Argand lamps. A delicate painting of a naval ship in battle hung above the mantel. In the corners of the fireplace wall were rounded corner candlestands with marble tops. On each stand was placed an ornate glass-and-brass candlestick. Toward the center of the room stood a Martha Washington chair with a closed Pembroke table set in front. On the Pembroke table was a matched silver tea and coffee service consisting of a coffeepot, a teapot, a sugar bowl, a creamer, and a slop bowl. Bow-shaped sugar tongs and matched teaspoons were set on the surface along with a pair of porcelain teacups and saucers. Against one wall was a secretary with a slant-front desk. Ceramic and silver pieces were displayed behind the glass panes of the upper doors. A painted oval-back side chair was located in front of the open desk area. A silver inkstand and a brass candlestick with hanging glass prisms accompanied the various papers on the desk surface. Against another wall was a spinet piano. Either end of the top surface of the piano supported a silver candelabrum. Sheet music rested on the opened stand above the keyboard. A side chair with a square open back and an urn-shaped splat provided seating for the musician. In front of the two windows on another wall were a pair of shield-back side chairs. Set between the windows was a rounded card table with a concave front. On the folded surface were a pair of cut-glass decanters and a Chinese porcelain bowl. Silk-embroidered pictures, in particular, mourning pictures, were hung on the walls. A glass chandelier was suspended from the center of the ceiling. A French Aubusson carpet covered the floor.

The dining room became a large separate room. The dining table had been extended to a large oval shape by the addition of wooden sections. An oval silver tray was placed at the center of the table with a central four-armed silver candelabrum. Two urn-shaped lidded cut-glass containers stood at either end of the tray. The table had no cloth. A wineglass, a silver tumbler, and a nonmatching set of a fork, knife, and spoon were at each place. At the center of the Chinese export plate was an eagle. Four blown-glass decanters were set near each corner of the table. Eight shield-back chairs were spaced around the table so that side chairs alternated with armchairs. A sideboard was located against the wall. At each end stood a side chair that matched the chairs drawn up to the table. A wooden urn-shaped knife case was positioned at each end of the sideboard. A pair of tall silver candlesticks flanked each knife case. Silver serving pieces were displayed on the sideboard surfaces. If the room were large enough, a pair of matching sideboards could be present. The second sideboard would allow even more silver and ceramic serving pieces to be shown. Against another wall was a breakfront Salem secretary. Ceramics and pieces of silver were seen behind the glass panes of the closed doors. Pale colors on the floor were provided by a French Savonnerie carpet.

The master bedroom showed the tester bed with either its head or side against the wall. On one side of the bed was a corner basin stand which supported a silver candlestick. On the other side of the bed against the wall was an oval table with a tambour door. This table had a silver Argand lamp and a book resting on its surface. A bow-front chest of drawers stood against a wall. A pair of silver candlesticks and an oval mirror on a stand were placed on top. A chatelaine was set there for the night. In front of each of a pair of windows on one wall was a bench with tall arms and no back. At right angles to the fireplace was a Federal sofa. In front of the sofa stood a drum table with an oil lamp and an unfinished embroidery piece on its surface. At the other side of the fireplace opening was a wing-back easy chair. Against the chair away from the fireplace was a ladies' worktable. On the tabletop were an oil lamp, a pincushion, and a pair of scissors. Against the wall in back of the easy chair stood a lady's tambour desk. A ceramic inkwell with a quill pen and a matching ceramic candlestick rested inside the tambour opening along with a closed diary. A shield-back side chair was positioned in front. A Persian carpet covered a large portion of the floor.

The Empire Period 1810-1840

Empire Interior Architecture

House interiors designed in the Empire style were based on those of the Federal period with Empire characteristics added. Greek Revival architecture appeared during the second quarter of the nineteenth century. The facade of Empire houses was based on stately Greek temples. The floor plan was similar to that of Federal houses but larger in scale. Exterior and interior woodwork carefully followed the classical orders. As in the change of the style of furniture from Federal to Empire, interiors became more heavily ornate. The framework of doorways and windows was composed of entablatures supported by pilasters. The entablature was a rectangular section supported by columns in Greek and Roman architecture. The section was composed of a narrow band called an architrave upon which rested a wider frieze. A molded band called a cornice topped the entablature. In Empire interior architecture, the frieze might have been plain or carved. Friezes were often gilded. Marble mantelpieces had a pair of tall classical figures for supports. Walls might have been painted mauve or pale blue with white woodwork that resembled chalk. This wall treatment echoed Wedgwood's jasperware.

Empire Furniture

The Empire and Federal styles coexisted in America for many years. The pure line of Federal fashion was based on Roman grace as seen at Pompeii; the Empire style was derived from England and France where classical furniture forms and stonework elements were copied, often literally. Classical features were forced into the design of house interiors and furniture. There was little consideration for comfort or scale as massive architectural features became the basis of design. Furniture was luxurious in the use of lush woods and metal ornamentation. Decorative motifs were swags, wreaths, torches, mythological figures, and later, Egyptian sphinxes and animal forms.

Thomas Sheraton began his furniture designs under the influence of England's neoclassicist, Robert Adam. Sheraton's later style adopted the French features seen in Directoire furniture. Legs and vase pedestals became heavier. Chairs curved back in the Greek fashion to foreshadow the Greek klismos chair. Sheraton used twisted turnings and arms with a spiral design.

Duncan Phyfe reproduced the later style of Sheraton and then developed an Empire style that was uniquely his own. He introduced the klismos chair, a popular

Duncan Phyfe klismos side chair with lyre splat and sabre legs that are ornamented by carved waterleafs and a dog's paw foot.

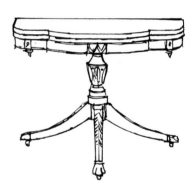

Duncan Phyfe folding card table on vase pedestal with carved waterleafs and brass caster feet.

chair form of the period, characterized by a continuous flowing line down the back, over the seat-rail, and down the incurved saber leg. The crest rail rolled backward. Phyfe also introduced Roman curule chairs. These had the klismos back and a curved X-shaped base, as seen on page 89. Tables produced by Phyfe used vase pedestals with tripod saber leg supports. Waterleafs appeared occasionally on the top surface of the legs. Legs ended in a brass animal paw or a squared foot. Card table tops were cloverleaf in shape, that is, the sides curved to form rounded corners and the front bowed out from the corners. Chair splats were carved cornucopias or lyres. Lyres also served as bases for tables, as seen in the Andalusia Bensalem, Pennsylvania, Thorne room. Later in his career, Phyfe became bogged down by heavy Empire features.

A French cabinetmaker by the name of Charles Honoré Lannuier brought the French Empire tradition to

Duncan Phyfe furniture pieces with a lyre splat or base are seen with curule chairs in a drawing room in Andalusia, Bensalem Township, Pennsylvania, 1834–1836. *Courtesy: Thorne American Rooms in Miniature, The Art Institute of Chicago*

this country. In his short career he introduced Americans to the decoration of marble columns, brass inlay, and ormolu, which consisted of gilded brass or copper mounts.

After 1810, the Empire style was adopted throughout America. Parts of furniture became scrolled, supports were winged or caryatid in form. Lion's or dog's paws served as feet, and lyres were used as splats or supports. The next decade (1820–1830) used these motifs in a grander scale. Brackets became carved leaves or wings. Turned feet seemed bulbous. Pedestals were massive. Stenciling techniques were employed to imitate the use of ormolu for furniture decoration. The last decade of the Empire period (1830–1840) displayed forms with heavy flat surfaces, plain large scrolls, and protruding columns. Plain or veneered surfaces of mahogany and rosewood replaced the earlier ormolu decoration and luxurious carving. Geometric and simple scroll supports were used in a variety of combinations on chairs, tables, sofas, and case pieces. "Scroll furniture" emulated the French Restoration style. Examples of scrolled pieces are seen in the Thorne rooms depicting a South Carolina ballroom and a Tennessee entrance hall.

The Egyptian form of the klismos chair used the rolled back, but a Greek form was also seen at this time. It had a top rail projecting beyond the upright

back supports. The Egyptian klismos chair was also made with arms that curved in the same manner as the back and seat-rail. The arms rested on incurved supports that mirrored the curve of the saber leg.

A window bench created by Phyfe was made up of the backs of two lyre-back klismos chairs facing each other. The cushion rested on an elongated U-shaped framework. The saber legs ended in dog's-paw feet.

Sofas now had upcurved ends. The Grecian squab described by Sheraton showed one end lower than the other. The back stopped short of the lower end by either rounding off at the seat-rail or by forming a scroll. Saber legs, scrolled feet, or curved cross-shaped supports were used on these classical sofa forms. The surfaces were upholstered, carved, or covered with rush and the back and arms were left open. The curving lines of the sofa hinted at the resurgence of the rococo style to occur during the Victorian period. Late in the Empire period, the front surface of the curved sofa arm became a cornucopia filled with fruit. These forms had ornate stenciled decoration. The feet became carved animal paws.

The Empire bed was a sleigh bed with outward curved ends. The feet might have been carved to resemble dolphins. Veneer and ormolu were used for decoration, though the beds were often seen plain.

Scrolled furniture is in evidence in a Charleston, South Carolina, ballroom. *Courtesy: Thorne American Rooms in Miniature, The Art Institute of Chicago*

A Grecian-style klismos chair common during the Empire period.

Side or pier tables of the Empire period had white or black marble tops. The tables were rectangular with an incurved lower shelf. A mirror formed the back wall between the top surface and the lower shelf. The rear legs were round or square columns. The front legs were seen in many forms. They might have been rounded columns painted white or made of marble; classically draped, carved female figures that were gilded; or gilded winged supports, carved to resemble half-swan or half-human figures with fish tails. The feet were in the shape of lion's paws or curved dolphins. Decoration was in the form of gilding and gold-colored wire inlay. It was this table style that was introduced by Lannuier.

The Empire card table followed the vase pedestal style of Phyfe (see page 92) or the style of the pier table. The folding top was supported by two turned supports placed in back of a single gilded winged support. These rested on a rectangular platform with incurved sides. The platform was placed on lion's-paw feet. Later tables had simpler supports and carved, scrolled aprons that predicted Victorian forms.

The rectangular sofa table had at each end a short drop leaf with canted corners. Four vase-shaped legs

An entrance hall from The Hermitage, near Nashville, Tennessee, 1835–1845, in which scrolled furniture pieces are seen. *Courtesy: Thorne American Rooms in Miniature, The Art Institute of Chicago*

Empire sofa circa 1820 with a seat constructed of fine thread to simulate the typical rush treatment. Hand-stenciled designs ornament the piece made by Elisabett. Available from the Washington Doll's House and Toy Museum.

A sleigh bed of the Empire period.

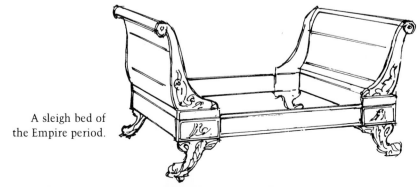

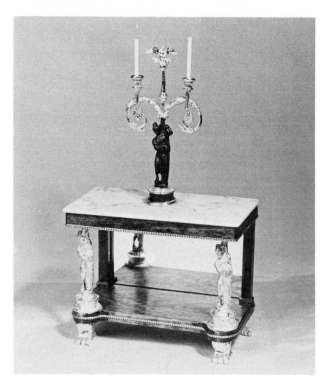

This splendid pier table by Virginia Merrill incorporates all of the Empire characteristics, including a mirrored back panel, marble top, gilt figures, lion's paw feet, and rich mahogany wood.

A Charles Honoré Lannuier card table with winged support.

Denis Hillman's extension dining table shows the heavier supports of the Empire period.

were supported by twist-turned stretchers, the framework of which rested on lion's-paw feet. The feet faced out to the side. A winged support was placed on each side stretcher.

A marble-topped round table usually rested on a massive central pillar. The central column was supported by three or four incurved legs ending in brass paw feet. This large round table was used for card playing. A wooden-topped round tea table may have had three column supports on an incurved triangular platform with lion's-paw feet. The paw feet had brackets in the form of carved leaves.

Dining tables now had brass clips to join sections together. A turned column on a tripod base served as a support. Later, sections of the table rested on four slender turned columns. The columns stood on an incurved square platform. Four saber legs, located at the corners, were carved with waterleafs. The legs ended in paw feet with casters. Still later, sectional dining tables used heavy vase pillars on small, square platforms with the same incurved legs, paw feet, and casters. An acanthus carved vase replaced the cluster of slim columns on the earlier Empire tables.

The Empire chest of drawers had projecting columns at the side under the first tier of drawers. The columns and the three bow-front drawers they framed rested on a platform. Lion's-paw feet protruded from beneath a vertical carved acanthus leaf.

Desk designs were heavy compared to the more delicate Federal pieces. The cylinder closing was popular on desks of this period. This round wooden device replaced the slant-front and tambour doors. A pierced gallery edged the back and sides of the top desk surface. Drawers, located underneath the desk area, reached almost to the floor where short, fluted vase shapes provided support.

Sideboards showed the cupboards getting deeper and closer to the floor. These Empire pieces made use of large plain surfaces. The three sections were divided by thin, classical columns supported by lion's-paw feet. The back of the top surface was edged with a stepped board that echoed the three-part division of the front surface. Carved pineapple finials divided the board into three parts. A gallery of short, turned spindles lined the sides of the top surface. Tambour doors enclosed the middle cupboard.

Brass drawer pulls on Empire furniture took the form of a lion's head. A swinging circular ring hanging in his mouth served as the handle for pulling open the drawer.

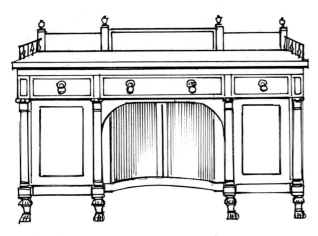

Slim columns and paw feet grace this Empire sideboard.

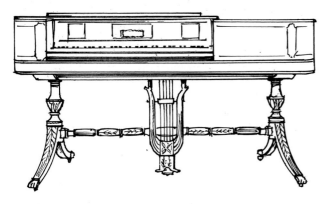

An Empire piano case with rounded corners, carved waterleafs, and a lyre support.

The piano case utilized the Empire supports consisting of vase pedestals with two saber legs that curved to the front and back. The single stretcher was reeded, turned, and carved. A lyre shape joined the pedals to the case. The veneered case had rounded corners.

Clocks in the styles described for the Federal period became more available and, therefore, more plentiful because of the use of less expensive wooden works.

Looking glasses of the Empire period were more heavily decorated and larger in size. The pier glass frame was wider and, in some instances, consisted of carved columns. The sculptured eagle had become grander in scale. The girandole mirror was an Empire form (see page 77). The round convex mirror was often equipped with gilt candle arms. The circular frame was ornately carved, typically with a circle of round balls. An eagle, dolphin, and greenery were the characteristic forms for carved decoration.

Shaker Furniture

The Shakers were members of a religious group striving to create a perfect society. They felt that by disciplining the body and setting aside material pleasures, they would attain absolute happiness in this life. The first Shaker settlement in America was formed in 1774 in the state of New York. The sect prospered until the 1850s, having spread as far west as Ohio and Kentucky. While Shaker architecture and furniture in no way reflected nineteenth-century classical styles, it did exist at the same time. Furniture and goods were sold to neighboring towns.

The interior architecture and furniture of Shaker communities reflected the simplicity and the discipline of Shaker life. Neatness and organization were encouraged by the network of built-in drawers and closets. Nests of oval boxes were made from thin strips of maple that were wrapped around a form after they had been steamed. The long points of wood at the seam were secured with copper rivets. A wooden strip with carved pegs lined the top portion of the stark plaster wall. Simple ladder-back chairs, as well as clothing, were hung from these pegs when not in use. The flat woodwork might have been mustard yellow. Bare floors, if colored at all, had to be reddish yellow. Shaker furniture always followed tradition; there was little change in style or form. The simple and controlled

A Shaker ladder-back chair by Ron Terrill. *Courtesy: Ron Terrill*

A Shaker table by Ron Terrill.
Courtesy: Ron Terrill

lines created a slender appearance as seen in the Shaker table. The straightforward design advocated sound construction and good proportions. This rural furniture was made from local woods such as pine, maple, walnut, and fruitwood.

Empire Upholstery

The upholstery covering Empire furniture was brighter in color than that used on Federal pieces. Bold hues of empire (kelly) green, bright blue, canary yellow, and cherry red added to the massive look of the furniture. Fabrics such as heavy, figured silks and satins, horsehair, leather, and velvets were used. Patterns depicted the Napoleon "N" motif, stripes, or eagles framed with a laurel wreath. Gold medallions were seen on bright colored grounds. Seats were set into the frame or boxed with cording and set on top of the frame. Brass tacks were used on occasion. Decorative tape trimmed a solid colored fabric on some seats. The tape followed at a distance the inside edge of the front and sides of the seat frame.

Empire Drapery Treatment

Windows in the Empire-styled houses were draped in the same manner as the Federal windows. Mull curtains, embroidered with metallic thread, were used, as were fabrics that matched the furniture upholstery. As time progressed, the French side panels became longer than floor-length and fell along the floor when they were tied back at the sides.

The sleigh bed often had a drapery wall treatment above it. The bed stood with its side, rather than its head, against the wall. A semicurved mahogany crown hung high above the bed, from which was suspended a pleated valance. Behind the valance were suspended two long panels of fabric. The panels were pulled to the side and tied at one or two places with tasseled cords as they moved down the wall toward the ends of the bed. When they spread to the width of the bed, the panels fell straight to the floor. A fringed cotton fabric printed in an allover pattern of portrait medallions was appropriate for this bed drapery treatment. Matching fabric covered cylindrical end pillows and the mattress, which was set into the sleigh frame. Window draperies probably matched also.

Empire Floor Coverings

Floor coverings in Empire and Federal houses were the same. However, during the Empire period in France, the delicate Aubusson designs became heavier. French Empire Aubusson carpets purchased by Americans were colored with bolder backgrounds of brown, olive green, and Napoleon "Empire" green. Patterns were created with laurel wreaths (see page 250), bumblebees, torches, shields, helmets, lions, sphinx heads, urns, and cornucopias.

Empire Needlework

Many handwork techniques were now executed by machines. Women were no longer required to perform knitting, the chain stitching of tambour work, the heavy embroidery of candlewicking, or the stuffing and cording of Marseilles work.

Silk-embroidery techniques of the Federal period continued in use until the 1830s, when tent-stitch Berlin work came into vogue. In the early 1800s in Berlin, A. Philipson first printed needlework patterns on paper. A fine network of lines formed squares, each of which represented a stitch in the pattern. These designs were hand-colored. The close guidance of the printed pattern left no creativity to the stitcher. Patterns depicted garlands, bouquets, vases, and landscapes. At first, designs were worked with wool or silk on a fine canvas. No background was stitched at this time, but a piece of colored silk might have been placed behind for a colored effect. Tent-stitch motifs were cut and appliquéd onto a dark-colored broadcloth. Or canvas was basted to broadcloth or horsehair, stitched, and then unraveled, leaving the stitched motif. Nellie Custis Lewis used this last technique when she created a dog and butterfly cover for her grandson's footstool (see page 191). Her work was done on a brown background.

Some of the most colorful and imaginative quilts were made from 1820 to 1870. Again, the three different quilting techniques of one-piece, pieced, and appliqué were usually combined. English roller-printed chintzes provided naturalistic appliqué motifs. In pieced quilts, embroidered squares were alternated with contrasting plain squares. Silk was used often in quilt construction at this time.

Empire Silver

Empire elements began to appear at the beginning of the nineteenth century. The delicate shapes and ornamentation of the Federal period gave way to the heavier forms of imposing Egyptian, Greek, and Roman styles. Silver pieces were enlarged and broadened. Ovals were lower, wider, and shaped with the vertical lobes of melon reeding. Decorative bands around rims, shoulders, and bases emphasized the horizontal axis. For the most part, the forms themselves were simple and geometric. Shapes were round or polygonal. The Greek amphora was the basis for vases and pitchers. Large oval bodies tapered into narrow cylindrical necks. Handles rose at least to the level of the mouth. Greek and Roman lamps, vases, and urns were models for other pieces. Egyptian motifs were seen in sphinx supports,

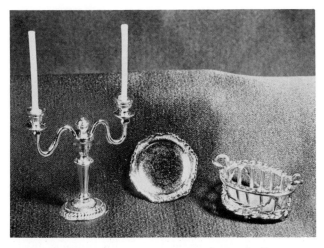

Assorted silver pieces as seen in Empire homes by Eugene Kupjack: a candelabrum, a plate, and a cake basket.

snakes coiled around bases, rims, and handles, and stylized plants and flowers used in borders. There was an extraordinary amount of mixing of the different forms and motifs. Patriotic symbols were also in evidence in the decorative mélange.

The real achievement of silver craftsmanship during the Empire period was in the beautiful sculpture of the cast ornamentation. Finials were created in the form of pineapples, floral bouquets, and animals. Handles and spouts ended in dolphin or animal heads. Supports took the form of caryatids, as they did in furniture design. Leaves were abundant in the allover ornamentation of silver pieces. Several strips of machine-made borders were combined on each piece.

Forms became gradually more and more ornate as the nineteenth century progressed. Goblets continued to be made in sets. Classical decorative motifs were applied to the oviform bowl and the trumpet base of the Federal period. The straight-sided beaker incorporated a molded rim and a band at the base before changing to the bulging curve of the Empire form. Melon reeding added to the heaviness of its appearance.

Flatware adopted a new handle style during the Empire period. Knives and forks continued to be made. Spoon handles became fiddle-shaped, that is, the broad bottom half of the handle tapered inward as it approached the bowl. Just before the juncture with the bowl, small pointed projections, or shoulders, jutted out. This same handle was used on the four-tined fork of the period. The bowl of the spoon was wider and more pointed at the end. No drops were seen on the underside of the bowl where it met the handle; there was a V-shaped outline only. Initials were engraved lengthwise down the handle. Four-tined forks and specialized spoons followed the spoon handle style. Nineteenth-century ladles had circular bowls with widely curved handles. Fish servers resembled pie servers. They were made of thin silver and were ornately pierced and engraved. Skewers were flat and severely tapered from an end one inch in width to a point at the other end. A round opening at the wide end served as a handle.

Serving pieces, such as salt cellars, cake baskets, and vegetable dishes, incorporated ornamental banding and cast decoration. Ornate classical motifs, such as a freestanding handle in the form of an irate asp, frequently decorated sauceboats. The spout ended in an animal head. Four cast feet were in the form of sphinxes or eagles. Occasionally, the boat was set on a matching tray to catch any dripping that might have occurred. The cruet stand had a molded, curved leaf edge on the tray, which was supported by four scrolled feet. The tall central handle ended in an ornately sculptured ring handle. Silver caster domes or glass stoppers topped glass bottles. Cayenne pepper, sugar, and salt were contained in the casters, while oil and vinegar were housed in the glass-stopped cruet bottles. As many as seven glass containers stood on the tray. The mustard pot now showed the glass liner supported only by a silver ring. Three cast legs supported the ring to which a hinged lid was attached. Pitchers adopted a bulb shape, which was molded into the lobes of melon reeding. This form was lidded with an open spout. Gadrooning and machine-stamped borders were wrapped horizontally around the piece. Heavy cast ornamentation adorned the high handle. An open pitcher form with no lid followed the lines of the ancient ewer. Leaves decorated the body, and the handle was in the form of a snake.

Sets of silver plates were produced during the Empire period. The plates were plain. Cast borders, such as gadrooning, edged the rim (see page 95). A small design was engraved at the center of the plate surface. These plates were coordinated with matching oval platters in graduated sizes.

A silver pitcher shaped like a ewer.

The tea service composed of matched pieces was still in style. There were now two teapots, which became melon-shaped with severely scrolled spouts. Each pot rested on four ball feet. The lid was topped by a rectangular or animal finial. The teapot later took on the antique ewer shape with its spout, feet, and finials all formed into animals. Ornamentation on this piece consisted of acorns, oak leaves, and heavy borders. The pot was supported by a round domed foot or by a plinth with four eagle or sphinx feet. The silver handles had ivory rings at the top and bottom for insulation. The coffeepot followed the shape of the teapot although it was taller. The creamer and sugar bowl also followed the basic design of the teapot. The creamer had an elongated curved lip, and the sugar bowl had two handles and a lid. The urn continued in use, but it was larger and more heavily decorated. The slop basin was circular with no handles or lid. Twice as large as the sugar bowl, it had a wide protruding rim to protect against splashing. There was no silver tea caddy be-

cause tea was in such abundance that it was unnecessary to house it in a special container. Tea tongs continued to be made in the bow shape. Ornamentation on the arms was probably heavier.

Trays of the Empire period had rims decorated with rich borders of stamped ornamentation and gadrooning. Some were supported by cast feet in the form of scrolls, eagles, or paws. Large cast handles were applied to the ends of heavier trays to assist in carrying them from place to place. Large, flat, oval trays with handles were still used with tea sets.

A chamber stick with a douter by Eugene Kupjack.

Candlesticks retained the use of the classical column with the urn-shaped socket. Empire ornamentation was applied to this Federal form. A short chamber stick was produced at this time. The height allowed for easy carrying from room to room. It was probably this candlestick form that was taken to the bedchamber at night. The shortened form took on the urn shape for its dwarfed shaft. The shaft rested on a tray, on which a douter, a cone used to snuff the flame, and, perhaps, a snuffer were supported on short columns. Branched candlesticks and candelabra appeared at this time (see page 95).

The Empire inkstand incorporated a candlestick in its design. The candlestick became the lid for the inkwell. Three legs were formed by foliated curves ending in an animal head.

Empire Britannia

Britannia metal proved to be more practical than the earlier pewter because of its durability and its ability to be made into a great variety of forms. The new metal was easily applied to Empire lines. Melon reeding and wide fluting decorated the popular pear and inverted pear shapes. Great height was given to objects by the use of pedestals. Some teapots became unusually tall and were formed into tapering cylinders. An octagonal teapot was also produced. New techniques provided crisp, sharp edges. Handles were scrolled and double-scrolled. Midbands on mugs became obvious ridges.

Lamps took on new emphasis as light sources during this period. Whale oil or other fluids served as fuel.

Some of the containers were made with britannia. Shapes for the lamp portion were bell, inverted bell, cylindrical, and others. These fuel containers might have been mounted on a shaft, similar in appearance to a candlestick. The shaft was supported by a domed base. The lamp portion was also made in a shortened form and was placed on a saucer or stood independently in a bell shape with a handle. Britannia candlesticks had a baluster-shaped stem that stood on a domed foot. The mid-sized shaft was topped by a tall, tulip-shaped, clear glass shade.

Empire Ceramics

During the Empire period, American potters broke away from the tradition of making only kitchen and dairy wares that were purely practical in design and use. During the second quarter of the nineteenth century, many of the English earthenwares, such as transfer-printed tablewares and spatterware, began to be produced in America. Stoneware was made in white, straw yellow, and brown, otherwise known as Rockingham. The brown-glazed Rockingham ware had been created in England at an earlier time. Stoneware was now made with molds rather than by the throwing technique. The mold technique was also adopted in England a few years earlier. Designs could now be molded in high relief onto the surface of pitchers, flowerpots, tea sets, jars, and mugs, as well as Toby jugs, spittoons, water coolers, and tablewares. Popular patterns were naturalistic plants and flowers, especially grapes on vines, hunting scenes, and romantic landscapes. Two forms unique to this period were apostle and hound-handled pitchers. Apostles stood side by side, each in a pointed arch. Hound-handled pitchers showed the hounds hunting in a landscape on the molded pitcher surface. The handle was shaped in the form of an outstretched hound.

At this time in Philadelphia, William Ellis Tucker produced the first successful American porcelain, fashioned after French porcelain. White classical forms were decorated with enamel-painted flowers or portraits, gilding, or local landscapes created with a rich red brown sepia. Tea wares, pitchers, and elegant vases with cast gilt bronze ormolu handles were shaped in the Empire style.

English ceramics also adopted the heavy classical shapes of the Empire period. Transfer-printed stonewares now showed motifs framed by a wide, elaborate floral border. Jug shapes were no longer barrel in form, but globular with wide, straight collars. Patterns were printed on the cream background in either blue or black.

Gaudy Dutch pottery was produced in England from 1810 to 1830. The wares were so named because of the bright, almost garish, flowers and foliage that were painted onto cream-colored plates and tea wares. The colorful designs resembled those of the Pennsylvania Germans in their combination of naturalism and stylization. These ceramics were expensive because they were hand-painted.

Spatterware was as colorful as Gaudy Dutch ware, but less expensive. The earthenware background was covered with monochromatic spattered decoration in a wide range of colors. A central motif might have been a peafowl, a tulip, or a schoolhouse. Forms were created in a wide variety of patterns from 1820 to 1850. A matching jug and washbowl composed a toilet set. Sets and individual pieces were produced in the form of platters, plates, water jugs, and tea and dinner dishes.

Lusterware continued to be a popular item from the 1820s to the 1840s. Tea and dinnerwares were seen. Globular pitchers had straight necks and copper or gold luster ornamentation. A silver resist design on a white background seemed to cover a teapot with dots. In the 1820s, other ground colors, such as apricot, pink, beige, yellow, and blue, appeared.

Castleford was a white jasper stoneware shaped into neoclassical forms with molded ornamentation. A highlight of brilliant blue was used to outline sections of the piece. The teapot was the most popular form.

Ironstone was heavy and white. Thus, it was particularly suitable for neoclassical Empire forms. Most forms were left undecorated, but a transfer-printed lacy design or sprigged ornament might have been seen. Many pieces were made from ironstone, such as sets of dinnerware and a matching jug and pitcher for the washstand.

Some European porcelains were seen in America at this time. Tea and dessert sets followed the styles initiated by Meissen and Sèvres. Urn-shaped vases were painted with a portrait of an eminent American against a dark ground. The background framing the medallion still appeared in Sèvres colors. They were decorated with more gilding and some ormolu handles.

Empire Glassware

During the Empire period, the American glass industry was finally coming into its own. While other technological traditions for creating glassware persisted, new methods opened glass factories to more creative possibilities and to a wider market in America. A uniquely American technique for making glass objects was the three-blown mold method. In this process, a gathering of glass was blown into a full-sized three-sectioned patterned mold. The end result resembled cut glass, although the facets were not as sharp. Thus, inexpensive wares could be offered with the cut-glass look. Three-blown mold glass forms consisted of a vari-

A glass flask with a molded design on the front surface.

ety of decanters, bottles, dishes, pitchers, and tumblers with straight or barrel-shaped sides. Flasks were made in full-sized molds and were used to contain liquids of all sorts, especially alcoholic. They were made in many attractive colors and patterned with symbols of important historic events.

A pressed-glass method was provided by a machine invented by Deming Jarves, who was associated with the Boston and Sandwich Glass Company. A plunger pressed lead glass, either clear or colored, into the mold. Early pieces were usually of clear glass and followed cut-glass designs, such as diamonds, scallops, or fans. From 1828 to 1840, lacy glass was produced. Forms took on oversized round or rectangular Empire shapes. They were covered with allover designs of leaves and flowers, cornucopias, arches, scrolls, and patriotic symbols. The background was stippled to create a glittering effect that was lost in the pressing process. The forms created in lacy glass patterns were numerous, such as cup or tea plates, salts, sauce dishes, and sugar bowls. Cup plates held teacups while tea was allowed to cool in the saucer. Patriotic subjects served as central motifs. Salt dishes were generally rectangular in shape with some basket, boat, or circular forms. Lamps were constructed with a lacy domed foot and a free-blown rounded stem and font, where oil was contained. Candlesticks now could be made in many shapes, the most popular of which was the dolphin. With these technological advances in the glass industry, mold designers and creators replaced glassblowers.

The traditional Southern Jersey style of glass production continued during this period, however. Free-blown and pattern-blown methods were still used. Empire

A glass candlestick whose shaft was molded in the form of a dolphin.

shapes were placed on baluster feet. Applied glass was still used to decorate glass objects with threads, swirls, and glass pieces moving over the surface. A new decorative technique was the looping of contrasting glass threads through the gather while the piece was being blown. The loops were wide or thin. Typical colors were a clear gather with turquoise threads or an aquamarine gather with white threads. Another interesting contrast was the use of a second color for the rim of an object. Bowls, pitchers, and vases were the standard forms, and some candlesticks, salts, decanters, compotes, and sugar bowls were made. Witch balls were hung in cottages in England to keep evil spirits at bay. These round balls were made of glass and served as lids for vases and pitchers (see page 274).

In Europe, glassblowers continued to create innovative decorative techniques. Cameos were made of a white paste and enclosed in glass. These medallions reflected the neoclassical look so popular at this time, as did Wedgwood's jasperware. Leadless glass tablewares were created in the city of Nailsea because of the expense of leaded glass in England. Dark green glass was spattered with chips of colored enamel. Light green glass was wrapped in white threads around the rim. Bottles, flasks, and jugs were covered with bold loops or stripes. Pale green glass had stripes of pink, white, and other colors.

Irish cut glass was now being produced in serving dishes to accompany dinnerware. Characteristics of the Irish cut glass of this period were bands of vertical flutes, which could be seen fanning around the lower portions of goblet bowls, and borders consisting of a continuous flow of arches, which were scalloped in outline.

Because of the achievement of high quality and the deterrent of protective tariffs, the demand increased for American free-blown and molded-glass objects, with cut or engraved ornamentation. Engraved designs included carefully executed leaves and flowers, ships, buildings, and national symbols. Cut patterns were diamonds and fans with diamond bands. Later, carving became flatter, and bold panels became dominant on the piece. Serving dishes were round or boat-shaped. Pitchers and decanters were squat and pear-shaped. Sugar bowls were sizable and round. Occasionally, a molding of vertical shaped pillars created wide bases around massive decanters, vases, cruets, and candlesticks.

Empire Metalwares

Traditional metalware craftsmanship was replaced by mechanical mass production during the Empire period. This new creative process led to the development of new forms for established objects. Copper tea kettles became sleeker with straight spouts. Andirons were made almost totally in America by the end of the eighteenth century because, earlier than Americans, the English had been forced to use coal. Coal had to be used for fires because wood supplies had dwindled around urban centers. Empire andirons continued to be short but they were heavier in form. The graceful shaft and legs of earlier forms were replaced by a heavy column and a large ball finial. A smaller ball-topped shaft was joined on the inside by a flat, curved arm. The support for the wood extended from the shorter shaft. When America turned to coal, grates were placed on the andiron supports so that andirons could still adorn the fireplace. Fireplace tools also continued to be used with coal fires.

Cast-iron stoves became popular at this time. They were designed in the rigid geometric shapes seen in Empire architecture. Decoration took the form of arches, columns, friezes, urns, flat curves, and linear decorative bands.

Lighting devices followed the Federal classical forms with heavy Empire outlines and ornamentation. Candlesticks had ponderous shafts with knops and balusters supported by round domed bases. Candelabra were composed of classical or patriotic figures, alone or in groups (see page 92). Neoclassical architectural features and national symbols were abundant. Shafts and sockets were often ornately embellished with suspended glass prisms. Bouillotte candle holders and oil lamps continued to be used during the Empire period.

Empire Room Arrangement

The same allocation of rooms seen during the Federal period was followed in homes decorated in the Empire style. A central round marble-topped table served as a gaming table, as revealed by the cards on the surface. A pair of Egyptian-style klismos chairs were drawn up to it. The table was positioned on the central design of a square Aubusson rug. An ormolu and cut-glass chandelier was suspended above. The fireplace faced the rug. At either end of the mantel stood a glass candlestick with a tall, clear glass shade. Centered on the mantel was a French gilt bronze clock with decorative figures. A girandole mirror hung on the wall above. Flanking the fireplace were a pair of pier tables on which were placed bronze and ormolu figures and matching porcelain urns decorated with portraits. Op-

posite the fireplace against the wall was an Empire sofa. At either end, a small, round marble-topped table supported an oil lamp. Flanking the central Aubusson carpet were two smaller carpets that mirrored its design. On one stood a round, wooden-topped table set for tea with a Tucker coffee and tea set consisting of many matching pieces of porcelain. Two Greek-style klismos chairs were placed at the table. At the opposite end of the room was a cylinder-top desk. A Greek-style klismos chair was positioned at the opening where papers, books, and a silver inkstand were placed. A pair of heavy silver candlesticks with tall, clear glass shades graced the top surface of the desk.

The Empire dining room, too, reflected the Federal furniture arrangement. A centrally located extension dining table was set for six with no cloth. Framed between a pair of silver candlesticks, a fruit-filled silver compote stood in the middle of the table. Matching sets of forks, knives, and spoons were set at each place. A wineglass and a colorful porcelain plate ornamented with an eagle were set within the silverware. Six Greek klismos chairs were spaced around the table. Against the wall were a sideboard and a side table. An oil portrait hung above each. A silver lidded ewer and a cut-glass decanter with matching tumblers were displayed on the heavy sideboard. A matching coffee and tea service stood on the side table. At each rear corner of the side table was placed a glass candelabrum with cut-glass prisms suspended from its two candle sockets. An English Axminster carpet imitating models from the Orient covered the dining room floor.

The Empire bedroom showed a sleigh bed whose side was placed against the wall. At one end of the bed stood a low, square table with a pair of silver candlesticks and a book on its marble surface. Against the wall a heavy Empire worktable supported an oil lamp and a wooden box containing sewing tools. A klismos chair stood next to the worktable. In a corner was located a small, round marble-topped table supporting a bouillotte candlestand with a dark green shade. A semicircular dressing table with a gathered skirt tacked around the top surface was set between two windows under a large, gilded pier glass. Two silver candelabra and a pair of ladies' gloves rested on the top surface. A Greek klismos chair provided seating for the lady using the dressing table. An ingrain, or Scotch, carpet covered the floor.

A double parlor in the house of a Georgia planter, 1850.
Courtesy: Thorne American Rooms in Miniature, The Art Institute of Chicago

The Victorian Period 1830–1870

Victorian Interior Architecture

In the early 1830s, the Greek Revival in architecture was joined by a Gothic style. Selected features of earlier Gothic architecture were incorporated according to the whim of the architect and the patron. Pointed arches separated the front and back parlors. Tre- and quatre-foils were deeply carved into dark paneling. A mantel with a square opening might have been wooden with carved Gothic details or marble with simple motifs. A carved wooden soffit might have lined the top edge of the wall surface. Door panels became slim vertical arches with trefoil or pointed tops. Wallpapers were embossed, perhaps with dark green stylized patterns dominating a cream-colored ground. Set at the ends of the room were bay windows with decorative stained-glass designs. No chandelier was present.

By 1835, the "Tuscan" style of architecture emerged. Tuscan was used to describe the most basic of the Roman architectural orders or types of columns. Roman architectural designs were revised during the Renaissance and were combined with Greek and Gothic features for country houses in Italy. The Renaissance Italian style was emulated by American Victorian architects. In this style, arches were rounded, as seen at

100

the opening of the marble fireplace and in the shape of niches set into the wall. The separation between two parlors was rectangular. The aperture was draped with fabric hung on rods and pulled back to either side. Rooms were no longer rectangular. Because of exterior architectural features such as towers, the end of a room might have extended beyond the normal front line of the house with canted corners. Ornate gold chandeliers hung from the middle of the ceiling and supported candles or gaslight globes.

Rococo architectural features became fashionable at the middle of the nineteenth century. Ceilings were decorated with elaborate plaster ornamentation. Twisted ropes of marble framed the arch of the fireplace opening. Marble mantels were heavily decorated with naturalistic motifs and cupids. Masks might have been placed above floral pendants hanging down either side of the fireplace. The outer edges of the mantel might have been rounded and scrolled. Wall surfaces were paneled, papered, or painted. The panels were carved arches designed with curves and foliage. The wallpaper depicted a large American panorama or an abstract pattern. The dominant color of the patterned paper was dark, the design was large. The floor surface was usually covered with one large rug or several small

A Victorian staircase with a bronze figure supporting a gaslight globe.

ones, or with wall-to-wall carpeting, so little or no wood flooring showed. The printed wallpaper combined with the patterned carpeting created a very ornate interior. Cornice molding was wide and often heavily carved. In mansions of this period, rococo motifs were painted in medallions on the walls and ceilings. Gold leaf was added to the ornate carved decoration. The hall staircase rose from a marble floor to the second story, often with no support from a wall. Dark wood was used for the carved, turned balusters and handrail. On top of octagonal newel posts stood bronze classical figures supporting round gaslight globes. Carpet runners partially covered the rich wood of the steps.

Victorian Furniture

Furniture produced during the Victorian period gave no evidence of a unique style of its own. There was a great deal of experimentation in materials, techniques, and interpretations of the old styles. The Victorian age was characterized by eclecticism. The romantic spirit of the times brought about a tendency to look to the past for stylistic suggestions. The increased dissemina-

tion of information exposed furniture designers to a great variety of sources of inspiration. Several stylistic periods were revived: Gothic, rococo, Elizabethan, and Renaissance. Rather than offering a succession of styles, cabinetmakers and manufacturers offered a menu of revivals from which the customer could select. Old forms were molded to suit current needs. Comfort and convenience became requirements for household furnishings because leisure time had increased. More often than not, stylistic motifs from different periods were combined. Furniture design of the period was grand and ornate. From the middle of the century, pieces were styled in suites (sets) so that matching pieces could furnish each room. Different styles were recommended for different rooms: Gothic for the hall and the library and rococo for the drawing room, the parlor, and the bedroom.

Victorian classical furniture differed from the forms of the Empire period in that they were even grander in scale and more elaborately ornamented. The pedestals of dining and marble-topped tables were heavier. Legs were composed of larger lion's-paw feet and florid leaf brackets. The columns on sideboards increased proportionally. Large spirals were in evidence as arm supports and leg supports on sofas.

The Victorian revival of the Gothic style in the 1840s was less popular in America than in England. Gothic traditions were accepted more readily in architectural design than in furniture. However, elements of the Gothic style were seen. Pointed arches shaped the panels on the doors of secretaries and wardrobes. The same arches were seen in the panels of a heavy pedestal base that supported a round extension dining table. The feet of the base were turrets. Chairbacks incorporated Gothic arches in the openwork design. Chairs had cane, wooden, or upholstered seats. The tall backs of chairs were also upholstered, with pointed crests carved with solid or open Gothic motifs. Carving designs consisted of cusps, crockets, and rosettes. Sharply pointed lancet arches and tre- and quatrefoils were borrowed from the tracery designs in earlier Gothic windows. Whatnot shelves were supported by carved tracery. At first, they stood about the height of a side table. In the 1840s, the piece became taller. By the 1850s, it was placed in a corner. Tre- and quatrefoils were seen in the carved openwork of a hall tree or in arches on heavy head- and footboards on beds. The steeple clock was a Gothic piece because its case resembled a Gothic cathedral.

The rococo style unearthed in the 1850s was characterized by prolific curves, exaggerated scale, and abundant heavy decorative carving. Victorian craftsmen interpreted the French fashion with a new technical process called lamination. John Henry Belter originated the technique of gluing thin sheets of wood together with the grain of each layer going in the opposite direc-

A Classical Revival sofa is displayed in the bedroom of a house in New Orleans. *Courtesy: Thorne American Rooms in Miniature, The Art Institute of Chicago*

tion from the previous layer. Furniture sections were then cut out and steamed in molds to create a curved shape. Ornate rococo motifs were then carved by hand. This furniture was generally made of rosewood, although some pieces were constructed from walnut or mahogany. Many craftsmen adopted this style, but it was most closely associated with Belter.

New shapes were made possible through Belter's technique, which allowed for the creation of complicated seating softened with lush upholstery. Rounded wooden surfaces were ornately carved with open patterns. Rococo chairs had high backs. The entire surface might have been carved or an upholstered back might have been crowned with a raised crest of pierced carving. On some chairs, the framework enclosing the back bowed out to frame an upholstered surface used for an armrest, as seen to the left of the sofa in Nic Nichols's parlor (see page 103). Cabriole legs ended in a short, tapering column or, rarely, the French scroll of the eighteenth century. Rear legs reversed the S-curve, with the convex portion at the foot. Sofas had backs in a triple-medallion shape with a carved crest surmounting the taller center section. The side sections might have been higher on other models. The tête-à-tête, or love seat, was made in the S-shape with one seat facing forward and one facing backward. This form was traditionally used for courting. A single-end sofa had a tall medallion-shaped back at one end, the sides of which

A corner whatnot shelf with Gothic tracery.

A side chair in the style of Henry Belter with beautifully carved naturalistic designs forming the openwork of the back, made by Thomas A. Warner. *Collection of Mary Lee Dearring Tracy*

A Gothic Revival hall rack made by Nic Nichols of Nic's Creative Workshop. *Courtesy: Nic Nichols*

A Victorian parlor made by Nic Nichols contains a matched suite of Rococo Revival furniture. *Courtesy: Nic Nichols*

A suite of medallion-backed Rococo Revival furniture consisting of a chair and sofa, available at Roy's Hobby Shop.

tapered in waves down to the seat toward the opposite end. An ornate vinelike crest surmounted the back.

The rococo fashion was adapted for many other forms such as a curvilinear ladies' desk and a serpentine bureau with an ornately framed mirror. Oval center tables were used in parlors. The top surface was marble. The legs were cabriole ending in a forward-turned scroll. The apron and stretchers were curvilinear and decorated with open carving. Whatnots were created in the rococo style. Shelves were supported by C- and S-shaped curves. An openwork crest rested on the top shelf and pierced carving trimmed the other shelves.

The balloon-back side chair was a popular furniture form of the rococo revival period. The open silhouette was made up of gentle curves. Rounded shoulders extended from a carved floral crest. They tapered in at the carved splat located midway down the back toward the seat. The curve continued to the floor to form the rear leg. As on the klismos chair, the back support curved forward along the side of the seat and down to form an incurved front leg. The inset seat was upholstered.

The Elizabethan revival lasted from the 1840s until the 1860s. The feature emphasized in this style was spiral turning. Stiff symmetrical seating with tall backs were typical. Spiral twists were used as supports in upholstered chairbacks. These same twisted turnings served as legs on some pieces. Spool turnings were split and applied to the surfaces of painted chests seen in sets of "cottage furniture."

Furniture designs were inspired in the 1850s by a revival of the Renaissance style. Forms were generally rectangular with architectural devices such as wide

wooden trim, heavy curved pediments serving as crests, molded busts or columns, and superimposed carved medallions. Victorian additions were machine-incised linear ornamentation and a turning in the shape of an acorn. Chairs were rectilinear and heavily upholstered. The front legs were rigidly turned and vaguely resembled the trumpet turnings of the William and Mary period. The Victorian Renaissance interpretation often incorporated baroque elements in the designs. Baroque classical heads might have been placed on the handrests of chairs.

Bedroom suites consisting of a bed, bureau, a washstand, and two nightstands were typical Renaissance revival forms. The massive pieces had heavy columnar supports and moldings framing the different surfaces. The carved pediment surmounting the tall headboard was matched by that above the bureau mirror. The bureau was composed of a long, low drawer section and a

A tête-à-tête, or love seat, in the Rococo Revival style.

Balloon-back rococo chair with a
washstand made by Harry Smith.

tall, ponderous mirror. The mirror was set in a central recess in the drawer arrangement.

The Renaissance étagère was the culmination of the smaller, less important whatnot. It became the Victorian version of the Jacobean court cupboard. If doors were present, they had mirrored panels. The piece continued to have shelves for display, but it became more substantial—sometimes standing more than seven feet tall. Corner or wall étagères were styled with Renaissance features, such as the arched crest, but they also incorporated baroque scrolls for shelf supports or rococo and Gothic framework around mirrored panels. The mirrored panels served as a background for small shelves and made the displayed objects appear even greater in number.

Renaissance features proved particularly suitable to

A Renaissance Revival bedroom suite available from The Miniature Mart. *Courtesy: The Miniature Mart*

other forms. A heavy wardrobe had a rounded crest and a single door with an oval mirror inset. The sideboard, whose base rested directly on the floor, had a wooden back topped by a curved crest. The surface of the sideboard was marble. Another marble shelf was set in the back and supported by scrolled consoles.

By the 1870s, upholstery had completely overtaken wooden frames and soon became the focus of seating forms, such as easy chairs, stools, and ottomans. Ottomans became circular sofas with no arms, rather than upholstered stools. They soon took the central position in the room formerly occupied by the marble-topped table.

Innovative furniture forms and materials emerged during the Victorian period. Around 1850, some furniture required mechanisms for adjustment or convertibility. Technical devices, which enabled chairs to recline, tilt, swivel, and fold up, were patented. The name "patent furniture" categorized these chair forms. Iron furniture was created for garden use and for stands to hold hats and umbrellas. Papier-mâché was used for chairs, tables, and stands, especially in England. Occasionally, this material was inlaid with mother-of-pearl. Papier-mâché forms were light in weight and colorful in decor. These fragile furniture pieces were intended more for room decoration than for heavy use.

Handles on drawers were seen in many styles. Different materials were used to create them. Carved wooden pieces curved out from the drawer front to provide a grip, as on the drawers of the basin stand on page 105. Round knobs were made of wood or cut glass. Gilt drawer pulls had ornate, round backplates with a suspended ring, seen on the Renaissance bedroom suite on page 105. As in all other aspects of Victorian furniture design, hardware styles were left to the whim of the designer.

Victorian Upholstery

Because of the emphasis on comfort, upholstery became very important during the Victorian period. Chair and sofa backs were heavily padded and framed with wood. Seats incorporated the use of springs, and upholstery was brought over the frame, sometimes with trim or, later, with deep fringe. Upholstered surfaces were smooth or tufted; a series of covered buttons were tied to create an indented pattern on the soft surface.

Appropriate fabrics for Victorian upholstery were heavy and lush, such as velvets, brocades, damasks, and, most particularly, horsehair. Horsehair, or haircloth, was a covering of finely woven horsehair and cotton, linen, or wool. This cloth was extremely sturdy. Typically, it was black in color with a plain woven surface or an impressed pattern. Woven fabrics took on

a new dimension with the invention of the Jacquard loom. Intricate patterns were abstract or naturalistic in design. Elaborate, realistic patterns were also seen on printed chintzes. Roses were a popular motif. Silks and velvets were considered extremely luxurious. Damasks were usually woven in one color with large floral designs. Berlin needlework patterns were prevalent on upholstered furniture pieces.

Colors during the 1830s and 1840s were pure and bright, such as scarlet, yellow, turquoise, and yellow green. Early in the 1850s, shades became darker, with crimson and bottle green receiving emphasis. Around 1855, the heavy Victorian colors of maroon, tan, and dark green appeared. At this point, three or four colors were used in one design instead of the earlier combination of one or two shades.

Victorian Drapery Treatment

Victorian drapery treatments were voluptuous and complicated. Ponderous fabrics, draped in elaborate arrangements, were excessively decorated with fringe, tassels, and braided trims. French curtains hung to the floor. They were held back at a low level with tasseled cords and, later, with fabric tiebacks. The tiebacks ended in rings and attached to a wall hook. They were decorated to match the valance. Carved, gilded cornices crowned the valances, especially in drawing rooms.

In the 1830s, pure classicism was still in evidence in interior decoration and furniture design. Drapery valances were seen in the simple style of a fringed fabric box-pleated at intervals. Sheer muslin undercurtains were used, especially in drawing or dining rooms. A more elaborate classical treatment was seen in valances with festoon drapery. Swags of fabric were hung over a rod in loops.

Another early valance style was Gothic in inspiration. This fashion was characterized by shaped valances. One silhouette echoed the Gothic arch because the bottom edge flowed down from the center to deep corners. Other silhouettes had level lower edges that

A draped window valance in the classical style.

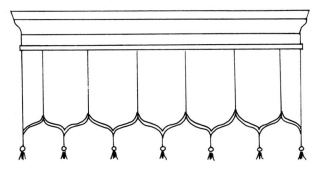

A Gothic valance panel.

were shaped in a repeated pattern of pointed arches. The edges were bordered with contrasting trim and often decorated with tassels.

The Elizabethan valance was more formal. It was shaped at the lower edge into curved and angled silhouettes that resembled strapwork. The flat shapes were trimmed with thin, contrasting color, and tassels were evenly spaced across the bottom. The French curtains might have hung from brass rings on a curtain rod suspended in front of the valance.

Festoons became much more elaborate when used with the rococo revival furniture. Separate pieces of fabric were hung in deep swags, forming an oval shape. Fringe and tassels were abundant.

Victorian valance designs soon bore no resemblance to any one historic style, but became the expression of the designer, who combined different stylistic elements in his own way.

During the 1850s, sheer muslins became decorated with white embroidery. The pleasant effect of sunlight coming through the patterned fabric was stressed, so a pair of undercurtains were hung together until just reaching the windowsill, where they were pulled back. A single sheer panel might have been used. It was pulled across the entire window opening and tied back to one side at the same low level as the French drapes. Lace or machine-made net curtains were used by themselves at the window later in the Victorian period.

Cambric window shades were made between 1830 and 1860. The fine, white linen fabric was decorated

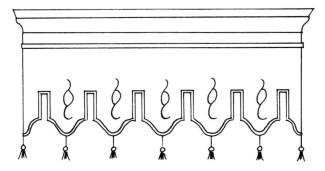

An Elizabethan valance panel.

with painted designs and realistic romantic scenes. These translucent shades hung alone at the window and were usually pulled to display the painted motifs.

Victorian Floor Coverings

The emphasis on softness and comfort was seen in the abundance of rugs and carpeting. Machine-weaving reduced the cost of floor coverings, so they were plentiful in all homes. Strips of carpeting mounted stairs and lined hallways. Striped or checked Venetian carpeting was the most popular and durable for this use. Wall-to-wall carpeting was laid so that it completely covered the wooden floors. This covering was mass-produced in Europe and in America. One popular example from England was Brussels carpeting. Medallions or realistic flowers were scattered over the entire surface. The carpeting was manufactured in strips. The strips were laid side by side and tacked to the wooden floor so that the designs matched and the floor was completely covered. Victorian carpeting and rugs favored dark, rich colors for the background, such as amethyst, forest green, and deep mazarine blue. Motifs were colored in lighter shades of mauve, lavender, robin's-egg blue, and fern green.

Individual rugs were machine-woven, hand-knotted, and stitched with Berlin wool. The styles of rug design followed those of furniture. At the beginning of the Victorian period, the motifs were classical in inspiration, as was seen in the use of acanthus leaves, flowers, and scrolls. Gothic styles were based on architectural features. Around 1840, a popular design was the diamond trellis, created with flowers and leaves, which covered the entire rug surface. In the 1850s, elaborate three-dimensional flowers, scrolls, and ferns complemented the furniture and interior architecture of the rococo style. Rugs continued to be imported from the Near East. There were many copies of the Turkish and Persian patterns.

Less formal ingrain carpets were made by simultaneously weaving two cloths so that they were interwoven. Geometric and striped patterns were created. The limited number of colors were seen in reverse on the back. During the Victorian period, the number of colors involved in this technique increased.

Needlework carpets were stitched throughout the Victorian period. The designs of these carpets, too, followed the fashion of the times. There were some examples of cooperative projects where individual panels, made by different people, were joined to make a large rug.

Hooked rugs became very popular at this time. They copied oriental styles and originated an unlimited number of primitive designs. In the late 1860s, E. S. Frost, a Yankee peddler, became interested in hooking rugs as he watched his wife at work. He developed zinc stencils so he could mass-produce on burlap designs he created or bought from New England farm women. His wagon became filled with hooked rugs and rug patterns, as well as with tinware and calico. Simplistic designs of birds or animals, such as eagles, dogs, or lions, were often surrounded by geometric or curved decorative borders. Floral motifs were abundant also.

Victorian Needlework

The Victorian woman was relegated to the home. She became the moral guardian of her domestic sanctuary. Industrialization and the presence of servants, an important status symbol, led to an increase in her leisure time. Her life outside the home was spent attending church activities, shopping, and "calling" on social acquaintances to advance the social position of herself and her husband. In the home, she was managing and stitching. Printing machines allowed for the dissemination of information for women through women's magazines, newspapers, and manner books. The most popular was Louis A. Godey's *Lady's Book*, which was first printed in 1830. Stitching techniques and patterns were made available to the entire female population through printed materials.

Tent-stitch needlework, from 1830 to 1870, consisted almost totally of Berlin work. The graphing method for this handwork was easily mass-produced by printing machines. A less expensive cotton canvas emerged. It was more coarse than the earlier silk canvas, the finest being twenty-four threads to the inch. Now a background was stitched in white, tan, or blue. Merino wool began to be used for a soft, angoralike needlework yarn. This wool was particularly well suited to the Berlin patterns. After 1850, the background was worked in very dark colors, such as claret, dark green, and black. The discovery of an aniline dye widened the color range of wools. In the 1860s, needlework pieces incorporated vivid colors, such as mauve, magenta, maroon, purple, pink, orange, and strong green and blue. Designs broadened to include three-dimensional arrangements of flowers, historical events, scenes from the Bible, Shakespeare, and copies of famous paintings. A plethora of needlework pieces decorated every possible article of clothing and home furnishing. Tent- and Irish-stitched projects covered pillows, pieces of furniture, pole screens, and wastebaskets. Wool-stitched canvas created slippers, rugs, pictures, frames, cigar cases, bellpulls, purses, and antimacassars (small coverings placed on chair and sofa backs to protect the upholstery fabric from being stained by hair oils).

Creativity on the part of the Victorian women was channeled into the making of quilts. The three quilting techniques were incorporated in the construction of one quilt. Now, appliquéd shapes were created by the stitcher, rather than by following a printed design on the fabric. Friendship quilts were created by different friends who appliquéd squares. The squares were framed with pieces of fabric and joined to make a top quilt layer. An overall stitched pattern seen on one-piece quilts was worked on the appliquéd and pieced surface. Colorful silk pieced quilts were also typical of Victorian quilting. Newspaper was used to stiffen the individual shapes when they were sewn together. Brightly colored crazy quilts were created with silk shapes and ribbons formed into fans. Each fan was framed with black velvet. An embroidered bird, flower, or butterfly was stitched on the fan section. Decorative stitching in a contrasting color surrounded each piece of fabric.

Victorian Silver

During the Victorian era, the neoclassicism of the Empire period persisted, for the most part. Also, silver design moved from the grand scale of the earlier style to romanticism. The classical urn shape with a tall curving handle was prevalent, as was the cylix, a shallow bowl on a pedestal foot. Victorians had a great deal of sentiment about the past and about nature. The stylistic revivals seen in furniture design occurred in silver production also.

The romanticism of the Victorian period was well suited to the earlier rococo style, which reached its culmination in the 1850s. It was characterized by a recurving line and luxurious naturalism. Victorian rococo forms were bulkier than those of the Chippendale period. They were elaborately decorated with sculptured decoration. Bases were a continuation of the body. They consisted of a curvilinear skirt resting on four foliated feet. Parts of rococo pieces were cast in natural forms, such as tree branches, which served as handles, and flowers and vegetables, which became finials.

The Renaissance revival occurred in the 1860s. This style emphasized flat surface decoration in the form of geometric bands and classical friezes. Legs and feet were composed of curved acanthus leaves or animal heads or feet. Handles and finials took the form of cast masks, swans, cupids, or lion heads. Other popular motifs were allegorical and mythological figures.

A great deal of experimentation characterized the Victorian period. The silversmith combined historical motifs in his own way and executed his work with a great deal of help from machinery. By 1860, silversmiths became salesmen for manufactured wares. The silver designer took over the creative aspects of silversmithing: factories executed his ideas. Jewelry stores and silver factories replaced silversmith shops. Mass production and the creation of "silver plate," base metal covered with a thin layer of silver, reduced the cost of silver pieces. Thus, silver was prolific in a great many American homes. Mechanization reproduced old techniques, such as engraving, piercing, flat chasing, casting, and embossing, and invented new ones that provided freestanding figures and realistic decoration in high relief. Also, because of new methods, surface variations were achieved.

While individual silver pieces were produced during the Victorian period, the emphasis was placed on matching sets. At this time, all flatware was made with the same handle shape and design. Not only spoons were made in a single design, but forks, knives, a variety of serving pieces, such as nut picks, and crumb, orange, cheese, and fish knives were also made in the spoon pattern. In the 1830s, handles had again turned up. The projections near the juncture of the handle and bowl had become rounded and then disappeared. The fiddle-shaped handle became pointed, and the shaft became very thin before joining the bowl. By the middle of the century, machine-stamped patterns of motifs such as acorns and leaves were applied to handles. This mass production of ornamentation enabled silver factories to produce a variety of patterns and handle shapes for sets of flatware.

Presentation pieces consisted of a single oviform goblet with engraving and molded design, or a set of simply engraved, straight-sided beakers with a molded base band. Elaborate dinner or tea services might also have been given to honor an individual's achievements. The dinner service included entrée dishes, a centerpiece, serving dishes for vegetables, and a lidded, cylix-shaped tureen. The tea service was composed of a tea kettle on a stand, two teapots, a coffeepot or urn, a sugar bowl, a creamer, a waste bowl, pitchers, a spoon holder, a domed butter dish, and bow-shaped tea tongs.

Other dining accessories were created individually. Salt cellars and mustard pots had blue or ruby protective glass liners set into pierced and molded silver frames. The frames were decorated with rococo curves, leaves, and shells. Silver fruit compotes were cylix in style with encrusted decoration or with pierced, flared sides. Cake baskets, too, were pierced in intricate patterns. Ewer-shaped pitchers now stood on molded pedestals. Their handles looped high above the body. Punch bowls had a taller domed foot, but retained the Chinese porcelain shape. Monteiths reappeared at this time, also with taller bases. A molded grape vine encircled the bowl. Centerpieces were considered luxurious. Along with candlesticks and candelabra, they were the perfect form for the fanciful expression of the designer. Allegorical figures, swans, or cupids supported one or more fruit containers in the form of baskets or chariots. Wild animals or exotic plants and flowers were placed playfully in the arrangement of the differ-

ent motifs. Candlesticks progressed from round shafts with round bases to rococo curves involving naturalistic forms. Twisted branches or intertwined grapevines formed the arms of candelabra. Also produced in silver were tea balls, punch strainers, and napkin rings.

A multitude of silver objects were created during the Victorian period. Thimbles and small boxes continued to be produced. Silver inkstands were decorated in the ornate Victorian style. Silver and glass card receivers were provided for a caller to deposit a card, according to the social custom of the time.

Victorian Britannia

Britannia ware continued to be made during the beginning of the Victorian period. Cake baskets, liquid fuel lamps, candlesticks, and spoons were produced, as well as cuspidors, picture frames, snuff and tobacco boxes, faucets, and the ear portion of hearing trumpets. In the 1860s, britannia was replaced by ornamental ceramics, pressed glass, and silver-coated electroplated objects.

Victorian Ceramics

By the middle of the nineteenth century, potters' shops where clay was thrown and turned on a wheel had been replaced by factories where ceramics were formed in molds. Americans were now producing many of the European wares, even porcelain. Stoneware took the place of redware, except for the creation of the most basic forms. Redware jugs had round bodies and narrow necks; pie plates had glazed interior surfaces; platters had flat bottoms; and pots had straight sides.

Stoneware became much more ornate. Designs were brushed or trailed in blue or brown. Earlier abstract plant and flower motifs became more realistic renditions of animals, people, trees, and houses seen in the countryside where the potter worked. A deer might be seen standing quietly in a pasture. Buff or dark gray forms were pots, jugs, or crocks and lidded bean pots, flasks, and barrel-shaped water coolers with a spout at the front.

Practical dishes for everyday use were produced in yellow, white, and Rockingham glazes. Flint enamel, a new glaze whose formula was patented by Christopher Webber Fenton of Bennington, Vermont, added spots or streaks of green, yellow, and blue to the brown Rockingham glaze.

Parian, a fine-grained porcelain that resembled marble, was first invented in England, but was used a great deal in America for statues, vases, and pitchers. As seen in other wares of the Victorian period, the molded decoration on the Parian pitchers completely took over the shape. Decoration was florid, naturalistic, and in high relief. If a corn husk pattern were the pitcher's decorative motif, the handle would be formed by leaves and a stalk, the spout by leaves, and the body by swirling corn, leaves, and husks. Another use for molded Parian forms was applied decoration on blue, or perhaps tan, pink, or green, objects. This decorative technique was used for ewers, vases, and pitchers. Parian motifs were naturalistic forms or sentimental scenes.

England continued to provide Americans with transfer-printed earthenware. Printing was now seen in more colors than blue and black. Light blue, sepia, green, and the ever-popular pink were also used to depict romantic fictional scenes, which replaced earlier historic subjects. Two colors might have been used on the same piece with one color designated for the central portion and the other for the border.

Rich porcelains were in great demand by Victorians. They were produced in bright colors and with elaborate decoration by factories such as Meissen, Sèvres, Haviland, and several English establishments. Rococo shapes were adopted and exaggerated to such an extent that curves moved in utter confusion. Dessert, dinner, and breakfast sets were created, as well as centerpieces, vases, ewers, and garden pots. Flowers, fruits, or scenes served as central motifs that were framed with rich gold borders. Molded colored porcelain flowers covered the surface of decorative pieces.

Irish Belleek pottery appeared during this period. Parian forms were covered with a luster of mother-of-pearl. The surfaces were extremely thin and were decorated with molded underwater forms, such as coral, mermaids, shells, and marine plants. Baskets shaped by Parian twigs were encrusted with flowers. Tea wares, vases, and small bowls were typical forms.

Interiors of Victorian homes were given the crowded, cluttered look so sought by housewives by the presence of innumerable statues and figurines. These pieces were displayed on whatnot shelves, étagères, and on special stands, if they were large. Parian statues were executed in the form of mythological, royal, nude, or sentimental figures with romantic titles (see page 112).

Rockingham ware formed lions, cow creamers, poodles, and deer. Other animal figurines represented horses, monkeys, birds, bears, and bird whistles. Toy banks were made in the shape of buildings or Empire chests of drawers.

More sophisticated figurines were produced in England and Europe. Staffordshire subjects represented famous people, such as kings, queens, actors, singers, historical personages. They were brightly colored and shiny. French bisque offered sentimental settings with children in pastel shades. Highly colored and glazed shepherds and shepherdesses were produced in France and Germany.

Victorian Glassware

An overabundance of detail characterized the Victorian period. Richness and ornateness were indications to the common man that luxuries were no longer available exclusively to the aristocrat. Eclecticism abounded in the design of glass objects as it did in all other art forms. Different styles and different decorative techniques were combined in great numbers on any one piece. Glass that had been colored, coated with silver, or frosted was used by itself or in combination with other colors of glass. Shapes became elongated. The ancient Greek jar, the amphora, was again popular for the shape of jugs, cruets, vases, and other vessels. Handles were placed high on the shoulder and often curved above the object. Pear-shaped glassware was also common. Goblets and wineglasses had bell, tulip, and round bowls with faceted and carved rims, stems, and feet. Colors were many and important.

Southern Jersey glassware styles continued relatively unchanged. The free-blown and pattern-mold blown pieces were still appreciated. Pressed glass changed around 1840 from the lacy patterns to those of plain geometric shapes, such as panels, thumbprints, flutes, and diamonds. These wares were called "pattern glass." In the 1850s, simple designs were placed on a ground of fine vertical ribs. Ribbed designs were replaced in the 1860s by a more ornate high-relief pattern. After the lacy patterns, pressed glassware was made in large sets of dishes. The choice of color became greater, with sets being offered in green, amber, blue, white, and amethyst with finishes ranging from transparent to translucent to opaque to frosted. Dish forms included in these sets were plates, cup plates, dishes, butter dishes, spoon holders, goblets, wineglasses, celery vases, and lamps. Paperweights became popular glass items. They were produced with flower or fruit centers on a striped background.

Luxury glass items made in America continued to follow European trends. Bohemian glass came in many types. The most popular in America was cased glass. The method for making this kind of Bohemian glass consisted of coating a basic glass with a thin layer of glass of another color. Ruby glass covering clear glass was a popular combination. A glass cutter would then cut away the ruby layer, leaving a design of clear glass. Another color combination for the overlay technique could have been a white opaque coating over colored glass. Bohemian glass was also made in clear and solid colors, such as ruby and black. It was characterized by elaborate engraved designs of naturalistic motifs or romantic scenes.

The repeal of the glass tax in England allowed for the creation of exquisite heavy cut glasswares. Deeply cut intricate designs covered the entire piece. Wineglasses, vases, and pitchers were made, but more elaborate pieces were also produced, such as a covered compote and dessert sets. The dessert sets included three sizes of goblets, a decanter, a ewer, a footed bowl, and a large centerpiece, all matched in design.

There were other types of glass produced in England at this time. A milky opal glass was painted with enamel colors and with gilt. Venetian-inspired wineglasses were fragile in appearance and delicately decorated. Chandeliers were enormous and, like the cut glass, consisted of a myriad of sparkling prisms.

Victorian Metalwares

Cast iron was used for a greater variety of forms during the Victorian period. Furniture for outdoor use, frames for mirrors, and bases for lamps were created in all of the styles revived at this time. Parlor stoves were designed in the rococo, Gothic, and Renaissance revival fashions. These stoves were also installed in other rooms in the house, such as the kitchen or the laundry. Timesaving devices were mounted on the stove, such as the bracket that holds several flatirons against the iron surface so a hot iron would always be handy. By the middle of the nineteenth century, cast-iron coal grates had completely replaced andirons. Fireplace tools were still used to handle the hot coals in the grates. Kitchen kettles and pots were joined by more sophisticated kitchen tools. Coffee grinders, cherry pitters, and apple peelers and corers were made of cast iron.

More sophisticated technology was incorporated with the production of metalwares. Brass kettles were prolific because they were made from a sheet of brass, which was spun on a lathe. Copper kettles became rare. Kitchen utensils, such as cylindrical dry and liquid measures, were produced.

The Yankee peddler sold kitchen utensils. This itinerant salesman could provide the rural Victorian household with plain tin items. Dairy and kitchen wares included coffee and teapots, milk cans, tea caddies, dishes, boxes, trays, colanders, pans, strainers, cookie cutters, measures, mugs, and dippers. Tin picture frames and mirrors had scalloped edges with pierced or punched designs. The same designs were seen on the tin sides of foot warmers. Here the pierced sides were framed with wood. Tin chandeliers hung in taverns and churches from the beginning of the nineteenth century. The chandeliers had gracefully curved arms that ended in plain candle sockets.

Japanned tinwares reached the peak of popularity during the Victorian period. Background colors were red, blue, green, and red-yellow-brown. Designs were stenciled in red, green, yellow, and bright blue. Hand-painted naturalistic ornamentation was also found. Banks, boxes, dishes, and trays were made. Trays were scalloped, rectangular, oval, octagonal, and coffin-shaped (created by canting the corners of a rectangular tray).

Lighting fixtures were made with japanned tin, iron, brass, and britannia. Ornate decoration took control of

An assortment of stoves that might be seen in Victorian homes.

the utilitarian form. Candelabra became uncontrolled intertwined rococo vines, leaves, and grapes. Chandeliers, sconces, and lamps were fueled with kerosene. Kerosene was made from oil, which was discovered in Pennsylvania in 1859. Gas provided light in private homes in cities after the Civil War. Stationary gas fixtures were attached to walls and ceilings. The fixtures were ornate, showing an abundance of decorative motifs from many of the revival styles.

Victorian Room Arrangement

Victorian floor plans varied with the architectural style of the house. Room use was standard, however. The parlor, or drawing room, followed basic trends, whether it was one large room or two rooms separated by a large doorway. Seating was not oriented around the fireplace. This emphasis had begun to disappear with the Empire period. An ornate chandelier was suspended above a round or oval table which had been centered in the room. Several side chairs and, perhaps, a sofa were scattered over the carpet. The sofa and chairs also might have been situated around the edge of the room along with a whatnot or étagère and various tables, such as an oval marble-topped table, a round side table, and a tilt-top papier-mâché table. Furniture surfaces were cluttered with ceramics, clocks, and lamps. Ceramics took the form of vases with heavy ormolu decoration, colorful figurines under glass domes and Parian statues. Clocks continued to be gilded with prolific molded ornamentation. Lamps were topped with frosted globes. Cut-glass prisms were often suspended from the bases of the globes. Shaped or tall col-

umnar shafts were made with colored ceramic material decorated with gilt. Ormolu formed the opulent bases. Scenic paintings with heavy gold-leaf frames were hung on the wall. Oval portraits might have been suspended from wire supported by a nail high above. Patterned carpeting covered the entire floor.

The Victorian dining room closely resembled that of the Empire period in the types of pieces in the room and their placement. A central-extension dining table displayed a silver centerpiece in which figures supported several dishes surrounding a large central container. A four-armed candelabrum was placed on each side of the centerpiece. An intricate glass chandelier was composed of many leafy branches that ended in incised frosted globes. The sideboard showed several cut-glass decanters, candelabra with five candle sockets, and a silver coffee and tea service on a large tray. A tall stand with a large Parian bust stood in front of the sheer undercurtains at the window. Gold-framed oil portraits decorated the walls. The pattern of the wall-to-wall carpeting differed from that of the neighboring room, but mirrored its colors.

In the bedroom, the Victorian bed was positioned with its head against the wall. All the furniture pieces matched. A night table with an oil lamp, a book, and eyeglasses stood next to the bed. On the other side, a matching nightstand supported a large ceramic pitcher set in a matching bowl. A towel rack was located nearby. Against the wall stood a bureau with an attached or matching mirror. Glass-topped bottles and ceramic boxes occupied the various surfaces on the bureau. A table that followed the style of the bedroom suite was centered under a globed gaslight chandelier.

Victorian accessories for the parlor.

The interesting scrolled base of the Victorian table was made by Elizabeth Scull. A dried flower arrangement is protected by a dome in the Victorian manner.

A ceramic fruit compote rested on the table surface on a Berlin-stitched mat. A tall, rectangular cheval fire screen stood low to the floor next to the fireplace. Over the mantel hung a large oil painting with an ornate gold frame. On the marble mantel shelf was displayed a clock whose case was embellished with elaborate gold decoration. A pair of ceramic candlesticks showed a shaft that had become a human figure, supporting a socket composed of leaves and flowers. At each end of the shelf was a ceramic vase covered with three-dimensional flowers. Oval portraits decorated the walls. Wall-to-wall carpeting with light medallion designs covered the floor.

2 Making Period Furniture and Accessories

Basic Needs for Getting Started

Fine-grained woods are essential in making miniature furniture according to "proper scale." A well-crafted piece of furniture can be distorted by using a wood with too large a grain. There are, however, many types of wood that are appropriate in scale and therefore used for making miniature furniture. Cuban mahogany, walnut, lemon and pearwood, cherry, and basswood are among the favorites. We tend to use basswood more than any other because of the very fine grain, and achieve an extraordinary finish by sanding very carefully, applying stain, and finishing with eight to ten coats of varnish. The piece is sanded lightly and rubbed with a piece of 0000 steel wool.

After selecting the wood, a scaled drawing of the piece you have chosen is drafted onto a piece of paper and the patterns are transposed onto the wood. Templates, a drafting pencil, and a protractor are very useful, as are a T square, calipers, and a compass.

A knife set and an awl provide the miniature maker with the necessary tools for carving and marking the wood with a small hole in preparation for drilling a hole. The jewelers' saw is used to cut the components of a furniture piece and files are for sanding small

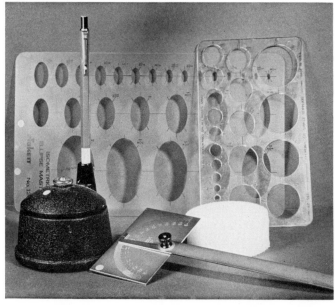

Oval and round templates standing in background, from left to right: variable taper lead pointer and draftsman's mechanical pencil, protractor, and clean pointer.

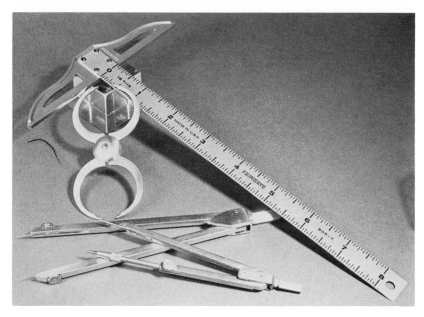

Assorted measuring tools from top: T square, loop calipers, straight calipers, and compass.

Knife set for carving, awl, 6" metal ruler, and jewelers' saw with 4" throat.

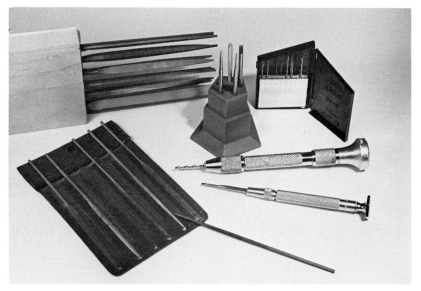

Sets of files, screwdrivers, and drill bits with holders.

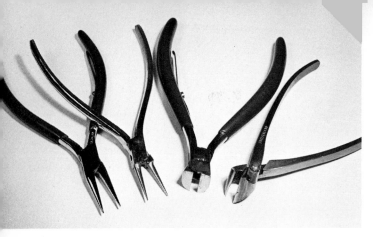

Various kinds of pliers and wire nippers.

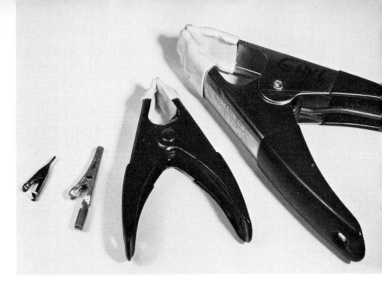

Graduated sized clamps.

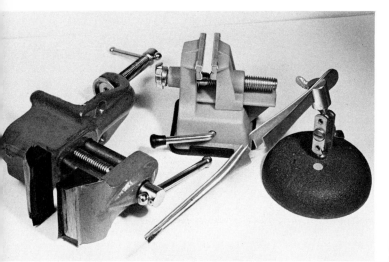

Holding devices: large and small vises, and third hand.

The Chopper and metal miter box with companion saw.

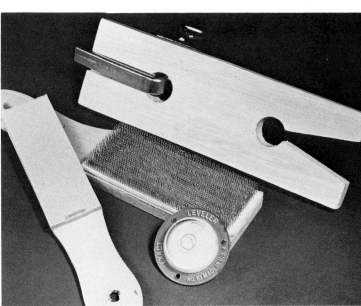

Pencil sharpening board, metal file cleaner, V-board and clamp, and leveler.

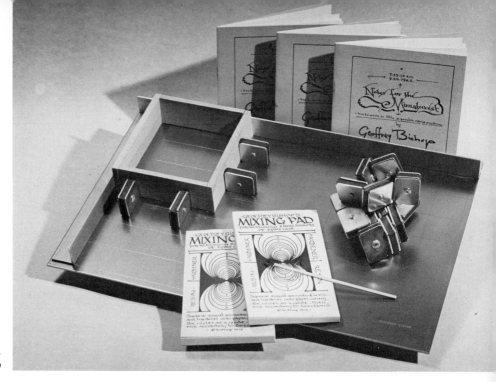

Geoffrey Bishop's magnetic jig.
Courtesy: Geoffrey Bishop

areas. Pliers and clamps are handy holders for small wood parts, as are a vise and a third hand. A V-board and clamp is a device that is used for resting the work as you cut and sand.

With the invention of "The Chopper," cutting lengths of stripwood and mitering corners have become easy tasks. This clever device holds the wood in place while the handle, which holds a razor blade attachment, is brought down on top of the strip, cutting a nice straight edge. A miter box and a saw are other useful tools for mitering an edge.

When gluing component parts, which requires even, straight corners, Geoffrey Bishop's magnetic jig is an important workshop accessory. It consists of a smooth iron bed with a 7" × 11" working area scribed with 1" squares. Along the sides is aluminum molding to ensure right angles. The work is held in place by four strong magnets.

Other useful tools include: wire nippers, small curved cuticle scissors, and other large scissors; assorted dental tools; adhesives (Titebond Glue®, 5 Minute Epoxy, Velverette, white glue, such as Elmer's or Sobo); acrylic paints, varnish, stain; toothpicks; and Artfoam.

There are a number of power tools available for advanced miniature makers. The Dremel Moto-Shop has all the attachments for sawing, sanding, grinding, and buffing, and a flexible shaft drill and accessories can be connected to a variable speed regulator. The Moto-Tool is for cutting, shaping, hollowing, polishing, sanding small pieces, and drilling. A jewelers' lathe is used for turning and as a drill press.

We have attempted to construct the furniture in this book, for the most part, by using simple tools rather than elaborate power tools, by using a jewelers' saw

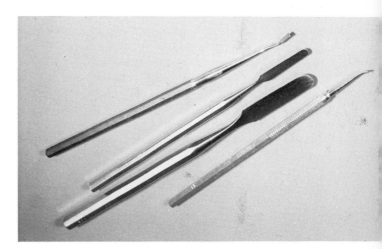

Assorted dental instruments.

instead of a power saw, for instance, and using a hand drill rather than a drill press. Turnings can be filed by hand with small files and a bit of patience.

General Methods

The methods described here apply throughout the furniture-making section of this book.

After cutting and sanding furniture parts, they should be stained before gluing together. Prestaining is done in case the glue seeps out onto the top surface. This makes it difficult for the stain to penetrate into the wood, leaving a blotchy surface. It is possible to assemble the pieces first if care is taken not to let any glue come onto the wood.

117

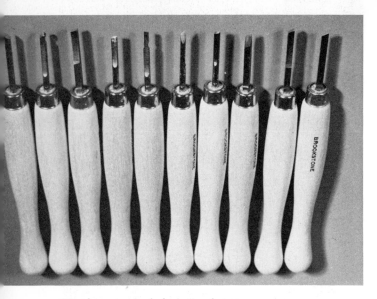

Wood-turning tools from Brookstone.

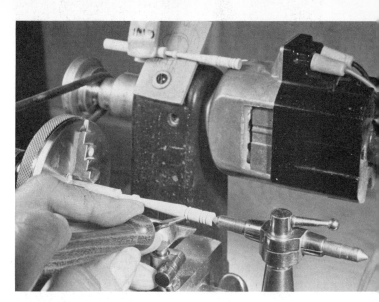

A sample turned leg, clamped in back of working surface for easy viewing.

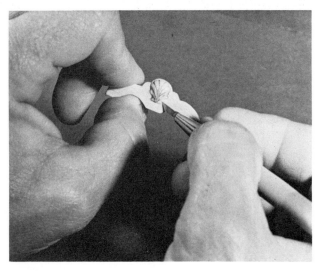

Rose Barell shown here carving a shell design of the top crest rail of a Queen Anne chair.

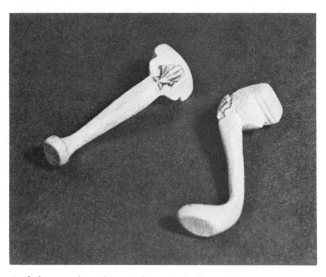

And the matching legs with same shell motif.

Turning a chair or table leg is accomplished by mounting a dowel between the centers on a jewelers' lathe, using turning tools. A sample leg is clamped into place in back of the working surface for easy viewing. If the leg is partially square, a rectangular piece is placed in a chuck for holding the square end. Calipers are used for measuring leg diameter and distances, so that all legs are uniform in size.

To make a shell carving on a chair rail and knee, superimpose a piece of wood about the same size and shape as the shell and carve the shape into the overlay piece using a small sharp carving knife.

Various shaped dowels and rectangles, when covered with sandpaper, make useful sanding sticks for shaping curves and corners on legs and other furniture parts.

A china cupboard very often has a rounded back. Use a cardboard tube, cut in half, vertically, and attach to the back.

Many period furniture pieces require a rush seat for finishing. The procedure is as follows: The four-step diagram indicates the process of the seat rushing, to be worked on an open wood frame. Pulling the thread taut, in the direction away from the worker, starting at arrow, go over bar #1 at left front corner and under, go over bar #4 and under and across front, over #2 and under, over and under #1, across to back, over and under #3, over and under #2, across frame, over and under #3, repeating until the seat area has been completely filled in. Should the seat be irregular in shape, the procedure is as follows: Work around the seat once.

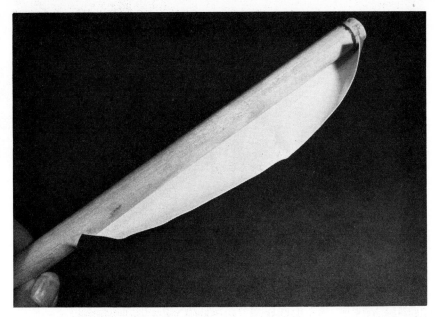

Cover a dowel with double-faced carpet tape (sticky on both sides) . . .

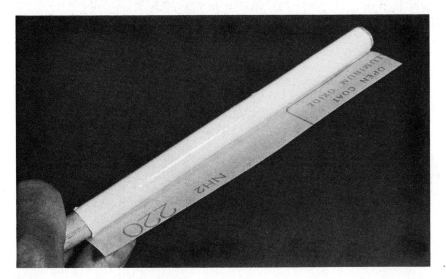

. . . and lay sandpaper over sticky tape . . .

. . . to make these sanding sticks, a round and a square.

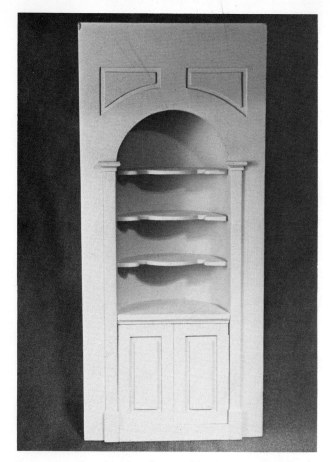

Front view of a cabinet with curved back.

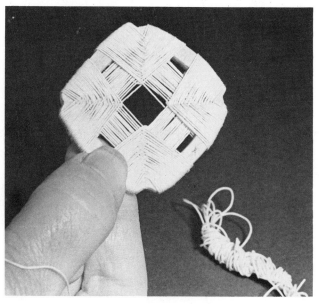

Numbered steps of diagram for rush seat.

#3 bar

#4 bar

#2 bar

#1 bar
front

A cardboard tube cut in half vertically forms the back of cupboard.

Here fine linen rigging, used in building ship models, is wrapped around a cardboard bobbin to make the "rushing" easier. When a point is reached where the bobbin no longer fits through the center hole, unwind the thread and use a threaded needle to finish the procedure until inside area is completely filled. Tie off thread on underside of seat.

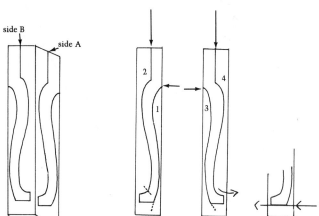

side B

side A

2

1

4

3

side A

side B

side A

← finishing cut

Fig. 1

Diagram for making cabriole legs.

Marbleizing a tabletop.

At the beginning of the second round, wrap the rush around each bar twice, and proceed with the next round in the usual way. Continue working the double wrap every other row until the threads are straight horizontally and vertically.

Cabriole legs are a predominant feature on period furniture. The basic steps described here may be applied to any size that you are working with. Trace leg pattern shape onto wood. This sample leg was cut from wood 3/8″ × 3/8″ × 2 3/8″. Figure 1 shows the direction of the legs when traced onto the two joining sides of the wood. The knees are facing each other. With side A on top, start the cut at arrow #1, cut to end of dotted line, using either a jigsaw or a jewelers' saw, and stop. Back saw out of cutting line. Proceed to arrow #2, cut to dotted line and stop, backing saw out of cutting line. Turn wood one turn with side B on top. Cut #3 as you did #1. Starting at arrow #4, cut this line completely through, as curved arrow indicates. Hold all leg pieces together as you cut. Turn piece again with side A on top, and slide blade into #2 cut and finish the cut in the direction of the arrow, as for #4. The final step is to cut completely across the bottom of the foot, allowing pieces to fall apart, leaving a cabriole shaped leg. Sand and shape foot to a spoon or slipper shape.

Marbleizing a surface is a rather simple procedure. Paint the surface of wood to a very smooth finish. Flood the painted surface with water, and using a size 1 brush, blend one color into large cloudlike shapes. Allow to dry. With a very fine brush, using a dark color acrylic, paint very thin lines, forming veins across the marble. Varnish the entire surface until a very smooth patina is formed.

A miniature maker's workbench.

A needlework designer in action.

Directions and Patterns

Chippendale Bed

A four-poster, Chippendale-style bed, supported by four cabriole legs, hand-painted with a flower and leaf design on a red ground.

BILL OF MATERIALS

Basswood, red acrylic paint, four cabriole legs, varnish, Titebond Glue, gold and black paint.

WOOD SIZES	THICKNESS
#1 headboard	3/32″ × 3 3/8″ × 3 1/4″
#2 footboard	3/32″ × 2 3/8″ × 3 1/4″
#3 sideboard	3/32″ × 1 7/16″ × 1 9/16″ (cut 4)
#4 turned post (square stock)	3/16″ × 3/16″ × 3 5/8″ (turn 4)
#5 side rail	1/8″ × 6″ × 1/4″ (cut 2)
#6 back and front rail	1/8″ × 3 7/16″ × 1/4″ (cut 2)

Cabriole legs may be purchased—#43111 from X-ACTO,® HOUSE OF MINIATURES,® or made according to directions on page 120.

PROCEDURE

Cut and sand all bed parts. Turn four posts and sand cabriole legs, shaping foot to a slender slipper foot. Glue side rails to outside of front and back rails, forming a frame. Attach four turned posts #4, using dowel joints, to four top corners on frame. Glue headboard and footboard between posts, recessing in from the edge 1/32″. Attach four sideboard pieces to posts, recessing as for front and back headboard. Glue cabriole legs at corners, using dowel joints for securing legs to bottom of bed frame. Paint bed with red paint and decorate, using design on pattern sheet. Varnish to a smooth patina.

A four-poster Chippendale bed.

#1 headboard

#3 sideboard

#2 footboard

#4 turned post

Pattern sheet for Chippendale bed.

Daybed or Couch

From the seventeenth century, daybeds were developed and used for reclining and sleeping. They often resembled chair styles of the period, and were also referred to as "long chairs." The adjustable headboard of this daybed is composed of three vase-shaped splats, surmounted by a gently curved crest rail. The covered cushion and pillow, made of fine petit point, was designed and worked by Susan Richardson. A graph for petit point is on page 204.

BILL OF MATERIALS

Basswood, dowels, 220 sandpaper, 5 Minute Epoxy, stain, varnish, fine brass or gold chain, four brass pins.

WOOD SIZES	THICKNESS
#1 seat	3/32″ × 1 13/16″ × 4 7/16″
#2 front leg	1/4″ dowel × 1 7/16″ (turn 2)
#3 back post and leg	3/16″ × 3/16″ × 3 1/16″ (turn 2)
#4 side leg	1/4″ dowel × 1 11/32″ (turn 4)
#5 front and side stretcher	3/16″ dowel × 1 3/8″ (turn 7)
#6 shoe	1/16″ × 3/16″ × 1 7/16″
#7 back splat	1/16″ × 5/16″ × 15/16″ (cut 3)
#8 crest rail	1/16″ × 1/2″ × 1 7/16″

PROCEDURE

Cut and turn all pieces from specified wood sizes, using pattern shapes on pattern sheet. Sand until smooth. Cut out half-round shape at each corner on front of seat for attaching top of #2 legs. Drill four holes on seat for dowel fitting of four legs #4. Pieces may be stained now or after the assembly is complete. Glue back splats, crest rail, and shoe to form back of bed. Set aside to dry. Epoxy front and side legs in place. Glue back post and leg section to back of daybed, securing joining with brass pins, inserted through post into seat. Fit and epoxy #5 stretchers in place between legs. Sanding will be necessary to fit stretchers properly. Stretchers may also be doweled into legs for stronger joining. If this is done, holes must be drilled completely through four side legs, 3/8″ from bottom, and on the back and inside of only the two front legs. Cut and fit three plain stretchers between side and back legs, as shown in illustrated drawing. Attach a 7/8″ chain from back post to crest rail. Varnish to a smooth patina.

The vase and ring-turned stretchers strengthen the capacious length and width of this elongated chair form.

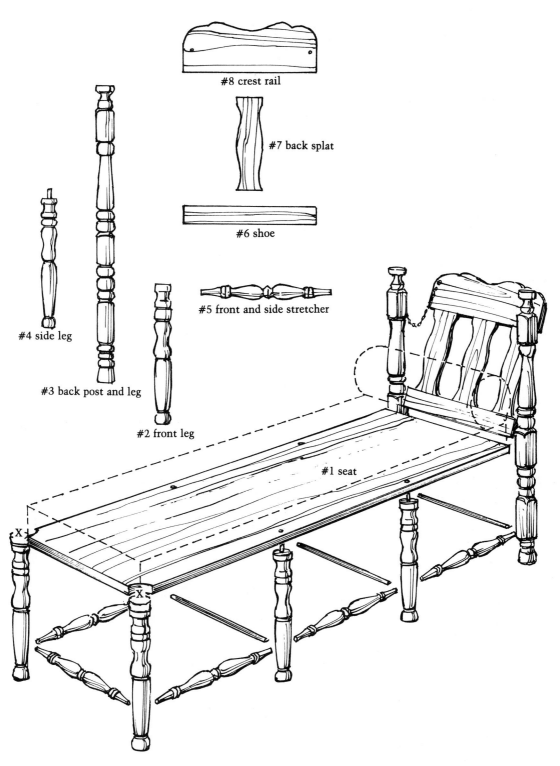

#8 crest rail

#7 back splat

#6 shoe

#5 front and side stretcher

#4 side leg

#3 back post and leg

#2 front leg

#1 seat

Pattern sheet for daybed.

Early-Eighteenth-Century Birdcage

These Dutch pieces were made of fine ceramics. We have used wood for making our miniature adaptation of this attractive piece. After painting with white acrylic paint, the design was painted blue and seven coats of varnish were applied to the surface, thus creating a very smooth finish that simulates the glossy appearance of ceramic.

BILL OF MATERIALS

Basswood, blue and white acrylic paint, Deft ® varnish, #72 gauge wire, 000 fine sable brush, pin vise with #72 drill, 5 Minute Epoxy.

WOOD SIZES	THICKNESS
#1 front and back	3/32″ × 1 17/32″ × 1 3/4″ (cut 2)
#1a crossbar	1/16″ × 1 9/16″ × 3/32″ (cut 2)
#2 side	3/32″ × 7/8″ × 7/16″ (cut 2)
#2a crossbar	1/16″ × 7/8″ × 3/32″ (cut 2)
#3 bottom	1/16″ × 7/8″ × 1 5/16″
#4 center arch	3/32″ × 1 17/32″ × 15/16″
#4a top divider bar	1/16″ × 11/32″ × 3/32″ (cut 2)

PROCEDURE

Cut all pieces from pattern shapes, using wood thickness as indicated. Sand and paint with two coats of white paint. Drill seven holes 1/16″ deep on both #1

pieces at bottom of opening. Drill corresponding holes in #1a pieces completely through the wood. Epoxy piece at X on #1 front. Blue design may be painted on at this time. Drill sixteen holes at inside top arch of #1, using hole spacing on pattern #4. Do not drill completely through wood. Drill corresponding holes in #4 center arched piece, completely through the wood. Drill five holes 1/16″ deep in top of #2 pieces. Drill corresponding holes 1/32″ deep in #2a pieces. Epoxy 3/8″ wire lengths into holes on these pieces. Epoxy free ends of wire into corresponding holes in #2 pieces. Epoxy these two assembled sides to #1 front. Insert wires into bottom and middle bar holes on #1 front section, snipping wire at top to fit curved arch. Insert 15/16″ long wire pieces into center arched section #4. Epoxy #4 at each end X to center of #2a, fitting wires into holes on #1 arched piece. Assemble #1 back, using the same procedure as #1 front. Epoxy this section to assembled cage, lining up the wires with drilled holes. Insert pieces #4a at top of cage. Insert vertical wires of back section as you did the front. Carve a tiny bird and epoxy onto a round perch, glue into place in cage. Glue bottom piece #3 in place. Finish with seven coats of Deft varnish until the finish has a smooth, soft patina. Use cup-shaped findings for side feeding cups and a brass finding for top finial. Epoxy in place.

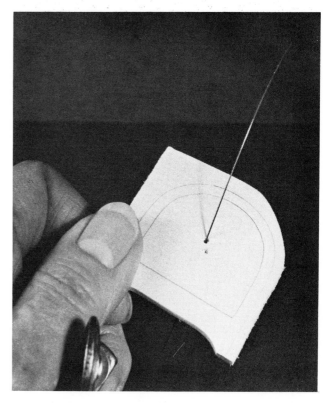

Drill a hole in center of area to be removed, insert saw blade, and cut out inside.

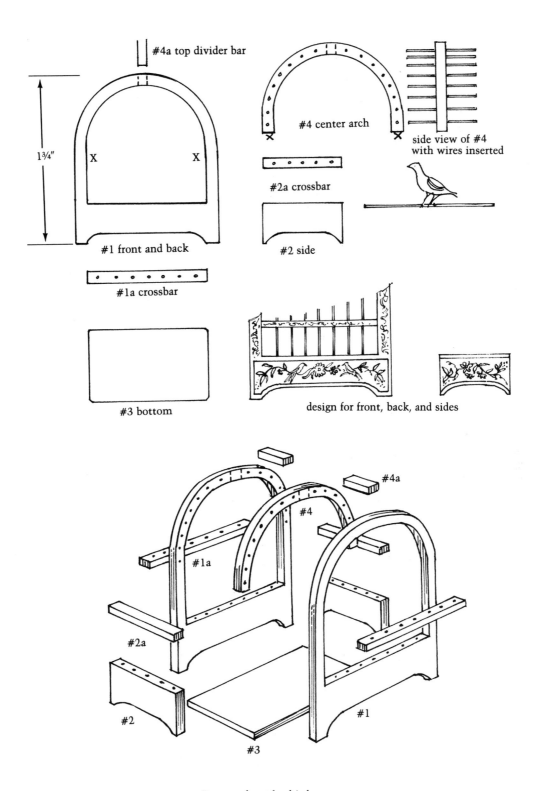

#4a top divider bar

#4 center arch

side view of #4
with wires inserted

1 3/4"

X   X

#1 front and back

#2a crossbar

#2 side

#1a crossbar

#3 bottom

design for front, back, and sides

#4a

#4

#1a

#2a

#2

#3

#1

Pattern sheet for birdcage.

Sand inside area with dowel sanding stick before cutting outside edge.

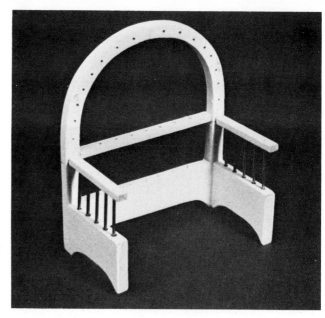

Two assembled sides attached to front.

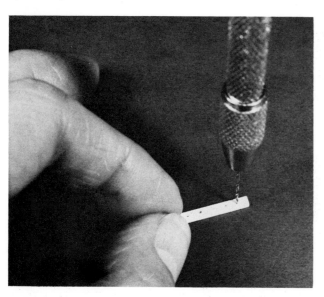

Drill five holes on #2a crossbar. Do not drill completely through.

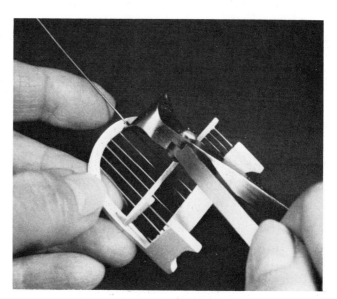

Snipping wire at top to fit curve of cage top.

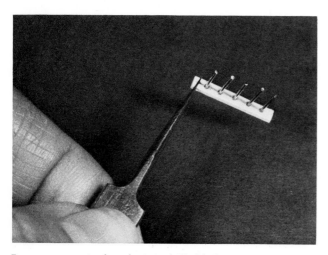

Epoxy precut wire lengths into drilled holes on #2a.

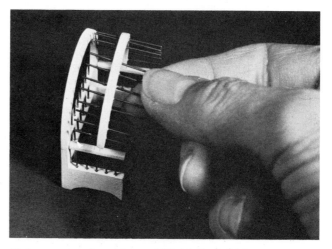

Lining up wires from #4 to drilled holes in #1.

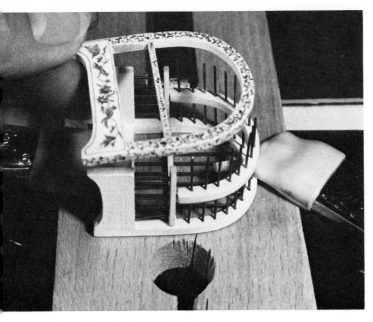

Attaching the front and back sections.

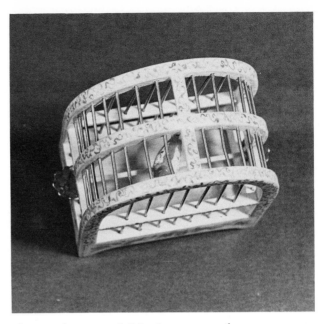

Showing placement of #4a pieces on top of cage.

Lacquer Cabinet

A black lacquer cabinet, after the style of Thomas Chippendale, an English cabinetmaker of the eighteenth century, painted with a black ground and varnished to a soft patina, to resemble the beautiful examples of the East. The design may be raised by applying gesso and painted gold or the piece may be decorated by applying gold leaf to the raised motif. The finish is similar to a method known as japanning. Chinese figures, trees, flowers, and birds are used on this piece. Animals may also be added to the design.

BILL OF MATERIALS

Basswood, black and red acrylic paint, gold-leaf paint, varnish, embossed gold paper trim, brass findings, four hinges (3/16″) manufactured by Houseworks Ltd. (#1120), white glue, 5 Minute Epoxy, 220 sandpaper.

Eighteenth-century cabinet, with a chinoiserie design painted on a black ground.

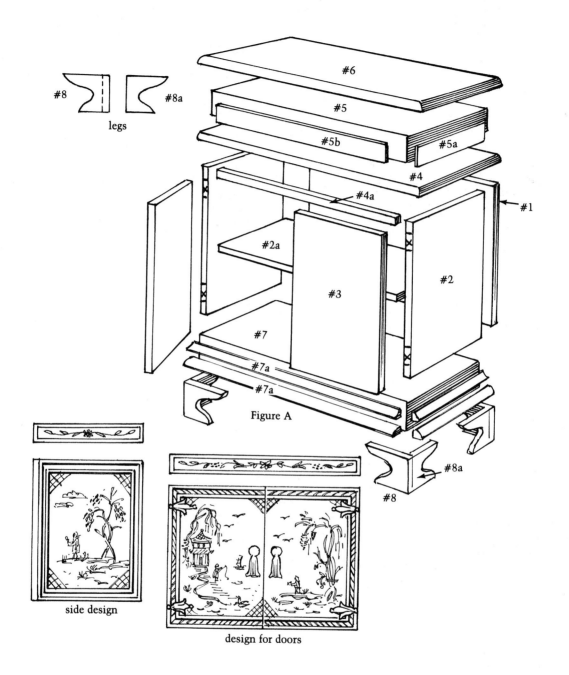

#8 #8a

legs

#6

#5

#5b #5a

#4

#4a #1

#2a

#3 #2

#7

#7a

#7a

Figure A

side design

design for doors

Pattern sheet for eighteenth-century cabinet.

WOOD SIZES	THICKNESS		
#1 back panel	3/32″ × 1 1/2″ × 2 1/8″	#5a side overlay	1/32″ × 1 1/16″ × 3/16″ (cut 2)
#2 side panel	1/8″ × 1 1/2″ × 1 3/16″ (cut 2)	#5b front overlay	1/32″ × 2 1/4″ × 3/16″
#2a inside shelf	1/16″ × 2 1/8″ × 1 3/32″	#6 top	3/32″ × 2 9/16″ × 1 3/8″
#3 door	3/32″ × 1 1/2″ × 1 5/32″ (cut 2)	#7 bottom base	3/16″ × 2 1/2″ × 1 3/8″
#4 horizontal layer	3/32″ × 2 9/16″ × 1 5/16″	#7a base molding	Cove 5/64″ and quarter round 3/32″
#4a door stop	1/16″ × 1/16″ × 2 1/8″ (cut 2)	#8 leg	1/16″ from pattern (cut 4)
#5 horizontal layer	1/4″ × 1 3/8″ × 1 3/16″	#8a leg	1/16″ from pattern (cut 4)

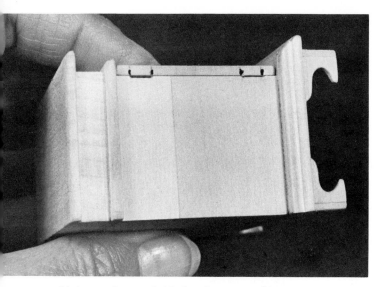

Lining up door and side for placement of hinges.

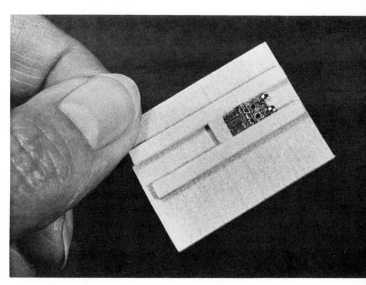

A jig made of wood to hold hinges while drilling holes for inserting pins. Hinges by Houseworks (#1120).

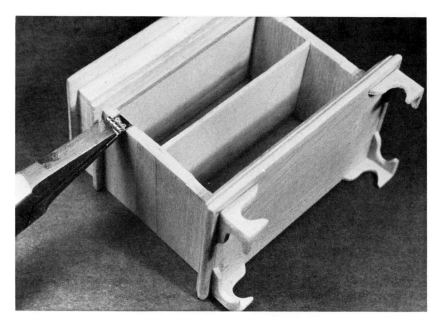

Measuring hinges to recessed area on side panel.

PROCEDURE

Cut and sand #1 and #2 pieces. Recess side pieces as shown in Figure A at X, 1/32" deep to accommodate hinges. Glue two side pieces to outside of #1 back panel. Glue shelf #2a at center of inside walls against sides and back. Cut doors #3. Sand until smooth. Cut #4, beveling two sides and front edges, and glue in place on top of assembled pieces, flush with back. Glue #4a pieces across top and bottom of cabinet as shown in Figure A. Cut and attach #5 in place on top of #4, flush with back. Cut #6 and sand, beveling two sides and front on the top edge as on #4. Glue on top of

assembled piece, flush with the back. Glue #5a and #5b in place. Cut #7 and glue to bottom of cabinet, keeping back of piece flush. #7a molding is formed by gluing 5/64" cove and 3/32" quarter round to #7 base, mitering two front corners. Cut and sand #8 and #8a, forming a right angle. Attach to cabinet bottom 3/32" from side and front edges, keeping back flush. Cabinet is painted black with two coats of acrylic paint and varnished until smooth.

Trimming is applied and design is painted with liquid gold paint. When completely dry, attach hinges and other findings.

WOOD SIZES	THICKNESS
#6 horizontal side bar	3/32″ × 3/32″ × 2 13/16″ (cut 4)
#7 horizontal front and back bar	3/32″ × 3/32″ × 1 3/8″ (cut 4)
#8 vertical corner post	3/32″ × 3/32″ × 1 1/4″ (cut 4)
#9 vertical side brace	3/32″ × 3/32″ × 1 1/16″ (cut 2)
#10 bottom of cradle	3/32″ × 1 11/16″ × 2 3/4″

PROCEDURE

Turn #1 and #2 pieces and cut #3 base feet. Sand until smooth. Assemble prepared pieces, using dowel joints for attaching horizontal braces. Epoxy four base feet to either side of posts. Stain. To assemble cradle, cut out remaining pieces and glue together as indicated on pattern sheet. Photograph shows cradle, held in place with spring clothespins, as pieces are glued into place. Trim edges of cradle with 5/64″ double bead wood molding. Stain needlepoint canvas and cut to fit sides, front, back, and hood. Glue into place and stain wood parts of cradle. Cut two brass strips 1″ long. Drill a small hole at the end of each piece and attach to front and back of cradle with small brass pins. Attach in the same manner to the posts. Varnish to a soft patina. Dress the inside with a mattress, pillow, and cover.

English Cradle

An early-seventeenth-century wooden cradle with caned sides and top, suspended between two turned posts, with two brass strips for rocking. Our adaptation of a cradle such as this, from a private collection, is made of basswood, using a #18-mesh needlepoint canvas to simulate the caning.

BILL OF MATERIALS

Basswood, stain, varnish, 220 sandpaper, 5 Minute Epoxy, 18-mesh needlepoint canvas, brass pins, thin brass strip 1/16″ wide.

WOOD SIZES	THICKNESS
#1 vertical post	3/16″ × 3/16″ × 4 1/4″ (turn 2)
#2 horizontal brace	1/16″ × 1/16″ × 3 1/4″ (turn 2)
#3 base foot	3/16″ × 7/8″ × 1/4″ (cut 4)
#4 cradle hood	3/32″ × 1/8″ × 1 1/2″ (cut 2)
#5 hood brace	3/32″ × 3/32″ × 1″ (cut 4)

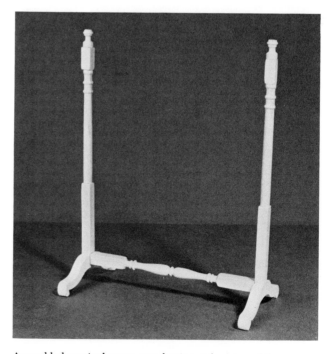

Assembled vertical posts, one horizontal post, and feet.

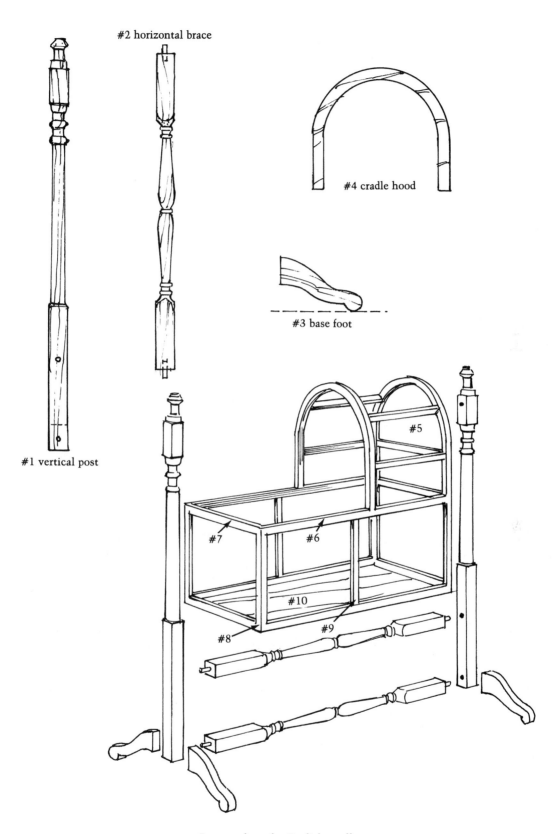

#2 horizontal brace

#4 cradle hood

#3 base foot

#1 vertical post

#5

#7   #6

#10

#8   #9

Pattern sheet for English cradle.

Cradle clamped in place after gluing.

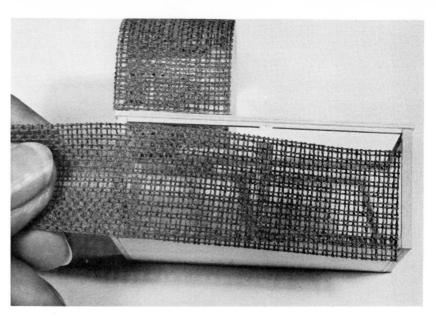

Fitting stained needlepoint canvas to body of cradle.

Attaching brass suspension strips to front and back of cradle.

Martha Washington armchair with a tree of life petit point design by Susan Richardson.

BILL OF MATERIALS

Basswood, 5 Minute Epoxy, Velverette glue, stain, varnish, Artfoam, 220 sandpaper, fabric or petit point, fine braid.

WOOD SIZES	THICKNESS
#1 back	1/4″ × 2 3/8″ × 1 11/16″
#2 seat	1/4″ × 2″ × 1 15/16″
#3 back leg	1/8″ × 1 3/32″ × 3/16″ (cut 2)
#4 front leg	3/16″ × 3/16″ × 3/16″ (cut 2)
#5 arm	1/8″ × 1 3/8″ × 3/16″ (cut 2)
#6 arm support	3/16″ × 1 1/8″ × 3/16″ (cut 2)
#7 side rail	1/16″ × 1/8″ × 1 13/13″ (cut 2)
#8 center rail	1/16″ × 1/8″ × 1 9/16″
#9 back rail	1/16″ × 1/8″ × 1 3/8″

PROCEDURE

Trace pattern pieces onto appropriate wood thickness. Cut out with jewelers' saw and sand until smooth. Pieces may be stained and varnished before assembling the chair. Front legs may be fluted or left plain. Epoxy arm supports to front legs using dowel joints. Drill hole at end of arms, as indicated on pattern, and insert dowel. After working petit point design, cover back and seat, using Velverette glue. When piece is completely dry, epoxy back to seat and epoxy back legs in place using dowel joints. Epoxy front leg and arm support assembly into slots at X. Measure carefully where arm will meet back, drill hole into back to accommodate dowel, and epoxy in place. Measure and attach rails 3/8″ from bottom of foot. Dry thoroughly before handling.

Martha Washington Armchair

The Martha Washington chair, also referred to as the lolling chair, was used widely in the Federal period. The style, an upholstered, open-arm, high-back chair, was considered to be of Chippendale or Queen Anne style, depending on the leg shape. The lolling chair was produced more often in Massachusetts than anywhere else in America. The chair presented here is in the style of Chippendale, with rounded crest, graceful serpentine lines, flaring arms with concave arm supports, set on top of square legs. The stunning petit point upholstery was designed and made by Susan Richardson. A graph for petit point is on page 225.

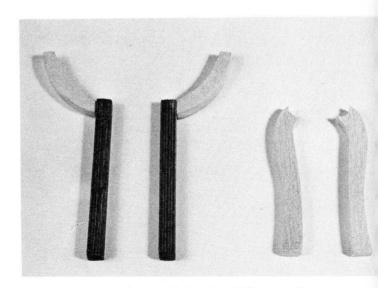

On the left, arm supports attached to legs. Right, curved arms.

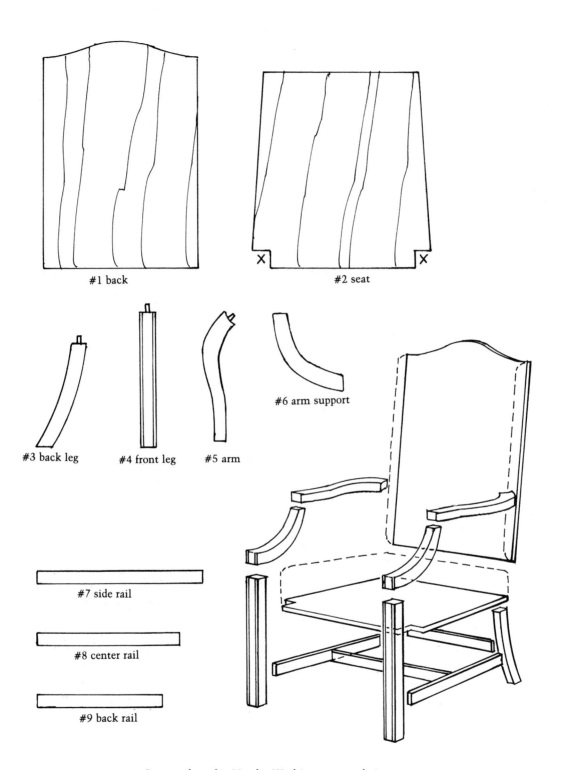

#1 back

#2 seat

#3 back leg

#4 front leg

#5 arm

#6 arm support

#7 side rail

#8 center rail

#9 back rail

Pattern sheet for Martha Washington armchair.

A dowel inserted into back of arm for insertion into seat back when assembling chair.

Covering seat and back with petit point.

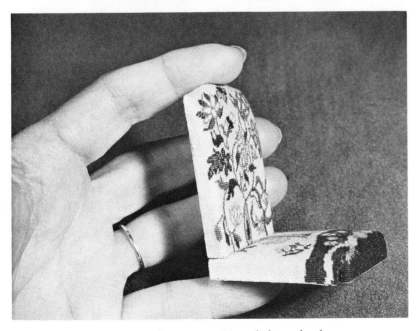

Chairback epoxied into place on seat. Note slight angle of the back in relation to the seat.

Attaching arm to back, using a dowel joint.

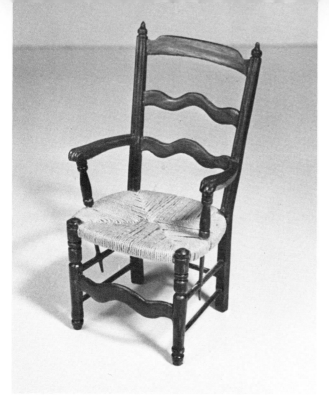

Country armchair with rush seat from an original by Eugene Kupjack.

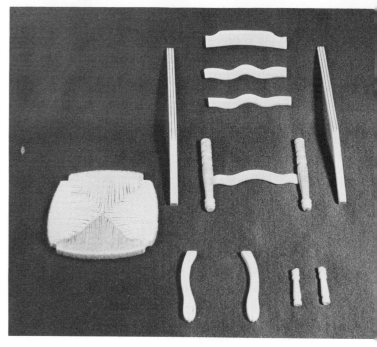

Chair component parts before staining.

Country Armchair

An informal chair with rush seat, made of basswood, stained to a dark mahogany, finished with two coats of dull varnish. The front legs are lathe-turned, as are the arm supports.

BILL OF MATERIALS

Basswood, 5 Minute Epoxy, stain, varnish, linen thread for the rush seat.

WOOD SIZES	THICKNESS
#1 leg and back post	1/8″ × 3/16″ × 3 1/4″ (cut 2)
#2 seat frame	1/16″ × 1 7/8″ × 1 11/16″ (cut 2)

Glue these two pieces of wood in a cross-grain direction before cutting shape.

#3 front stretcher	1/8″ × 1 3/8″ × 3/8″
#4 top cross slat	1/8″ × 1 1/2″ × 5/16″
#5 cross slat	1/8″ × 1 7/16″ × 1/4″
#5a cross slat	1/8″ × 1 3/8″ × 1/4″
#6 front leg	3/16″ dowel × 1 1/2″ (turn 2)
#7 arm	1/8″ × 1 1/4″ × 1/4″ (cut 2)
#8 arm support	1/8″ dowel × 11/16″ (turn 2)
#9 side and back stretcher	1/16″ dowel (cut 5)
#10 finial	1/16″ dowel (turn 2)

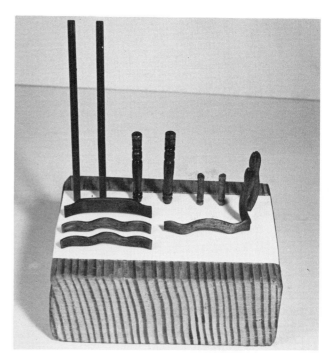

After staining, pieces are set aside to dry on a block of wood covered with double-faced tape, which allows them to dry upright.

PROCEDURE

Cut #1 from pattern, using appropriate wood size. Rout or carve two horizontal grooves from top to X on front face of top post, to create a fluted effect. Before cutting #2 seat frame, glue the two specified pieces of wood together in a cross-grain direction to provide greater strength to the frame while working the rush seat. Drill a hole on each side of frame at O, angling the

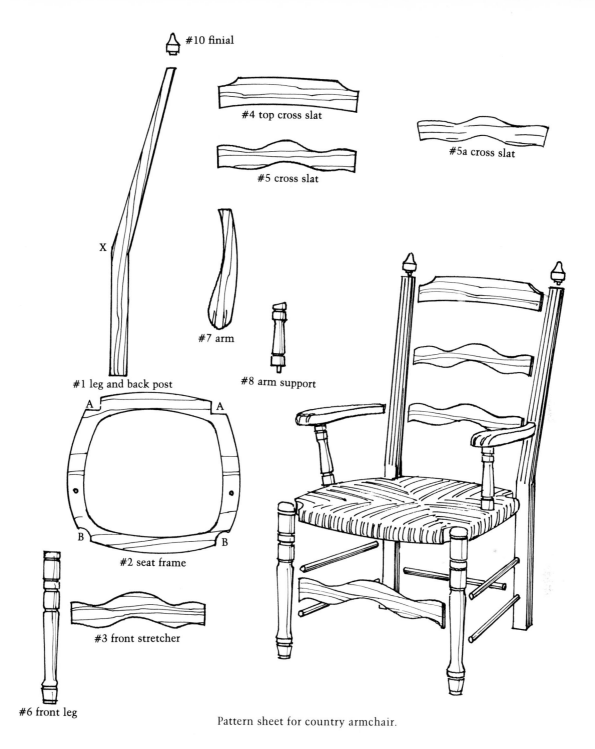

#10 finial

#4 top cross slat

#5 cross slat

#5a cross slat

X

#7 arm

#8 arm support

#1 leg and back post

A   A

B   B

#2 seat frame

#3 front stretcher

#6 front leg

Pattern sheet for country armchair.

hole slightly toward the back to accommodate dowel insert from arm support. Cut #3 front stretcher from pattern, shaping piece to a slight concave form until stretcher measures 1/16″ thick. Cut #4, #5, and #5a cross slats and sand to shape as for #3. Turn front legs #6 to pattern shape and cut arms, carving two grooves at handhold section to form knuckles on each arm front. Turn arm supports, forming a dowel at the bottom of each turning, to be inserted at O on seat frame. Sand all pieces until smooth. Stain and varnish and set aside to dry. Work rush seat as illustrated in diagram on page 118.

ASSEMBLY OF PIECES

Epoxy back leg and post sections into slots A on seat frame. Attach #4, #5, and #5a slats in place. Epoxy front legs into slots at B. Epoxy #3 cross front stretcher between front legs 1/2″ from the bottom of leg. At this point, it will be necessary to measure the distance between the legs to determine the length of #9 stretchers. These may be doweled into the legs or very carefully glued with epoxy. Assemble arm and arm supports and epoxy into place, from back post to the top of seat frame, inserting dowel into previously drilled hole. Turn two finials and attach to the top of back posts.

A Louis XV bergère covered with silk hand embroidery.

Bergère

Adapted from the style of Louis XV, this barrel-shaped chair suggests comfort and ease. A very elegant chair with upholstered seat and back, and closed arms that flow gently into the turned arm supports and slender legs. The very delicate design on the seat and back are embroidered on a thin silk fabric.

BILL OF MATERIALS

Basswood, 5 Minute Epoxy, Titebond Glue, soft turquoise acrylic paint, gold embossed paper trim, varnish, 220 sandpaper, Artfoam, silk fabric, DMC embroidery floss, fine embroidery needle.

WOOD SIZES	THICKNESS
#1 seat	1/8″ × 2″ × 2 1/8″
#1a barrel back, consists	3/16″ × 2″ × 2 1/2″ (cut 1)
of 8 layers	1/4″ × 2″ × 2 1/2″ (cut 7)
#3 back leg	3/16″ × 1″ × 1″ (cut 2)
#4 handhold	1/8″ × 11/32″ × 3/16″ (cut 2)
#5 cushion base	3/16″ × 1 13/16″ × 1 13/16″
#6 front leg and arm	
support	3/16″ × 3/16″ × 2″ (turn 2)

PROCEDURE

Trace #1 pattern on indicated wood and cut seat along solid line with jigsaw or jewelers' saw. Sand and set aside. The barrel back is shaped from eight layers of wood, each layer glued in the opposite direction, cross-grained to provide extra strength for the shaped back. We have glued six layers of wood, flat sides touching and traced pattern #1 with dotted line A between X and Y on edge of the wood, as shown in photograph. Dotted line B forms inside cutting line. Glue the two remaining pieces of wood, trace pattern, and cut out shape as for the previous six layers. Glue the two shapes together, one on top of the other, forming the curved back. Sand inside and outside surfaces until smooth. Glue curved back to seat, keeping outside edges flush. Using pattern #2, trace shape onto back for cutting line, to form top curve and arm. Cut with jewelers' saw and sand. Cut and attach handhold pieces to end of arm section. Turn #6 pieces from pattern, sand and glue into place fitting into notches at C. Cut back legs #3 and epoxy into bottom of seat with dowel joints at O as indicated on pattern. Paint assembled chair with acrylic paint and varnish. Cut seat cushion #5 and glue Artfoam on top. Work embroidery from design on pattern sheet. Cover lightweight cardboard with back embroidered piece, and glue to inside shape of back. The raw edge will be covered with gold trimming. Cover cushion, centering design very carefully, and glue to seat. Trim chair with embossed gold paper trim or ready-made fine braid. (Special note: Do not draw outline of seat cushion onto fabric along dotted line; the pencil lines would show when piece is upholstered. This is just a guideline for placing embroidery design.)

Showing line of pattern after being traced on layered wood.

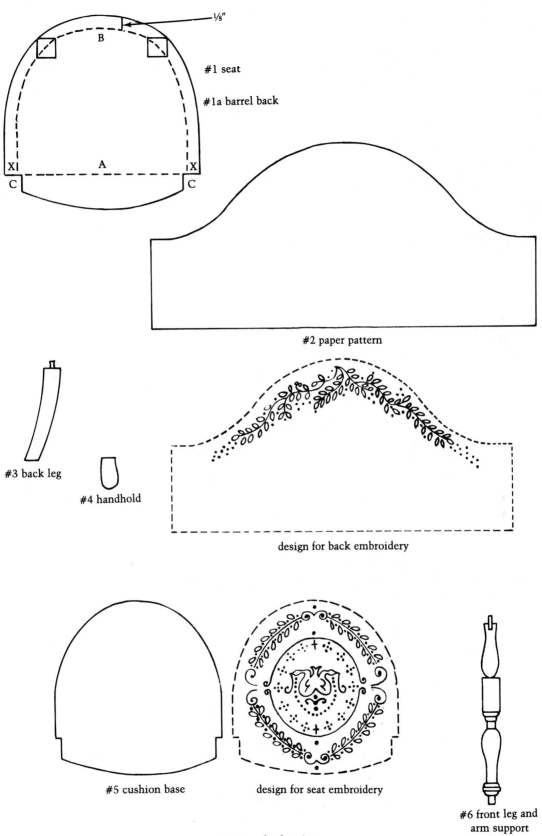

1/8"

B

#1 seat

#1a barrel back

X   A   X
C   C

#2 paper pattern

#3 back leg

#4 handhold

design for back embroidery

#5 cushion base

design for seat embroidery

#6 front leg and
arm support

Pattern for bergère.

Cutting inside line of shaped back from layered wood with jigsaw.

Piece marked with X is the cutout shape of the barrel back of the chair.

Pattern used for tracing shape on wood to form the curve at top and arms after cutting.

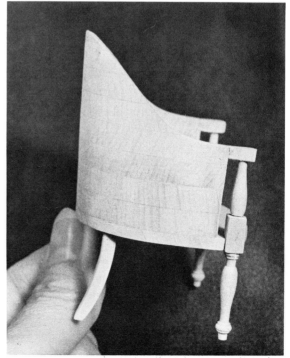

Assembled chair, ready for painting.

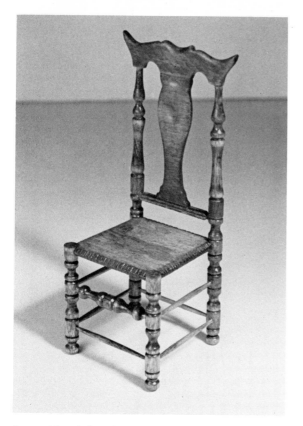

A transitional chair by Eugene Kupjack.

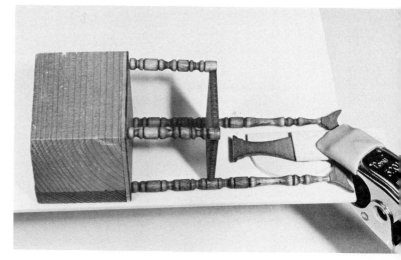

A spring clamp holds work in place while parts are glued together.

Transitional Country Chair

This transitional chair with Queen Anne splat and William and Mary turnings is stained with an Early American oil stain. For finishing, two coats of dull varnish were applied. The seat may be made of applied rush seating or a cushion pad may be placed over a plain wooden seat.

BILL OF MATERIALS

Basswood, stain, 220 sandpaper, Titebond Glue, 5 Minute Epoxy, varnish, round wooden toothpicks.

WOOD SIZES	THICKNESS
#1 crest rail	3/32" × 7/16" × 1 3/4"
#2 splat	3/32" × 1 11/16" × 9/16"
#3 back leg and post	3/16" dowel × 3 7/16" (turn 2)
#4 seat	1/8" × 1 3/8" × 1 3/8"
#5 front leg	3/16" dowel × 1 1/2" (turn 2)
#6 shoe	3/32" × 3/32" × 1 1/8"
#7 front stretcher	3/16" dowel × 1 3/16"

PROCEDURE

Cut, sand, and stain all chair parts. Glue #2 splat to crest rail at X. Turn #3, #5, and #7 from pattern shapes. Drill holes at O areas as indicated on pattern sheet. Epoxy #3 turned leg and post. Epoxy front legs into slots on seat, and attach seat to back posts, fitting legs into slots. Glue #6 shoe into place at bottom of slat, between parallel posts. Attach turned stretcher between front legs, inserting ends into already drilled holes. Measure six plain stretchers, using round toothpicks, that have been sanded to 1/16" rounds. Stain and insert into already drilled holes in legs. Clamping your work while gluing will keep chair parts from slipping. Make a padded cushion to cover seat or a rush seating may be used (see page 118).

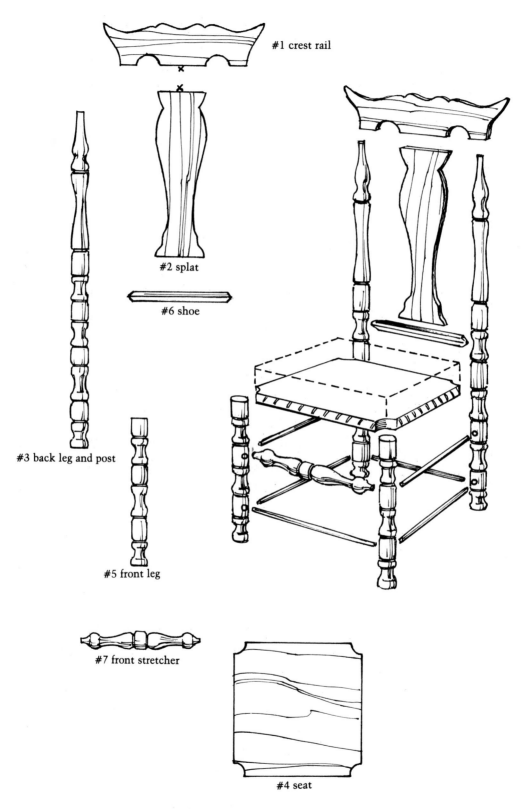

#1 crest rail

#2 splat

#6 shoe

#3 back leg and post

#5 front leg

#7 front stretcher

#4 seat

Pattern for transitional chair.

Hepplewhite chair, circa 1795. Painted birch. In the collection of the Museum of Fine Arts, Boston. *Courtesy: Museum of Fine Arts, Boston*

Hepplewhite Chair
(circa 1795)

A Hepplewhite chair of the Federal period, adapted from a chair of the same style from the Museum of Fine Arts, Boston. The delicate, classic lines, encompassing square, tapered legs that terminate in spade feet, with suitable motifs of grapes, urns, bellflowers, and paterae, make this chair a charming reproduction of the character of the period. The central plume, set within an oval back, resembles the Prince of Wales feathers, an insignia of the Prince of Wales, and is held together with small bowknots. The top and base of the plume are decorated with rich green leaves and bunches of grapes, with a delicate vine intertwined on the oval frame. The chair is painted with a black ground and varnished to a soft patina.

BILL OF MATERIALS

Birchwood, 220 sandpaper, black acrylic paint, 5 Minute Epoxy, varnish, small brass pins, Artfoam, pure silk fabric, 0000 paintbrush, assorted paint colors for decorating.

WOOD SIZES	THICKNESS
#1 back	1/8" × 2" × 1 3/8"
#2 seat and cushion base	1/8" × 1 7/8" × 1 3/8" (cut 2)
#3 shoe	1/8" × 1/4" × 1"
#4 back leg	3/16" × 1/4" × 2 1/16" (cut 2)
#5 front leg	1/8" × 1/8" × 1 5/16" (cut 2)
#6 plume	1/16" × 1 3/4" × 1 3/16"

PROCEDURE

Cut back oval, sand to shape as indicated on pattern sheet #1a. Cut back legs and sand to shape. Epoxy legs to back oval at shaded areas. Cut #3, shaping sides to fit into place between back legs at shaded areas. Attach with 5 Minute Epoxy. Trace #6 plume shape onto

An adaptation of the Hepplewhite chair in the Museum of Fine Arts, Boston.

145

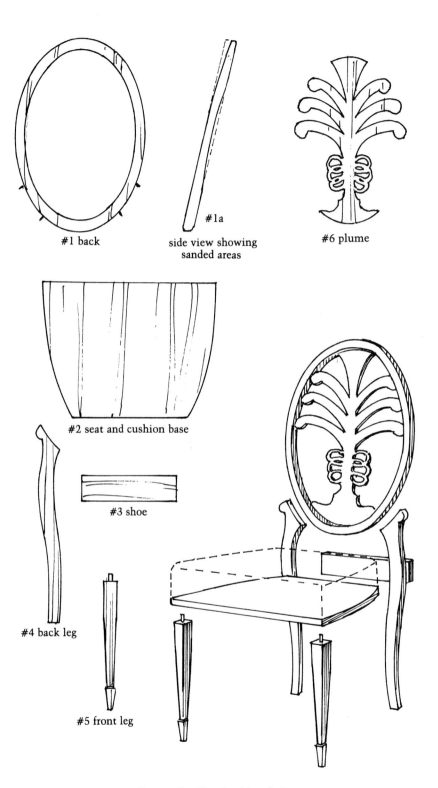

#1 back

#1a
side view showing
sanded areas

#6 plume

#2 seat and cushion base

#3 shoe

#4 back leg

#5 front leg

Pattern for Hepplewhite chair.

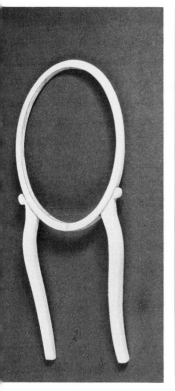

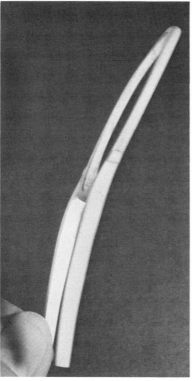

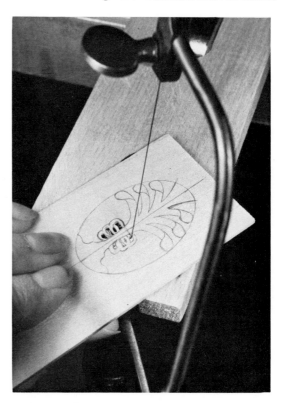

Position of legs in relation to oval back.

The side view, showing curved shape.

Using a jewelers' saw with a fine blade, cut out inside design.

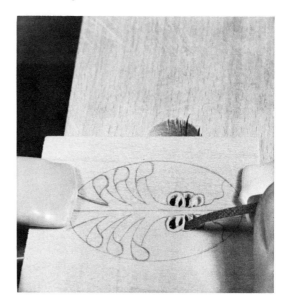

Piercing inside of bowknot design with a fine hand drill.

Sand pierced areas, using a strip of emery cloth, working in an up-and-down motion.

wood. Using a fine drill, pierce inside of bowknots and cut very carefully with a jewelers' saw. Sand with fine emery cloth, cut into thin strips. Cut around outside edges of plume design, being careful not to cut ends of plumes too short or they will not fit into oval. Epoxy plume shape inside oval frame. Apply black paint to frame and top vase and paint plumes and bows with a soft gold color. Hand-paint a delicate design as shown in photograph of finished chair. Varnish back assembly completely. Cut cushion base and front legs, sand until smooth. Paint legs black and varnish. Glue Artfoam on top of cushion base and glue to seat. Cover with fabric to bottom edge of seat and trim edge with braid or small brass pins. Attach back section to seat and front leg assembly with dowel joint with 5 Minute Epoxy.

Queen Anne chair ready for staining and varnish. See page 258 for completed chair.

Queen Anne Chair
(circa 1740–1760)

The first Queen Anne chair seats were trapezoidal in shape, later becoming horseshoe-shaped. We have chosen to adapt the latter because it is a more interesting outline for our petit point designs. Because the seat frame is very thin vertically, we have provided a separate, solid inside base to give added support to the applied frame. The cabriole leg has a rounded knee, which follows the curve of the seat, with the lower shape terminating into a slipper foot. The parallel back posts are shaped to follow the form of the splat, which flows into the plain top crest rail. The upright splat is a typical, solid vase shape. Two lovely petit point designs, charted for this chair, were designed and worked by Susan Richardson. A graph for petit point is on page 258.

BILL OF MATERIALS

Basswood, stain, varnish, 220 sandpaper, 5 Minute Epoxy, Titebond Glue, Velverette glue, Artfoam, #38 silk gauze, DMC (mouline special) embroidery floss, size 25 needle.

148

WOOD SIZES	THICKNESS
#1 seat frame	1/4″ × 1 9/16″ × 1 5/8″
#2 seat inside base	1/8″ × 1 1/2″ × 1 1/2″
#3 back splat	1/8″ × 1 1/2″ × 11/16″
#4 top rail	1/8″ × 1 5/8″ × 11/32″
#5 back post and leg	3/16″ × 3″ × 1/8″ (cut 2)
#6 shoe	1/8″ × 1 1/8″ × 1/4″
#7 strip under splat	1/32″ × 11/16″ × 1/16″
#8 cabriole leg	1/2″ × 1/2″ × 1 1/4″ (cut 2)
#9 cushion base	1/8″ × 1 7/16″ × 1 7/16″

PROCEDURE

Trace pattern #1 onto 1/4″ wood. Place pattern #2 within the traced lines and draw around shape. Cut inside line and sand. Cut outside line, replace cutout shape; use this piece as a support jig while sanding outside frame. This will hold piece and keep it from breaking. Using pattern #2, trace and cut shape from wood. Sand and glue shaped frame to #2 seat on the outside, keeping bottoms flush. Cut #3 splat, and sand to shape by using a drum sanding attachment on the Dremel Moto-Tool. The shaded areas on the pattern sheet indicate the portion to be shaped to a concave curve, thus forming a cyma curve. Cut top rail, post, and leg pieces, sand until smooth. Assemble #3, #4, and #5 shapes, using epoxy glue. Cut shoe and glue #7 strip across the top. Attach seat assembly to back, using dowels inserted through shoe into seat. Dry thoroughly. Cabriole legs #43111 from X-ACTO,® HOUSE OF MINIATURES ® may be sanded and applied or the legs may be cut from directions on page 120. Legs are attached to seat bottom with dowel joints at X. Stain and varnish chair completely. Cushion base is cut from pattern #2, reducing outside shape by 1/32″ all around to allow for the upholstery. Work petit point design and cover cushion base, glue to the top of seat.

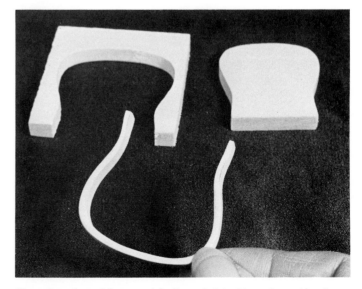

Horseshoe-shaped frame, with discarded inside and outside pieces.

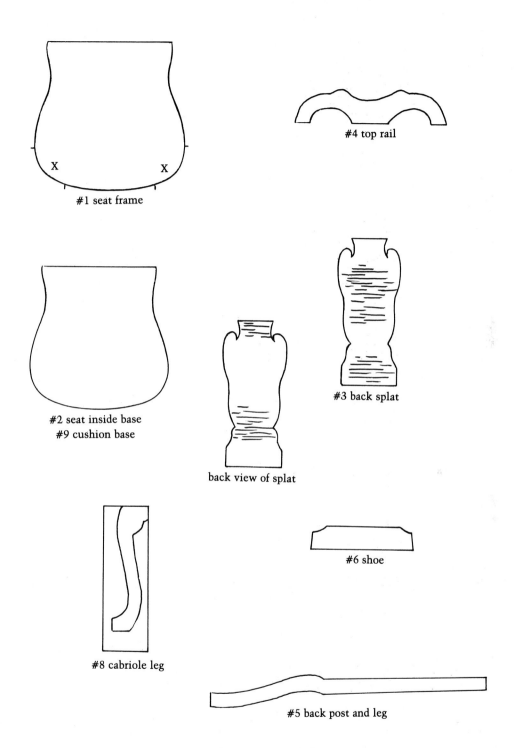

#4 top rail

#1 seat frame

#2 seat inside base
#9 cushion base

back view of splat

#3 back splat

#6 shoe

#8 cabriole leg

#5 back post and leg

Pattern for Queen Anne chair.

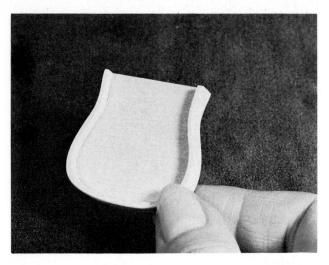

Attaching seat to shaped frame.

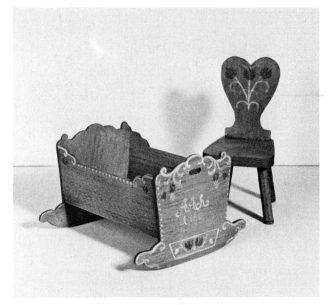

Austrian painted cradle and chair, circa 1840.

Shaping splat to form a cyma curve, using drum sanding attachment of Dremel Moto-Tool.

Austrian Cradle
(circa 1840)

A cradle painted a soft green color, decorated with rust and yellow. A rather crude but charming style of peasant furniture.

BILL OF MATERIALS

Basswood, white glue, 220 sandpaper, acrylic paint, commercial antique glaze.

WOOD SIZES	THICKNESS
#1 front and back	1/16″ × 2 5/16″ × 1 5/8″ (cut 2)
#2 side	1/16″ × 2 9/16″ × 15/16″ (cut 2)
#3 bottom	1/16″

PROCEDURE

Cut #1 and #2 from indicated wood sizes and sand until smooth. Glue sides to front and back pieces. Measure inside area and cut bottom piece to fit. Glue into place to form cradle bottom. Paint with acrylic paint and apply antique glaze. When dry, decorate with design on pattern sheet.

Austrian Chair
(circa 1840)

A painted chair that matches Austrian cradle. Again showing the simple lines of the peasant influence.

BILL OF MATERIALS

Basswood, white glue, 220 sandpaper, acrylic paint, commercial antique glaze.

WOOD SIZES	THICKNESS
#1 back and front	1/16″ × 1 3/8″ × 1 1/16″
#2 seat	3/16″ × 1 1/4″ × 1 3/16″
#3 leg	3/16″ dowel × 1″ (cut 4)

PROCEDURE

Cut #1 and #2 from indicated wood size. Miter bottom edge of #1 very slightly and glue to seat at X. Back will tilt back slightly. Cut four legs, angling top and bottom edges slightly, as indicated on pattern. This will splay the legs as shown in photograph. Paint and decorate.

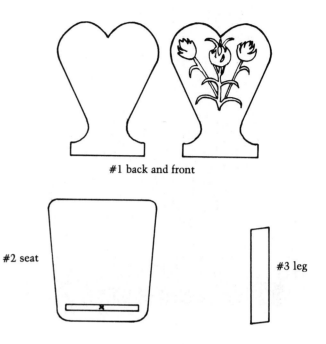

#1 back and front

#2 seat

#3 leg

Pattern for Austrian chair.

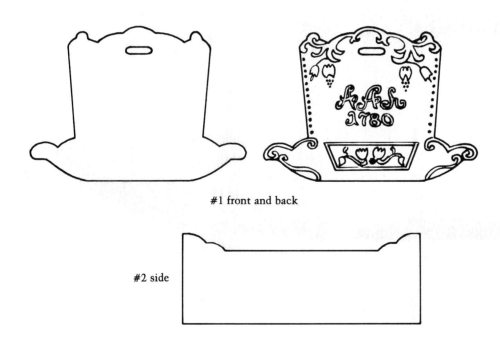

#1 front and back

#2 side

Pattern for Austrian cradle.

151

French Lyre Clock

French lyre clock, painted blue and trimmed with ormolu and gold braid.

Re-created from a late-eighteenth-century lyre-shaped clock, which was supposedly made for Queen Marie Antoinette, with a case of Sèvres porcelain, ormolu mounts, and a painted enamel dial. This clock represented a most magnificent timepiece of the period. We have made our lyre frame of wood and varnished the painted area to a high gloss to simulate the effect of Sèvres porcelain. The laurel wreath piece surrounding the face is a brass finding.

BILL OF MATERIALS

Basswood, blue paint, varnish, 5 Minute Epoxy, three brass wire lengths for strings, embossed gold paper trim, a 5/16" paper clockface, brass finding.

WOOD SIZES	THICKNESS
#1 lyre frame	1/16" from pattern
#2 face base	3/32" × 7/16" circle
#3 top oval base	1/4" × 1/4" oval
#4 center oval base	1/32" × 9/32" oval
#5 third oval base	1/16" × 3/8" oval
#6 bottom oval base	1/16" × 1/2" oval

PROCEDURE

Cut #1 lyre frame, sand, and drill three holes as indicated on pattern. Cut #2 face, using template circle size 7/16". Paint face white and glue paper clockface at center. Decorate outer edge of wood with leaves and flowers. Cut #3, #4, and #5 ovals from pattern. Sand #3 very carefully, scooping outside edges to form a waist. Glue base pieces together, cutting and attaching bottom base piece #6. Drill three holes in top of #2 to accommodate three brass wires. Epoxy brass wires into #2 holes and glue into place between sides of frame, lining up brass strings with top holes. Paint with blue paint and varnish. Decorate with a brass finding across top and around clockface. Trim edges of frame and bottom ovals with fine gold braid.

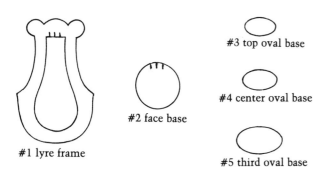

#1 lyre frame

#2 face base

#3 top oval base

#4 center oval base

#5 third oval base

#6 bottom oval base

Pattern for French lyre clock.

Cut #1 and #2 pieces, sand, beveling top edges of both shapes, and glue together. Paint black and marbleize, with gray paint, as described on page 121. Dry thoroughly and varnish. Cut the shank from the back of the clock button, using nippers, and epoxy into the brass base. When dry, attach to the back of the elephant, using a third hand to hold the work securely while drying. Epoxy elephant to base, again using the third hand to hold in place, and allow to dry overnight. Glue four brass feet in place under base.

Elephant clock, adapted from
a late-nineteenth-century timepiece.

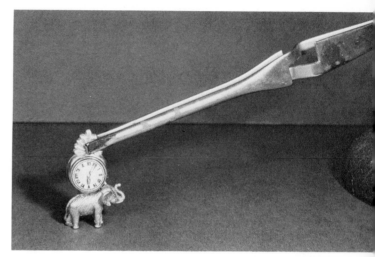

A third hand used to hold work in place after gluing with epoxy.

Elephant Clock

A whimsical clock, adapted from a timepiece of the late nineteenth century. Appropriate, perhaps, for use on a Victorian mantel. The elephant stands on a wooden base that has been painted to simulate a piece of marble.

BILL OF MATERIALS

Basswood, black and gray acrylic paint, a 000 paintbrush, varnish, brass elephant, brass finding to hold clockface, clock button, four brass feet, 5 Minute Epoxy.

WOOD SIZES	THICKNESS
#1 base	1/16″ × 13/16″ × 3/8″
#2 top	1/16″ × 5/8″ × 1/4″

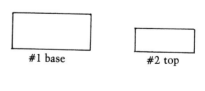

#1 base   #2 top

side view of base

Pattern for elephant clock.

Louis XVI gilded canapé. Embroidery design by Stephanie Matthews.

Louis XVI Gilded Canapé

A French style sofa, of the late eighteenth century, adapted from a design by George Jacob. This piece is made of basswood, painted, sanded, and gilded. The back is square with slightly curved open arms, decorated with embossed gold decorative strips; slender tapering turned legs; upholstered with a hand-embroidered pure silk fabric. Many of these elaborately styled sofas may be seen today at Malmaison and Versailles in France.

BILL OF MATERIALS

Basswood, acrylic paint, 5 Minute Epoxy, gold paint or gold leaf, two 1/8″ wooden balls, gold embossed paper trim, Velverette glue, fine silk fabric, DMC embroidery floss, Deft varnish, 220 sandpaper, Artfoam.

WOOD SIZES	THICKNESS
#1 seat	3/16″ × 4 1/2″ × 1 7/16″
#2 back	3/32″ × 4 1/2″ × 2″
#3 cushion base	3/16″ × 4 7/16″ × 1 11/32″
#4 arm and side	1/8″ × 2 1/8″ × 1 13/16″ (cut 2)
#5 leg	3/16″ dowel (turn 4)
#6 crossbar	1/16″ × 4 1/2″ × 3/32″

PROCEDURE

Cut #1 seat to proper size and sand until smooth. Miter back edge to an 80° angle as shown on pattern sheet. Cut #2 back and sand. Drill hole at each corner of #1 seat 3/32″ in from each edge. Cut #3 cushion base, sand, and set aside. Cut #4 arm sections. Sand both pieces together, clamping work to V-board. Glue seat to back; the mitered angle will give a slight angle to the back. Glue arm sections into place on outside of back and seat. Clamp securely while drying. Turn legs, using pattern shape as guide. Insert dowels in top of each leg and epoxy these dowels into already drilled holes on seat corners, forming dowel joints. Glue crossbar across back of sofa at X. Assembled piece may be stained or painted with bole paint and gold leafed.

Embroidery procedure: Place silk fabric in an embroidery hoop. Sketch design on a piece of transparent paper. Tape design to the back of the silk and, from the right side, trace the design very lightly with pencil onto the silk. Remove paper pattern from the back of silk and work the design with one thread of DMC cotton embroidery floss. The colors in this piece were worked in soft pink, rose, turquoise, and yellow. When working cushion design, the point where the long threads cross are tied or couched down at each junction with a cross-stitch. The basket, flowers, and bows are all stem stitch with the exception of a few French knots here and there.

Upholstery procedure: Cover seat top with Artfoam for padded surface. Cut a piece of cardboard, slightly smaller than back and cover one side with Artfoam. Cover both pieces with embroidered silk using Velverette glue. Dry thoroughly and then glue back piece and upholstered seat into place. Finish sofa by applying gold embossed paper that simulates beaded trim. Varnish with three coats of Deft.

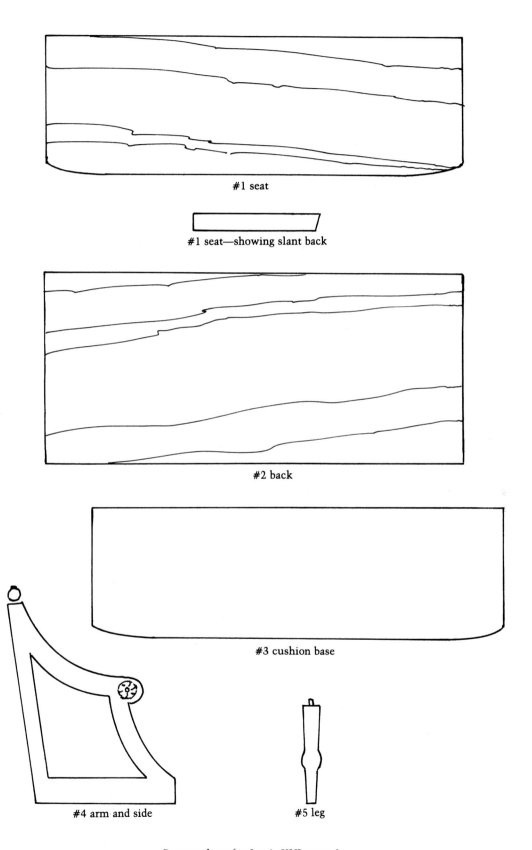

#1 seat

#1 seat—showing slant back

#2 back

#3 cushion base

#4 arm and side

#5 leg

Pattern sheet for Louis XVI canapé.

156

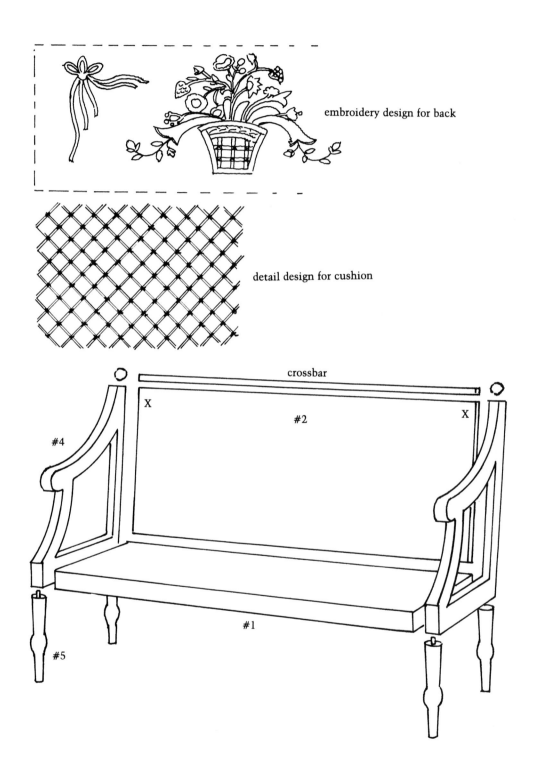

embroidery design for back

detail design for cushion

crossbar

X

#2

X

#4

#1

#5

Pattern sheet for Louis XVI canapé.

Two arm pieces, clamped to V-board and sanded together with dowel sanding stick.

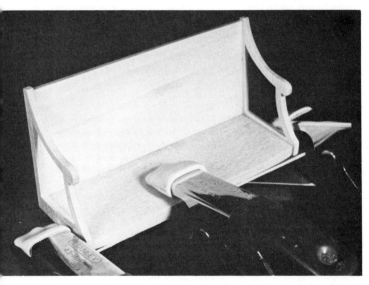

Spring clamps used to hold piece securely in place while drying.

Canapé after applying bole paint, ready for gilding.

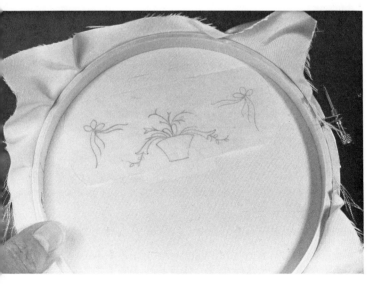

Silk fabric stretched over embroidery hoop with design sketched on thin transparent paper taped to back of work, ready to be traced onto the face of fabric by holding piece up to the light.

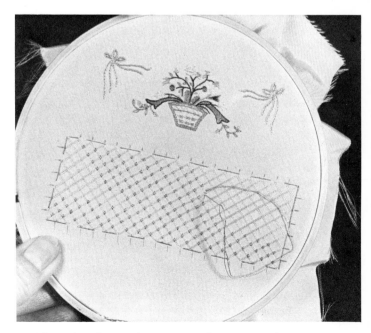

Couching threads at each junction with a cross-stitch.

Victorian desk, made by Karen Kuchinskas, hand-painted design by Linda Wexler.

Black Lacquer Desk

A Victorian period desk, painted with a black ground, lacquered to a high gloss and hand-painted with roses, vines, and gilt. The desk was made by Karen Kuchinskas, and the design was hand-painted by Linda Wexler.

BILL OF MATERIALS

Basswood, stain, black acrylic paint and assorted colors, gold paint, lacquer, 220 sandpaper, brass pins, emery board, files, 5 Minute Epoxy, Titebond Glue.

WOOD SIZES	THICKNESS
#1 desk bottom	3/32″ × 1″ × 2 5/16″
#2 side	3/32″ × 1 1/16″ × 7/16″ (cut 2)
#3 back	3/32″ × 2″ × 7/16″
#4 drawer guide	3/16″ × 1 3/16″ × 7/16″ (cut 2)
#5 crossbar	3/32″ × 1/16″ × 1 3/4″
#6 writing surface	1/16″ × 2″ × 1 3/8″
#7 top side	1/16″ × 1 1/4″ × 11/16″ (cut 2)
#8 top back	1/16″ × 2 1/4″ × 11/16″
#9 top shelf	1/16″ × 2 1/14″ × 5/8″
#10 undershelf panel	1/16″ × 2 1/4″ × 1/4″
#11 drawer front	1/16″ × 1 7/8″ × 3/8″
#12 drawer back and front	1/16″ × 1 9/16″ × 5/16″ (cut 2)
#13 drawer side	1/16″ × 1 3/16″ × 5/16″ (cut 2)
#14 drawer bottom	1/16″ × 1 9/16″ × 1 1/16″
#15 leg	1/8″ × 1/8″ × 2 3/8″ (cut 4)

PROCEDURE

Cut #1, #2, and #3 and glue sides and back on top of #1, 1/32″ from edge. The corner notches will be formed at the four corners for fitting the legs. Cut and glue two drawer guides #4 parallel to #2 sides. Glue #5 crossbar in place across top front, between guides, to form an opening for the drawer. Cut #6 writing surface and glue to top of assembled bottom section, flush with the back. The sides and front will overhang the bottom. Cut and glue two sides #7 to outside edges of the top back #8. Attach to top of writing surface with Titebond Glue. Glue shelf and undershelf sections into place. Solid wood blocks may be attached behind this section on both sides to indicate drawers as shown on pattern sheet at A. Cut and glue two fake drawer fronts 1/32″ × 3/8″ × 5/32″ to front of #10. Assemble drawer sections as indicated on pattern sheet to fit into the opening of your desk. Legs may be lathe-turned or shaped by hand, using an emery board and small files. Epoxy legs into four notched corners. Stain the inside areas, including the writing surface. All other areas are painted with black paint. Hand-paint design and lacquer entire piece.

Construction of bottom, sides, side block guides, and top crossbar, with desk surface piece ready for gluing.

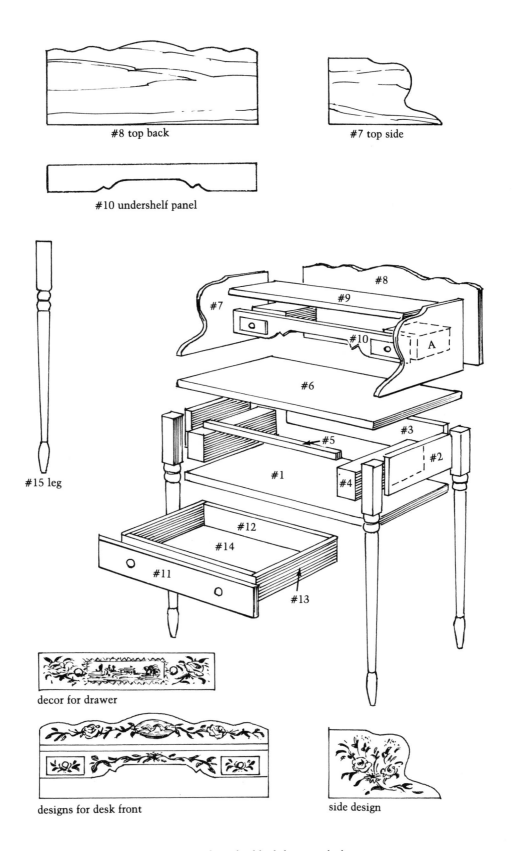

#8 top back

#7 top side

#10 undershelf panel

#15 leg

#7

#8

#9

#10

A

#6

#5

#3

#2

#4

#1

#12

#14

#11

#13

decor for drawer

designs for desk front

side design

Pattern sheet for black lacquer desk.

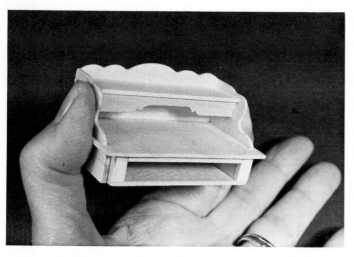

Assembled desk top with notches formed at corners for legs.

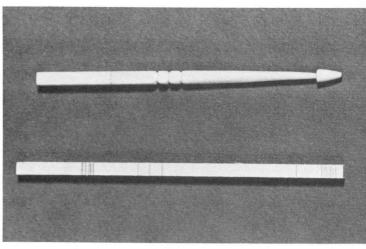

Marked leg piece ready for turning, shown at top after turning either by hand or by lathe.

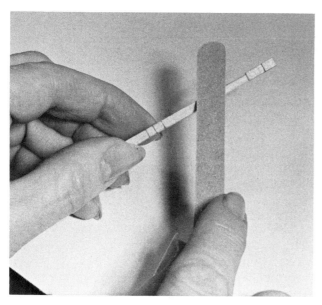

Leg piece being shaped by hand with an emery board.

Fitting legs into corner slots.

Ladies' desk, circa 1770. Adapted from an antique desk by Rose Barell.

WOOD SIZES	THICKNESS
#1 top	1/16″ × 1 13/16″ × 15/16″
#2 back	1/16″ × 1 11/16″ × 1″
#3 side	1/16″ × 1 11/16″ × 1″ (cut 2)
#4 inside curved strip	1/16″ × 1 3/4″ × 1″ (cut 2)
#5 inside curved panel	1/16″ × 1 5/16″ × 7/8″ (cut 2)
#6 writing surface	1/16″ × 1 3/4″ × 1 15/16″ (cut 2)
#7 back apron	3/32″ × 1 5/8″ × 3/8″
#7a side apron	3/32″ × 1 1/2″ × 3/8″ (cut 2)
#8 drawer bottom	1/16″ Cut to fit your desk opening.
#9 drawer front	3/32″ Cut to fit your desk opening.
#9a drawer side and back	1/16″ Cut to fit your desk opening.
#10 roll top	
#10a strip	1/16″ × 1/16″ × 1 11/16″
#10b tambour strip	3/64″ half-rounds
#11 leg	1/8″ × 1/8″ × 2 1/2″ (cut 4)
Interior Section:	
A. inside divider	1/32″ × 1/2″ × 9/16″ (cut 3)
B. inside shelf	1/32″ × 1/2″ × 1 9/16″
C. inside back	1/8″ × 7/8″ × 1 9/16″

PROCEDURE

Trace pattern pieces onto indicated wood sizes. Using a jewelers' saw or jigsaw, cut out and sand shapes until smooth. Pieces may be stained now or after piece is assembled. Glue #4 inside curve to #3 sides, keeping top edges flush. Glue these assembled side pieces to outside edges of back #2 at X. We have used a magnetic jig for holding wood firmly in place after gluing. The next step is to form the rolltop section. Cut a piece of the mending fabric the width of your piece from side to side and approximately 1 1/2″ deep. Glue one strip of #10a on the edge of one end of the fabric. Proceed gluing half-rounds #10b to fill the fabric piece. Stain both sides of the roll top, dry thoroughly, and apply two light coats of Deft varnish on wood-strip side only. When dry, drill two holes in #10a section as indicated on pattern sheet. Roll top must now be placed under #4 inside curve, and #5 panel glued into place matching X at back of desk. Do not fit this too closely against roll top; it must move freely in the track. To assemble bottom section of the desk, glue two sides and back apron shapes to the two surface pieces #6, recessing the aprons 1/32″ from edges as indicated in photograph. Assemble the drawer parts #8, #9, and #9a, sanding and fitting to allow the drawer to slide in and out with ease. Stain and dry thoroughly. Attach to upper section of desk, keeping back flush. Drill hole for knob in center of drawer front. Taper legs #11 by pulling leg along sandpaper to form a gradual taper, to a bottom measurement of 1/16″ × 1/16″. Stain leg

Ladies' Desk
(bureau à cylindre)
(circa 1770)

A Hepplewhite period desk, with a tambour cylinder roll top that slides into the body via a track or groove on each side. The interior is fitted with an arrangement of three partitions resting on a narrow shelf. A particularly nice piece for use in a room setting or house where the wall space is limited to a narrow piece of furniture. The writing surface may be covered with a small patterned or marbleized paper or very thin leather.

BILL OF MATERIALS

Basswood, 220 sandpaper, 5 Minute Epoxy, white glue, stain, Deft varnish, marbleized paper or thin leather, iron-on mending fabric, two small brass pins, one brass knob for drawer.

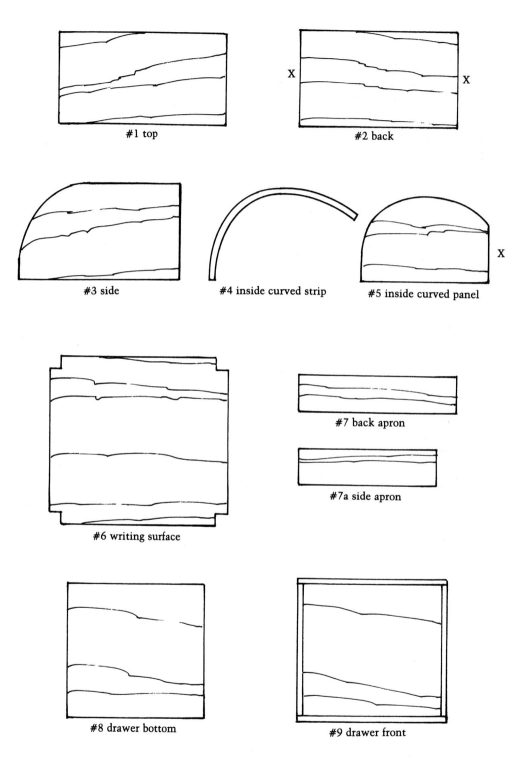

#1 top

#2 back

#3 side

#4 inside curved strip

#5 inside curved panel

#6 writing surface

#7 back apron

#7a side apron

#8 drawer bottom

#9 drawer front

Pattern for ladies' desk.

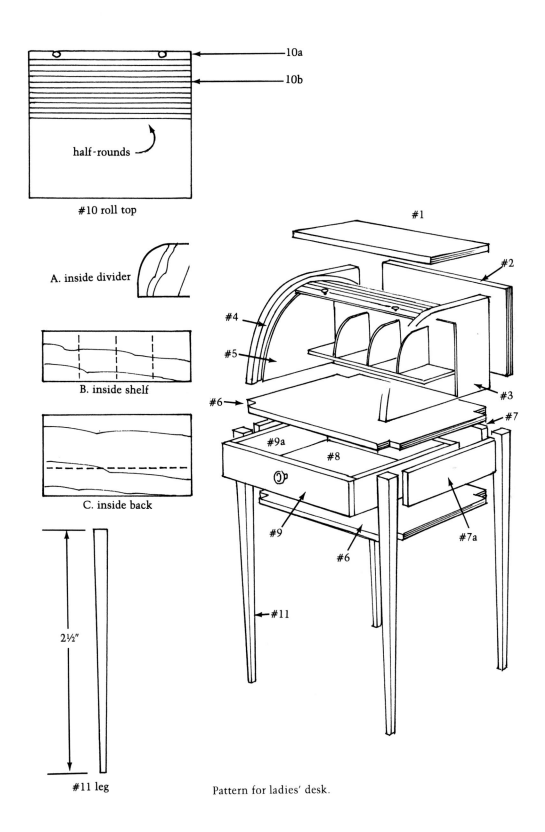

10a

10b

half-rounds

#10 roll top

A. inside divider

B. inside shelf

C. inside back

2½"

#11 leg

#1

#2

#4

#5

#3

#6

#7

#9a

#8

#9

#7a

#6

#11

Pattern for ladies' desk.

Magnetic jig holding assembled work after gluing.

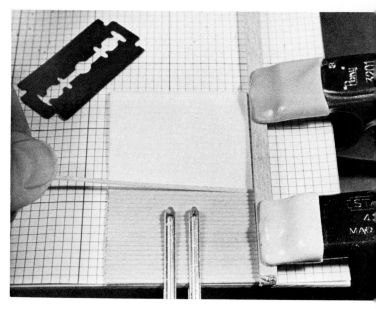

Measuring half-rounds, to be superimposed on fabric for roll top.

Roll top in closed position, before attaching top.

Assembled bottom section of desk, with drawer partially open.

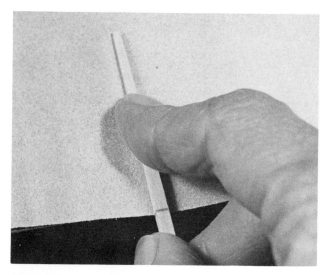

To taper legs, press down on 220 sandpaper, pulling piece toward you. Shape four sides, tapering bottom to 1/16" × 1/16".

shapes, dry completely, and epoxy into four corner slots. Glue #1 top in place, flush with back of desk. Cut paper or leather to proper size to fit writing surface and glue into place. Assemble interior sections, A, B, and C, by matching component parts to dotted line areas, as shown on pattern sheet. Sand to fit into your desk, making sure the sliding roll top clears the interior fittings when rolled down to the closed position. Stain any parts that were not previously treated and varnish completed desk to a soft patina. Attach brass pull and knobs with 5 Minute Epoxy.

Eighteenth-century harp by Eugene Kupjack.

Eighteenth-Century Harp

Reducing a 5 1/2-foot harp to a 5 1/2-inch harp is no small matter. The same harmonious shape is purely decorative, allowing the "harmonic curve" to give even tension to the strings, which are stretched over an open triangular frame consisting of three main parts, the column, the string arm, and the body. The full-size eighteenth-century harp was played by plucking the strings with the fingers, depressing the pedals to variable degrees, and altering the pitch by tone or semitone.

The harp became popular in Ireland during the eleventh century, with the earliest example of a six-stringed instrument found in Suffolk in the seventh century.

The harp was most often elaborately decorated with carving and scrolls, hand-painted, gilded, and further ornamented with figures, cupids, and other popular motifs, including a crown top.

BILL OF MATERIALS

Basswood, sheet brass .010, 51-gauge brass rod, nylon thread, brass pins, gold leaf, 5 Minute Epoxy, stain, white glue, varnish, and paint.

WOOD SIZES	THICKNESS
#1 body of harp	1/32″ × 3 11/16″ × 1 5/8″
#2 soundboard	3/32″ × 3 11/16″ × 7/8″
#3 string arm	1/4″ × 2 3/8″ × 1″
#4 column	3/8″ dowel × 5″
#5 base one	1/4″ × 1 1/4″ × 1 3/16″
#6 base two	3/32″ × 1 5/16″ × 1 1/4″
#7 notched strip for strings	1/32″ × 3 11/16″ × 1/8″
#8 underpiece	1/32″ × 3 11/16″ × 1/16″
#9 foot	3/16″ × 1/4″ × 11/16″ (cut 4)

PROCEDURE

Cut #1 and #2. Sand until smooth. Soak #1 in hot water for a quarter hour to soften wood for bending. Bend around #2 to form a half-cone shape. Epoxy in place, using a jig setup as a support to hold work while drying for eight hours. Cut #3 and sand a groove at wide end as shown on pattern sheet (top view) to prepare end for fitting with round column top. Turn column #4 to shape. Glue #5 on top of #6. Cut #7 and underpiece #8 and glue together, keeping one side flush, leaving a 1/16″ overhang. With a very fine saw blade, cut thirty-one notches, one halfway across #7 on the overhang side. These notches will be used to hold knotted strings in place on the soundboard. Cut four feet, carving each foot into a claw shape. Stain #3, #5, and #2. Paint #6 and #1 with black paint. Gold leaf or paint #4, the four feet, and any ornamentation that you choose for the column top. Cut brass from pattern #3.

To assemble: Epoxy brass shape to string arm #3. Drill thirty-one holes along top, 1/16″ from the edge, and another thirty-one holes along the bottom edge of the arm for the tuning pins. Epoxy the notched strip to #2 in the center. Paint a scroll or flower design along each side of the strip. Epoxy column #4 to base at the narrow end of the base, using a dowel joint to secure connection. Epoxy body of the harp to wide end of base unit. Epoxy string arm between these two units and set aside to dry. Drill holes for three pedals that have been flattened at one end about 1/4″ to shape. Insert pedals into holes using epoxy glue. Glue feet on bottom of base. Attach any other decorative piece with epoxy glue. Varnish to a soft patina.

Stringing the harp: Tie a knot in the end of thread, dip end into white glue, and tuck the knot into notch with knot fitting into space underneath. Tweezers are handy for this procedure. Continue this step until thirty-one strings are securely glued into place, letting the free ends hang down out of the way. When completely dry, bring each thread up, one at a time, and thread through top hole on string arm. Dip brass pin

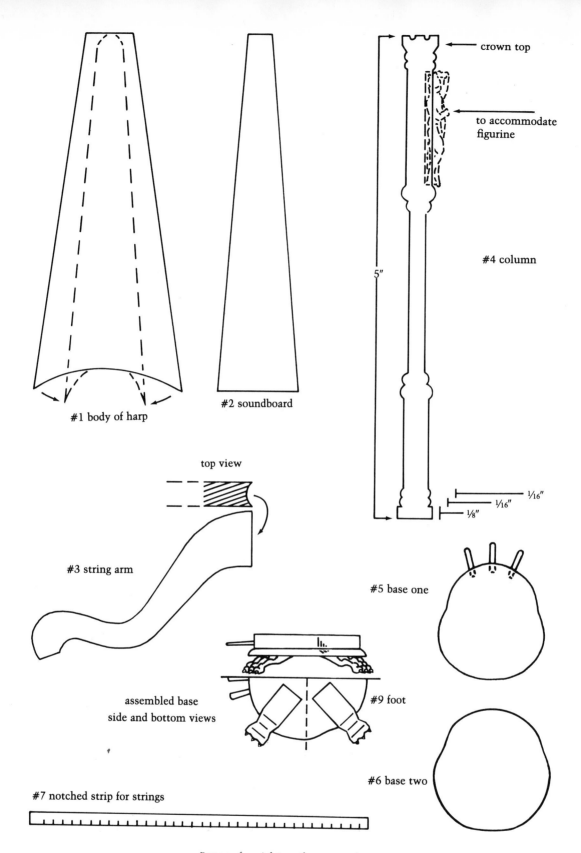

crown top

to accommodate figurine

#4 column

5"

1/16"

1/16"

1/8"

top view

#3 string arm

#5 base one

assembled base
side and bottom views

#9 foot

#1 body of harp

#2 soundboard

#6 base two

#7 notched strip for strings

Pattern for eighteenth-century harp.

into epoxy and put through hole with thread and pull thread tightly from the back. Do not push pin completely into hole; allow pin to protrude about 3/32″. Cut off pin and thread in the back. Epoxy tuning pins into holes at the bottom of arm, extending the same distance as top row of pins. Cut off the heads of pins on the bottom row only on the front side. Paint every fourth string red, or use a red felt-tipped pen.

An eighteenth-century needlework frame, with baskets for holding yarn.

Standing Needlework Frame

An eighteenth-century turned-base embroidery frame, used for stretching canvas or fabric. Tape was mounted around the edges of the canvas or fabric, which in turn was laced to the sides of the frame. The real frame was adjustable. Our adaptation of this frame, which stands only 3″ high, is too delicate to attempt such a feat. We have, however, made the tiny baskets for holding the yarn.

BILL OF MATERIALS

Mahogany wood, stain, varnish, 220 sandpaper, Elmer's white glue, 5 Minute Epoxy, brass pins, #24 mono canvas, round wooden toothpicks, two 1/8″ round wooden beads.

WOOD SIZES	THICKNESS
#1 post top (square stock)	3/16″ × 3/16″ × 7/8″ (turn 2)
#2 post bottom	3/16″ dowel × 1 1/4″ (turn 2)
#3 foot stand	1/8″ × 1 5/8″ × 3/8″ (cut 2)
#4 stretcher	3/16″ dowel × 2 1/8″
#5 frame top and bottom	1/16″ dowel × 1 7/8″ (cut 2)
#6 frame side	1/16″ dowel × 1 1/8″ (cut 2)
#7 corner block	3/16″ × 3/16″ × 1/4″ (cut 4)

PROCEDURE

Basket assembly: Wrap a piece of #24 canvas that has been dipped in warm water tightly around a 3/8″ bead, twisting the loose end as shown in photograph. Paint with white glue to stiffen, and allow to dry. Remove bead from canvas and cut excess from loose end to form a small round basket. Cut a small hole in the rounded bottom to fit over post #2. Trim top edge of basket with one thread from the canvas.

Frame assembly: The vertical posts must be turned in two pieces to be able to attach the baskets in the center of the post. Turn the top and bottom separately, the top from square stock, the bottom from a round dowel. Insert dowel on #2 into already drilled hole on top of foot stand, place basket with small hole at the bottom over top of post, and slide down to within 3/4″ of the post bottom. Glue into place. Attach top #1 with a dowel joint, and secure with epoxy. Attach stretcher between the two vertical posts with a dowel joint. Construct frame from illustration on pattern sheet. Drill a hole at each side at O for brass pin to hold wooden bead. The frame is attached to the base by the pin and bead inserted into slot on top of the post. Stain and varnish complete frame to finish.

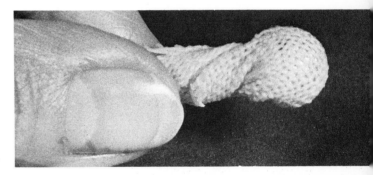

Wrapping wet canvas around a bead to form rounded shape for small basket.

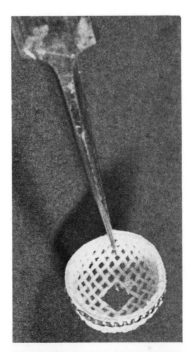

Finished basket, showing cutout at bottom.

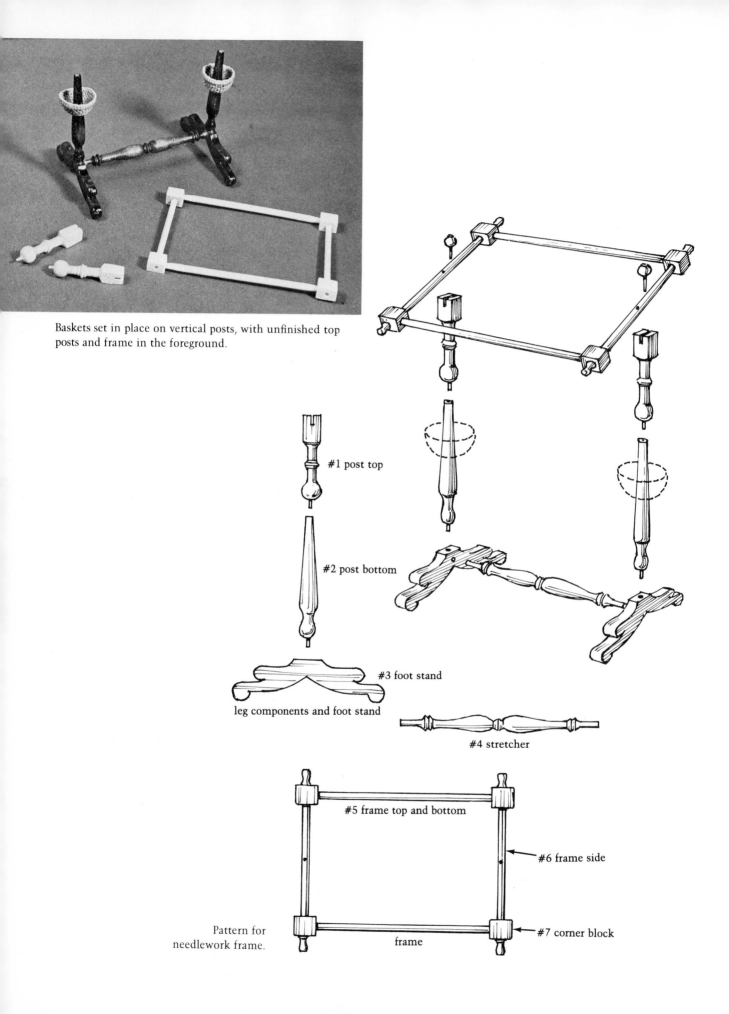

Baskets set in place on vertical posts, with unfinished top posts and frame in the foreground.

#1 post top

#2 post bottom

#3 foot stand

leg components and foot stand

#4 stretcher

#5 frame top and bottom

#6 frame side

#7 corner block

Pattern for needlework frame.

frame

Mahogany Chippendale looking glass, circa 1750–1780.

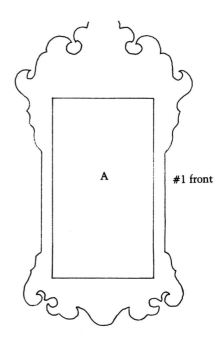

Pattern for Chippendale looking glass.

Chippendale Looking Glass
(circa 1750–1780)

This mahogany mirror, adapted from a style made in New England, has a scroll-shaped frame with a gilded-leaf inner molding.

BILL OF MATERIALS

Mahogany wood, stain, 220 sandpaper, 1/32″ thin mirror, gold leaf or gold paint, Titebond Glue.

WOOD SIZES	THICKNESS
#1 frame	3/32″
#2 inside molding, top and bottom	1/32″ × 1/32″ × 1 1/16″ (cut 2)
#3 inside molding side	1/32″ × 1/32″ × 1 7/8″ (cut 2)

PROCEDURE

Trace pattern for frame onto wood. Drill hole at center and insert blade of jewelers saw through hole and cut out inside portion at A. Sand inside edges until smooth. Cut outside shape of frame and sand, beveling edges slightly. Stain and varnish. It is easier to gold leaf

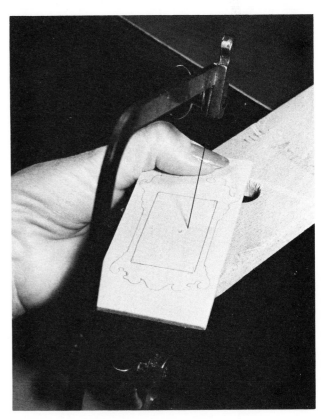

Cutting out center portion of looking glass, resting on V-board, using a jewelers' saw.

or paint entire molding strip and cut to size after allowing it to dry completely. Miter each corner and glue into place, keeping molding flush with frame top. The molding forms a lip on the back of frame for holding the mirror.

Sanded looking glass ready for staining.

Eighteenth-century japanned looking glass with black ground and gilt painting.

Japanned Looking Glass

The looking glass with figures, birds, pagodas, and trees painted with gold paint on a black ground appeared in many great homes in the eighteenth century. The designs were copied from oriental lacquerwork, and the ornamental painting was raised with a ground of gesso or whiting and finished with gold leaf. Our mirror, an adaptation of the eighteenth-century style, is painted black with the design painted in thick gold paint and varnished to a soft patina.

BILL OF MATERIALS

Basswood, 220 sandpaper, Titebond Glue, black acrylic paint, varnish, gold leaf or gold paint, 1/32″ thin mirror.

WOOD SIZES	THICKNESS
#1 outer frame	1/16″ × 3 1/2″ × 1 1/2″
#2 overlay frame	1/16″ × 2 7/8″ × 1 1/2″

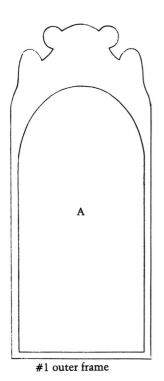

#1 outer frame

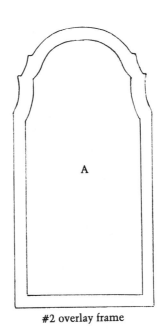

#2 overlay frame

Pattern for eighteenth-century looking glass.

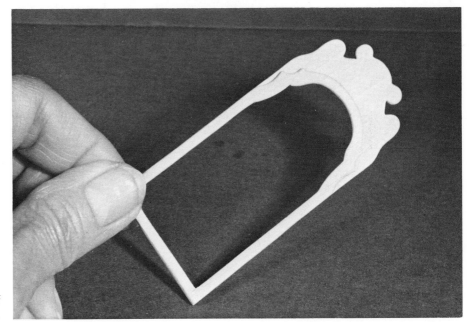

Gluing overlay frame on top of
outer frame.

PROCEDURE

Cut inside area of #1 and #2 at A, using same procedure as for Chippendale looking glass. Cut outside edges, beveling them slightly. Glue #2 on top of #1, keeping bottom edges flush. Paint and varnish entire piece and decorate. Have thin mirror cut to shape to fit into back opening and epoxy into place.

A lampshade crowns figurine base. (Lamp stands 2″ tall.)

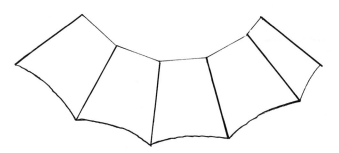

Pattern for lampshade.

Lampshade

To be used on a preassembled lamp base made with findings, as shown in photograph.

BILL OF MATERIALS

White paper of medium weight, Velverette glue, 5 Minute Epoxy, silk fabric, fine braid for trimming shade.

PROCEDURE

Cut shade from pattern, using white paper. Mark four vertical lines, using a hard pencil. Bend shade slightly on the four ruled lines using a 6″ ruler as a guide. With Velverette, glue very sparingly the silk fabric to paper shade, one panel at a time. Cut away excess fabric to shape of paper. Secure all edges with diluted glue to keep from raveling. Bend panels again to shape. Glue back seam. Cut a piece of paper to fit across the top of opening and glue fabric onto this piece. Attach to top of shade with white glue and trim completed shade with braid. Attach to lamp base with long brass pin inserted in hole at top of shade and epoxy to back of figure on base.

Gluing fabric to shade one panel at a time.

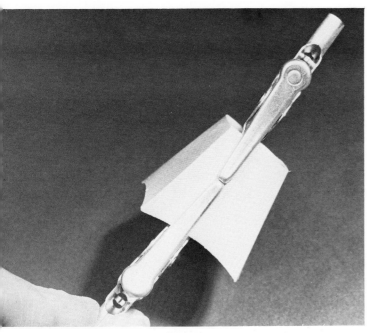

Back seam held in place by alligator clamps after gluing.

Shade with brass pin in place through top hole, ready for assembling. The two brass findings and brass pin are available from Eastern Findings (round piece #7075, flower tree #829).

A wheel barometer.

Barometer

The barometer is an instrument for measuring the weight or pressure of the atmosphere. Barometers were first introduced in English retail shops in the 1670s, and have become a popular weatherglass guide about the weather ever since. The dial of this wheel barometer is framed behind a convex glass, with a thermometer placed on the upper portion of the frame.

BILL OF MATERIALS

Basswood, stain, varnish, brass wire, white glue, 5 Minute Epoxy, 1/2″ round dowel, a 22mm watch glass.

WOOD SIZES	THICKNESS
#1 base	1/16″ × 1 3/32″ × 3 5/16″
#2 pediment	1/16″ × 7/16″ × 1/8″ (cut 2)
#3 pediment	1/32″ × 5/16″ × 3/32″ (cut 2)
#4 crossbar	1/32″ × 9/16″ × 1/16″
#5 overlay circle	1/16″ × 1 1/16″ circle
#6 small overlay circle	1/16″ × 7/16″ circle

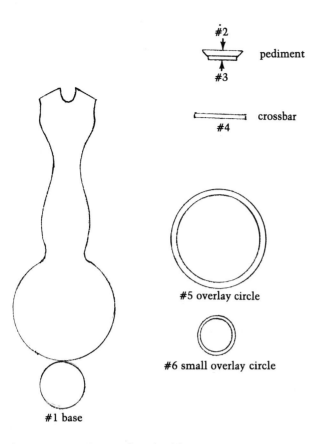

pediment #2

#3

crossbar #4

#5 overlay circle

#6 small overlay circle

#1 base

Pattern for wheel barometer.

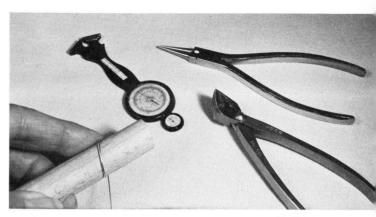

Forming brass wire around 1/2" wooden dowel.

PROCEDURE

Cut and sand all wood pieces. Glue pediment pieces in place at top of barometer, keeping pieces flush with the back. Glue #5 and #6 circles as shown in photograph. Glue #4 crossbar across top 1/4" below pediment. Stain and varnish barometer completely. Paint a dial and thermometer on a piece of white paper and glue into place. Glue a 22mm watch glass over dial. Bend wire around a 1/2" wooden dowel to form shape to fit glass and glue over glass, forming a bezel around the glass. Snip a white nylon bristle from a brush and glue on top of thermometer strip to simulate glass tube. Using a jig setup, bend a piece of thin wire, pressing it down firmly onto the wire jig, with a piece of wood that has been notched. This will form a shape to hold down the nylon bristle.

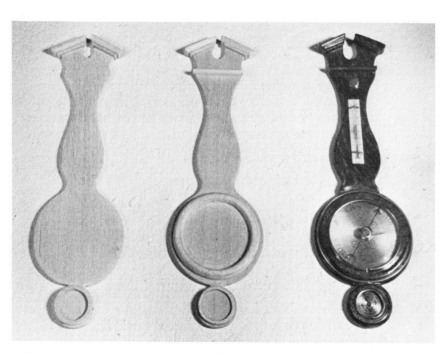

Pediment and circles attached to base.

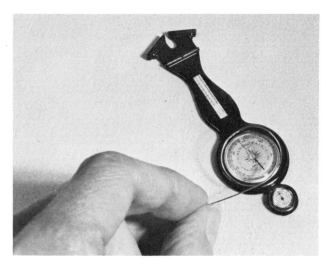

Measuring brass wire shape around convex glass.

Measuring piece of nylon bristle, taken from a brush, to simulate glass thermometer.

Jig setup for shaping wire to fit over thermometer.

Library steps.

Library Steps

A four-step, cherry wood library stair, for use in a miniature house as a functional piece of furniture in a den or library.

BILL OF MATERIALS

Cherry wood, stain, varnish, 3/16" wooden ball, 5 Minute Epoxy, Titebond Glue, 220 sandpaper.

WOOD SIZES	THICKNESS
#1 steps A and B	1/16" from pattern
	3/32" from pattern
#2 steps A and B	1/16" from pattern
	3/32" from pattern
#3 steps A and B	1/16" from pattern
	3/32" from pattern
#4 steps A and B	1/16" from pattern
	3/32" from pattern
#5 post	1/8" dowel × 6 3/8"
#6 brace (square stock)	3/16" × 3/16" × 3/4" (turn 8)

PROCEDURE

Cut and sand #1, #2, #3, and #4. Glue B sections to the bottom of A sections, keeping scoop-out at narrow ends even. Epoxy braces #6 into notches on underside of each step. Assemble all steps, one above the other, keeping back edges flush. Attach bottom of braces to each step below. Epoxy post into recess curves on each step. Epoxy bead at post top. Stain and varnish entire piece.

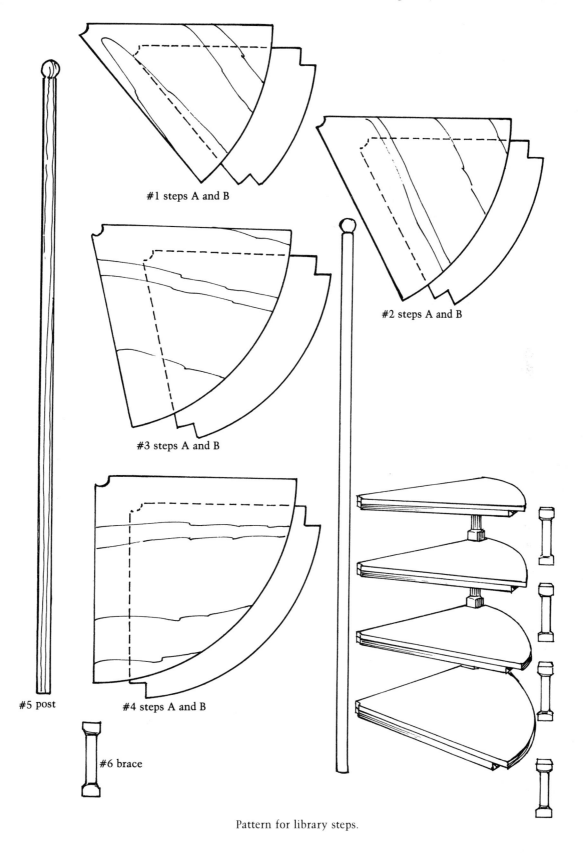

#1 steps A and B

#2 steps A and B

#3 steps A and B

#5 post

#4 steps A and B

#6 brace

Pattern for library steps.

Pole fire screen. The base and pole are from Andrews Miniatures. The top panel is made from directions. The William and Mary pastoral scene in petit point was designed and stitched by Susan Richardson.

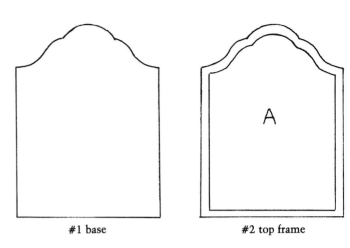

#1 base   #2 top frame

Pattern sheet for pole screen frame.

PROCEDURE

Cut #1 base from pattern, sand and stain back and sides only. Varnish until smooth. Cut #2 frame on inside line. Sand very carefully, then cut outside edge, supporting shape while cutting or the wood will split. Sand, stain, and varnish. Using Velverette, glue finished petit point onto unfinished side of #1 to within 1/16" from the edge. Dry thoroughly. Glue frame #2 over petit point, making sure the edges are flush and even. Attach to pole with epoxy glue.

Pole Fire Screen

A useful and decorative item, used as a shield from the heat of a fireplace. The base of this screen is from Andrews Miniatures (item #214), with a top frame of our own design. The William and Mary pastoral scene in petit point is by Susan Richardson. A graph for petit point is on page 213.

BILL OF MATERIALS

Basswood, stain, Deft varnish, 5 Minute Epoxy, Velverette glue, a 1/8" wooden bead.

WOOD SIZES	THICKNESS
#1 base	1/16" × 1 1/2" × 2"
#2 top frame	1/16" × 1 1/2" × 2"

Gluing frame over petit point panel.

178

Round piano stool with silk upholstery.

Round Piano Stool

Ornamental stools were used for seating at a dressing table or as a window seat. This small round stool with silk upholstery is a piano stool, supported by curved legs and a circle stretcher.

BILL OF MATERIALS

Basswood, 15/16" brass ring, four 1/8" wooden balls, stain, varnish, 5 Minute Epoxy, Velverette glue, fabric, Artfoam, embossed gold paper strip or braid, circle template.

WOOD SIZES	THICKNESS
#1 top, bottom, and seat	1/16" × 1 1/8" circle (cut 3)
#2 center core	3/32" × 1 1/16" circle
#3 leg	1/8" × 1/4" × 1 1/16" (cut 4)

PROCEDURE

Cut three circles from pattern #1 or by using a template with circle size 1 1/8". Sand until smooth, put circle aside for covered top. Cut circle #2. After sanding, glue three circles together, placing #2 in the center. Cut legs from pattern, drill a hole in the top of each leg, and insert a dowel into each hole. Drill corresponding holes into stool bottom at X. Epoxy legs in place, along with a 15/16" brass ring. Apply four wooden balls at bottom of legs. Stain and varnish stool. Glue Artfoam on top of remaining circle, cover with fabric, and attach to top of stool. Trim edge with gold paper trim.

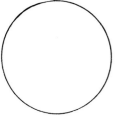

#1 top, bottom, and seat

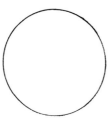

#2 center core

#3 leg

Pattern for round stool.

Susan Richardson designed this fashionable balloon motif in fine petit point for the panel of the eighteenth-century cheval fire screen.

Cheval Fire Screen

An adjustable screen, mounted on a supporting frame suspended between two vertical turned columns, used for protection from the heat of a fire. The petit point panel is vertically adjustable for the convenience of swinging the frame to a suitable angle. Needlework is used for the panel covering. A graph for petit point is on page 216.

BILL OF MATERIALS

Cherry wood, stain, varnish, 220 sandpaper, brass pins, 1/8" double bead molding, Velverette glue, 5 Minute Epoxy.

WOOD SIZES	THICKNESS
#1 vertical post	3/16" × 3/16" × 3 1/8" (cut 2)
#2 base foot	1/8" × 1 5/16" × 1/2" (cut 2)
#3 panel	1/16" × 2 3/8" × 1 7/8"
#4 crossbar	3/32" × 1 15/16" × 3/32" (cut 2)

PROCEDURE

Turn posts #1 and glue to base piece #2 using a dowel joint. Cut crossbars and drill small holes at center for brass pin inserts. Attach to posts at top and bottom, spacing carefully to allow ample space for panel to swing freely. Cut #3 panel. Stain and varnish all parts except panel front. Stain and varnish double bead molding, to be used later for framing petit point. After working the canvas, glue to nonstained side of the panel with Velverette glue. Frame with double bead molding, mitering the four corners. Attach panel to frame by inserting brass pins through top and bottom crossbars into panel.

#4 crossbar

#1 vertical post

#2 base foot

#3 panel

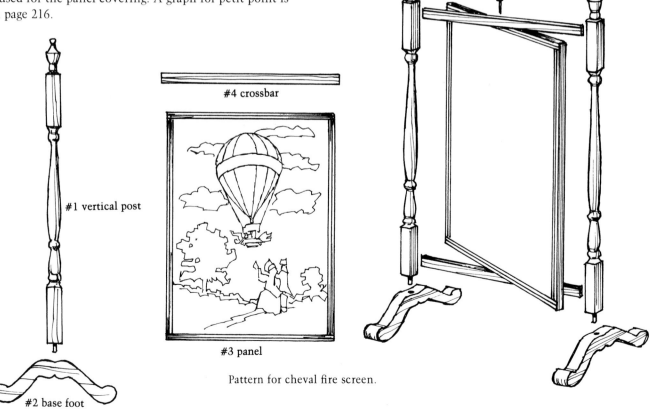

Pattern for cheval fire screen.

A Louis XV occasional table, from one made by Eugene Kupjack.

Louis XV Table

An occasional table of the Louis XV period, identified by free lines and curves, elegant style, and the use of metal ormolu mounts. A rectangular top is supported by four slender cabriole legs with typical ornate decoration. The miniature version of this table is adapted from one made by Eugene Kupjack. The finish is a very light stain and the top is painted to simulate inlay. The edge is trimmed with a gold embossed paper.

BILL OF MATERIALS

Basswood, stain, 220 sandpaper, varnish, 5 Minute Epoxy, dark brown paint, Titebond Glue, gold or brass jewelry findings for ormolu trim, gold embossed paper strip.

WOOD SIZES	THICKNESS
#1 top	1/16" × 1 7/16" × 1"
#2 front and back apron	1/16" × 3/4" × 5/16" (cut 2)
#3 side apron	1/16" × 7/16" × 5/16" (cut 2)
#4 leg (square stock)	1/4" × 1/4" × 2 1/8" (cut 4)
#5 base	3/16" × 1 1/8" × 11/16"

PROCEDURE

Cut #2, #3, and #5. Glue front and back apron to base piece. Glue side aprons to sides of base, flush at the top, forming notches at corners for legs. Cut and glue top #1 to assembled base. Cut four cabriole legs, as illustrated on page 120. Epoxy legs into corner notches. Stain entire piece. Dry thoroughly. Paint a 1/8" border around the top edge with dark brown paint and paint dark brown lines on front and side aprons to simulate a grained wood. Varnish to a soft patina. Trim the top edge with embossed gold paper trim, and epoxy gold jewelry findings at top and bottom of legs.

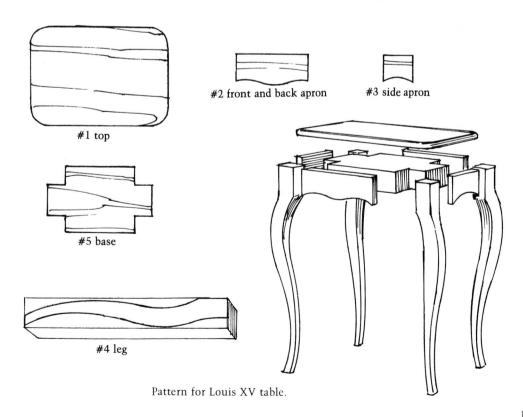

#1 top

#2 front and back apron

#3 side apron

#5 base

#4 leg

Pattern for Louis XV table.

Early-eighteenth-century William and Mary stool with rampant lion petit point design.

William and Mary Stool

An eighteenth-century stool, very often used with a well-designed William and Mary lowboy as a dressing table ensemble, with a handsome mirror of the same period. The stool was also used as an occasional piece in a sitting room. A graph for petit point is on page 222.

BILL OF MATERIALS

Basswood, stain, varnish, Titebond Glue, 5 Minute Epoxy, Artfoam, #38 silk gauze for petit point.

WOOD SIZES	THICKNESS
#1 front and back rail	1/8″ × 1 5/8″ × 3/16″ (cut 2)
#2 side rail	1/8″ × 15/16″ × 3/16″ (cut 2)
#3 corner post	1/8″ × 1/8″ × 3/16″ (cut 4)
#4 stool top	1/32″ × 1 7/8″ × 1 3/16″
#5 quarter-round	3/64″ × 1 7/8″ (cut 2)
	3/64″ × 1 3/16″ (cut 2)
#6 corner brace	1/16″ × 5/16″ × 5/16″ (cut 4)
#7 stretcher	1/16″ × 1 7/8″ × 1 1/4″
#8 leg	1/4″ dowel × 1″ (turn 4)
#9 finial	1/8″ dowel
#10 ball foot	3/16″ round wooden bead (4)
#11 padded seat	1/8″ × 1 5/8″ × 15/16″

PROCEDURE

Cut #1, #2, and #3 with jewelers' saw. Sand and glue rails and corner posts to form a frame. Cut #5 quarter-round pieces, mitering corners, and glue to stool top #4, forming a recess to hold padded seat onto top of frame. Cut and glue #6 corner braces to inside frame of stool. Cut #7 stretcher, drilling five holes as indicated at O on pattern. Leg and finial dowels will be inserted into these holes. Turn #8 legs and #9 finial, forming a dowel at top and bottom of each leg and at the bottom of the finial. Glue legs and finial to stretcher. Dry thoroughly and glue assembled piece to bottom of seat frame into previously drilled holes. Glue ball feet #10 under stretcher. Stain and varnish entire piece. Cut #11 padded seat, fitting carefully into frame opening. Be sure this is not a tight fit; allowance must be made for petit point covering. Glue Artfoam to the top of #11 and cover with petit point or other fabric and glue into frame. Trim edge of padded seat with handmade braid.

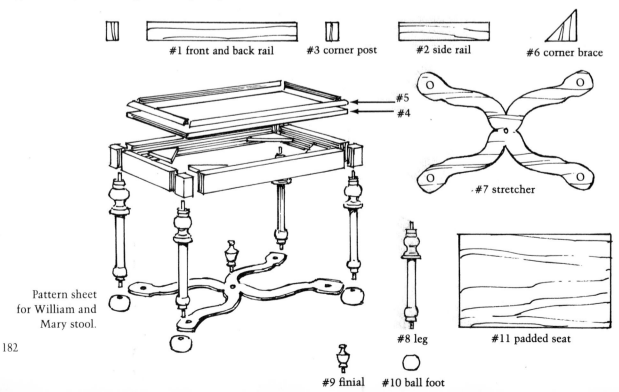

#1 front and back rail   #3 corner post   #2 side rail   #6 corner brace

#5
#4

-#7 stretcher

Pattern sheet for William and Mary stool.

#8 leg

#11 padded seat

#9 finial   #10 ball foot

Eighteenth-century gaming table, with recessed corner ovals for holding counters or money. The delicate pastoral scene was designed and stitched by Susan Richardson.

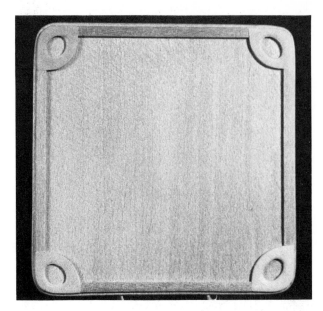

Gaming tabletop with overlay pieces glued in place.

Eighteenth-Century Gaming Table

New York cabinetmakers excelled in the design and manufacture of card tables during the Chippendale period. The eighteenth century brought designs of English origin. The shaped frieze, flowing into graceful cabriole legs, gives this miniature table the flavor of the Queen Anne period. Recessed ovals, holders for counters or money, were placed outside the playing area on the corners or sides. Many of the old tables were made with corner turrets used to hold candlesticks that provided light for game playing. A graph for petit point top insert is on page 203.

BILL OF MATERIALS

Mahogany wood, white glue, Titebond Glue, Velverette glue, stain, varnish, 220 sandpaper.

WOOD SIZES	THICKNESS
#1 top	1/16" × 2 9/16" × 2 9/16"
#2 overlay side strip	1/32" × 1 5/8" × 1/8" (cut 4)
#2a corner overlay piece	1/32" from pattern (cut 4)
#3 undertable base piece	3/16" × 1 15/16" × 1 15/16"
#4 side apron	1/8" × 1 15/16" × 7/16" (cut 4)
#4a leg bracket	1/4" × 3/16" × 3/16" (cut 8)
#5 cabriole leg	3/8" × 3/8" × 2 3/8" (cut 4)

PROCEDURE

Cut #1 top and sand until smooth. Cut #2a corners and cut oval centers out completely, sanding inside with a small file, at X. Glue to the corners of top 1/32" from edge. If necessary, sand corners of top to follow curve of overlay piece. Cut #2 strips and glue to top edges between corner pieces as shown in #2b, top view on pattern sheet. Glue #3 to the bottom of #1, centering very carefully. Cut and glue #4 aprons to outside edges of #3, forming notches for legs at X, as shown in bottom view on pattern sheet. Cut cabriole legs as demonstrated on page 120, and sand to form a pad-shaped foot. Cut #4a leg brackets, shaping to the curve of the leg. Glue into place at notched corners. Stain table and when completely dry varnish until smooth.

Assembled table ready for stain and varnish.

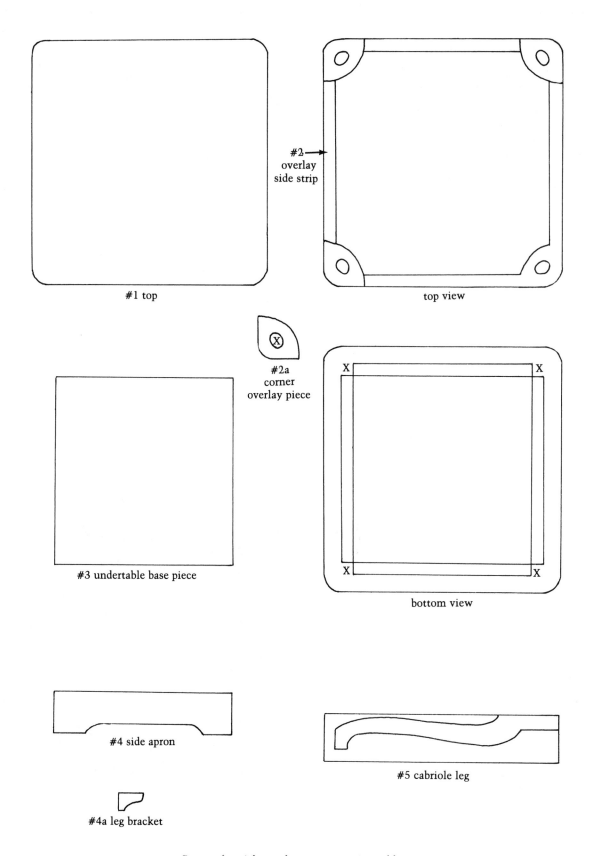

#1 top

#2 → overlay side strip

top view

X   #2a corner overlay piece

#3 undertable base piece

bottom view

#4 side apron

#5 cabriole leg

#4a leg bracket

Pattern for eighteenth-century gaming table.

A small oval tea table, supported by four tapered legs, with curved end handles. Made by Eugene Kupjack.

edge of slot #1, glue a wedge of wood 1/32" thick, tapering to O, and in slot #2, glue a wedge of wood 1/16", tapering to O. The wedges raise the bottom portion of the leg, holding it in a position to form a taper when sanded. Cut four leg pieces 1/8" square to 1 1/2" lengths. Mark an X on one side of each leg. Place one leg in #1 slot with X at the bottom, and sand top with a flat metal sander or an emery board until it becomes flush with the vertical posts. Try not to sand the posts. Remove leg from the slot and turn one turn, place into slot #1 again and sand again. Remove leg, place into slot #2, with X on top and sand. If leg wobbles in jig, slip a 1/32" × 1/16" strip of wood alongside of leg as a wedge. Remove leg and turn one turn to unsanded side, replace in slot #2, and sand remaining side. The result is an evenly tapered leg. Glue legs into slots. Cut handles and shape them by using a drum sander attachment on the Dremel Moto-Tool or a 1/2" dowel wrapped with 220 sandpaper. Sand until piece is the shape of #4 on pattern piece. Cut out opening on handle using a drill; file out opening with a fine round file. Epoxy handles at table ends 1/32" from rounded edge. Sand piece thoroughly, stain, and varnish.

Oval Tea Table

A small oval table, supported by tapered legs, finished in dark mahogany, and varnished to a soft patina.

BILL OF MATERIALS

Mahogany wood, stain, varnish, 220 sandpaper, Titebond Glue.

WOOD SIZES	THICKNESS
#1 top	1/16" × 1 3/4" × 1 3/16"
#2 base	1/4" × 1 1/2" × 1 1/8"
#3 leg (square stock)	1/8" × 1/8" × 1 1/2" (cut 4)
#4 handle shape	1/4" × 7/8" × 1/4" (cut 2)

PROCEDURE

Cut #1, sand until smooth, beveling top edges. Cut #2 base, cutting four notches for legs. Sand notches with a 1/8" square of wood wrapped with sandpaper. This will make notches the exact size for leg fittings. Glue base to top.

To taper leg: Form a jig, using a base piece of wood 4" × 1" × 1/4". Glue a strip 1/8" × 1/8" × 1 1/8" across the width 1 1/2" from the edge. Glue three 1/8" × 1/8" × 1 1/2" lengths vertically, 1/8" apart, marking #1 and #2 at the top of each slot. At the bottom

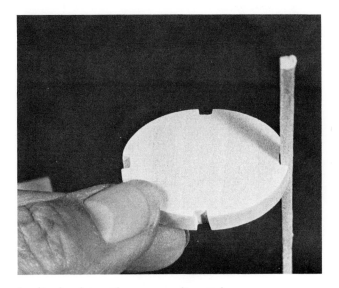

Sanding leg slots with square sanding stick.

185

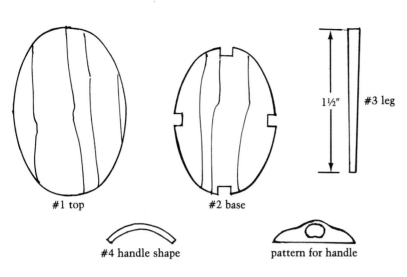

#1 top   #2 base   1½″   #3 leg

#4 handle shape   pattern for handle

Pattern for tea table.

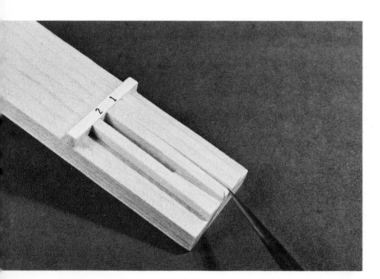

Place leg in jig slot #1 to hold piece for sanding.

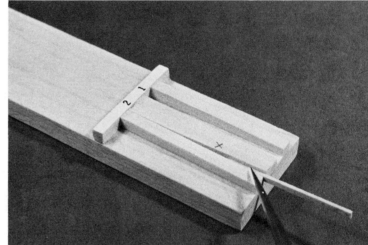

Leg placed in slot #2 with X on top, ready for sanding.

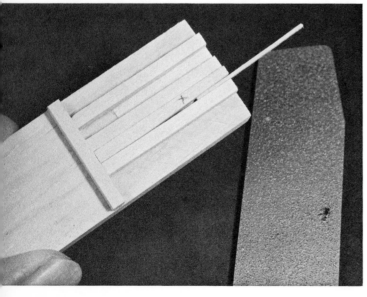

Flat metal sander used for tapering leg as it lays in bed of jig setup.

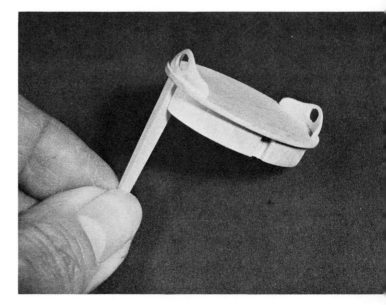

Attaching leg with glue into slot.

Velvet-covered harp bench.

Harp Bench

An upholstered bench with leg sections painted black and decorative painting in gold. Three turned stretchers support the legs and the top cushion is covered with red silk velvet.

BILL OF MATERIALS

Basswood, black acrylic paint, gold paint, varnish, 220 sandpaper, braid for trimming, Artfoam, fabric for upholstery, Elmer's glue, 5 Minute Epoxy, Velverette glue.

WOOD SIZES	THICKNESS
#1 seat	1/8″ × 2″ × 1 1/2″
#2 base leg	1/8″ × 2″ × 1 1/4″ (cut 2)
#3 crossbar stretcher	1/8″ dowel × 1″ (turn 3)
#4 cushion base	1/8″ × 2″ × 1 1/2″

PROCEDURE

Cut and turn all parts from shapes on pattern sheet. Drill holes in #2, as indicated on pattern sheet. Do not drill holes completely through wood. Glue Artfoam on top of cushion base. Epoxy turned stretchers into drilled holes on base leg sections. Glue assembled bottom section to seat #1. Paint with black acrylic paint and decorate with gold-painted scroll-and-leaf design. Epoxy padded cushion to the top of seat. When completely dry, cover with velvet fabric, extending it down over the sides to edge of seat. Trim bottom edge with braid or other finishing trim.

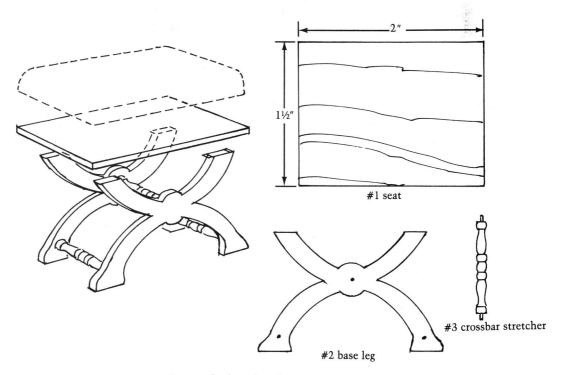

#1 seat

#2 base leg

#3 crossbar stretcher

Pattern for harp bench.

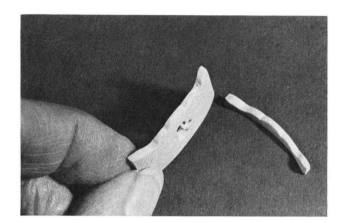

Side table.

Side Table

An occasional table for use in a bedroom or sitting room with tapered Queen Anne shaped legs and an open front.

BILL OF MATERIALS

Basswood, stain, varnish, Titebond Glue.

WOOD SIZES	THICKNESS
#1 top	$1/16'' \times 1\ 9/16'' \times 1\ 3/16''$
#2 side	$1/16'' \times 9/16'' \times 3/4''$ (cut 2)
#3 back	$3/16'' \times 1\ 1/8'' \times 3/4''$
#4 front apron	$3/16'' \times 1\ 1/8'' \times 1/8''$
#5 bottom	$1/16'' \times 1\ 1/8'' \times 7/8''$
#6 leg (square stock)	$1/4'' \times 1/4'' \times 2\ 3/16''$ (cut 4)

PROCEDURE

Cut and sand top #1, beveling top edges. Cut #2 and #3, and drill a hole at designated spot. Using a round file, shape as indicated on pattern sheet. Cut front apron #4, shaping this piece and #3 back to form a convex curve. Cut bottom #5, matching curve to the shaped apron and back. Glue front apron to bottom section, flush at top, then glue back into place, with bottom scallop protruding evenly below #5. Glue sides to sides of bottom section, forming notches at each corner for fitting legs. Attach assembled pieces to #1 top, distributing overhang evenly on all sides. Cut four legs as shown on page 120. Glue into corner notches. Table pieces may be stained before assembling or when fully constructed. Varnish to a smooth patina.

Shaping front and back apron pieces to a convex curve.

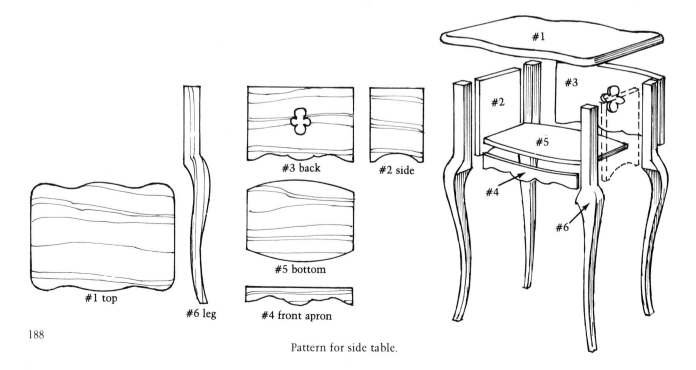

#3 back

#2 side

#5 bottom

#1 top

#6 leg

#4 front apron

#1

#3

#2

#5

#4

#6

Pattern for side table.

Sheraton canterbury for storing papers, magazines, and music. Made by Rose Barell.

PROCEDURE

Glue #6 sides to the outside of #8 1/16″ from front edge. Glue back section to the outside of #8 as indicated in diagram. Attach second piece of #8 to the top of assembled pieces, forming an opening for the drawer and notches at the corners for the legs. Turn legs from shape on pattern sheet and glue into place at corners. Glue #4 horizontal top side rails between leg posts, and #5 side posts from top to bottom. Assemble the inner section by cutting all top dividers, fitting and attaching two vertical posts #3 at the bottom of each divider. Glue this center construction inside canterbury, lining up each section carefully. Construct drawer to fit into opening. Pieces may be stained after cutting and before assembling or upon completion. Varnish, and attach hardware. The brass pins are inserted into bottom of each leg for finishing.

Canterbury

A Sheraton-style canterbury, with vertical partitions, used for papers, magazines, and music, adapted to a miniature size by Rose Barell. In Thomas Sheraton's *Cabinet Dictionary of 1830*, a similar piece was first made for "a Bishop of Canterbury."

BILL OF MATERIALS

Cherry wood, stain, Titebond Glue, 5 Minute Epoxy, varnish, one drawer pull, four brass pins.

WOOD SIZES	THICKNESS
#1 center divider	1/16″ × 1 1/2″ × 3/8″
#2 divider	1/16″ × 1 1/2″ × 1/8″ (cut 4)
#3 divider vertical post	1/16″ × 3/32″ × 5/8″ (cut 10)
#4 horizontal side rail	1/16″ × 3/32″ × 1″ (cut 2)
#5 vertical side post	1/16″ × 3/32″ × 11/16″ (cut 6)
#6 side	1/16″ × 3/8″ × 1″ (cut 2)
#7 back	1/16″ × 1 1/2″ × 3/8″
#8 bottom	3/32″ × 1 1/2″ × 1 1/16″ (cut 2)
#9 leg (square stock)	1/8″ × 1/8″ × 1 5/8″ (turn 4)
#10 drawer bottom	1/32″ × 1 13/32″ × 15/16″
#11 drawer side	1/16″ × 15/16″ × 5/32″ (cut 2)
#12 drawer front and back	1/16″ × 1 1/2″ × 5/32″ (cut 2)

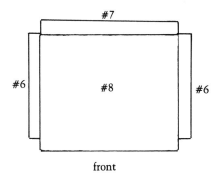

Diagram for bottom of canterbury.

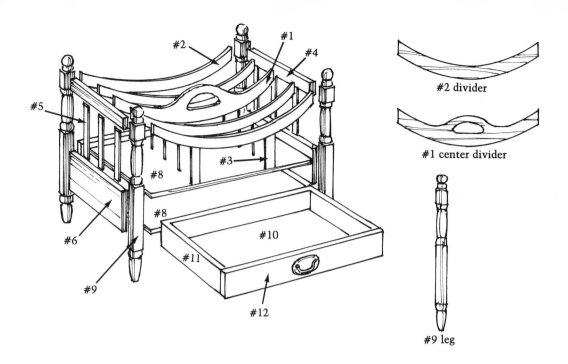

#2 divider

#1 center divider

#9 leg

Pattern for canterbury.

3 Charted Needlework

Many details of the original design of a period piece will be lost as it is reproduced in miniature. When selecting the elements to be included, the goal to be kept in mind is that of creating an impression, not an exact replica of the original.

Loss of detail is prevalent in the reinterpretation of early needlework. Today, full-sized designs are worked on canvas that has ten to twenty-four threads to the inch. Seventeenth-, eighteenth-, and early-nineteenth-century patterns were stitched on fine canvas composed of between 22 and 52 threads to the inch. An even greater challenge than reproducing period designs on a large scale is reducing the pattern to a scale of one inch to one foot on silk gauze with a thread count of twenty-four to thirty-eight. A good example is the replica of the stool design of a puppy chasing a butterfly created by Nellie Custis Lewis. The graph, intended for 38-count silk gauze, would lack important details if it were stitched on a larger canvas, for example 14-count canvas (see page 197).

The amount of detail in the original piece determines the difficulty of needlework reproduction. A simple design, such as the balanced, geometric hatchment, coat-of-arms, is not as difficult to copy.

On the other hand, the approximately 1 1/2′ × 3 1/2′ tent-stitch Fishing Lady picture at the Boston Museum

A stool covered with brown broadcloth on which is stitched "Puppy Chasing a Butterfly," created by Nellie Custis Lewis for her grandson. Woodlawn Plantation, Mount Vernon, Virginia; property of the National Trust for Historic Preservation.

Replica of the Nellie Custis Lewis "Puppy Chasing a Butterfly" stool, designed and stitched by Susan Richardson.

Miniature hatchment, adapted from the photograph below, by Susan Richardson.

Hatchment coat of arms, American 43.75 Saltonstall, Winthrop Dudley, and Roswell. *Courtesy: Museum of Fine Arts, Boston*

Needlepoint picture entitled "The Fishing Lady" was stitched during the eighteenth century in America. Pictures such as this, depicting scenes of the Boston Common, were hung over the mantel. *Courtesy: Museum of Fine Arts, Boston. Seth Sweetser Fund. Accession 21.2233*

of Fine Arts is more of a challenge. The museum piece is composed of a great many elements, not all of which can be used. The miniature depicts hilly terrain, swans on a pond, with fewer houses and trees set in the landscape. A pair of strolling figures is missing; animals in the foreground have been omitted.

A similar selection of detail occurs in the reproduction of the gaming tabletop. The floral border is created with simpler flowers. The central landscape with the shepherd boy and shepherdess is duplicated to a degree, but with fewer animals and simpler terrain. The smaller bird has been eliminated.

The eyes on the figures and animals stitched on 38-count canvas are frequently too large when the tent stitch is used, even though the stitch crosses only one canvas intersection. If the eyes are worked in a vertical direction over a single canvas thread, however, they will be small enough to be in proper proportion to the face. This technique was used in both the Fishing Lady picture and the gaming table insert.

Because it typically covers four threads, the Irish stitch, which forms a flame design, is often too large to be used in the intricate miniature patterns. However, if 72-count silk gauze is used, the Irish-stitch design can

Miniature version of "The Fishing Lady" in the collection of the Museum of Fine Arts, Boston. Designed and stitched by Susan Richardson.

Needlepoint top of Queen Anne gaming table, made in England in the eighteenth century. William E. Nickerson Fund. *Courtesy: Museum of Fine Arts, Boston. Accession 49.330*

be included successfully in a specified area. The fire screen with a carnation pattern made by Rose Barell is a fine example of this delicate handwork. Flame motifs can be worked on a 38-count canvas if an "Irish stitch" is created by working three vertical tent stitches. The vertical stitches move in full steps with no overlap. This method allows for the tall peaks and subtle shading that are characteristic of the William and Mary canvas work as seen on the daybed and chair cushion on pages 204 and 205.

Irish-stitch designs became smaller and more complicated during the Queen Anne period. The vertical stitch of the Bible cover and folding pocketbook following in this chapter has been reduced to a single tent stitch in order to duplicate the intricate pattern on a small scale.

The following graphs offer the reader a variety of period pieces that we hope will contribute to the growing demand for historical accuracy in miniature needlework. Authentic colors are artfully combined to enhance the designs. The number following the graph symbol and color name indicates the manufacturer's number for that particular shade. A majority of the graphs are worked on size 38 silk gauze to allow for more detailed duplication; however, the piece may be made smaller or larger by changing to another size canvas.

It is best to begin the execution of a design with the central motif and work outward. The background is filled in last, using the basket-weave stitch wherever possible because this stitch ensures the retention of the original shape of the piece. The tent stitch is also known as the continental stitch; the Irish stitch is the proper eighteenth-century term for the bargello stitch.

Susan Richardson's adaptation of the Museum of Fine Arts gaming tabletop.

Fire screen with carnation pattern, worked on 72-count silk gauze. Designed and stitched by Rose Barell.

Painting on Silk Gauze

1. On a piece of paper, draw the design to scale, keeping in mind the limitation of the canvas count.
2. Ink the final miniature pattern so that it will show through the silk gauze.
3. Cut the gauze to allow generous borders (about 1" to 2") around the painted design. Pin the gauze on top of the pattern at the corners. The silk canvas should not buckle.
4. Apply acrylic paint that has been slightly thinned with water. Very fine brushes (000 and 10-0) are used with a dabbing motion.
5. When the painting is completed, remove the gauze and allow to dry.
6. Edge the canvas with slightly diluted white glue, and dry.
7. Stitch the design.

The painting technique provides a stitching guide, which is easily covered when the design has been worked. If a shortcut is taken so that the design is only inked on the canvas, care must be taken not to use dark ink where a light color thread is to cover. Should this happen, white paint can be used to cover the dark ink before the thread is worked.

Graphed Needlework Designs

Puppy Chasing a Butterfly Stool Cover

#38 silk gauze
DMC embroidery floss, 1 thread
- White 712
- / Yellow 676
- o Dark gold 434
- ∧ Dark brown 3371
- ✓ Tan 841
- ☐ Brown 898 background

An adaptation of the "Puppy Chasing a Butterfly" stool at Woodlawn Plantation, Mount Vernon, Virginia; a property of the National Trust for Historic Preservation. The Woodlawn Plantation stool needlework design was made by Nellie Custis Lewis for her grandson.

The miniature version was designed and stitched by Susan Richardson.

The design was worked first, filling in the background color to fit this particular stool. You may, however, adjust your design to fit your own piece. The edges were trimmed with a gold braid, or you can braid three threads of the background color and glue around the edge. For finished stool, see page 192.

Graph of "Puppy Chasing a Butterfly" design. Permission to adapt this design in miniature granted by the Woodlawn Plantation, Mount Vernon, Virginia; property of the National Trust for Historic Preservation.

Graph of hatchment.

Hatchment

#38 silk gauze
DMC embroidery floss, 1 thread
*   Red 321
•   White blanc neige
x   Light gray 762
✓   Gray 318
/   Light gold 676
∧   Dark gold 680
□   Black 310 background

A hatchment is described as an embroidered coat of arms on a lozenge-shaped ground.

The miniature version offered here, designed and stitched by Susan Richardson, is an adaptation of the American Hatchment Coat-of-Arms, 43.75 Saltonstall, Winthrop Dudley, Roswell. Courtesy, Museum of Fine Arts, Boston (see page 192).

The completed petit point is mounted on a thin board and mounted in a black frame with gold trim.

The Fishing Lady

#38 silk gauze
DMC embroidery floss, 1 thread

•	White 712	U	Medium brown 434
□	Light aqua 504 background	+	Brown 801
/	Medium aqua 502	2	Dark brown 3371
0	Dark aqua 500	3	Light gray 415
*	Skin 543	4	Gray 318
✓	Red 918	5	Light purple 3042
▽	Pink 224	6	Purple 327
–	Light blue 800	7	Pale yellow 3047
∧	Blue 312	8	Gold 676
x	Tan 422	9	Black 310

The Boston Museum of Fine Arts has granted us permission to adapt in miniature their needlepoint picture "The Fishing Lady," American 8th CY-21.2233 Seth Kettell Sweetser Fund. Courtesy, Museum of Fine Arts, Boston.

Pictures such as this were used over a mantel. Susan Richardson's design very closely resembles the original, which may be seen on page 193.

Add an attractive wooden frame with small candle sconces on either side, and this miniature is ready for hanging.

Graph of "The Fishing Lady."

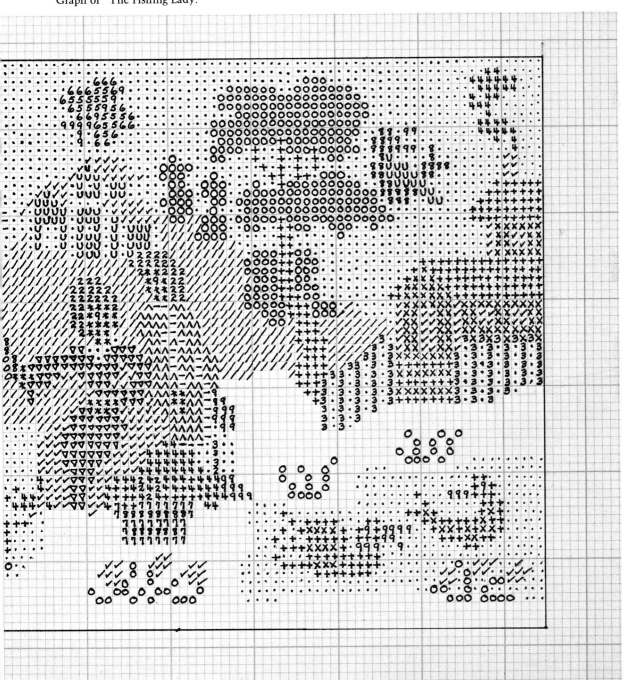

Petit Point Gaming Tabletop

#38 silk gauze
DMC embroidery floss, 1 thread

2	Black 310	3	Blue 931
*	White blanc neige	∧	Medium blue 799
x	Dark gold 680	–	Light blue 800
o	Gold 676	4	Red 816
z	Pale yellow 3078	5	Brown 434
✓	Dark green 890	6	Skin 543
•	Medium green 3346	7	Light purple 3042
/	Light green 3348	8	Dark purple 327
□	Dark blue 924 background		

With the inspiration provided by a visit to the Museum of Fine Arts, Boston, Susan Richardson adapted this version of the needlepoint top of a Queen Anne gaming table. While the tabletop at the museum provides an exquisite and intricate design (see page 194), this "small wonder" depicts a likeness that many miniature makers will enjoy. So, make the table yourself (page 183) and insert this charming design, and you will have a gem.

Graph of gaming tabletop.

Daybed Pad and Pillow

#38 silk gauze
DMC embroidery floss, 1 thread

White 712	Blue 927
Light green 472	Medium blue 926
Dark green 471	Dark blue 924
Light green 472	White 712
White 712	Rose 233
Light blue 928	Red 221

Made with the tent stitch in alternating rows of colors in the order indicated above, this finely designed daybed pad and pillow can be used to cover the William and Mary daybed on page 124. The flame design is typical for this period.

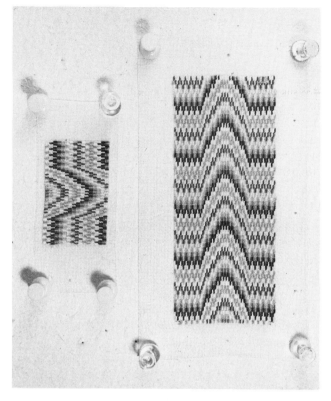

Flame-stitch design for daybed of the William and Mary period. Designed and stitched by Susan Richardson.

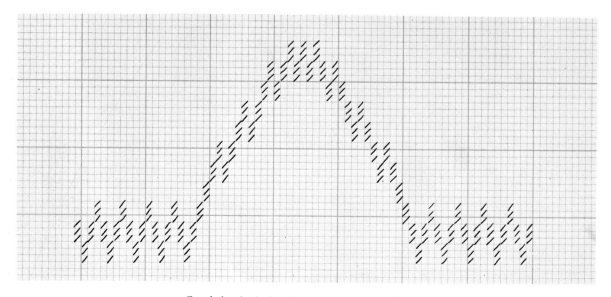

Graph for daybed upholstery petit point design.

Flame Design Chair Cushion

#38 silk gauze
DMC embroidery floss, 1 thread

Dark blue 924	Dark green 3051
Blue 926	Dark rose 355
Medium blue 927	Rose 223
Light blue 928	Medium rose 224
Light green 3053	Light rose 225
Green 3052	

Using a column of tent stitches, work the above colors alternately, covering the area you want to use for the size cushion your piece requires. The color combination in this design is truly beautiful. We have used it to cover a banister-back chair made by Marty Dinkel of The Mouse Hole.

Chair cushion used during the Jacobean and William and Mary periods.

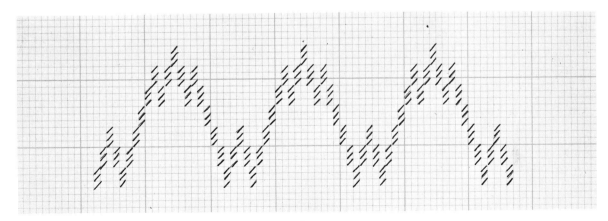

Graph of flame design for chair cushion.

Bible Cover

#38 silk gauze
DMC embroidery floss, 1 thread

/   Gold 680
□   Yellow 3047 background
o   Blue 930
x   Pink 223
✓   Red 355
•   Light gold 676

After working the design in petit point, cut a piece of wood 7/8″ × 1 1/4″ × 1/4″. Measure your finished design to make sure it will wrap around the block of wood leaving a slight overhang at top, bottom, and one side. Turn under silk gauze at stitching line and glue into place. Paint sides of wood block to finish and glue Bible cover to wood with Velverette glue.

Bible covered with petit point in a carnation design.

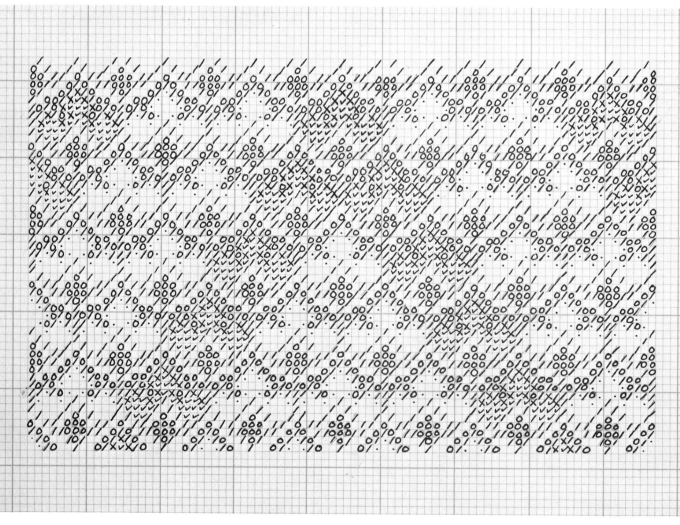

Graph for Bible cover.

The carnation pattern decorates this tiny pocketbook.

Irish-Stitch Pocketbook

#38 silk gauze
DMC embroidery floss, 1 thread
- • Red 355
- ✓ Dark green 367
- x Rose 758
- ☐ Gold 676 background

This pocketbook, no bigger than your fingernail, is worked in an Irish stitch on a silk canvas. The pocketbook is a fold-over clutch type that is attached on each side with tiny stitches after folding under the silk gauze. The flap is held down with a loop and tiny seed bead.

Pocketbook with Floral Design

#38 silk gauze
DMC embroidery floss, 1 thread
- x Pink 224
- ✓ Red 221
- o Yellow 745
- • Gold 680
- / Green 934
- ☐ Light green 469 background

Another tiny pocketbook, this one with a floral design surrounded with green leaves. After working the design, dampen the piece and block on a board, stretching taut, and dry overnight. Remove from board, cut off excess gauze to 3/16" of stitches, and turn edges under with Velverette glue. Fold bottom of pocketbook up over body and turn down the flap. A small piece of ribbon or braided thread is attached to underside of flap and used to tie pocketbook closed.

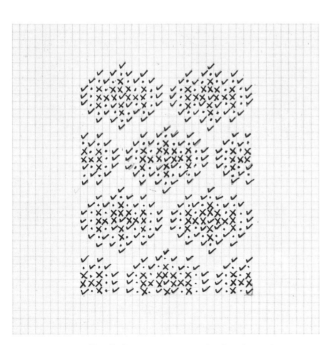

Graph for carnation pocketbook.

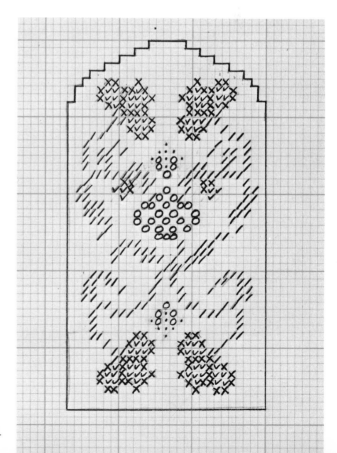

Graph for floral pocketbook.

Candlescreen

#38 silk gauze
DMC embroidery floss, 1 thread
- •   Brown 829
- □   Yellow 676 background
- ∧   Green 469
- ✓   Rose 355
- o   Light rose 224

    Work petit point design from graph. Construct a surrounding frame and, after mounting petit point on a thin piece of wood, attach. The post is carved from a toothpick and the bottom is made from two 1/6″ pieces of wood. The entire stand is varnished and stained.

Hand fire screen and candlescreen with carnation and flame designs.

Hand Fire Screen

#38 silk gauze
DMC embroidery floss, 1 thread
- /   Light rose 758
- □   Aqua 927 background
- ✓   Rose 355
- •   White blanc neige

    Hand-held fire screen with carnation design. The handle can be made by carving a toothpick. Stain, varnish, and attach it to the two layers of petit point.

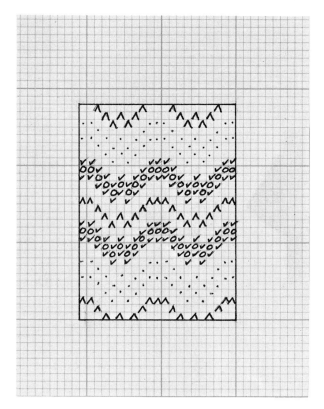

Graph for candlescreen.

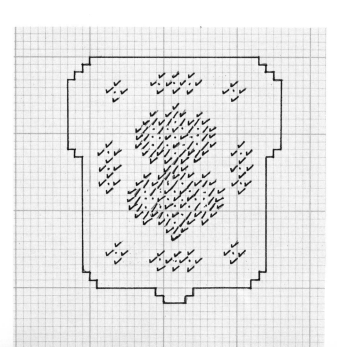

Graph for hand fire screen.

Wall pocket for storing letters and books near the bed.

Wall Pocket

#38 silk gauze
DMC embroidery floss, 1 thread
x   Brown 433
✓   Dark green 890
☐   Light green 3348 background
∧   Rose 356
•   Gold 676

When stitching canvas, work design with part A face up and part B face down so that when the bottom is folded up over A, the right side will be facing forward. Run a line of diluted glue along stitching line of A to keep edges from fraying when they are cut and turned to inside. Turn top edges to back, forming steps on the top half. Fold bottom section up over top to form a pocket. Fold sides and glue to back. Braid a small loop and attach to top.

A minute pocket to hang on the wall near a tiny bed for letters or books. When stitching canvas, work the design with part A face up and part B face down so that when the bottom is folded up over A, the right sides will be facing forward. Run a line of diluted glue along stitching line of A to keep edges from fraying when they are cut and turned to the inside. Turn top edges to the back, forming steps on the top half. Fold bottom section up over the top to form a pocket. Fold sides and glue to back. Braid a small loop and attach to the top.

Graph for wall pocket.

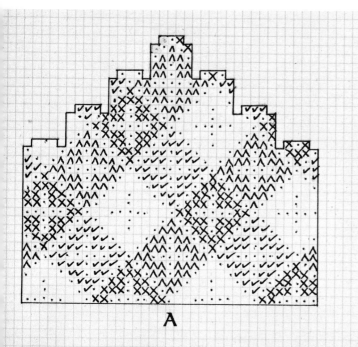

A

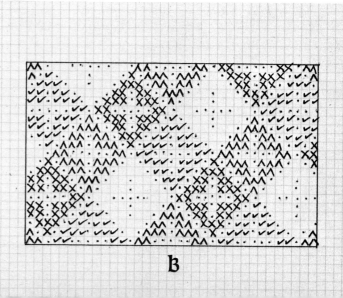

B

Petit point slippers with a flame pattern.

Slippers

#38 silk gauze
DMC embroidery floss, 1 thread
- • Blue 926
- B. Light blue 928
- x Red 355
- □ White blanc neige background

This slipper, a little less than 1 inch long, is to be worked in the flame pattern as indicated by the color symbols above and on the pattern. When the petit point is completed, run a line of glue around all edges to secure the stitches. Cut along stitching line. Bring the two straight back edges together and secure with Velverette glue. From the shaped slipper, measure a pattern for the sole onto paper. Using pattern, cut sole from a very thin fabric such as suede cloth or from another suitable material.

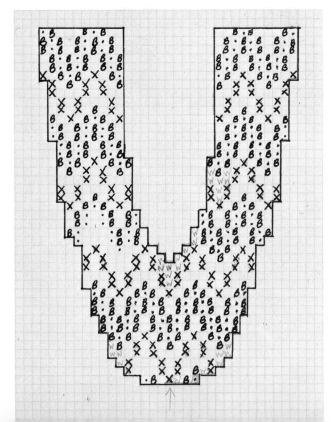

Diamond Pillow

#38 silk gauze
DMC embroidery floss, 1 thread
- | Orange 407
- | Green 3053

A variation of the Irish stitch: over one thread, over three threads, over one thread, skip one, over one thread, over three threads, over one thread, skip one. Continue in this manner across the row, and across the next row, fitting the stitches into the previous row. When the pillow is the size that you have already predetermined, turn under the edges, line the back with a fine silk fabric, leaving one end open to allow for stuffing with cotton, and stitch end closed with very small stitches.

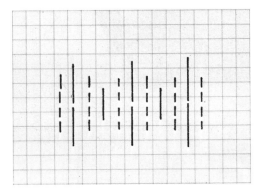

Decorative pillow with diamond design.

Graph for diamond pillow.

Graph for patterned slippers.

Oriental Butterfly Pillow

#38 silk gauze
DMC embroidery floss, 1 thread

/   Dark blue 930
V   Yellow 727
o   Red 356
□   White 712 background

Using a tent stitch, follow graph for design and finish as for diamond pillow.

Oriental butterfly pillow.

Graph for butterfly pillow.

Graph of stag fire screen.

Stag Fire Screen

#38 silk gauze
DMC embroidery floss, 1 thread

x	Black 310	o	Dark brown 640
•	Light green 927	W	White blanc neige
/	Dark green 3051	∧	Light gray 762
R	Red 815	G	Gray 318
✓	Light brown 840	▢	White 712 background

After completing petit point design, make a frame to fit the outside shape, mount the work on a thin piece of wood, and glue the frame to panel. The base of this frame is a fire screen available from Andrews Miniatures.

Fire screen design of a stag in a landscape typical of crewel embroidery designs of the eighteenth century.

Graph of pastoral fire screen.

Pastoral Fire Screen

#38 silk gauze
DMC embroidery floss, 1 thread

•	Dark green 890	W	White blanc neige
□	Light blue 800 background	G	Gold 680
		B	Blue 312
∧	Brown 632	L	Medium blue 775
−	Medium green 469	R	Dark rose 221
o	Light green 472	P	Rose 356
✓	Black 310	S	Flesh 225
/	Gray 414	x	Dark brown 3371

Work pattern as for previous designs. Mount completed work on a thin piece of wood. Directions for making the frame are on page 178.

This fire screen shows a gentleman and his lady in a pastoral setting. Bucolic landscapes were typical themes in colonial needlework.

These flowers set in a vase were designed and stitched by Claudine Wilson on 48-count canvas. The finer gauze allows a great deal of realism.

Flower Vase Fire Screen

#38 silk gauze
DMC embroidery floss, 1 thread

R	Dark red 902	■	Medium green 3346
o	Medium red 816	L	Light green 703
•	Red 666	B	Blue 3325
x	Hot pink 604	b	Pale blue 828
\	Medium pink 963	W	White 712
/	Pale pink 225	☐	Gray 415 background
G	Dark Green 890		

After working the design, mount the petit point on a thin piece of wood. See page 178 for directions for making frame. This piece was designed for a fire screen available from Andrews Miniatures.

Graph of flower vase fire screen.

Balloons were the vogue in eighteenth-century France. A balloon design decorates this cheval fire screen designed in the French style.

Balloon Fire Screen

#38 silk gauze
DMC embroidery floss, 1 thread

W	White blanc neige	o	Dark green 890
x	Black 310	/	Medium green 937
•	Dark aqua 502	+	Light green 3346
✓	Light aqua 504	–	Blue 931
G	Gold 676	L	Dark blue 311
R	Dark rose 355	☐	Light blue 828 background
P	Rose 224	B	Brown 801

A French balloon scene decorates this charming fire screen panel which, when completed, will be set into a cheval-type frame. Directions on how to make the screen are on page 180.

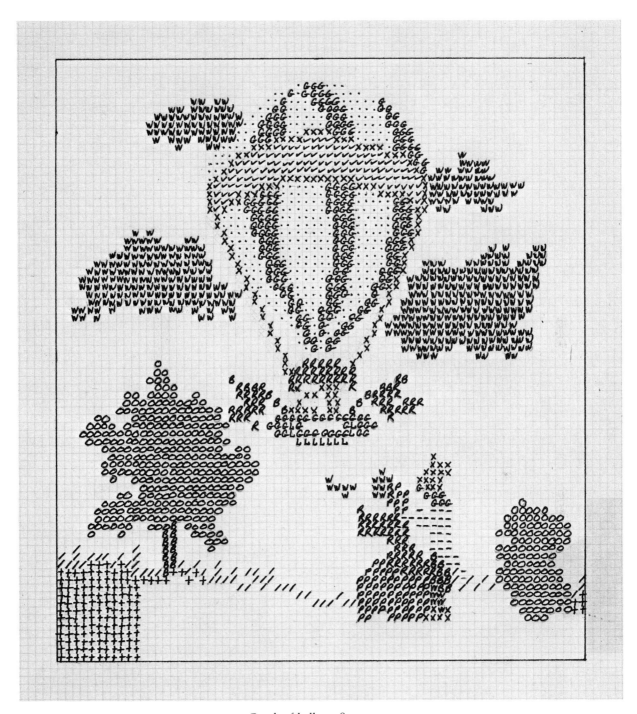

Graph of balloon fire screen.

Graph for mourning picture.

Early-nineteenth-century mourning picture with a weeping willow, a lady dressed in a classical-style gown, and a tomb topped by an urn.

Mourning Picture

#38 silk gauze
DMC embroidery floss, 1 thread

x	Dark green 935	•	Light blue 927
□	White blanc neige background	▽	Medium blue 926
✓	Olive green 733	/	Dark blue 500
o	Dark aqua 501	K	Black 310
*	Light aqua 501	S	Skin 543
		∧	Gray 415

An early-nineteenth-century mourning picture to be worked in petit point on size 38 silk gauze and framed for hanging.

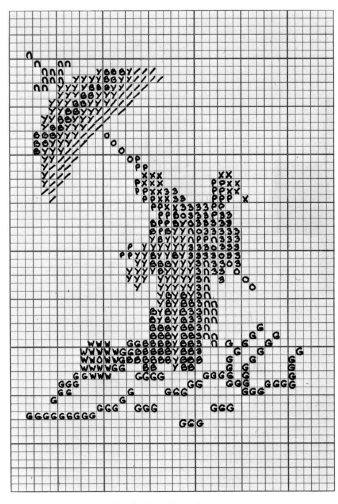

Graph for oriental design.

Design with an oriental theme to be used for a fire screen, a
pillow, or a picture.

Oriental Design

#38 silk gauze
DMC embroidery floss, 1 thread

X	Black 310	∩	Medium blue 931
P	Flesh 832	G	Green 3052
3	Light blue 813	/	Orange 758
B	Rust 356	W	White blanc neige
o	Brown 839	□	Blue 311 background
Y	Gold 3013		

A superb color combination enhances this piece of
oriental petit point. The finished work can be framed
or applied to a fire screen.

Eighteenth-Century Tapestry

An eighteenth-century tapestry stitched on 48-count canvas by Claudine Wilson.

#48 silk gauze
DMC embroidery floss, 1 thread
Silver metallic thread

I	Dark red 814	3	Cream 739
•	Medium red 304	6	Gold 422
◣	Bright red 666	9	Dark green 890
Γ	Flesh 225	B	Brown 801
/	Pink 963	C	Light blue 928
Y	Black 310	☐	Blue sky 3325 background
O	Medium blue 799	☐	Gray clouds 415 background
4	Dark blue 824		
X	White	☐	Green grass 3345 background
∧	Ecru		
S	Silver metallic thread	8	Light green 503
		△	Medium green 3346

A magnificent tapestry, worked on very fine silk gauze, with a well-planned combination of colors. This piece can be framed or used as a fire screen panel.

Graph of eighteenth-century tapestry.

Rampant Lion Stool Cover

#38 silk gauze
DMC embroidery floss, 1 thread
/ Gold 676
☐ Black 310 background

A well-designed cover, to be used on a William and Mary stool. Directions for making the stool are on page 182.

A stylized design of a rampant lion with floral motifs for a stool of the Jacobean or the William and Mary period.

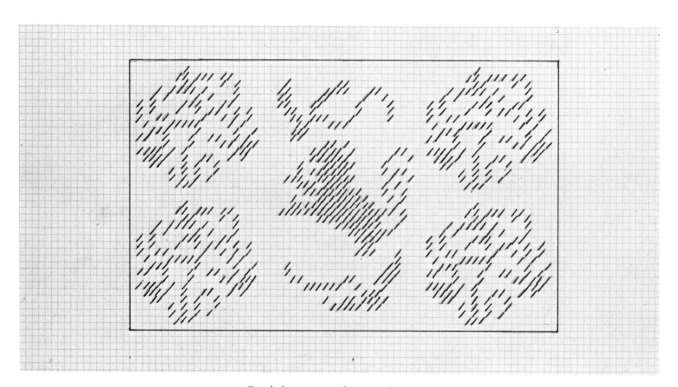

Graph for rampant lion stool cover.

Balloon Stool Cover

#38 silk gauze
DMC embroidery floss, 1 thread

✓ Rose 356
Y Gold 676
∧ Black 310
o Brown 898
• Dark aqua 500
□ Medium aqua 502 background
/ Light aqua 504
x Dark gold 680

The eighteenth century introduced the ever-popular balloon motif, shown here covering a harp bench. Directions for making the bench are described on page 187.

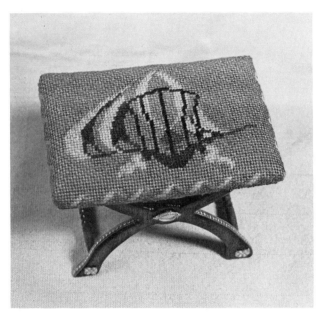

A balloon motif, popular during the eighteenth century in France, is seen here on a harp stool.

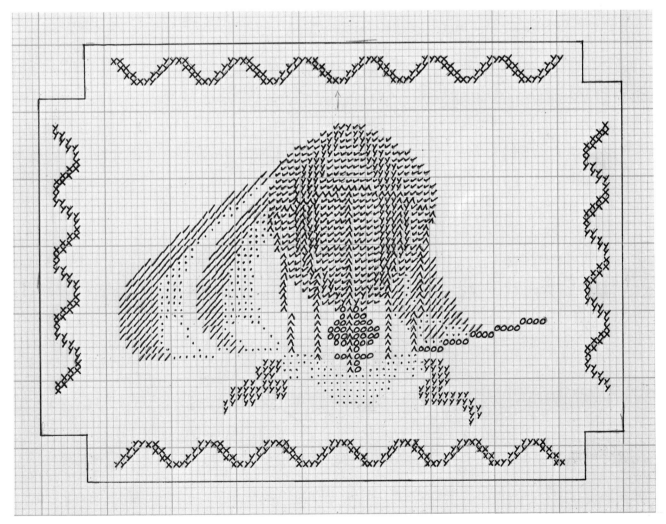

Graph for balloon stool cover.

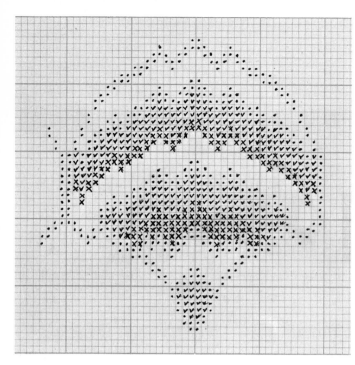

Graph for Queen Anne seat cover.

Queen Anne Seat Cover

#38 silk gauze
DMC embroidery floss, 1 thread
✓   Blue 828
•   Medium blue 826
x   Gold 725
☐   White 712 background

The clever application of a Queen Anne seat design taken from a wallpaper motif. The chair can be made (see page 148), and the completed work applied over a wooden base.

Kay Weiger reproduced a wallpaper design for the seat of a Queen Anne chair.

Tree of Life Chair Cover

Tree of life motif adapted to a lolling chair of the Chippendale period. Designed by Susan Richardson.

#38 silk gauze
DMC embroidery floss, 1 thread

5	Pink 225	+	Black 310
6	Dark Pink 223	B	Brown 433
7	Red 355	M	Medium brown 729
l	Light blue 775	T	Light tan 680
2	Medium blue 931	W	White blanc neige
o	Navy blue 336	/	Gray 318
3	Light green 3348	✓	Medium gray 762
4	Medium green 3347	□	Yellow 676 background
•	Dark green 895	x	Brown 433

This exquisitely designed chair covering by Susan Richardson is graphed in three sections: the back, the seat, and the rear. The color codes are the same for all three sections. The chair on which to mount the petit point is described on page 135.

Graph for back of tree of life chair.

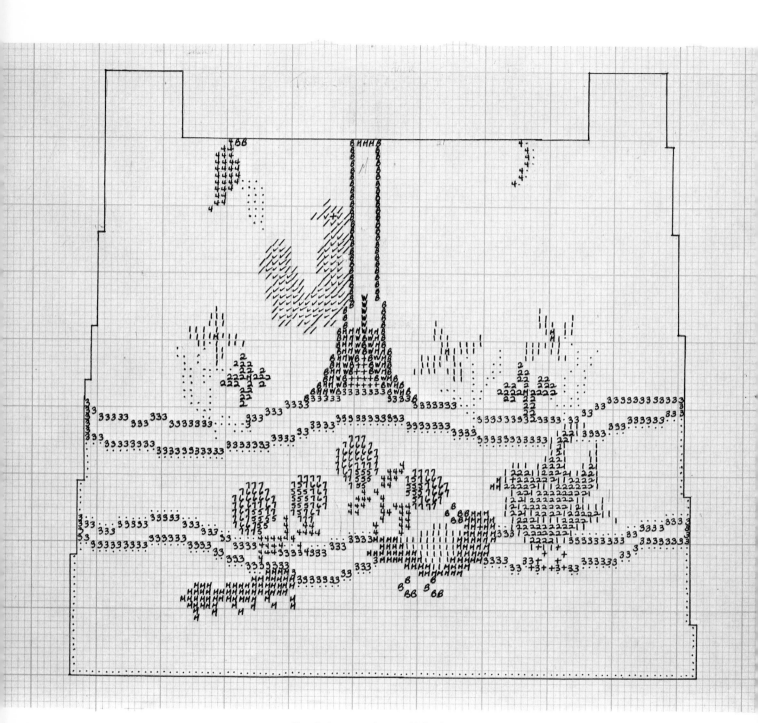

Graph for seat of tree of life chair.

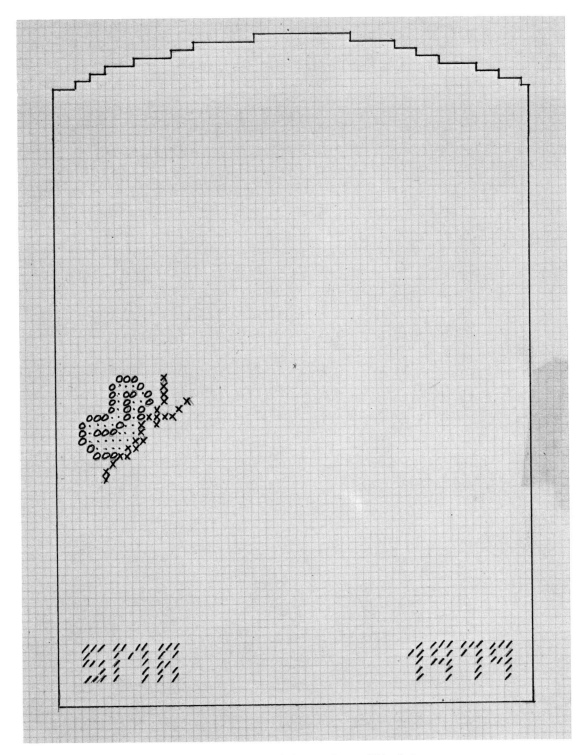

Graph for the rear upholstery of tree of life chair.

Chippendale Side Chair Seat Cover

#38 silk gauze
DMC embroidery floss, 1 thread

•	Dark rose 355	D	Dark gold 680
Λ	Rose 407	z	Dark Green 3346
o	Pink 225	Y	Medium green 471
V	Light yellow 3047	x	Light green 472
C	Medium gold 729	/	Light blue 800
G	Light gold 676	□	Dark blue 336 background

A lovely floral designed petit point covers the seat of this exquisite Chippendale chair, made by Harry Cooke. The same design can be adapted to fit a variety of size chairs.

The petit point design on this Chippendale side chair, made by Harry Cooke, was a popular motif. The flower-filled vase was inspired by Robert Furber's floral designs.

Graph for Chippendale side chair seat cover.

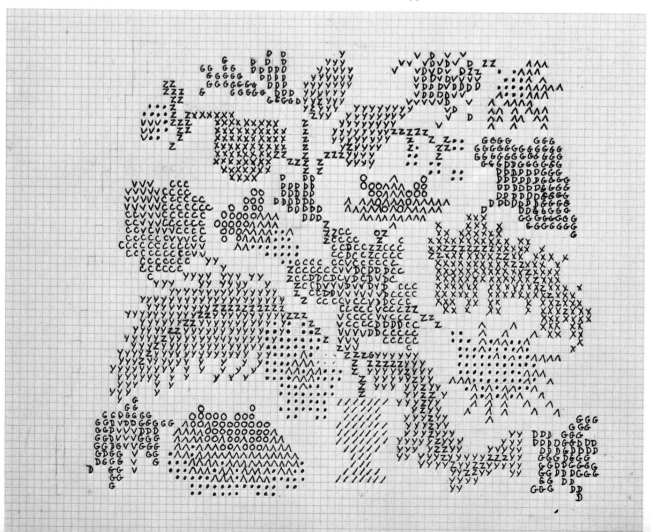

The Chinese influence was strongly felt during the Chippendale period. A blue monochromatic design is used here on a white ground.

Chinese Settee Seat Cover

#38 silk gauze
DMC embroidery floss, 1 thread
/   Navy blue 336
o   Medium blue 312
✓   Light blue 334
•   Pale blue 800
□   White 712 background

The completed seat cover was set into this charming settee, available in kit form from X-ACTO,® HOUSE OF MINIATURES.℠

Graph for Chinese settee seat cover, turned on page.

Bouquet Design for Gaming Tabletop

#38 silk gauze
DMC embroidery floss, 1 thread

▽	Blue 927	T	Turquoise 926
x	Green 3053	✓	Light pink 225
P	Pink 3354	B	Brown 3045
Y	Yellow 3047	o	Light blue 928
W	White blanc neige	☐	Dark blue 924 background

A very delicate design for an insert to enhance the top of a table. Page 183 will show you how to make a gaming table, using this motif for the top.

A bouquet of flowers provides the pattern for this Queen Anne gaming table insert.

Graph for bouquet design on gaming table insert.

A table carpet with a pastoral border inspired by sixteenth-century English carpet.

English Table Carpet

#28 silk gauze
DMC embroidery floss, 1 thread

□	Light blue 927 center background	R	Red 221
/	Dark blue 930	3	Rose 407
o	Dark green 934	W	White blanc neige
∨	Green 936	4	Gray 414
∧	Light olive 3013	*	Black 310
•	Olive 3012 border background	G	Gold 680
		x	Brown 632
		S	Flesh 739

A carpet used for covering a table, worked on size 28 silk gauze. For finishing the edges, cut excess border 1/2" from stitching line. Run a line of diluted glue next to last row of stitches. After work is completely dry, turn edges under and glue to back of carpet, mitering each corner. This makes a very nice, thin, smooth edge on all sides. See page 20 for carpet placed on a table in a setting.

Graph for English table carpet on next two pages.

A tree of life motif, common during the Queen Anne period, decorates this floor carpet.

Tree of Life Carpet

#28 silk gauze
DMC embroidery floss, 2 threads

□	Ecru center background	2	Light gray 648
•	Brown 840 border background	3	Dark gray 414
		K	Black 310
/	Navy 311	4	Tan 738
*	Medium blue 931	5	Brown 632
z	Light blue 932	6	Dark brown 829
G	Dark gold 680	7	Medium brown 433
✓	Medium gold 676	8	Dark rose 221
Y	Light gold 3047	9	Rose 223
x	Dark green 500	P	Pink 225
o	Medium green 469	L	Lavender 316
—	Light green 472	∧	Purple 315
W	White blanc neige		

A very attractive period carpet with a wonderfully coordinated color arrangement. The outside border code has not been filled in completely with the small dot. We felt it is easier to follow a chart when some areas are partially marked (upper left corner). This is also true in the terrain at x and –. The animals are much more legible when they are not surrounded by symbols.

Graph for tree of life carpet on pages 236 and 237.

An early-nineteenth-century carpet with Aubusson motifs of shells, ribbons, and floral vines. Designed by Susan Richardson; stitched by Lois Sterling.

Shell Aubusson Carpet

#24 silk gauze
DMC embroidery floss, 2 threads
/   Dark green 3051
☐   Light green 3053 background
•   White 822
x   Rose 407
✓   Red 221

The soft greens and shades of rose forming the shell and vine motif of this carpet place it as an Aubusson type of floor covering.

Graph for Aubusson carpet, with shell motif on pages 238 and 239.

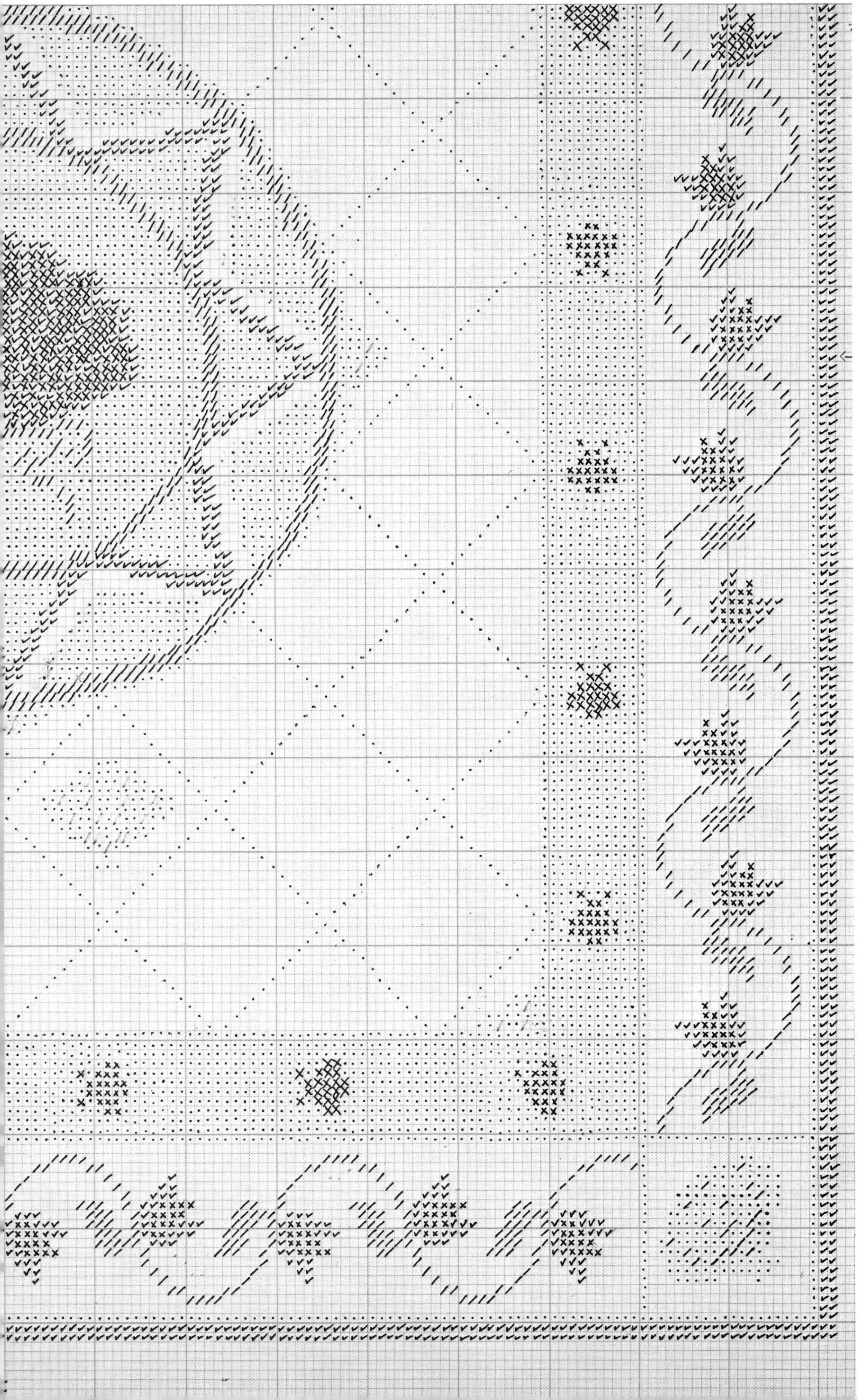

Another Aubusson design for Federal homes shows a vase filled with flowers. A matching rug using some of the same motifs might accompany it on the floor.

Flower Vase Aubusson Carpet

#28 silk gauze
DMC embroidery floss, 2 threads

✓	Red 355	—	Green 3347
•	White blanc neige	G	Gold 676
☐	Blue 927 background	●	Light pink 225
x	Dark blue 926	O	Pink 224
K	Dark green 890		

Graph for vase with flowers Aubusson.

Matching Carpet

This carpet might accompany the flower vase Aubusson when there is a need for two rugs to be used together, but not necessarily to match exactly. The two charts may also be used to make a third carpet, larger than the two charted here. Three carpets were often used in a large room of a Federal period home. Page 80 shows the rugs used as one unit.

Graph for similar carpet, which might accompany vase with flowers Aubusson.

Kay Weiger's carpet design resembles an Aubusson with an allover design of stylized flowers.

Aubusson Carpet

#38 silk gauze
DMC embroidery floss, 1 thread
o   Green 3053
V   Rose 899
•   Pink 3354
x   Gold 725
/   Green 3347
▲   Deep rose 3687
□   Eggshell 712 background

A Greek carpet design in the Aubusson style. The soft colors make it adaptable for a setting where an overall pattern is needed. Kay Weiger designed and worked this carpet, and charted one side, the top, and one flower motif so that it can be made to any size.

Graph for Aubusson carpet with stylized flowers.

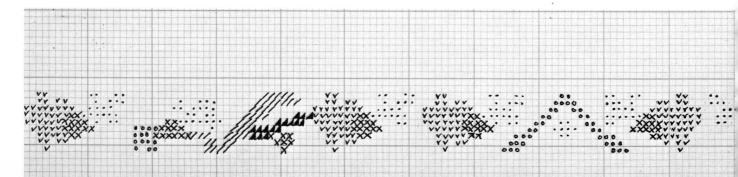

The Aubusson style is reflected in this carpet by Kay Weiger
with a central motif, which resembles a patera, surrounded
by wreaths of flowers.

Patera Aubusson Carpet

#24 silk gauze
DMC embroidery floss, 3 threads
x   Pink 224
o   Medium rose 225
V   Rose 223
/   Green 3053
□   Eggshell 712 background

A mélange of flowered wreaths surround the pa-
teralike center motif of this beautiful carpet. The
colors are a combination of soft rose, pink, and green.

Graph for patera Aubusson on pages 248 and 249.

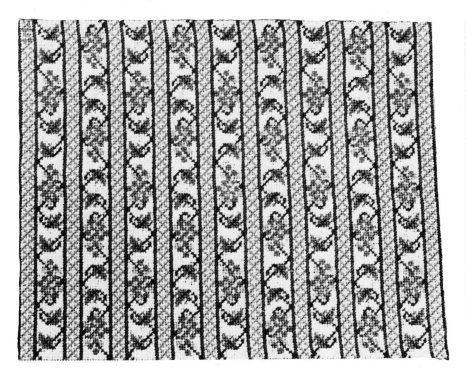

Early-eighteenth-century canvas stitched carpets were often
designed in borders. A curved design alternated with a more
geometric stripe. Grapes are a standard Federal motif.
Designed by Susan Richardson; stitched by Lois Sterling.

Federal Border Carpet

#24 silk gauze
DMC embroidery floss, 2 threads

L	Lavender 316	/	Dark blue 924
P	Purple 315	o	Light blue 926
G	Dark green 934	□	Yellow background 746
✓	Olive 3011		

An eighteenth-century bordered carpet, displaying
the typical grape-and-leaf motif that was popular in the
Federal period.

Graph of Federal border carpet turned on side.
Each stripe alternates its vertical direction.

This circular carpet is appropriate for Empire floors with an eagle surrounded by laurel wreaths in Napoleon green and gold colors.

Circular Eagle Carpet

#28 silk gauze
DMC embroidery floss, 2 threads

☐   Emerald green 890 background
o   Dark gold 680
/   Light gold 3047
—   Dark brown 632
x   Black 310

An Empire carpet displaying exceptionally well executed designs that conform to the shape and size within a confined area. The round edge can be maintained if, upon completion, the outside edge is unraveled and the threads are woven one by one through the back stitches.

Graph of circular eagle carpet.

Geometric carpet design.

Geometric Carpet

#24 canvas
Penelope wool thread, 1 strand

D	Medium blue 322	W	White 992
P	Pink 702	R	Dark red 716
N	Dark blue 325	□	Aqua 692 background
B	Light blue 562	∩	Rose 143
/	Beige 691	Z	Dark green 254

The geometric design of this carpet has its place in the appropriate setting. It emphasizes a more tailored look.

Graph of geometric carpet design on pages 254 and 255.

Turkish carpet by Claudine Wilson.

Turkish Carpet

#24 silk gauze
DMC embroidery floss, 3 threads

x   Beige 738
\   Peach 402
△   Golden yellow 676
V   Golden beige 613
•   Brick 920 inner background
o   Navy blue 823
□   Brick 920 background

Exceptionally well-executed designs are found in this Turkish carpet by Claudine Wilson. The colors blend well in a coordinated theme of shapes and curves. The edge is fringed, as were many of the old Turkish carpets.

Graph for Turkish carpet on pages 256 and 257.

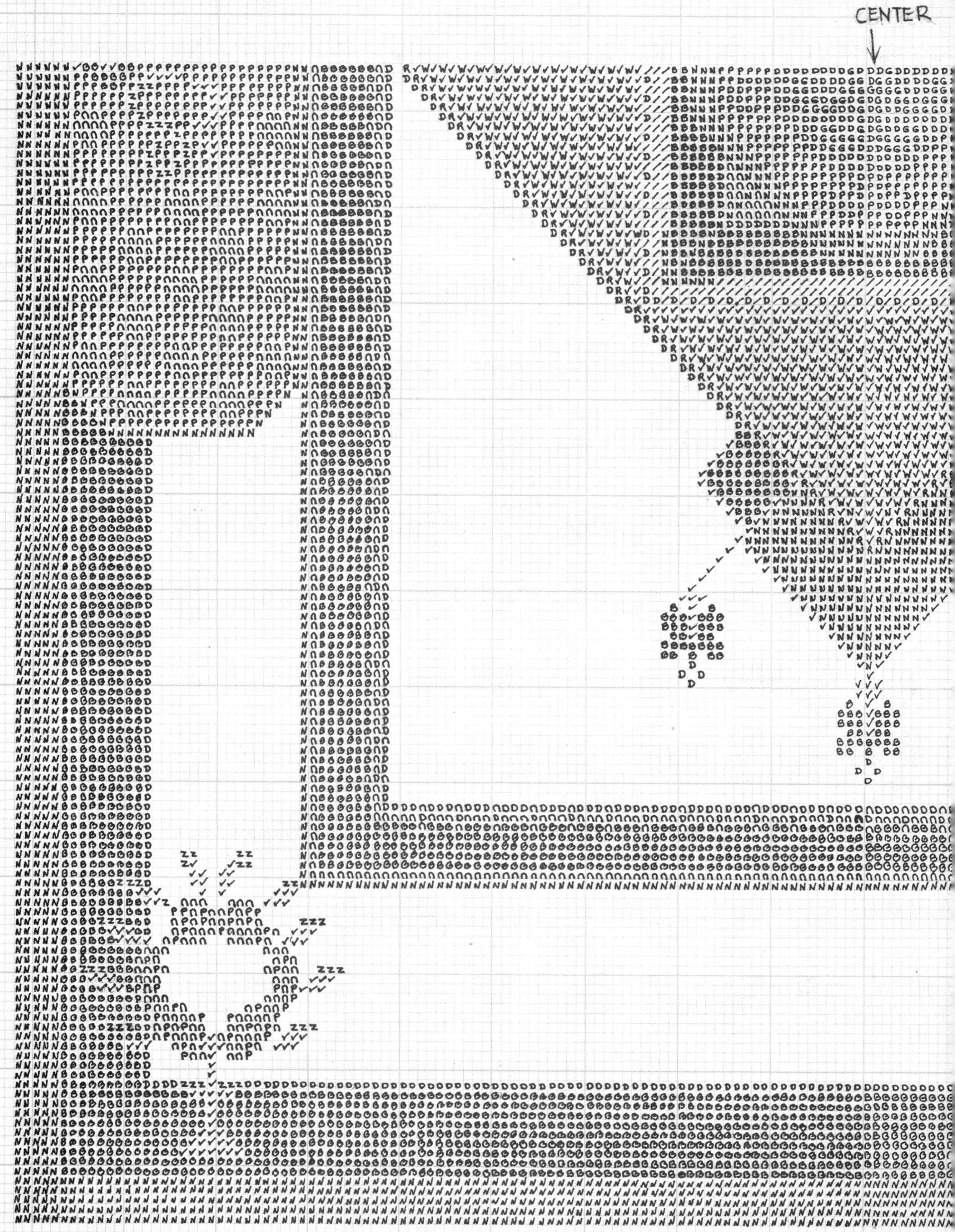
CENTER

255

— CENTER

613

613

613

920

402

Graph for Turkish carpet.

257

613

920

613

4082

← CENTER ROW
DO NOT REPEAT

Two Queen Anne Chair Seat Designs
Woman with Basket
Woman with Pails

#38 silk gauze
DMC embroidery floss, 1 thread

x	Dark green 890	W	White blanc neige
∧	Medium green 469	S	Flesh 543
∨	Green 471	P	Pink 224
•	Light green 472	—	Brown 801
0	Blue green 501	*	Dark brown 3371
R	Red 498	K	Black 310
B	Blue 312	+	Gray 414
G	Gold 676	□	Yellow 745 background

A common treatment for the Queen Anne balloon seat is a central pastoral scene with a frame of assorted flowers. Design by Susan Richardson.

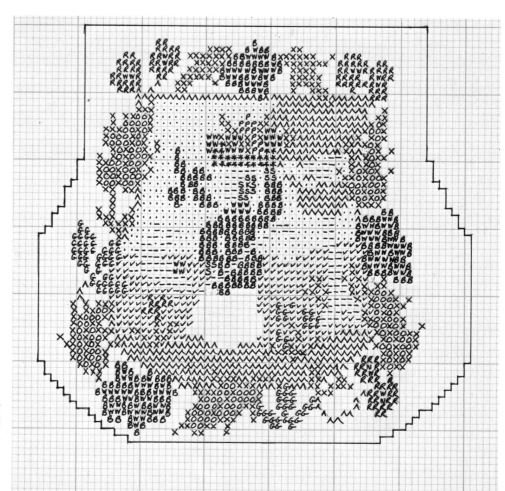

Graph for balloon seat cover of woman with a basket of flowers on her head.

The execution of these designs is truly remarkable, with the inclusion of so many details worked into a chair seat no bigger than a 1 1/2-inch square. The colors are coordinated, so they may be used as a pair, and the designs, woman with a basket on her head and woman with two pails, are typical for Queen Anne period chairs as seen in many museums. These were designed and worked by Susan Richardson. Instructions for making the chair for these pieces are on page 148.

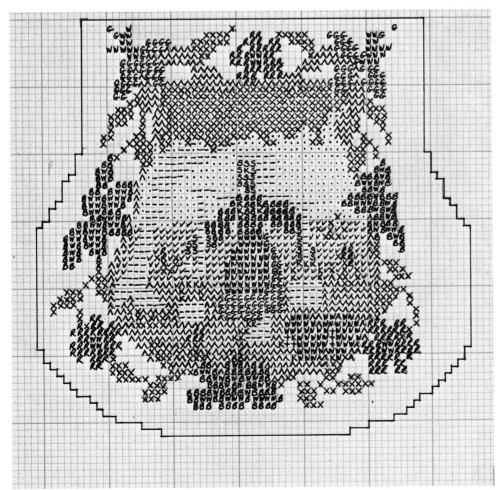

Graph for balloon seat cover of woman carrying milk pails.

4 A Collection of Works by Well-Known Artisans

The number of artisans making miniatures today is innumerable. Little people, medium people, and grown-up people are entering the wonderful world of "making and collecting" furniture and accessories, houses, dolls, and anything small enough to hold in the palm of your hand.

There are kits, plans, and books on the subject. And a supply source that can fill every need.

There is a wealth of opportunity for creating a small vignette or setting from the miniatures one has made or collected. A simple glass enclosure houses just such an assortment, as this intriguing example shows, with a banister-back chair, a carpet-covered table, a hand-painted portrait, a porcelain bowl, candlesticks, and a partially rolled sampler resting on the floor.

At the other extreme, a more formal and elaborate example has been created in this French-style music room, boasting a harpsichord, a gilt settee, and an eighteenth-century harp, complete with harpist.

On a more whimsical note, here is a vignette enclosing two white mice in a setting entitled "Saturday night bath."

A Christmas theme and a corner shop add to the variety of ideas for a small vignette.

Shifting the scene to the outdoors, as shown in the setting "Summers at the shore," presents an entirely unique idea. It is complete with a "live" green lawn,

miniature shrubs, trees, and garden plants, which took Kathleen Pitney two years to grow—in all, twenty-six different varieties of plant material. The real lawn, the same grass used on the putting greens of a golf course, is mowed with a pair of fine scissors. The three-sided porch on the Victorian-style house was designed and made by Jane Hotchkiss. The house and garden are situated on a bluff overlooking a quiet harbor. The entire scene is so lifelike you can almost imagine yourself in the wicker chair on the porch, watching the boats in the harbor. The hanging basket holds real dried ferns. The doors to the house are screened, the path of seashore stones (actually baked birdseed) divides the lush lawn and leads to a fence-enclosed garden (the fence was made from wooden coffee stirrers). Unfortunately, the live plant material in this setting cannot be maintained indefinitely. The plants are dismantled after being on exhibit and the tiny plants are returned to a greenhouse where they are kept alive until the diorama is displayed again.

A permanently sealed lamp base is another way of displaying a miniature setting, as Dusty Boynton's cleverly designed arrangements show.

Miniaturists are designing and making furniture pieces to accommodate attractively worked petit point. Such a piece is the Chippendale game table by Terry Rogal, with a needlework insert designed by Susan

Eighteenth-century music salon, adapted from an original design by Eugene Kupjack. Made by Virginia Merrill. The embroidered settee and chair are by Stephanie Matthews.

A William and Mary setting in a glass enclosure showing a table covered with a carpet and a banister-back chair with Irish-stitch seat pad. The carpet and pad are graphed in Chapter 3. The oil painting is by E. W. Allen, Jr., of Artist's Workshop. The candlesticks are by Eugene Kupjack and the bowl is by Priscilla Lance and Deborah McKnight.

"Saturday Night Bath," a whimsical composition with two white mice as the occupants.

This shallow vignette depicts a
Christmas scene. Designed and made
by Priscilla Lance.

Miniature room setting entitled "Sunday, Time for Renewal." Designed and made by Dusty Boynton. *Courtesy: Dusty Boynton*

Richardson and stitched by Joan Carson.

Fire screens, chair seats, and accessories such as pillows, pictures, and bellpulls are more examples of pieces that needlework designers are focusing on. Kits are popular for those who wish to have it all in "one package": canvas, thread, and complete directions. Stenciled or hand-painted furniture offers "another look" for the collector. Lovely paneled screens, desks, tables, and a number of other interesting and well-designed styles are available to complete a room decor.

Properly scaled dolls add to the overall conception of a miniature setting; so do a variety of accessories.

Furniture selection is the first consideration when planning a vignette, room setting, or decorating a miniature house. Keep in mind the period and style you want to achieve. We have gathered a number of exceptionally fine pieces, made by well-known artisans or manufacturers, for the reader to study. There are many other makers of furniture and accessories who are not represented here. They may be found by attending a show of miniatures, visiting an attractive shop, or through the advertisements in miniaturist magazines. Many of the photographs shown here reveal a miniature maker's approach and ingenuity in the construction and finishing of a particular piece of furniture. If this were not a book about miniatures, you would imagine it to be a life-size piece.

This miniature home setting titled "Sunday, Time for Renewal" was designed especially for the miniature room exhibit at the 1980 Philadelphia Flower Show. The artisan worked for six months to create a house and its environment within the prescribed limits of 26 by 40 inches. The design enables the viewer to see three interior rooms in detail, the exterior of the house, and the whole as it exists in the landscape that surrounds it. Deliberate touches reflect determination to catch a living, fleeting moment as opposed to a preservation: the baseball on the roof, the sneakers as they

Elmer Tag's Corner Shoppe is a well-constructed and perfectly designed miniature, waiting to be filled with minuscule gifts. This is the lower level of a two-level structure. The leaded glass door panels and transom, as well as the dentil molding and decorative corbel brackets, were also made by Elmer Tag. *Courtesy: Elmer Tag*

This diorama by Katina Mills speaks for itself.

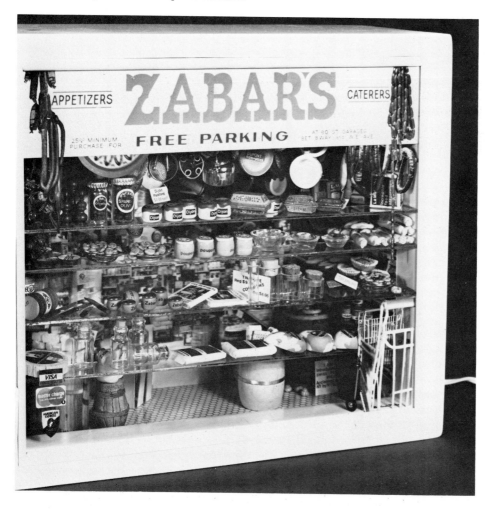

"Summer at the Shore," a display setting with a live-grass lawn and plants by Jane Hotchkiss and Kathleen Pitney.

lay, the open newspaper—unmistakable marks of the people who live there. The wallpapers, room colors, and lighting evoke not a decorator but the eclectic nature of a real home.

Supported by two bonsai trees, the hammock awaits the family, the water in the birdbath summons the birds, the goldfish pool is fed by natural water flow. The plant material and grass are all living. The interior includes solid cherry pegged floors, individual laid walnut parquet, cherry paneling, hand-hewn beams, a marble floor, and functioning glass doors. The home won a blue ribbon in Philadelphia and was subsequently shown in the Small Wonders II exhibit in Saint Davids, Pennsylvania, and at the International Guide of Miniature Artisans show at the Statler Hilton Hotel in New York City.

Another arrangement with dried plants.

A useful application of a small room in a permanently sealed lamp base. Designed and made by Dusty Boynton. *Courtesy: Dusty Boynton*

Another lamp base setting, this one enclosing a group of Queen Anne furniture, by Dusty Boynton. *Courtesy: Dusty Boynton*

This shallow setting can hang on the wall. A shop full of dolls. From The Enchanted Dollhouse.

A table piece entitled "For My Valentine," by Dusty Boynton. *Courtesy: Dusty Boynton*

Chippendale gaming table made by Terry Rogal, with Irish-stitch insert designed by Susan Richardson and stitched by Joan Carson.

An example of petit point applied to furniture. Made by Claire Dinsmore.

Fire screen and chair from Andrews Miniatures. The needlework is available in kits from C. J. Originals.

Two samplers worked on size 38 gauze, available in kits from C. J. Originals.

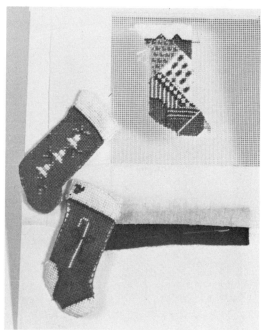

Another kit offers you a choice of Christmas stockings. To be worked on size 38 silk gauze. From C. J. Originals.

Embroidered items from C. J. Originals.

Cantitoe Corners offers "The American Museum Quilt Series" all in kit form. This quilt is "The Bird of Paradise."

"The Pride Of Iowa" miniature quilt is another in the museum series from Cantitoe Corners. *Courtesy: Cantitoe Corners*

A six-panel screen. Hand-painting on a black ground by Nancy Weaver.

Linda Wexler's hand-painted six-panel screen and ladies' desk are decorated with a chinoiserie hand-painted motif, and the desk with delicate flowers and scrolls.

Set of three tables, again showing Linda Wexler's exquisite painting. Tables made by Donald Dube.

Hillhouse Handmade Miniatures produces a line of nineteenth-century cottage furniture with authentic stenciled designs.

A Pennsylvania painted chest, from The Hoffman Collection. Hand-decorated by David Williamson.

Provincial cradle, circa 1890, Château de Romezay, Montreal, Canada. From Hillhouse Handmade Miniatures.

This magnificent hand-sculpted porcelain doll was designed and made by Galia Bazylko.

Susan Sirkis made this lovely eighteenth-century doll.

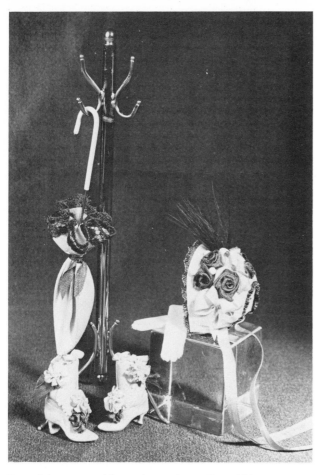

Parasol, bonnet, and boots from The Doll's Cobbler.
Collection of Gloria Hurme

U.S.F. *Constitution* in miniature measures 3″ × 3 1/2″.
"Old Ironsides," famous for her brilliant actions in the War
of 1812, now lies quietly at the Boston Navy Yard. Made by
Ron Stetkowicz.

Trunk-Full-of-Dolls. The
trunk by Diane Kennedy
and the dolls made by
Elaine Bohensky. Both
items from The Burkey Place.

Early American tray, Queen Anne period. Made by Rose Barell. The two decanters have ground glass stoppers, hand-blown by Francis Whittemore.

A blackamoor, used as a decorative piece.

To add charm to your settings, these charming flower arrangements and fruit pyramid are available from The Paisley Shop.

An elaborate hand-blown chandelier built around a hollow base with eight arms and several tiers decorated with approximately 700 tiny glass beads. Made by Gerry Rynders of The Glassblowing Shop.

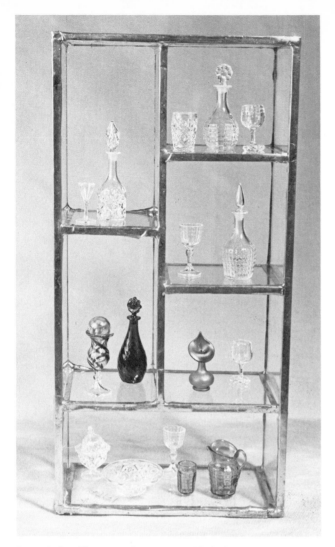

Pressed, free-blown, and pattern molded glass pieces by Ferenec Albert. The Tiffany vase, second shelf, second from the right, is a hand-blown piece by Frances Whittemore.

A magnificent chair of the Louis XV period, with curvilinear lines emphasizing the graciousness of the period. The caned seat and back are extremely well executed.
Made by Terry Rogal.

A full-size pen nib dwarfs the tiny inkwells and readable books.

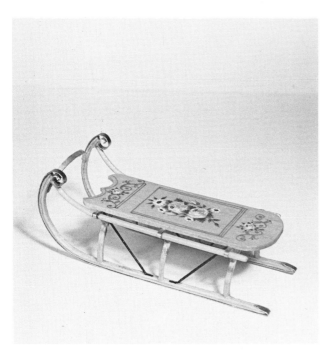

"Paris Cutter" sled with a top decoration of flowers and leaves, from Hillhouse Handmade Miniatures.

Brass birdcage and horse tricycle made by Alex Fried. Available from Dearring Tracy Ltd.

Assortment of baskets, made by Roberta Partridge of The Bird House.

Fanciful swan bed and small cradle made by Frank Matter; from Andrews Miniatures.

Miniature paintings by E. W. Allen, Jr., of Artist's Workshop.

A Venetian parlor stove
by Eugene Kupjack.

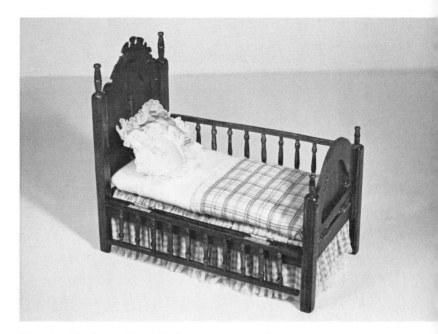

Victorian "Anderson Youth Bed," circa 1830, made of black walnut.
By Linda Jamison of Suite Dreams.

Donald Buttfield's bentwood fish stand.

A magnificent secretary desk made in England by
George Early. From a private collection.

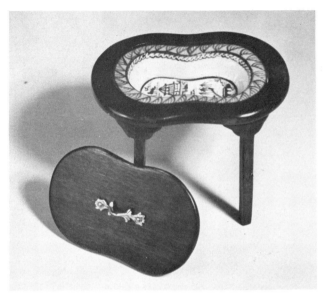

Music stand, made for Virginia Merrill by W. Foster Tracy.

A bidet with removable top made by Virginia Merrill. The porcelain liner is by Deborah McKnight.

William and Mary side table with elaborate apron, serpentine stretcher, bun feet, circa 1690; and a pair of reeded yoke banister-back side chairs, circa 1765. Made by Don Buckley. *Courtesy: Don Buckley*

Classic corner cupboard with fluted stiles, heavy molding, raised panel doors, and butterfly shelves. Flanked by a pair of mid-eighteenth-century ladder-back armchairs with medial arm stretchers. Made by Don Buckley.
Courtesy: Don Buckley

A four-poster bed with crewel bed hangings and bedspread, bed steps, candlestand, lowboy, bonnet-top highboy, all available from Roger L. Gutheil, Inc. *Courtesy: Roger L. Gutheil, Inc.*

A San Francisco Victorian row house, with elaborately carved detail. The three-story structure with an attic and a tower was made by Jim Marcus, the gifted builder of such Victorian dollhouses. The quality of his work and the result of his accuracy of reproduction places him at the top of the list as an artist, historian, and master miniaturist.

A bedroom setting with furniture available from R-Stuff.

R-Stuff offers this lovely
wing chair and Queen
Anne table for a room
setting or the interior
of a miniature house.

A big Christmas in a small box, by Dusty
Boynton. *Courtesy: Dusty Boynton*

5 Ready Reference Chart

PERIOD	Jacobean	William and Mary	Queen Anne
FURNITURE **Craftsmen**	Turners and joiners.	Cabinetmakers.	Cabinetmakers.
Wood	Oak.	Walnut and maple.	Mahogany.
Style	Turned supports. Painting, carving, applied turnings and knobs (sometimes painted black).	Slender turned supports: cup and trumpet turnings. Ball, bun, or Spanish foot. Arched crests. Sinuous crossed stretchers. Ram's horn handholds. Arched aprons. Veneer, marquetry, japanning.	Cabriole leg with pad, slipper, trifid, or claw-and-ball foot. Spoon back. Solid vase splat. Hoop back. Angular or balloon seat. Broken scrolled pediment with finials. Arched apron with drops. Natural wood-grain surfaces. Carved shells. Japanning.
Hardware	Wooden knobs for storage piece handles.	Diamond-shaped plate with teardrop handle; larger matching key escutcheon with engraved decoration. Both of brass.	Brass batwing-shaped plate with wide U-shaped handle; matching key escutcheon.

FORMS
Seating
	Chests.
	Benches.
	Joint stools.
	Settles.
	"Great chairs":
	   Brewster.
	   Carver.
		Stools.
		Wing chairs.
		Banister-back chairs.
		Boston chairs.
		Caned Carolean chairs.
		Corner chairs.
			Stools.
			Open-back side chairs.
			Open-back armchairs.
			Upholstered-back side chairs.
			Upholstered-back armchairs.
			Slipper chairs.
			Corner chairs.

Chippendale	Federal	Empire	Victorian
Cabinetmakers.	Cabinetmakers.	Cabinetmakers.	Cabinetmakers and factories.
Mahogany.	Mahogany.	Mahogany and rosewood.	Mahogany, rosewood, black walnut, iron, and papier-mâché.
Pierced splat. Bow-shaped crest rail. Angular seat. Broken scrolled pediment. Scalloped apron. Fretwork and openwork galleries. Cabriole leg with claw-and-ball foot. Chippendale straight leg. Marlborough leg on a plinth. Pierced leg brackets. Carved acanthus leaves and cobochon on knee.	Tapered straight leg (perhaps with spade foot) or reeded round leg. Shield, heart, oval, and square chairbacks. Carved splat. Vase pedestal base. Triangular broken pediment, flat top, or gently curved pediment. Doors with framed glass panels. Satinwood inlay in linear or classical motifs. Reeding. Veneered surfaces. Carved or brass cast classical motifs (urns, swags, bellflowers) mythological figures, or patriotic symbols.	Duncan Phyfe: Klismos and curule chairs. Vase pedestal with tripod saber leg supports. Carved waterleafs. Animal's paw or squared brass foot and perhaps casters. Lyre splats and supports. Lannuier: Marble columns, brass inlay, and ormolu mounts. 1810: Scrolled furniture parts. Winged or caryatid supports. 1820: Leg brackets of carved leaves or wings. Bulbous feet. Stenciling instead of ormolu. 1830: Heavy flat surfaces. Plain large scrolls. Protruding columns. Plain veneered surfaces.	Classical Revival (1830–1850): Leaf bracket on lion's paw foot. Large columns. Spirals for arm and leg supports. Gothic Revival (1830–1860): Pointed arches. Carved cusps, crockets, rosettes, and tracery. Tre- and quatrefoils. Rococo Revival (1850–1870): John Henry Belter. Curved surfaces created by lamination process. Ornate hand-carved rococo motifs in open patterns. Cabriole front leg. Convex rear leg. Elizabethan Revival (1840–1860): Twisted spiral turnings. Renaissance Revival (1850–1870): Crests of heavy curved pediments. Superimposed medallions. Acorn turnings. Molded busts. Rectilinear and architectural. Armchairs with heavy upholstery, handholds of carved heads, and trumpetlike leg turnings.
Larger brass batwing plate, often pierced, with elongated U-shaped handle and matching key escutcheon; each end of U-shaped handle suspended from small round disc with thin frame around key escutcheon.	Round or oval backplate with swinging handles; flat, circular protruding handles used as drawer pulls. Both styles of brass.	Brass lion's head with circular ring in mouth.	Carved wooden grips; round ornate gilt backplate with suspended ring; wooden or glass knobs.
Open-back side chairs with pierced splat or ladder back. Open-back armchairs. Lolling chairs. Open-back settees. Upholstered-back settees. Serpentine-back sofas.	Open-back side chairs. Open-back armchairs. Back stools. Lolling chairs. Wing chairs. Barrel-shaped easy chairs. Open-arm chairs with low	Klismos chairs. Curule chairs. Window benches. Sofas, e.g., Grecian squab.	Classical Grecian squab sofas. Gothic high-back side chairs. Rococo side chairs with tall back composed of carved openwork. Rococo upholstered high-back side chairs.

PERIOD	Jacobean	William and Mary	Queen Anne
FORMS			
Seating (con't)	Wainscot. Ladder-back. Cromwellian.		Wing chairs. Settees with upholstered or open back or arms. Sofas, rarely.
Beds	Straw mattresses on pallets. Stump bedsteads. Tester bedsteads.	Daybeds. Tester bedsteads. Folding trestle beds.	Daybeds. Low-post beds. Tester beds. Field beds.
Tables	Trestle tables. Chair tables. Settle tables. Stretcher tables. Butterfly tables. Gateleg tables.	Gateleg tables. Butterfly tables. Hutch tables. Tavern tables. Splay-leg tables. Porringer tables. Mixing tables.	Rectangular tea tables. Round tea tables. Drop-leaf tables with oval opened surface. Handkerchief tables. Folding card tables. Marble-topped pier or center tables. Candlestands. Mixing tables.
Case Pieces	Chests. Court cupboards. Press cupboards. Blanket chests. Bible boxes. Spice cabinets.	High chests with four to six legs. Dressing tables. Desks-on-frames. Slant-top desks. Desks and bookcases (secretaries). Tall case clocks.	Shell cupboards. Kas. High chests. Dressing tables. Desks-on-frames. Slant-top desks. Secretaries. Tall case clocks.
MISCELLANEOUS		Pier glasses. Pole screens.	Longer pier glasses. Pole screens.

Chippendale	Federal	Empire	Victorian
Corner chairs. Wing chairs. Stools.	upholstered back to match sofa. Windsor chairs. Sheraton fancy chairs. Hitchcock chairs. Boston rockers. Sheraton-styled sofas. Baltimore cabriole-styled sofas. Hepplewhite-styled sofas. Window benches.		Rococo medallion-back sofas. Rococo tête-à-têtes. Rococo single-end sofas. Rococo balloon-back side chairs. Elizabethan tall-back side chairs. Renaissance armchairs. Patent furniture, e.g., swivel chairs. Papier-mâché chairs. Upholstered ottomans.
Tester beds. Low-post beds. Field beds.	Tester beds. Field beds.	Sleigh beds.	Renaissance bedroom suites. Elizabethan cottage furniture.
Rectangular tea tables. Piecrust tea tables. China tables. Center or pier tables. Folding card tables. Rectangular drop-leaf dining tables. Handkerchief tables. Pembroke tables. Spider gateleg tables. Kettle stands. Basin stands.	Worktables. Pembroke tables. Drum tables. Rent tables. Sofa tables. Folding card tables. Side or pier tables. Sectioned dining tables. Corner basin stands. Pole screens. Music stands. Cellarettes. Mixing tables. Drawing tables. Dressing tables.	Side or pier tables. Folding card tables. Round tables with marble tops and central supports. Round wooden-topped tables with three columns as support. Sectioned dining tables.	Classical pedestal-based tables. Gothic pedestal-based dining tables. Rococo oval center tables. Papier-mâché tables.

High chests.
Dressing tables.
Chests of drawers:
   Flat front.
   Serpentine front.
   Reverse serpentine front.
   Block front.
   Bombé.
Chest-on-chests.
Kneehole dressing tables or desks.
Slant-top desks.
Secretaries.
Breakfronts.
Tall case clocks.
	Chest-on-chests.
	Chests of drawers.
	Dressing chests.
	Commodes.
	Sideboards.
	Slant-top desks.
	Tambour desks.
	Ladies' desks.
	Secretaries.
	Salem secretaries (breakfronts).
	Piano cases.
	Tall case clocks.
		Chests of drawers.
		Desks with cylinder closings.
		Sideboards.
		Piano cases.
			Classical sideboards.
			Rococo ladies' desks.
			Rococo bureaus with mirror.
			Renaissance wardrobes.
			Renaissance sideboards.

Bracket clocks.
Knife cases.
Pier glasses:
   Fretwork.
   Architectural.
   Rococo.
Pole screens.
	Case-on-case clocks.
	Banjo clocks.
	Girandole clocks.
	Pillar and scroll clocks.
	Pier glasses:
	   Broken scrolled pediment with gilding. French putty.
	   Tabernacle.
	Chimney glasses.
	Girandole mirrors.
	Wine coolers. Canterburies.
		Heavy pier glasses.
		Girandole mirrors.
			Gothic whatnot shelves.
			Rococo whatnot shelves.
			Renaissance étagères.
			Gothic steeple clocks.

PERIOD	Jacobean	William and Mary	Queen Anne
In America			
In England	William and Mary style using veneers, marquetry, and japanning on walnut to create: daybeds, tall-back chairs, high chests, drop-front desks, tall case clocks, and upholstered wing chairs.	Early Georgian style: chairbacks lower; pierced splats; cabriole legs with claw-and-ball feet; carved mahogany wood.	Georgian style: chest of drawers, desk, console table. Claw-and-ball feet, ogee bracket feet, mask and shell carving.
In France			
Upholstery	Knife-edged cushions. Cromwellian chair upholstery. Turkey work. Leather with brass tacks. Embroidered linens. Velvets. Satins. Tent-stitch patterns in flames, crests, flowers, and landscapes.	Knife-edged cushions with tasseled cords. Squab for daybed. Round end pillow for daybed. Flame patterns popular. Bright colored silk velvets; brocades; brocatelles; damasks; silks; embroideries, chintzes; calicoes; blue-and-white furniture checks; tapestrylike needlework scenes framed with flowers; printed linens, e.g., blue resist and copperplate prints; wools in red, green, gold, or blue.	Upholstery and gaming table inserts. Canvas work; crewel embroideries; blue resist-printed linens; copper-printed linens; leathers; velvets; silks; brocades; brocatelles.
Drapery	Italian brocatelles, damasks, and crewel-embroidered linens. Window-length panels hung on a rod on casement windows. Full set of hangings on tester bed which completely enclosed it. Straight edges and no gathering on valences and bases.	Wooden shutters. Fabrics same as upholstery, except for leather. Crewel-embroidered linens show tree of life motif. At window: floor-length side panels with scalloped valance; Venetian curtains.	Wooden shutters. Venetian blinds after 1750. Upholstery fabrics except leather, and crewel-embroidered linens at windows. Side panels with scalloped valance, Venetian and festoon drapery styles. Bed curtains located only at head of bed and did not enclose sleeping area.
Floor Coverings	Animal skins. Oriental and English carpets on table only.	Oriental and English carpets on table and floor.	Carpets only on floor. Oriental carpets. English needlework carpets. Painted floorcloths. Rag-woven (or list) carpets.

Chippendale	Federal	Empire	Victorian

Windsor chairs.
Pennsylvania German painted furniture:
    Scrolled-back chairs.
    Dower chests.
    Chests of drawers.
	Windsor chairs.	Shaker furniture:
		    Ladder-back chairs.
		    Long tables.	

Neoclassicism with inlay, controlled carving, and painting.	Regency style.	Regency style.	Gothic and oriental revivals.
	Napoleon Empire style.	Restoration style.	
Blue, red, or green silk damasks. Velvets. Leathers. Copper-printed cottons with blue oriental motifs. Blue resist linens. Crewel-embroidered linens. Tent-stitch canvas.	Silks (plain, striped, and/or embroidered), leathers, damasks, horsehair, floral chintzes, red copperplate cottons with historical scenes. Pale colors in the drawing room and bedroom; darker colors in dining room and study. Brass tacks in straight line or swags or scallops. Later replaced by contrasting tape.	Heavily figured silks and satins. Leathers. Velvets. Brass tacks and decorative tape. Motifs: Napoleon "N," stripes, eagles framed with laurel wreaths, gold medallions on bright grounds.	Black horsehair; velvets; brocades; damasks; Jacquard woven fabrics; printed chintzes; silks; Berlin needlework. Colors: 1830–1840: scarlet, yellow, turquoise, and yellow green. 1850: crimson and bottle green. 1855: maroon, tan, and dark green.

Damasks, velvets, and printed textiles. Venetian draperies. Festoon draperies. Floor-length panels with scalloped valance. On bed, scalloped hem on valances and bases. Ornamental headcloth and curtains at head of bed only. Decorative tape trim on printed textiles.	French draperies with a valance of festoons, a flat scalloped panel, or a pole draped with fabric.
	Fringe trim.
	Mull curtain panels. On bed, valances have scalloped hem or straight with cording swags on the surface. Fringed silk or satin embroidered spreads. Festooned hangings tied with cords.
	Matching drapery and upholstery in rooms.
		Federal-style window treatment with Empire upholstery fabrics, except leather and mull. Sleigh bed has crown drapery treatment.
		Matching drapery and upholstery in rooms.
			French curtains topped by variety of valances:
			Classical (1830s):
			    Box pleats or festoons.
			    Sheer muslin undercurtains.
			Gothic: Pointed arch silhouette.
			Elizabethan: Strapwork silhouette.
			Rococo: Festoons.
			Sheer muslins: used for undercurtains; embroidered with white designs in 1850s; sheer single panel.
			Lace or machine-made net curtains used alone at window later in period.
			Cambric window shades: 1830–1860.

"Turkish" carpets. Floral needlework carpets. Rag-woven carpets. Scotch carpets. Painted floor coverings. Grass mats in summer.	Carpets: Oriental; French Savonnerie and Aubusson; English Axminster; needlepoint; rag-woven; Scotch. Hooked rugs modeled after Aubusson examples.	Carpets: French Empire Aubusson; English Axminster; rag-woven; Scotch; and hooked.	Machine weaving: wall-to-wall Brussels carpeting, striped or checked venetian stair carpeting, individual rugs, ingrain carpets. Oriental rugs from the Far East.

Floor Coverings (con't)

Needlework	Strip sampler. Crewel-embroidered bed hangings with tree of life, bucolic, and flame pattern motifs. One-piece quilts with floral and geometric patterns. Knit stockings and mittens.	Strip sampler. Crewel-embroidered linens for drapery fabric, petticoat borders, and pockets. Tent-stitch upholstery and hatchments. Flame patterned upholstery and cushions. One-piece quilts. Knit stockings and mittens.	School samplers. Crewel-embroidered hatchments, bed hangings, window draperies, upholstery fabrics, pockets, petticoat borders, clothing decoration, and pictures for wall. Tent-stitch upholstery, pocketbooks, and pictures, e.g., fishing lady pictures. Irish-stitch upholstery, tablecloths, standing or hand fire screens, wall pockets, pocketbooks, book covers, candlescreens. One-piece quilts. After 1750, pieced quilts. Knit stockings and mittens.
Silver	Architectural. Based on Italian Renaissance style. Raised panels, chased floral patterns, engraved heraldic designs, flat strapped handles. Caudle cup, dram cup, punch bowl, beaker, tumbler, small cups, spout cup, tankards, mugs. Porringers. Medium-sized spoons: slip-end, Puritan, and trifid; sucket fork. Standing salts, trencher salts, and elliptical sugar boxes. Salvers on trumpet foot, chafing dishes. Candlesticks: clusters of columns for shaft and mid drip pan and square base.	Baroque basis: heavy, three-dimensional details; curves in motion; gadrooning; repoussé; cast elements; richness from combination of decorative techniques; ear-shaped cast handles (often with caryatid). Papboats, caudle cups, dram cups, beakers, tankards, mugs, canns. Porringers. Trencher salts, standing salts, casters, sugar boxes. Footed salvers; monteith bowls. Teapot; coffeepot; chocolate pot. Candlesticks: round stop fluted columns with square bases, mid and socket drip pans. Coral-and-bells; small boxes. Inkstand (standish).	More abundant in homes. Curvilinear silhouette; S-curve of spouts, handles; pear shape of containers; engraved ornamentation; midband; domed lid. Mugs, tankards, canns, round bottomed tumblers, presentation loving cups. Porringers. Spoons for eating and serving, strainer spoons, tea tongs. Sets of three casters; trencher salts. Salvers on three or four short feet, chafing dishes, sauceboats. Teapot, coffeepot, chocolate pot, milk pot, sugar bowl, tea caddy, tea kettle on stand. Candlesticks: octagonal lobed base with baluster shaft, no drip pan. Snuffer on tray.

Chippendale	Federal	Empire	Victorian
			Hand-knotted individual rugs with Victorian motifs. Berlin needlework rugs. Hooked rugs, e.g., designed by E. S. Frost. Colors: background of amethyst, forest green, deep mazarine blue; design of mauve, lavender, robin's-egg blue, and fern green.
School samplers. Crewel embroidery on petticoat borders, potholders, hatchments, clothing. Tent-stitch game table inserts. Tent- and Irish-stitch pocketbooks, upholstery, pincushions, hand and pole fire screens, wall pockets, and tablecloths. Quilts: one-piece, pieced, and appliqué. Knit purses.	School samplers. Silk-embroidered pictures, e.g., mourning pictures. Tambour work for drapes and dresses. Candlewicking for bedspreads. Marseilles quilting. Quilts: one-piece, pieced, and appliqué often combined. Knit lace edgings for tablecloths, pillowcases, and collars.	Silk embroidery until 1830. Then Berlin canvas work. Quilts: one-piece, pieced, and appliqué. Silk fabrics often used. Three techniques combined.	Berlin work 1830–1870: tent- and Irish-stitch pillows, upholstery, wastebaskets, slippers, rugs, pictures, frames, cigar cases, bellpulls, purses, antimacassars. Quilts: one-piece, pieced, and appliqué techniques combined. Silk pieced quilts. Friendship quilts. Crazy quilts.
Three-dimensional ornamentation of cast appliqués, repoussé, and gadrooning; naturalistic motifs; asymmetrical curves; piercing; pear and inverted-pear shapes; feet: claw-and-ball, shell; domed or double-domed lids with finials. Beakers, canns, mugs, tankards. Porringers. Spoons in various sizes with curved handle; concave bowl facing up when set on table; strainer spoon, punch ladle with shell bowl; tea tongs in scissor and bow shapes. Trencher salts and casters with glass cruets on tray. Punch bowl and strainer; chafing dishes; sauceboats; dish rings; salvers. Teapot; taller matching coffeepot; tea kettle; milk pot; sugar bowl; slop bowl; tea caddy. Candlesticks with square base and portable bobeches. Snuffers on a tray. Inkstands.	Symmetry, simplicity, and precision; French feet; classical shapes: urn, oval, inverted helmet; beading, reeded molding, fluted sides, cast finials, engraving. Sets emphasized. Goblets, cups, beakers, mugs, canns. Knives, four-tine forks, and spoons, each in own pattern. Down-turned handle. Caddy spoon, marrow spoon, salt and mustard spoons. Salt cellars, casters, and mustard pots. Chafing dishes with saucepans, sauceboats, papboats, sauce tureens, soup tureens, punch bowls with strainer, bread and cake baskets, toast racks, baking dishes, pitchers, and trays, some flat. Porringers. Teapot on fitted tray, coffeepot, lidded sugar bowl, creamer, slop bowl, bow tea tongs, urn. Candlesticks: fluted or reeded columns on square, round, or oval base; shaft slightly shaped; urn socket.	Heavy broadened forms; pear and inverted-pear shapes; horizontal decorative bands; gadrooning; melon reeding; cast ornamentation; classical shapes: amphora; Egyptian motifs: sphinx supports, coiled snakes, stylized plants and flowers; patriotic symbols. Goblets and beakers. Dinner plates. Knives, four-tine forks, and spoons, each in own pattern; fiddle-shaped handle with projections where bowl joins handle; ladles with circular bowls; fish servers; and skewers. Salt cellars, cruet stands, and mustard pots. Cake baskets, vegetable dishes, sauceboats with tray, pitchers, and trays. Two teapots, coffeepot, creamer, sugar bowl, urn, slop bowl, bow tea tongs. Candlesticks: tall classical columns with urn socket and Empire decoration; short chamberstick; candelabra. Inkstands.	Prolific in homes. Rococo recurving line and naturalism; sculptured decoration; naturalistic forms become parts of objects. Renaissance classical friezes; machine engraving, piercing, flat chasing, casting, embossing, freestanding figures. Large sets of objects. Oviform goblet as presentation piece. All flatware pieces in matching pattern: forks, knives, spoons, nut picks, and crumb, orange, fish knives; handles turned up; no projections at bowl juncture; pointed handle. Salt cellars and mustard pots. Dinner service: entrée dishes, centerpiece, vegetable dishes, tureens. Fruit compotes, cake baskets, ewers, punch bowls, monteiths. Tea service: tea kettle on stand, two teapots, coffeepot or urn, sugar bowl, creamer, waste bowl, pitchers, spoon holder, domed butter dish, bow-shaped tea tongs.

PERIOD	Jacobean	William and Mary	Queen Anne
Silver *(con't)*			
Pewter	Follows silver in form, but simple, crude ornamentation. Spoons; standing salts; trencher salts; tankards; mugs; few candlesticks; flagons; liquid measure; sadware with wide rim that becomes narrow and triple reeded: saucers, plates, soup plates, dishes, basins, chargers; porringers.	More abundant. Eating utensils and food containers: porringers, sadware with triple-reeded rim, flagons, tankards, mugs, standing salts, trencher salts, trifid-end spoons, few candlesticks, and chandeliers.	Sadware with single-reeded rim, spoons with trifid end, mugs and tankards with midbands and domed lids, beakers, porringers, teapots, sugar bowls, creamers.
Britannia			
CERAMICS			
In America	Redware with trailed slip; stoneware.	Redware and stoneware for practical forms.	Redware, stoneware, and sgraffito pottery.
In England	Redware. Stoneware: delftware: influenced by oriental porcelains; blue designs on white ground: two-handled posset pots with lid, globular wine bottles, blue dash chargers, "Merrymen" plates, barrel-shaped mugs, cylindrical tygs, fuddling cups, barbers' bowls, tablewares.	Delftware: red, green, purple, and yellow added to blue designs; some trek; round, octagonal, scalloped, or wavy edge on plates; tiles; teapots; cups; mugs; sugar bowls; creamers; tea caddies; sauceboats; tureens; monteiths; labels for necks of wine bottles; bricks; punch bowls with ladles; and puzzle jugs. White sprigged salt-glazed stoneware. Lead-glazed earthenware.	Staffordshire: agateware; tortoiseshell; "image toys"; salt-glazed stoneware: tablewares, "pew groups"; delftware: multicolored Chinese shapes and motifs; round, octagonal, or scalloped plates with wide rims; tiles.

Chippendale	Federal	Empire	Victorian
	Inkstands; sewing equipment; thimbles, hooks, needle cases, bodkins, chatelaine hooks; brooches, crosses, earrings, armbands, medals. Presentation pieces: tureens, punch bowls, and tea services.		Candlesticks and candelabra: fanciful arrangement of freestanding figures and naturalistic forms. Tea balls, punch strainers, napkin rings, thimbles, small boxes, inkstands, card receivers.
Prolific in homes. Forms follow silver, but simpler ornamentation. Teapot, sugar bowl, creamer, sadware with smooth rims, tankards, flagons and mugs with midbands and domed and double-domed lids, beakers, spoons, porringers.	Decline in demand for pewter: mugs, sadware with single-reeded rim. Neoclassical shapes.		
	Hard, bright, durable pewter with no lead. Used for traditional pewter forms: plates, mugs, porringers. Simple decoration.	Followed silver forms with melon reeding and wide fluting. Pear or inverted-pear shape; pedestals; scrolled and double-scrolled handles. Lamps: bell, inverted-bell, and cylindrical shapes on saucer, on a shaft with domed base, or independent. Candlesticks: baluster shaft on domed foot or mid-sized shaft topped by tall tulip clear glass globe.	Cake baskets, liquid fuel lamps, candlesticks, spoons, cuspidors, picture frames, snuff and tobacco boxes, faucets, ear portion of hearing trumpets. In 1860s replaced by ceramics, pressed glass, and silver-coated electroplated objects.
Redware, stoneware, sgraffito plates, bowls, mugs, platters, cooking utensils, and pitchers.	Redware, stoneware, sgraffito pottery with trailed slip or incised designs	Stoneware made in molds with naturalistic high-relief designs in white, yellow, and Rockingham brown: pitchers, flower pots, tea sets, jars, mugs, Toby jugs, spittoons, water coolers, tablewares, hound-handled and apostle pitchers. Spatterware. Transfer-printed tablewares. Tucker porcelain.	Stoneware instead of redware, except for most basic items; ornate decoration in blue or brown; everyday dishes in yellow, white, or Rockingham brown. Parian ware: statues, vases, pitchers, appliqués on blue, tan, pink, or green objects. Parian and Rockingham figurines.
Transfer-printed creamware. Frazackerly. Bianco sopra bianco. Jackfield wares. Cauliflower and pineapple forms. Toby jugs.	Wedgwood jasperware. Transfer-printed creamware in blue or black. Leeds creamware. Lusterware.	Transfer-printed creamware: elaborate floral border; Empire shapes; blue and black. Gaudy Dutch pottery. Spatterware. Lusterware. Castleford. Ironstone.	Transfer-printed creamware in light blue, sepia, green, and pink designs, two colors on same piece common. Porcelains in demand: dessert, dinner, and breakfast sets; centerpieces; vases; ewers; and garden pots. Staffordshire figurines.

PERIOD	Jacobean	William and Mary	Queen Anne
Other **China**		Some Chinese porcelain: tea caddies, globular teapots, platters, bowls, plates with central armorial design.	China Trade porcelain from England. German salt-glazed stoneware.
GLASSWARE **In America**	No glass products available in colonies until the eighteenth century, when England mastered glass production.	Glasshouses produced window glass and bottles. Few glass objects in colonies.	Southern Jersey: windowpanes and bottles; bowls; pitchers; and jars in green and amber.
In England		Wineglasses; cone, round, and waisted bowls; baluster stem with tear; flat or domed round foot with plain or folded edges; some painted or engraved ornamentation.	Drinking glasses: wine, ratafia, syllabub, and sweetmeat; graduated footed plates; chandeliers; sconces; candelabra.

Chippendale	Federal	Empire	Victorian
Japanese Kakiemon and Imari; Meissen; Sèvres; Chelsea; and Worcester.	Direct trade with China: large dinner and tea services in Fitzhugh, Nanking, and Canton patterns. Sèvres urns from France.	European porcelains: Meissen tea and dessert sets; Sèvres urn-shaped vases.	Irish Belleek tea wares, vases, and small bowls. French bisque children; French and German shepherds and shepherdesses.
Free-blown and pattern-molded glassware: tumblers, mugs, wineglasses, decanters, salt containers, sugar bowls, creamers, bottles, and jars; clear, green, and amber.	Free-blown and pattern-molded glass. Southern Jersey: bird finials and applied decoration; green, amber, blue and amethyst; bowls, pitchers, dishes, compotes, sauce dishes, lidded sugar bowls. Amelung glassware: close to European products; lidded tumblers and goblets; stoppers; flasks; and decanters. Bakewell cut glass: decanters, drinking glasses, large punch bowls, and centerpieces for fruit.	Three-blown mold: decanters, bottles, dishes, pitchers, tumblers, flasks. Pressed glass: clear glass resembling cut glass; lacy glass (1828–1840) cup or tea plates, salts, sauce dishes, sugar bowls, and lamps; dolphin candlesticks. Southern Jersey free-blown and pattern-mold glass: Empire shapes on baluster feet; applied glass decoration; looping; bowls, pitchers, vases, candlesticks, salts, decanters, compotes, sugar bowls, and witch balls for stoppers.	Eclecticism of styles and techniques. Glass colored, coated with silver, frosted, and combined with other colors. Goblets and wineglasses with bell, tulip, and round bowls; carved rims, stems, and feet; in many colors. Amphora shape for jugs, cruets, and vases; tall handles. Southern Jersey wares unchanged. Pressed glass with plain geometric shapes (panels, thumbprints) in large sets of plates, cup plates, dishes, butter dishes, spoon holders, goblets, wineglasses, celery vases, and lamps; green, amber, blue, white, or amethyst in transparent, opaque, or frosted finish. Paperweights with flower or fruit centers on striped background. Bohemian glass: cased glass, e.g., ruby over clear; clear and solid colors, e.g., ruby or black.
Wine and water goblets and decanters: lighter in weight; straight stem with air twist; funnel- or bucket-shaped bowl with straight or S-curved sides; decanters with sloping shoulders. Deep blue glass toilet water bottles, patch boxes, finger bowls, and wine coolers with gold decoration. Opaque white glass vases, bottles, tea caddies, candlesticks, mugs, basins, cruets, and plates; polychrome oriental motifs. Chandeliers with high canopies. Candelabra with hanging drops, spires, V-shaped indentations on arms. Candlesticks with straight shafts.		Cameo decorative technique. Leadless glass tablewares in Nailsea.	Cut glass: wineglasses, vases, pitchers, covered compotes; dessert sets: three sizes of goblets, a decanter, a footed bowl, and a large centerpiece. Milky opal glass gilded and painted with enamels. Delicate Venetian wineglasses. Chandeliers with myriad sparkling prisms.

PERIOD	Jacobean	William and Mary	Queen Anne
In Ireland			
Metalwares and Accessories	Cast iron: crane, mechanical spit, tongs, mortars, skillets, pots, caldrons, andirons, lamps (tallow, fat, or grease), hinges, and latches. Copper pots and kettles. Brass: skimmers, thimbles, pins, pots, kettles, trivets, plate warmers, bed warmers, mortars, lantern clocks, pendulum clocks, chandeliers, candlesticks. Wooden bread peels.	Cast iron: tools, kitchen utensils, andirons, firebacks, grates for logs, kitchen vessels, and candlestands. Copper tea kettles. Brass: tools; andirons with baluster shafts, ball finials, and perhaps creeper andirons; fenders; bed warmers; candlesticks with baluster shafts and drip pans; chandeliers with Dutch baluster shafts; large spoons and ladles; pots; saucepans; toasters; goffering irons; irons; clock jacks; kettles. Foot warmers. Wooden bread peels and bowls.	Cast iron: firebacks; candlestands; kitchen utensils and vessels; Franklin stoves (1740). Standard copper tea kettle with European variations. Brass: tin-lined saucepans; dippers; bed warming pans; kettles; bow or serpentine fenders; andirons with baluster shafts and cabriole legs, and claw-and-ball, snake, or penny feet; candlesticks; chandeliers with globular shafts and S-curved arms; wall sconces; hall lanterns; clock dials and works. Decorated tinware: gold ornamentation on red, black, or tortoiseshell ground; candlesticks, teapots, tea caddies, trays, boxes of different sizes.

Chippendale	Federal	Empire	Victorian
	Cut glass in heavy classical shapes: decanters, glasses, jugs, salt cellars, dishes, bowls, punch glasses, cruets, rummers, and candlesticks. Chandeliers: globe on shaft replaced by urn. Sconces.	Cut glass: serving dishes as well as dinnerware.	
In kitchen: brass, copper, iron, and tin utensils and vessels. Highly polished brass in other rooms of house. At fireplace: brass fenders in bow or serpentine shape with curved top edges; andirons with columnar shafts and urn finials, or short steeple versions; tools. Lighting with rococo decoration and curved arms; candlesticks, candlestands; chandeliers; sconces; and lanterns. Clockfaces and works of brass. Japanned tinware included colors in gold designs; tea caddies; boxes; candlesticks; and oval, square, rectangular, and scalloped trays.	Brass, copper, iron, and tin kept in kitchen. More formal rooms had silver, glass, and britannia objects. Fireplaces equipped with brass tools; engraved andirons with classical column shafts and urn finials; short steeple andirons; bow or serpentine fenders. Lighting emphasized glass; some brass chandeliers with urn on shaft; hall lanterns; wall sconces with glass globes; candlesticks; candelabra; bouillottes; oil lamps, e.g., Argand lamps. Clockfaces of brass, but wooden works. American japanned tinware: landscapes and flowers on trays, boxes, tea caddies, and candlesticks.	Cast-iron stoves and coal grates. Copper tea kettles, sleek with straight spouts. Brass fireplace tools and andirons with short, heavy columns and large ball finials; creeper andirons perhaps; candlesticks with heavy baluster shafts on round domed bases; candelabra composed of figures with glass prisms suspended from shaft and socket; bouillottes; and oil lamps. Mechanical mass production.	Cast iron: outdoor furniture; mirror frames; lamp bases; parlor stoves; coal grates; kitchen vessels and tools, e.g., coffee grinders, cherry pitters, apple peelers and corers. Copper kettles rare. Brass kettles mass-produced and prolific; fireplace tools; cylindrical dry and liquid measures. Tinware from Yankee peddler: coffee and teapots; milk cans; tea caddies; dishes; boxes; trays; colanders; pans; strainers; cookie cutters; measures; mugs; dippers; picture frames; mirrors; chandeliers. Japanned tinware very popular: red, blue, green, and red-yellow-brown ground colors with painted or stenciled designs in red, green, yellow, and bright blue; banks; boxes; dishes and trays with scalloped, rectangular, oval, octagonal, or coffin shapes. Lighting fixtures: japanned tin, iron, brass, and britannia; ornate naturalistic designs for candelabra, chandeliers, sconces, and lamps.

6 Terminology

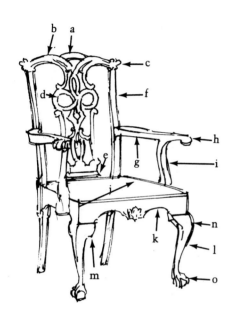

Chippendale Armchair

a Crest
b Bow-shaped crest rail
c Ear
d Pierced splat
e Shoe
f Rear chair support (stile)
g Arm
h Handhold (terminal)
i Arm support
j Seat frame
k Apron (skirt)
l Cabriole leg
m Leg bracket
n Knee
o Claw-and-ball foot

Chippendale High Chest of Drawers

a Central cartouche finial
b Urn finial
c Plinth
d Broken scrolled pediment
e Lattice
f Cornice
g Frieze
h Engaged column with fluting
i Apron (skirt)
j Cabriole leg
k Carved acanthus leaf

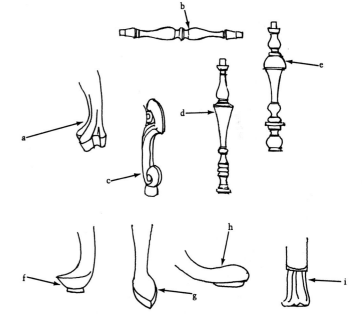

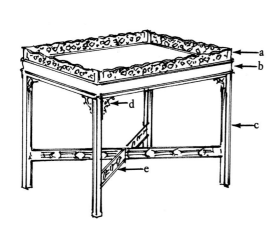

Chippendale China Table

a Pierced gallery
b Frieze
c Chippendale leg
d Pierced bracket
e Crossed fretwork stretchers

Feet and Turnings

a Trifid foot
b Vase-and-ring turning
c Flemish scroll
d Trumpet turning
e Cup turning
f Pad foot
g Slipper foot
h Snake foot
i Spanish foot

Glossary

amphora A Greek or Roman vessel that is tall and thin with two handles and a contracted neck.

apron A shaped element under a chair seat, dressing table, or tabletop.

arm support The vertical supporting member at the front of an arm.

bevel A 45-degree planed or sanded edge of a surface.

bonnet top A hood formed by a broken scrolled pediment, running front to back on top of a Chippendale case piece of furniture.

boss An oval or circular applied ornament of wood or silver.

bracket A supporting member on a table, chair, or chest, at the junction of the leg top.

cabriole leg A cyma-curved leg that curves outward at the knee, gradually curving inward at the ankle.

cartouche An ornamental motif of an unrolled scroll, with curved edges.

caryatid A supporting column shaped like a female figure.

cast To shape with liquid metal in a mold.

chasing Linear decoration on a metal surface formed with a blunt tool that removes no metal.

Chippendale style A style of furniture originated by Thomas Chippendale, an English cabinetmaker in the eighteenth century.

clock dial The face of a clock or watch with graduations of time and two pointer hands.

console A bracket projecting from a surface to support a freestanding object or a cornice.

cornice Molding that projects along the top of an entablature, a window, or a tall case piece.

cove molding A concave molding.

crocket A three-dimensional ornament of carved bent leaves on spire and gable edges in Gothic and Gothic Revival architecture; sometimes seen on furniture of those styles.

cusp A projecting point formed by the meeting of curves.

cyma curve A line that changes direction, creating a double curve.

dentil molding A progression of evenly spaced rectangular blocks, usually suspended from a cornice.

dish top A round tabletop with a raised rim.

dovetail A joint where the ends of two wooden members are fastened together at right angles by fitting one piece, which is cut like a flaring tenon, into the cavities of the adjoining member.

dowel A round wooden peg that projects from the end of one member, made to fit into a drilled hole in an adjoining member.

drop An applied or free-hanging ornamental turned pendant; in silver, the joining reinforces the back of the bowl of a spoon and its stem.

emboss To form raised ornamentation on a paper, metal, or fabric surface.

entablature The upper section of a column composed of a molded cornice, a flat frieze, and a molded architrave; in interior architecture, the wooden trim over doorways and windows and lining the upper portion of walls.

escutcheon The ornamental metal plate that surrounds a keyhole on a case piece of furniture.

fluting A progression of parallel semicircular channels cut into a surface.

foliated Decorated with leaves.

fretwork A latticelike ornamental pattern which is applied, cut in low relief, or freestanding; seen frequently on Chippendale, Federal, and nineteenth-century revival styles.

gesso The Italian word for plaster of paris, which provides a base for paint and gilt on furniture surfaces, such as mirror frames.

hatchment An embroidered coat of arms on a lozenge-shaped ground.

Hepplewhite, George An eighteenth-century English cabinetmaker who originated the style of furniture that bears his name.

jigsaw A powered sawing machine with a vertical motion moved by a vibrating action.

lathe A wood or metal turning machine.

lattice Openwork formed by crossed wooden strips.

melon reeding A semicircular relief motif with the lobed appearance of the outside of a melon.

miter To cut the end of a piece of wood at an angle to join with an intersecting member of the same angle.

miter box An instrument for sawing mitered edges.

modillion A carved block that resembles an ornate bracket, as seen in a building cornice.

occasional table One used for more than one area.

ogee bracket foot A furniture support consisting of two brackets, which are mitered to form a corner. The free edges are usually scrolled. On the ogee foot, the bracket surfaces are rounded in a cyma curve.

ormolu Ground gold or gold leaf covering brass or bronze, used as mounts on furniture of certain styles, such as Empire and Victorian.

overmantel Paneled wall surface above fireplace mantel.

oviform Shaped like an egg.

palmate In reference to leaves, shaped like a hand.

panel A piece of wood set into a frame or used as an overlay.

patina A soft, aged effect, resulting from finishing, aging, or polishing the surface of a piece of furniture.

pattern-mold blown glass Glass that has been blown or forced into a mold, patterned with protuberances and depressions, and expanded after removal.

pediment A motif adapted for case pieces of furniture such as secretaries and cabinet tops, as an ornamentation.

period furniture Belonging to a particular period style.

piercing On furniture, open patterns carved in galleries, stretchers, and chairbacks; in metalwork, open designs formed by cutting away metal.

quillwork Seventeenth- and eighteenth-century decoration consisting of rolled paper that was gilded, colored, and shaped into designs; boxes, mirror frames, and sconces ornamented with paper filigree, mica metal threads, or shells.

raked Inclined from the perpendicular direction.

ram's horn terminal Handhold on William and Mary armchair that curves down and spirals, resembling a ram's horn.

rosette A stylized flower motif set in a square, oval, or circle, as seen in nineteenth-century classical revival styles.

rush seating A form of weaving, used to fill and form a seat frame.

soffit The upper portion of a projecting cornice.

splat A central vertical part of a chairback.

stop fluted pilaster An engaged rectangular or half-round pillar that protrudes slightly from the surface; paths of fluted grooves "stopped" by bands of ornamentation.

strapwork Applied or carved decorative bands of flat, interlaced designs.

tracery Delicate open pattern as seen in Gothic windows, carved in wood for solid or pierced decorative detail, in, for example, Gothic Revival styles.

trammel Raising and lowering device for hanging pots from a crane, in a fireplace, and for lamps in the colonial times.

trefoil A three-lobed motif, often seen on Gothic and Gothic Revival furniture.

trifid A foot split into three carved toes, separated by weblike clefts.

vise A tool with jaws for holding wood members that are to be worked on. It is usually attached to a workbench.

volute A scroll, seen on classical capitals, as on the Ionic style.

wood overlay The placement of one layer of wood on the surface of another.

Bibliography

Apra, Nietta. *Empire Style*. London: Orbis Publishing Limited, 1972.

———. *The Louis Styles*. London: Orbis Publishing Limited, 1972.

Aronson, Joseph. *The Encyclopedia of Furniture*. New York: Crown Publishers, Inc., 1965.

Beard, Geoffrey. *The Work of Robert Adam*. London: John Bartholomew and Son Limited, 1978.

Bishop, Robert. *Centuries and Styles of the American Chair 1640–1970*. New York: E. P. Dutton & Co., Inc., 1972.

Bishop, Robert, and Coblentz, Patricia. *The World of Antiques, Art, and Architecture in Victorian America*. New York: E. P. Dutton & Co., Inc., 1979.

Boyer, Louise A. *The Complete Guide to Furniture Styles*. New York: Charles Scribner's Sons, 1969.

Burckhardt, Monica. *Mobilier Régence Louis XV*. Paris, France: Editions Massin.

Campbell, Christopher M. *American Chippendale Furniture 1755–1790*. Dearborn, Michigan: The Edison Institute, 1975.

Chamberlain, Samuel and Narcissa G. *New England Rooms: 1639–1863*. New York: Hastings House, Publishers, Inc., 1972.

Comstock, Helen. *American Furniture*. New York: The Viking Press, 1962.

Davidson, Marshall B. *Three Centuries of American Antiques*. American Heritage. New York: Bonanza Books, 1979.

Distin, William H., and Bishop, Robert. *The American Clock*. New York: E. P. Dutton & Co., Inc., 1976.

Downs, Joseph. *American Furniture, Queen Anne and Chippendale Periods*. New York: Bonanza Books, 1952.

Durant, Mary. *The American Heritage Guide to Antiques*. New York: American Heritage Publishing Co., Inc., 1970.

Dutton, Ralph. *The Victorian Home*. London: B. T. Batsford Ltd., 1954.

Dyer, Walter A. *Handbook of American Styles*. New York: The Century Company, 1918.

Edwards, Ralph, and Ramsey, L.G.G., eds. *The Connoisseur Period Guides, Early Victorian: 1830–1860*. New York: Reynal and Co., 1958.

Fales, Martha Gandy. *Early American Silver*. New York: E. P. Dutton & Co., Inc., 1973.

Fry, Plantagenet Somerset. *The World of Antiques*. London: The Hamlyn Publishing Group Limited, 1970.

Gammond, Peter. *Musical Instruments in Color*. New York: Macmillan Publishing Co., Inc., 1976.

Goodison, Nicholas. *English Barometers 1680–1860*. Woodbridge, Suffolk, England: Baron Publishing, 1977.

Gottshall, Franklin H. *Heirloom Furniture*. New York: Bonanza Books, 1957.

Hagler, Katherine Bryant. *American Queen Anne Furniture*. Dearborn, Michigan: The Edison Institute, 1976.

Hanley, Hope. *Needlework Styles for Period Furniture*. New York: Charles Scribner's Sons, 1978.

———. *Needlepoint in America*. New York: Charles Scribner's Sons, 1969.

Harris, Nathaniel. *Victorian Antiques*. New York: Golden Press, 1973.

Hepburn, Andrew H. *Great Houses of American History.* New York: Bramhall House Books, 1972.

Hinckley, F. Lewis. *A Directory of Antique Furniture.* New York, Bonanza Books, 1953.

———. *Directory of Historic Cabinet Woods.* New York: Bonanza Books, 1960.

Hummel, Charles F. *A Winterthur Guide to American Chippendale Furniture.* New York: Crown Publishers, Inc., 1976.

Kelly, Austin P. *The Anatomy of Antiques.* New York: The Viking Press, 1974.

Kettell, Russell Hawes. *Early American Rooms 1650–1858.* New York: Dover Publications, Inc., 1967.

Kirk, John T. *Early American Furniture.* New York: Alfred A. Knopf, 1970.

———. *American Chairs: Queen Anne and Chippendale.* New York: Alfred A. Knopf, 1972.

Krieger, Glee. *A Gallery of American Samplers.* New York: E. P. Dutton & Co., Inc., 1978.

Lanier, Mildred B. *English and Oriental Carpets at Williamsburg.* Williamsburg, Virginia: The Colonial Williamsburg Foundation, 1975.

Lea, Zilla Rider, ed. *The Ornamental Chair.* Rutland, Vermont: Charles E. Tuttle Company, 1960.

Margon, Lester. *Masterpieces of American Furniture.* New York: Architectural Book Publishing Co., 1965.

———. *Masterpieces of European Furniture.* New York: Architectural Book Publishing Co., 1965.

Marlow, Andrew W. *Fine Furniture for the Amateur Cabinetmaker.* New York: Bonanza Books, 1960.

Molesworth, H. D., and Kenworthy-Browne, John. *Three Centuries of Furniture in Color.* New York: The Viking Press, 1972.

Montgomery, Charles F. *American Furniture—The Federal Period.* New York: Bonanza Books, 1978.

Montgomery, Florence. *Printed Textiles.* New York: The Viking Press, 1970.

Ormsbee, Thomas H. *Field Guide to American Victorian Furniture.* Boston: Little, Brown and Company, 1952.

Ritz, Gislind M. *The Art of Painted Furniture.* New York: Van Nostrand Reinhold Company, 1971.

Rush, Richard H. *Antiques as an Investment.* New Jersey: Prentice-Hall, Inc., 1968.

Sack, Albert. *Fine Points of Furniture: Early American.* New York: Crown Publishers, Inc., 1950.

Scobey, Joan. *Rugs and Wall Hangings.* New York: The Dial Press, 1974.

Seale, William. *Re-creating the Historic House Interior.* Nashville: American Association for State and Local History, 1979.

Stanforth, Deirdre. *Restored America.* New York: Praeger Publishers, Inc., 1975.

Stillinger, Elizabeth. *Decorative Arts in America 1600–1875.* New York: E. P. Dutton & Co., Inc., 1972.

Swan, Susan Burrows. *Plain & Fancy.* New York: Rutledge Book/Holt, Rinehart and Winston, 1977.

Sweeney, John A. H. *The Treasure House of Early American Rooms.* New York: Bonanza Books, 1978.

———. *Winterthur Illustrated.* New York: Chanticleer Press, 1963.

Synge, Lanto. *Furniture in Color.* Poole, Dorset, England: Blandford Press, 1977.

Warren, David. *Bayou Bend.* Houston: The Museum of Fine Arts, 1975.

Willsberger, Johann. *Clocks and Watches.* New York: The Dial Press, 1975.

Supply Sources

Please send a self-addressed stamped envelope for a reply from any of the sources listed here.

ACCESSORIES

Broadswords Miniatures
68 Blackburn Road
Summit, New Jersey 07901
    Colonial accessories
    Hand-painted furniture
    Nautical accessories

Chestnut Hill Studio, Ltd.
P.O. Box 907
Taylors, South Carolina 29687

The Dollhouse Factory
157 Main Street
Lebanon, New Jersey 08833

The Enchanted Doll House
Manchester Center
Manchester, Vermont 05255

Jacqueline and Jason Getzan
39–530 South State Street
Ann Arbor, Michigan 48109
    Stained-glass lamps and
        windows—custom-made
    Hardwood canes, ebony
    Copper kitchen items
    Metal furniture

Roger L. Gutheil, Inc.
510 English Road
Rochester, New York 14616

Brass andirons
Brass candle holders
Lamps, sconces, chandeliers

It's a Small World
542 Lincoln Avenue
Winnetka, Illinois 60093

The Miniature Mart
1807 Octavia Street
San Francisco, California 94109

The Mouse Hole
111 Eagle Rock Avenue
Roseland, New Jersey 07068

Paige Thornton
P.O. Box 29217
Atlanta, Georgia 30359

Washington Dolls' House and Toy
   Museum
5236 44th Street N.W.
Chevy Chase
Washington, D.C. 20015

BASKETS

The Bird House
18 East High Street
Ballston Spa, New York 12020

> Assorted baskets
> Food

BOOKS IN MINIATURE

Borrower's Press
Route 1, Box 174
Winterport, Maine 04496

Mosaic Press
Department 8
358 Oliver Road
Cincinnati, Ohio 45215

Barbara Raheb
P.O. Box 7563
North Van Nuys, California 91409

Carol Wenk Miniatures
P.O. Box 2603
Lakewood, Ohio 44107

BRICKS

Binghamton Brick Co., Inc.
Upper Broad Avenue
P.O. Box 1256
Binghamton, New York 19302

> Real Tom Thumb bricks

Mini Brick and Stone Co.
343 Route 46
Fairfield, New Jersey 07006

BUTTONS

JHB Imports
1955 South Quince Street
P.O. Box 22395
Denver, Colorado 80231

> Clock buttons

CHINAWARE AND POTTERY

CNC Pottery
8 Pershing Road
Glens Falls, New York 12801

> Wheel-thrown pottery

Barbara Epstein
P.O. Box 1205
Crested Butte, Colorado 81224

Priscilla Lance
65 North Maple Avenue
Ridgewood, New Jersey 07400

> Hand-painted porcelain
> Chinese export
> Christmas vignettes

Susan's Miniatures
8480 Misty Blue Court
Springfield, Virginia 22153

Wee Treasures by Jean Yingling
1645 Glenwood Circle
State College, Pennsylvania 16801

COPPERWARE

Copper Miniatures, Harry G. Littwin
3904–52nd Street, W.
Bradenton, Florida 33505

> Kitchen appliances
> Pots, pans, and utensils
> Fireplaces, log carriers
> Coal buckets

DOLL CLOTHES PATTERNS

Ledgewood Studio
6000 Ledgewood Drive
Forest Park, Georgia 30050

> Period patterns for dolls
> Ribbons and trimming
> Flowers, shoe buckles, buttons
> Size 12 fine needles

DOLLHOUSES

Craft Creative Kits—a Division of
   Craft Products
Department 70
St. Charles, Illinois 60174

Jim Marcus
1332 Versailles Avenue
Alameda, California 94501

> Victorian dollhouses
> by commission

Miniature Mansions of Cheshire
P.O. Box 546
Cheshire, Connecticut 06410

> Dollhouses and shops

The Ha'Penny
R.F.D. 2, Box 13A
Chester, New Hampshire 03036

DOLLS

Galia Bazylko
911–220 S.W.
Edmonds, Washington 98020

> Hand-sculpted miniature dolls

The Burkey Place
227 Hoffman Street
Elmira, New York 14905

Gail Curry
10663 Lime Kiln Road
Grass Valley, California 95945

> China-head dolls with ornate
> hairdos and silk bodies

The Ha'Penny
R.F.D. 2, Box 13A
Chester, New Hampshire 03036

House of Tiny Treasures
5260 North Bartholow Road
Eldersburg, Maryland 21784

> Beautifully detailed bisque dolls

Paris Hill Shop
Box 74
Paris, Maine 04271

> Handmade jointed wooden dolls
> by Renee

Marty Saunders
91 Surfside Road
Minot, Massachussets 02055

Susan Sirkis
11909 Blue Spruce Road
Reston, Virginia 22091

FINDINGS

Baskin and Sons
732 Union Avenue
Middlesex, New Jersey 08846

Bergen Arts and Crafts
P.O. Box 689
Salem, Massachusetts 01970

Blue Swan Studio
P.O. Box 391
New Vernon, New Jersey 01976

> Brass elephants and findings for
> clocks
> Clock buttons

Boutique Trims
P.O. Drawer P
21200 Pontiac Trail
South Lyon, Michigan 48178

Eastern Findings
19 West 34th Street
New York, New York 10001

JAF Miniatures
8400 East 105th Street
Kansas City, Missouri 64134

FLOWERS, FRUITS, AND VEGETABLES

David and Barbara Krupick
3848 Luzon Street
Fort Myers, Florida 33901

    Shell flower arrangements
    Greenhouses
    Flower shops
    Turned ware

The Paisley Shop
104 E. Lancaster Avenue
Wayne, Pennsylvania 19087

    Williamsburg bouquets
    Containers
    Decoy arrangements

Posy Patch Originals
P.O. Box 38123
Atlanta, Georgia 30334

Wee Friends Too
1908 North Spruce Street
Little Rock, Arkansas 72207

    Flowers and plants

Gail Wise
61 Knickerbocker Road
Demarest, New Jersey 07627

    Miniature fruits and vegetables

FURNITURE

Andrews Miniatures
Patrick and Center Streets
Ashland, Virginia 23005

    Furniture and accessories

Hernania Anslinger
320 South Ralph Street
Spokane, Washington 99202

Don Buckley
Box 736
Main Street
Salisbury, Connecticut 06068

    Custom miniatures of the
      eighteenth century
    Country furniture
    Room settings
    Hand-carved shorebird decoys

Chestnut Hill Studio Ltd.
Box 907
Taylors, South Carolina 29687

    Period furniture and accessories

Cottrell Limited Editions
P.O. Box 161
Greenland, New Hampshire 03840

Dearring-Tracy Ltd.
South Montrose, Pennsylvania 18843

    Furniture and accessories of the
      finest quality
    Musical instruments
    Petit point rugs

Dolphin Originals
7302 Hasbrook Avenue
Philadelphia, Pennsylvania 19111

    Wicker and upholstered
      furniture

Warren Dick
P.O. Box 1662
Cottonwood, Arizona 86326

Roger L. Gutheil, Inc.
510 English Road
Rochester, New York 14616

    Eighteenth- and nineteenth-
      century furniture
    Shadow boxes
    Brass candle holders and
      andirons

Heirloom Replicas—Emily Good
2515 S. Solano Drive
Las Cruces, New Mexico 88001

Hillhouse Handmade Miniatures
45 Jamieson Road
Holden, Massachusetts 01520

    Very fine hand-stenciled
      furniture

The Hoffman Collection
Box 531
Summit, New Jersey 07901

    Country classic furniture

Douglas Kirtland
91 Canandaigua Avenue
Canandaigua, New York 14424

    Fine quality period and
      contemporary furniture

Elena Lamb Designs
11 Hartley Road
Great Neck, New York 11023

Nicole Walton Marble
3528 Ocean View
Glendale, California 91208

    Eighteenth- and nineteenth-
      century furniture
    Rare woods and ivory

Miniatures Ltd.
161 Linden Drive
Fair Haven, New Jersey 07701

    Fine furniture custom-made

Nic Nichols
405 St. Louis Avenue
Point Pleasant Beach, New Jersey
  08742

    Custom-made Victorian
      furniture

Edward G. Norton
Wesley Avenue
Westbrook, Connecticut 06498

    Custom furniture reproductions
    Houses and shops

George Passwaters
P.O. Box 761
Camden, New Jersey 08101

    Fine Queen Anne and Early
      American furniture
    Brass items

Terry Rogal Miniatures
212 Bridgetown Pike
Langhorne, Pennsylvania 19047

    Custom-made furniture of the
      finest quality

R-Stuff Miniatures
85 Morse Lake Road
Bloomingdale, New Jersey 07403

    Handcrafted Queen Anne and
      upholstered furniture

d. Anne Ruff
1100 Vagabond Lane
Wayzata, Minnesota 55391

Simms Miniatures
111 Edgewood Lane—P.O. Box 291
Williamsburg, Virginia 23185

    Eighteenth-century furniture
    Knife boxes
    Sterling silver flatware

"Sweet Dreams," Linda Jamison
630 South Linden Avenue
Pittsburgh, Pennsylvania 15208

    Victorian cribs
    Fancy beds.

Betty Valentine
114 E. New State Road
Manchester, Connecticut 06040

Washington Dolls' House and Toy
  Museum
5236 44th Street N.W., Chevy Chase
Washington, D.C. 20015

Nancy Weaver
Route 2 Cherokee Road
Cedartown, Georgia 30125

    Hand-painted oriental screens

Hal Weston
710 Merrick Avenue
East Meadow, New York 11554

Wexler-Duke Miniatures
718 Merrick Avenue
East Meadow, New York 11554

    Period screens, mirrors
    Custom chinoiserie

GAZEBOS AND
GREENHOUSES

David and Barbara Krupick
3848 Luzon Street
Fort Myers, Florida 33901

Ann Gatto
589 Third Avenue
New York, New York 10017

    Handcrafted and custom-
    designed gazebos

Braxton Payne
60 Fifth Street N.E.
Atlanta, Georgia 30308

    Greenhouses
    Garden tools

GLASSBLOWING

Albert Custom Glassblowing
P.O. Box 304A, Route 1
Putnam Valley, New York 10579

Milton Breeden
111 North 5th Street
Millville, New Jersey 08332

Glassblowers Workshop
1212 South Coast Highway
Laguna Beach, California 92651

Miniature Artistic Glassblowing
198 Pelhan Street
Pembroke, Massachusetts 02359

The Glassblowing Shop—Gerry
  Rynders
491 Brumley Road, Unit 14
Scarborough, Ontario MIJ IA4
    Canada

Crystal chandeliers
Glassware

The Whittemores
P.O. Box 1416
North Wales, Pennsylvania 19454

    Lead crystal hand-blown
    glassware

LEATHER

Berman Leather
147 South Street
Boston, Massachusetts 02111

Saks Arts and Crafts
207 N. Milwaukee Street
Milwaukee, Wisconsin 53202

Talas
Division of Technical Library Service
104 Fifth Avenue
New York, New York 10011

    Very thin skiver leather

LEATHER GOODS IN
MINIATURE

The Doll's Cobbler
1930 Falls Avenue
Cauahoga Falls, Ohio 44223
Sylvia Roundtree

    Doll shoes
    Boots and saddlery

Village Miniatures
910 Clayton Road
Ballwin, Missouri 63011

    English riding saddles with
    pewter stirrups, buckles and
    plates

LIGHTING

Cir-kit Concepts, Inc.
608 North Broadway
Rochester, Minnesota 55901

Elect-a-lite
742-B East Arctic Avenue
Santa Maria, California 93454

Illinois Hobby Craft Inc.
605 N. Broadway
Aurora, Illinois 60505

Kes Miniatures
P.O. Box 13742
Orlando, Florida 32809

    Miniature electric systems

MIRROR AND GLASS

Glass Smith Shop
7 Bank Street
Summit, New Jersey 07901

    Microthin mirror and glass

MISCELLANEOUS

Artfoam
100 East Montauk Highway
Lindenhurst, New York 11757

    May be purchased in a hobby
    or art supply store

James Bliss and Company
Dedham, Massachusetts 02026

    Linen rigging thread for rushing

J. J. Morris Co.
394 Elm Street
Southbridge, Massachusetts 01550

    Tiny brass screws

NEEDLEWORK

C. J. Originals
R.D. 2
Lebanon, New Jersey 08833

    Needlepoint
    Crewel
    Cross-stitch quilt kits
    Petit point rugs, bellpulls,
    tapestries, pictures, pillows,
    fire screens; all in kits

The Daisy Chain
Department N, P.O. Box 1553
Parkersburg, West Virginia 26101

    Silk and metallic threads
    Swiss silk gauze, 24–72 mesh
    English needles

Kay's Creations
2086 Fairwood Lane N.E.
Atlanta, Georgia 30345

    Hand-painted designs on canvas
    Petit-point rugs and bellpulls
    Oriental, traditional, and
    contemporary designs to work
    yourself

Knit Wit Shop
26 Beechwood Road
Summit, New Jersey 07901

    Needlework supplies

Miniatures 'N' Needlework
133 Onondaga Street
Corning, New York 14830

>Original works and kits, which include embroidery, hooked rugs, needlepoint, bargello, crewel
>Stained glass and paintings

Margot Gallery, Inc.
26 West 54th Street
New York, New York 10019

>Silk gauze, silk thread, and DMC embroidery floss

Needlework Designs—Susan Randolph
P.O. Box 804 NS
Huntington Beach, California 92648

>Swiss silk gauze, sizes 54, 40, 30, 24, 18, all 40" wide, retail and wholesale

Needleworks in Miniature—Barbara Cosgrove
P.O. Box 1138
Indian Rocks Beach, Florida 33535

>Museum-quality rug kits and finished models

Stitch Witchery
Denbrook Village P.O. Box N
Denville, New Jersey 07834

>DMC embroidery floss, silk gauze, Appleton yarn and other supplies

The Threaded Needle—Jean and Tom Holtey
1620 Massachusetts Avenue
Lexington, Massachusetts 02173

>Full color range DMC cotton floss, Medici wool, DMC pearl cotton, silk gauze
>Complete needlework and knitting supplies

Claudine Wilson
211 Sherwood Road
Beaconsfield, Quebec #H9W2H1

>Custom-made rugs, tapestries, and fine screens

The Whittemores
P.O. Box 1416
North Wales, Pennsylvania 19454

>A complete line of needlework supplies

PAINTINGS AND ETCHINGS

Artist's Workshop
E. W. Allen, Jr.
Box 476
Montclair, New Jersey 07042

>Miniature paintings to order

Beckwith Miniatures—Judy and Jim Beckwith
Box 6455
Bridgewater, New Jersey 08807

>Watercolor paintings in miniature

Karen Hardy
Fox Hunt Road
New Vernon, New Jersey 07976

>Oil paintings to order

The Little Farm Workshop—Jane Conneen
820 Andrews Road
Bath, Pennsylvania 18014

>Hand-colored etchings, herbs, wild flowers, Pennsylvania Dutch designs, birth and marriage certificates

PAPER TRIM

Harrower House
37 Carpenter Street
Milford, New Jersey 08848

>Gold embossed paper trim
>Decoupage supplies

QUILTS AND WOVEN COVERLETS

Cantitoe Corners—Deanna Mayer Vondrak
36 West 20th Street
New York, New York 10011

>"The American Museum Quilt Series" kits

Lillian A. Gaines
212 6th Street
Independence, Kansas 67301

>Handwoven coverlets

The Little Old Lady in Sneakers
Jinx R. Cutter Richmond
37 School Street
Hyannis, Massachusetts 02601

>Quilts, finished and in kits
>Stuffed toys
>Pillows and table linens

Jean Mason
45 Nelson Street
Quincy, Massachusetts 02169

>Handmade quilts

Old Curiosity Shop
Mobery Lake
British Columbia, Canada

>Quilts and afghans

ROOMS, VIGNETTES AND SHOPS

Dusty Boynton
Clay Court North
Locust, New Jersey 07760

>Custom-designed interior settings

Coad Canada Puppets
1384 Hope Road
North Vancouver, B.C.
Arlyn and Luman Coad

>Vignettes
>Handcrafted puppets

E. J. Kupjack and Associates
12 Main Street
Park Ridge, Illinois 60068

>Period rooms by commission

Dioramas by Katina Mills
P.O. Box 300
Cherry Lane Mendham, New Jersey 07945

>Custom-designed dioramas

Originals by Tag
R.D. 6, Box 249
Newton, New Jersey 07860
Elmer and Jean Tag

>Custom-designed Victorian shops
>Sleds
>Country kitchens
>Wheel-turned pottery

Wizard's Workbench
Route 1
Tamassee, South Carolina 29686
Norma De Camp

>Custom-made dioramas

SCULPTURE

Mini Contractors Supply
2616 N.W. 57th Street
Oklahoma City, Oklahoma 73112

>Miniature sculpture
>Architectural ornaments
>Old South garden accessories
>Pool and wall fountains and statuary

SHIP MODELS

Ron Stetkewicz
Foster Road
Cairo, New York 12413

> Ship models and furniture

TINTYPES

Tintypes in Miniature
c/o Alfred Forsberg
82 Grassy Sprain Road
Yonkers, New York 10710

TOLEWARE

Mary O'Brien's Yankee Notions
52790 Brooktrails
South Bend, Indiana 46637

> Deed boxes, stenciled trays, and other toleware

TOOLS

Anchor Tool and Supply Company, Inc.
231 Main Street
Chatham, New Jersey 07928

> Offers a catalog of fine tools for the craftsman

Brookstone Company
127 Vose Farm Road
Peterborough, New Hampshire 03458

> A free catalogue of "hard-to-find" tools, many useful to the miniaturist

Dremel Manufacturing Division
4915 21st Street
Racine, Wisconsin 53406

> Dremel Moto-Shop
> Dremel Moto-Tool
> Accessories

New England Hobby Supply Inc.
70 Hilliard Street
Manchester, Connecticut 06040

> The Bell Yankee Chucker
> Copy Cat duplicating device for lathe turning

Northwest Short Line
P.O. Box 423
Seattle, Washington 98111

> The Chopper

Wood Works
P.O. Box 874
Danville, California 94526
Geoffrey Bishop

> Magnetic holding jig

TRIMMING AND RIBBON

Linda Ballentine
6000 Ledgewood Drive
Forest Park, Georgia 30050

Arlene Bellinger
5521 East Morris
Wichita, Kansas 67218

Janice Naibert
165 Emory Lane
Rockville, Maryland 20853

TURNINGS AND SPINDLES

The Calico Dollhouse
Route 130 and Quarry Lane
North Brunswick, New Jersey 08902

> Finely turned spindles and turnings of maple, walnut, and mahogany, wholesale and retail

The Doll House Factory
P.O. Box 456
157 Main Street
Lebanon, New Jersey 08833

Houseworks Ltd.
3937 Oakcliff Industrial Court
Atlanta, Georgia 30340

> Dollhouse accessories, available in hobby and miniature shops

WOOD

Albert Constantine and Sons, Inc.
2050 Eastchester Road
Bronx, New York 10461

> Wood and wood inlays

Craftsman Wood Service Company
2272 South Mary Street
Chicago, Illinois 60608

The Miniature Mart
1807 Octavia Street
San Francisco, California 94109

> Doors
> Moldings

Northeastern Scale Models, Inc.
P.O. Box 425
Methuen, Massachusetts 01844

> Milled basswood
> Stripwood
> Structural shapes
> Model railroad supplies

Shaker Miniatures
2913 Huntington Road
Cleveland, Ohio 44120

> Hardwoods
> Mirror

WROUGHT-IRON MINIATURES

The Village Smithy
R.D. 5 Hemlock Trail
Carmel, New York 10512

Miniature Shops

ARIZONA

Sylvia's Dolls
3602 N. 24th Street
Phoenix, Arizona 85016

CALIFORNIA

The Dollhouse Factory
628 Santa Cruz Avenue
Menlo Park, California 94025

Mini Bazaar
400 Westminster Avenue
Newport Beach, California 92660

Mostly Miniatures
13759 Ventura Boulevard
Sherman Oaks, California 91423
and
310 Fifth Avenue
San Diego, California 92100

Willow Glen Miniatures
1110 Brace Avenue
San Jose, California 95125

FLORIDA

Poppenhuizen
8 S. E. Fourth Avenue
Delray Beach, Florida 33444

Miniland
2720 N. State Road 7
Margate, Florida 33063

ILLINOIS

The Beehive Studio Inc.
746 Judson Avenue
Highland Park, Illinois 60035

My Own Little World
422 W. Touhy
Park Ridge, Illinois 60068

The Red Oak Dollhouse and Miniature
   Shop
The Red Oak
Bishop Hill, Illinois 61419

MARYLAND

Millison's Dropstitch Studio
509 W. Cold Spring Lane
Baltimore, Maryland 21200

MASSACHUSETTS

The Elf Shelf
Route 28 at Academy Place
Orleans, Massachusetts 02653

The Enchanted Cottage Inc.
353 H. North Market
Faneuil Hall Marketplace
Boston, Massachusetts 02109

The Little Doll House
129 Littleton Road
Westford, Massachusetts 01886

The Miniature Shop
Depot Galleries
86 Thoreau Street
Concord, Massachusetts 01742

MISSOURI

Tin Lizzie
1304 W. Manchester Road
Ellisville, Missouri 63011

NEW JERSEY

The Dollhouse Factory
P.O. Box 456
157 Main Street
Lebanon, New Jersey 08833

The Emporium
71 Main Street
Chester, New Jersey 07930

The House of "Little"
13 N. Main Street
Mullica Hill, New Jersey 08062

Jean Johnsons Doll Houses
Brielle, New Jersey 08730

Mini Mall Miniatures
304 Morris Avenue
Spring Lake, New Jersey 07762

The Mouse Hole
111 Eagle Rock Avenue
Roseland, New Jersey 07068

Roy's Hobby and Toy Shop
38 Maple Avenue
Summit, New Jersey 07901

NEW YORK

B. Shackman & Co., Inc.
85 Fifth Avenue
New York, New York 10003

OHIO

Dian's Dollhouse Shoppe
125 N. Mulberry Street
Box 1653
Mansfield, Ohio 44901

Enchanted Toy Shop
23812 Lorain Road
North Olmsted, Ohio 44070

Little Bit Shoppe
4909 North Dixie Drive
Dayton, Ohio 45414

OKLAHOMA

Isn't It? (A Small World)
2121 E. 3rd Street
Tulsa, Oklahoma 74008

PENNSYLVANIA

Denny's Little House
708 E. Lancaster Avenue
Berwyn, Pennsylvania 19312

The Paisley Shoppe
104 E. Lancaster Avenue
Wayne, Pennsylvania 19087

Poppenhuizen
New Market
2nd and Pine Streets
Philadelphia, Pennsylvania 19147

Shoppe Full of Dolls
39 North Main Street
New Hope, Pennsylvania 18938

TENNESSEE

Little Treasures
F-1 Mountain Mall
Parkway at River Road
Gatlinburg, Tennessee 37738

VERMONT

Eagle's Nest
53 Prospect Street
Rutland, Vermont 05701

The Enchanted Doll House
Manchester Center
Manchester, Vermont 05255

VIRGINIA

Washington Dolls' House & Toy
   Museum
5236 44th Street N.W., Chevy Chase
Washington, D.C. 20015

Index

Pages in italics refer to photographs, graphs, or drawings.

About the Authors

VIRGINIA MERRILL is one of the foremost craftsartisans in the field of miniatures. She has exhibited and sold her works nationwide. Her two previous books on miniatures have been best sellers: *The Complete Book of Making Miniatures* and *Needlework in Miniature*. She teaches classes in miniature making in her hometown of New Vernon, New Jersey.

SUSAN MERRILL RICHARDSON is the daughter of Virginia Merrill and lives in Winchester, Massachusetts. She graduated with a B.A. and an Ed.M. from Smith College. She is a teacher and designer of needlework and a lecturer on the subject of miniatures.